IBM SYSTEM/360
ASSEMBLER LANGUAGE
DISK/TAPE
ADVANCED CONCEPTS

ANAHEIM PUBLISHING COMPANY
Specialist in Data Processing Textbooks

INTRODUCTION TO DATA PROCESSING

Our Computerized Society, Logsdon & Logsdon
The Computers In Our Society, Logsdon & Logsdon
The Computers In Our Society Workbook, Logsdon & Logsdon
Introduction To Flowcharting and Computer Programming Logic, Shelly & Cashman

BASIC

Programming In BASIC, Logsdon
Programming In BASIC With Applications, Logsdon

STRUCTURED COBOL

Introduction To Computer Programming Structured COBOL, Shelly & Cashman
Advanced Structured COBOL Program Design and File Processing, Shelly & Cashman

COBOL

Introduction To Computer Programming ANSI COBOL, Shelly & Cashman
ANSI COBOL Workbook, Testing & Debugging Techniques & Exercises, Shelly & Cashman
Advanced ANSI COBOL Disk/Tape Programming Efficiencies, Shelly & Cashman

RPG II

Computer Programming RPG II, Shelly & Cashman

RPG

Introduction To Computer Programming RPG, Shelly & Cashman

SYSTEMS ANALYSIS AND DESIGN

Business Systems Analysis and Design, Shelly & Cashman

ASSEMBLER LANGUAGE

Introduction To Computer Programming IBM System/360 Assembler Language, Shelly & Cashman
IBM System/360 Assembler Language Workbook, Shelly & Cashman
IBM System/360 Assembler Language Disk/Tape Advanced Concepts, Shelly & Cashman

FORTRAN

Introduction To Computer Programming Basic FORTRAN IV-A Practical Approach, Keys

PL/I

Introduction To Computer Programming System/360 PL/I, Shelly & Cashman

JOB CONTROL - OPERATING SYSTEMS

DOS Utilities Sort/Merge Multiprogramming, Shelly & Cashman
OS Job Control Language, Shelly & Cashman
DOS Job Control for Assembler Language Programmers, Shelly & Cashman
DOS Job Control for COBOL Programmers, Shelly & Cashman

FLOWCHARTING

Introduction To Flowcharting and Computer Programming Logic, Shelly & Cashman

IBM SYSTEM/360

ASSEMBLER LANGUAGE

DISK/TAPE

ADVANCED CONCEPTS

By:

Thomas J. Cashman, CDP, B.A., M.A.
Long Beach City College
Long Beach, California

&

Gary B. Shelly
Systems Programmer
Computer-Tek, Inc.
Anaheim, California

ANAHEIM PUBLISHING COMPANY
1120 E. ASH
FULLERTON, CALIFORNIA

First Printing
October 1970

Second Printing
May 1974

Third Printing
April 1976

Fourth Printing
March 1977

Fifth Printing

June 1978

Library of Congress Catalog Card Number: 78 - 22880

Printed in the United States of America

ISBN 0 - 88236 - 060 - 4

PREFACE

The System/360 utilizes many peripheral devices in addition to a card reader/ punch and a printer. Included among these peripherals are direct-access devices and magnetic tape devices. It is essential that a business programmer have a knowledge of these devices, their uses, and the instructions and programming techniques required to utilize these devices.

This book is designed to present both an introduction to magnetic tape and direct-access devices and the programming methods used for these devices under the Disk Operating System (DOS). A prior knowledge of basic assembler language such as presented in the text INTRODUCTION TO COMPUTER PROGRAMMING IBM SYSTEM/360 ASSEMBLER LANGUAGE is assumed.

Every effort has been made to present the concepts of direct-access and magnetic tape processing in a simplified manner through the use of realistic programming problems, numerous examples and illustrations, and completely documented and fully programmed examples. The approach used is to first introduce the student to a typical application, explain the computer instructions and DOS macros required to process the data, and conclude the chapter with an illustration of the input, output, and complete program to solve the problem. Each of the problems illustrated has been fully tested and run on a System/360 Model 30 operating under DOS.

The eight programs presented in the text explain the following concepts and operations: Magnetic tape sequential processing, sequential updating, DASD sequential processing, DASD indexed sequential processing (including sequential retrieval, random retrieval and updating, loading and adding records), the modular concept of programming, self-relocating requirements and techniques, overlays, and Physical IOCS. In addition, the binary data format is introduced together with fixed-length arithmetic instructions, and the associated register instructions. The explicit instruction format is used extensively throughout the text.

A comprehensive set of appendices is included for student reference covering such topics as the System/360 character set, the System/360 instruction set, and hexadecimal and decimal conversions. The appendices are intended to serve as reference material but it is suggested that the student be introduced to the material covered so that it can be used in a meaningful manner. In addition, a programming assignment is presented at the end of each chapter which should be coded by each student and run on a System/360.

When the student has completed the study of the material contained in the text, he should have a firm grasp of the capabilities of the System/360 when programmed in Assembler Language. He should be able to write programs utilizing magnetic tape and direct-access devices by using the instructions contained in the standard instruction set and the decimal instruction set. He should also be able to make decisions as to file usage and file organization for magnetic tape and direct-access devices.

It should be noted that several of the instructions available in the standard and decimal instruction sets and some of the macros available under DOS are not discussed. It is felt, however, that the student will be able to reference the appropriate IBM manual to acquire a knowledge of the material not presented in this text. In addition, it has been the authors' experience that a knowledge and understanding of DOS file management and the associated macros and techniques makes the transition to IBM's Operating System (OS) a relatively easy process. Thus, it is felt that a programmer with an understanding of the DOS concepts presented in this text can move to OS with little difficulty.

This text used in conjunction with the previous volume INTRODUCTION TO COMPUTER PROGRAMMING, SYSTEM/360 ASSEMBLER LANGUAGE, and SYSTEM/360 ASSEMBLER LANGUAGE PROBLEM TEXT should provide colleges and private business schools with a comprehensive set of instructional materials for an in depth course of instruction in Assembler Language. In addition, ideas and techniques presented in this text will provide instructional and reference material for the experienced Assembler Language programmer.

The authors would like to thank International Business Machines for providing the photograph used in Chapter 1, and for permission to use this illustration in the text.

Gary B. Shelly

Thomas J. Cashman, CDP

TABLE OF CONTENTS

CHAPTER 1

INTRODUCTION TO MAGNETIC TAPE AND DIRECT-ACCESS DEVICES

INTRODUCTION

The System/360 may utilize many types of "peripheral devices", that is, devices which are connected to the Central Processing Unit, to input data to the system and receive output. Although the card reader, card punch and the printer are important input/output units, two other types of devices play a vital role in the complete System/360. These devices are magnetic tape drives and direct-access disk drives.

The following is an illustration of a System/360 with magnetic tape and disk storage drives.

Figure 1-1 System/360 with tape and disk drives

MAGNETIC TAPE

Magnetic tape used with computer systems is similar to the tape used in audio tape recorders. Physically, the tape is composed of a plastic material normally one-half inch wide and coated on one side with a metallic oxide on which data may be recorded in the form of magnetic spots. The data recorded on magnetic tape may include numbers, letters of the alphabet, or special characters. Data is recorded in a series of parallel channels or tracks along the length of the tape. It is the presence or absence of magnetic spots on the tape that forms the representation of meaningful characters.

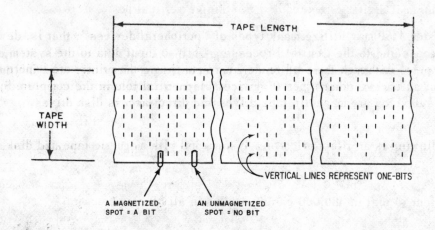

Figure 1-2 Data recorded on a section of magnetic tape

Computers using the Extended Binary Coded Decimal Interchange Code normally use 9 channel magnetic tape. The tape consists of 9 horizontal channels with one of the channels reserved for parity checking. The following diagram illustrates the coding structure and bit configurations for 9 channel tape.

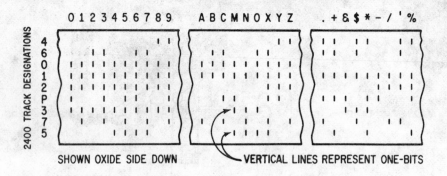

Figure 1-3 Nine Channel Tape

1.2

The bit assignments indicated are based upon the coding structure of EBCDIC using the zoned decimal format. It should be noted that the bit assignments were selected for maximum reliability and performance. Those bits utilized most frequently in representing data are recorded near the center of the tape. The bit positions used less frequently are recorded on the outer edges of the tape where reading or writing errors are more likely to occur. The numbers to the left of the tape segment reference positions 0-7 of the byte. Note that position 7 of the byte is the second channel from the bottom on 9 channel tape. Bit position 6 is the second channel from the top, etc. For example, the bit configuration for the number "one" in EBCDIC is 1111 0001. This same bit configuration is contained on 9 channel magnetic tape by referencing the bit positions as indicated.

When using 9 channel tape, data may also be recorded in packed decimal format allowing 2 decimal digits to be recorded in a single vertical position.

An important advantage of the use of magnetic tape is the density of recording, that is, the number of characters which may be recorded per inch. Although the density of magnetic tape varies, the IBM 2400 series of magnetic tape units may record or read data with a density of 800 bytes per inch or 1600 bytes per inch.

Magnetic tape is wound on plastic reels 10½ inches in diameter. A full reel contains approximately 2,400 feet of usable tape, but lengths as short as 50 feet can be used. It is interesting to note that a fully utilized 10½ inch reel of magnetic tape can contain data equivalent to that in 480,000 cards punched in all 80 card columns.

Magnetic tape is mounted on a magnetic tape unit for processing. During reading or writing, tape is moved from the file reel through a vacuum column, across a read-write head, through another vacuum column and to the machine take-up reel. Reading or writing takes place as the tape is moved across a read-write head. The tape-transport speed of the magnetic tape units varies from approximately 18.75 inches per second to 200 inches per second.

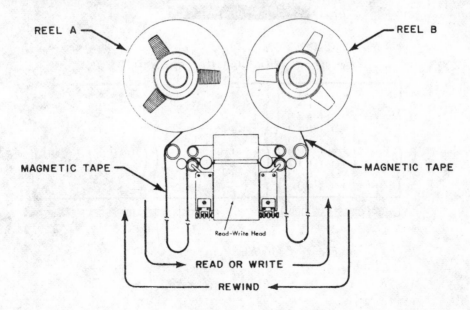

Figure 1-4 Schematic of a magnetic tape drive

1.3

Because of the density of magnetic tape and the speed at which the tape is transported past the read-write head, extremely fast input/output speeds are possible. To obtain the ''effective'' data transfer rate, that is the speed at which data may be transferred to the Central Processing Unit from magnetic tape, the tape transport speed is multiplied by the tape density. For example, a magnetic tape unit with a tape transport speed of 112.5 inches per second, processing magnetic tape with a density of 800 bytes per inch has an ''effective'' data transfer rate of 90,000 characters per second!

The picture below illustrates the IBM 2401 magnetic tape unit.

Figure 1-5 2401 Magnetic Tape Unit

The following chart summarizes the characteristics of some commonly used magnetic tape units.

2401			
	Model 4	Model 5	Model 6
Bytes per second	60,000	120,000	180,000
Density (bytes per inch)	1,600	1,600	1,600
Tape speed (inches per second)	37.5	75.0	112.5
Nominal Interrecord gap (inches)	.6	.6	.6
Nominal IRG time (milliseconds)	16.0	8.0	5.3
Rewind time, including reload (minutes)	3.0	1.4	1.0
Rewind and unload time (minutes)	2.2	1.5	1.1

Figure 1-6 Chart of characteristics of magnetic tape units

SEQUENTIAL FILE PROCESSING

Although tape drives operate in different modes, they all process data in a sequential access method. Sequential processing means that records are read or written one after another. Card readers and card punches operate in a sequential manner because cards are read or punched one after another. Thus, when using magnetic tape, records are read and written sequentially. In addition, the records stored on magnetic tape are normally arranged sequentially on the basis of some central field or "key" such as the item number of individual records, the salesman number, etc.

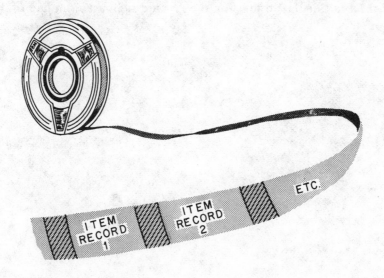

Figure 1-7 Illustration of records arranged sequentially on magnetic tape

After each record is written sequentially on a magnetic tape, there is an inter-block-gap (IBG) created (also called an IRG or inter-record-gap). This inter-block or inter-record-gap is a blank space on the tape approximately .6 inch long and indicates to the magnetic tape drive that the end of the record has been reached. This inter-block-gap is necessary to allow for the starting and stopping, acceleration and de-celeration, of the magnetic tape unit, and is required for correct reading and writing of records. Data to be read begins with the first character after an inter-block-gap and continues to the next inter-block-gap.

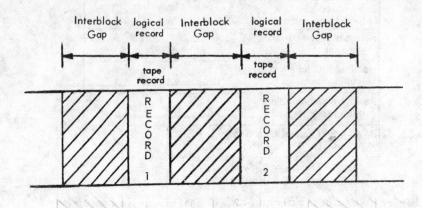

Figure 1-8 Illustration of records stored on magnetic tape

When writing on tape, the records are written sequentially with inter-block-gaps between each record. During writing, the gap is automatically produced at the end of each record or block of records.

When all the records of the FILE (that is, the group of related records on the tape) have been written by the program, a special character called a TAPE MARK is written. When a tape mark is written on the tape, it signifies that the file has been completely written. Thus, when the tape is read by another program, the tape mark will indicate the end of the file (similar to the way the /* card indicates the end of data when reading cards).

1.6

BLOCKING

In Figure 1-8, the records are shown to be written one by one in a sequential manner with inter-block-gap between each record. In many instances, it is advantageous to BLOCK the records. BLOCKING refers to the process in which two or more individual records (referred to as "logical records") are grouped together and written on a magnetic tape creating a "physical record" or "block". (See Figure 1-9)

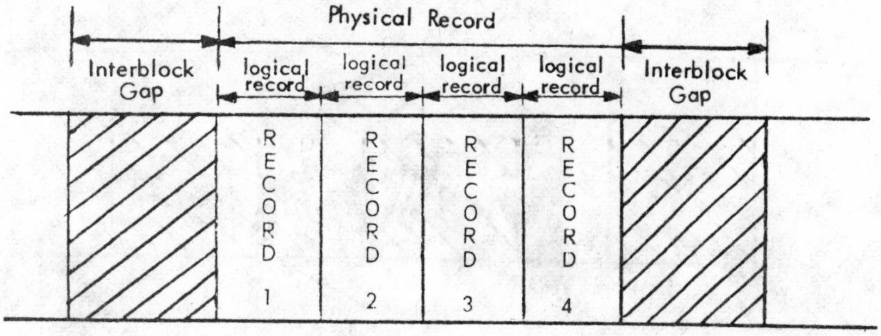

Figure 1-9 Illustration of blocked records

Blocking has two major advantages: (1) More records can be written on the tape because a number of records are recorded between each inter-block-gap, thus reducing the number of gaps on the tape; (2) The records can be read faster because two or more records can be read before the read operation is stopped by the inter-block-gap. The limiting factor in blocking records is the amount of core storage available for input/ output operations, as there must be enough room in core to store the complete block of data to be processed. Thus, the larger the block of records, the more core storage that must be allocated for storing the block. For example, if fifty 80 byte records comprise a physical record, then 4,000 bytes of core storage are required when the physical record is transferred from magnetic tape to core or from core to magnetic tape. The programmer or analyst must make the determination as to what size block can be used so that there is enough core storage available and the blocking is efficient as possible.

The number of logical records comprising the "physical record" is called the BLOCKING FACTOR.

TAPE MARKERS

Magnetic tape must have some blank space at the beginning and end of the tape to allow threading through the feed mechanism of the tape unit. Special markers called "reflective strips" are placed on the tape to enable the tape unit to sense the beginning and end of the usable portion of the tape. The tape unit senses these markers as either the LOAD POINT marker which indicates where reading or writing is to begin or as the END-OF-TAPE marker which indicates approximately where writing is to stop.

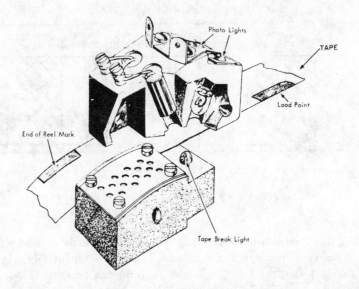

Figure 1-10 Load Point and End-Of-Tape Markers

The markers are small pieces of transparent plastic with a thin film of aluminum on one side. At least 10 feet of tape must be allowed from the beginning of the tape to the LOAD POINT marker and approximately 14 feet are normally allowed between the END-OF-TAPE marker and the end of the tape.

TAPE UNIT POSITIONING

When a magnetic tape is loaded onto a magnetic tape drive, the tape is positioned at the LOAD POINT. As the tape is read or written, it progresses by being taken up on the take-up reel. Thus, when the reading or writing of the tape file is complete and the tape mark has been written or read, there will be tape on the take-up reel. Two commands are available to return the tape to the "user reel"——the rewind command and the rewind and unload command. When the rewind command is executed, all the tape on the take-up reel is wound back on the "user reel" until the load point is reached. At that time the tape drive is readied and the tape is ready to be read or written again. When the rewind and unload command is used, the tape is wound back on the "user reel" and then the tape is unloaded, that is, it is taken out of a "ready" status and it is possible for the operator to dismount the tape.

There are times when one file is larger than one VOLUME (that is, one reel of tape). When this happens, a tape mark is written at the end of the first volume and a second volume must be mounted by the operator so that the file may be continued. When this situation occurs, the file is called MULTI-VOLUME file. It is also possible to have more than one file on a tape volume. This is called a MULTI-FILE volume.

FILE PROTECTION DEVICE

Because the writing operation automatically erases any previous information on the tape, a file protection device is provided to prevent accidental erasure. A plastic ring must be fitted into a circular groove on the tape reel to enable writing to occur on the tape (no ring – no write).

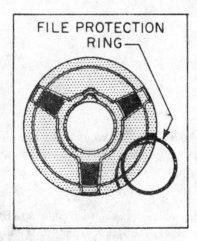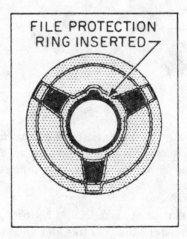

Figure 1-11 File protection ring

When this ring is removed only reading can take place. This technique tends to prevent accidental writing on a reel of tape as the operator must insert the ring in the reel for writing to occur.

TAPE LABELING

Installations utilizing magnetic tape as a form of input normally maintain a tape "library". This library may consist of hundreds and even thousands of reels of tape containing the data to be processed. It is essential, therefore, that an effective means of identifying the individual reels of tape be developed. To identify the individual reels of tape, techniques of tape "labeling" have been developed. These techniques consist of recording as the first records on each reel, information that uniquely identifies the reel. The label at the beginning of a reel is called a "HEADER LABEL". Labels written at the end of the reel are called "TRAILER LABELS".

STANDARD LABELS

With the Disk Operating System information for the recording of labels on magnetic tape is obtained from the Job Control cards utilized with the problem program. In actual practice magnetic tape labels include three basic types: a Volume Label, a Header Label, and a Trailer Label.

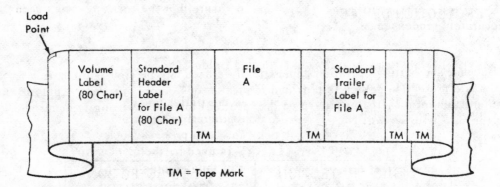

Figure 1-12 Standard tape labels

The volume label identifies the tape volume with the volume number assigned to it. This volume number is usually unique to the reel of tape and is used to ensure the proper volume is being used in tape processing.

The header label immediately follows the volume label with only an IBG between them. The header label is, like the volume label, 80 bytes in length.

When a tape is used as input to a program, the header label is checked to insure that the proper magnetic tape file is being used. A header label normally contains the following fields.

1. LABEL IDENTIFIER – identifies header labels.
2. TAPE SERIAL NUMBER – identifies a particular reel of tape.
3. FILE SERIAL NUMBER – identifies a tape file. This number may often be the same number as the tape serial number of the first reel of tape in the file.
4. SEQUENCE NUMBER – ensures that reels within a file enter the system in sequence.
5. FILE IDENTIFICATION – identifies the name of the file.
6. CREATION DATA – dates the creation of the file.
7. RETENTION CYCLE – indicates the obsolescence data concerning a file.

These fields are basic to a header label. Additional control information may be desired in a particular application.

A trailer label is used by the program to ensure that the entire reel has been accurately processed.

A trailer label may contain the following fields.

1. LABEL IDENTIFIER – identifies the trailer label.
2. BLOCK COUNT – is used by the program to ensure that the indicated number of blocks has been processed.
3. TAPE DATA RECORD COUNT – is used by the program to ensure that the indicated number of tape records has been processed.

Trailer labels may contain additional information necessary to a particular application.

STANDARD LABELS WITH USER LABELS

User labels may be used with standard DOS labels to provide more label information. For example, they may contain additional dating information or additional file identification.

The format of a tape file with standard and user labels is illustrated below.

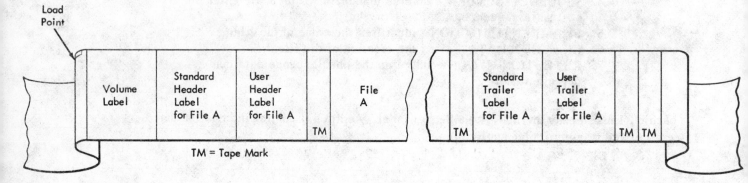

Figure 1-13 Standard and User labels

NON-LABELLED AND USER-LABELLED TAPES

In addition to the standard labels previously described, DOS supports non-labelled tapes and user-labelled tapes.

Non-labelled tapes are exactly that—there is no label on the tape. The tape begins with either the first data record or a tape mark and then the first data record.

User-labelled tapes have only user-labels on the tapes—no standard labels are supplied. Thus an installation could use strictly their own labels and not use IBM's standard labels at all.

The non-labelled tape ends with just a tape mark following the data and the user-labelled tapes can have whatever the user wishes.

RECORD FORMATS

Records on a tape or on a direct access device can be of several formats. These formats are chosen by the programmer or analyst depending upon the use of the record and what type of data will be contained in the record.

The three types of records are FIXED, VARIABLE and UNDEFINED. In addition, the fixed and variable length records may be BLOCKED or UNBLOCKED.

A FIXED-LENGTH record is one which always contains the same number of bytes. Thus, when a file is defined as having fixed-length records and the record length is 120, all records on the file contain 120 bytes. Normally, the fields in the record are defined by DS statements in the same manner used for the card reader and the printer.

Fixed-length records can be blocked or unblocked. When they are unblocked, each physical record will be 120 bytes long. When the fixed-length records are blocked, the physical record contains more than one logical record. Thus, if a blocking factor of five is used, that is, there are five logical records for each block or physical record, then the BLOCKSIZE or block length would be 600 bytes (120 bytes/rec times 5 recs/block).

A VARIABLE-LENGTH record is one which may contain a variable number of bytes in each record. That is, each record may contain the same or a different number of bytes. Variable-length records are used when different amounts of data may be available for each record.

The example below illustrates the use of variable-length records.

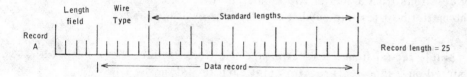

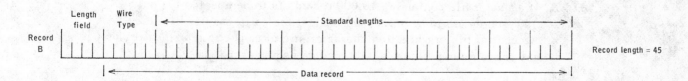

Figure 1-14 Variable-length records

The data record consists of the wire type and all the standard lengths the wire comes in. Some wire types have only a few standard lengths while others have a large number of standard lengths. It can be seen that if fixed-length records were used, a large amount of space would be wasted on the tape for those wire types which had only a few standard lengths. Thus, variable-length records were used for this file.

The length-field at the start of the record contains the length of the record. This field is used by the I/O module and must be supplied by the program each time a variable-length record is written.

Variable-length records may be either blocked or unblocked, depending upon the application.

An UNDEFINED record is a record which may be any length desired by the programmer. This type of record may be used whenever the length of the record is unknown. Undefined records differ from variable records in that there is a maximum length specified for variable length records and none specified for undefined records. Also, variable-length records can be blocked by the DOS input/output routines whereas any blocking for undefined records must be done by the programmer. Undefined records cannot be specified as blocked.

Although magnetic tape is an effective input/output media because of its high density and fast data transfer rate, the use of magnetic tape has several significant disadvantages. These disadvantages include the following:

1. Because records are stored on magnetic tape sequentially, transactions against master files stored on tape must be batched and sorted into sequence before processing.

2. Additions or deletions from a master file require that a new file must be created no matter how few the number of additions or deletions.

3. To extract a single record from a magnetic tape file (for example, the last record stored on a tape reel) requires that each record on the file be examined until the proper "key" identifying the record is found, at which time the record is processed as required.

4. In file updating procedures where there is little activity against the file the use of magnetic tape is normally inefficient. For example, if a master file containing 10,000 records is to be updated but only 100 records are to be processed against the entire master file, the sequential file organization characteristic of magnetic tape requires that the entire master file of 10,000 records be processed.

LOGICAL IOCS

The file management routines of the Disk Operating System are collectively referred to as the Logical Input/Output Control System (LIOCS). LIOCS performs those functions necessary to locate and access a logical record for processing. LIOCS routines perform the following functions:

1) Blocking and deblocking records.

2) Switching between input/output areas when two areas are specified for a file.

3) Handling end-of-file and end-of-volume conditions.

4) Checking and writing labels.

It should be noted that the input/output macros issued in a program (such as OPEN, GET, PUT, DTF, etc) are part of LIOCS.

DIRECT ACCESS STORAGE DEVICES

Another type of input/output device which is an effective storage media for many applications is a DIRECT ACCESS STORAGE DEVICE (DASD). Direct access storage devices may process files organized sequentially as with magnetic tape but also offer the advantage of "random" retrieval of individual records from a file. Although a number of direct access devices are currently available, the IBM 2311 disk drive is one of the most widely used direct access storage devices and serves as a general example for similar units. The 2311 disk storage drive is illustrated below.

Figure 1-15 2311 Disk Drive

The 2311 disk drive is a single unit which allows the mounting of removable disk "packs" (2316 disk packs). The packs when removed from the drive are enclosed in protective covers. Each pack consists of six disks mounted on a vertical shaft. The disks are 14 inches in diameter and are made of metal with a magnetic oxide coating on both sides of the disk. There are ten recording surfaces on each pack. The top surface of the upper disk and the bottom surface of the lower disk are not used for recording data.

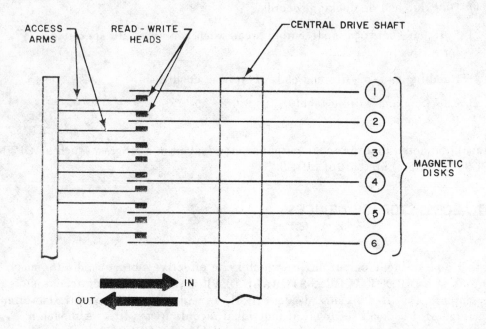

Figure 1-16 Schematic of Disk Unit

The disks rotate at 2400 revolutions per minute. To transfer data to or from the recording surface requires some type of "access" mechanism. On the 2311 disk drive the access mechanism consists of a group of access arms consisting of read/write heads that move together as a unit in and out between the recording surfaces of the disk pack. These comb-type access arms can move to 203 different positions on the surface of the disk as there are 203 discrete recording positions within a disk surface. It should be noted that only 200 positions are normally used for recording data. Three alternate areas are supplied if any of the first 200 positions are defective.

RECORDING OF DATA

Data is recorded on the surface of the disks in the form of magnetic spots along a series of concentric circular recording positions on each disk recording surface.

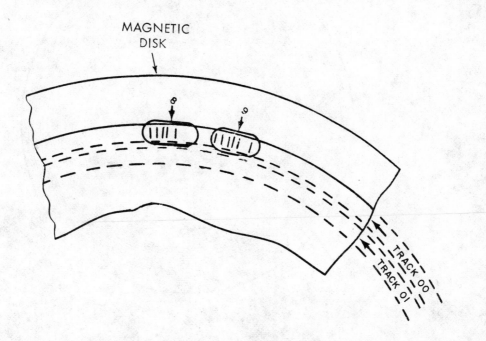

Figure 1-17 Segment of Disk Recording Surface

The recording surface of each disk pack is divided into many tracks. A TRACK is defined as a circumference of the recording surface. It should be noted that the tracks are concentric, not spiral like a phonograph record. Data is recorded serially bit-by-bit, eight bits per byte, along a track. On the 2311 disk drive there are 200 tracks per surface (plus 3 alternates) with each track capable of storing a maximum of 3,625 bytes.

The following is a schematic drawing illustrating the 200 tracks on a recording surface.

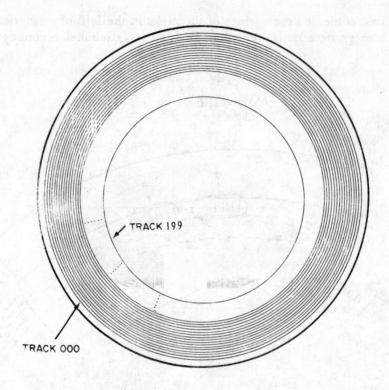

Figure 1-18 Schematic of Disk Recording Track Position

It should be noted that only 200 tracks can be defined for use by the programmer and that the 3 alternate tracks are used if any of the 200 tracks are defective.

CYLINDER CONCEPT

Each concentric circle as one looks "three dimensionally" from the top of the disk pack is called a CYLINDER. A "cylinder of data" is defined as the amount of data that is accessible with one positioning of the access mechanism. This is an important concept since movement of the access mechanism represents a significant portion of the time required to access and transfer data.

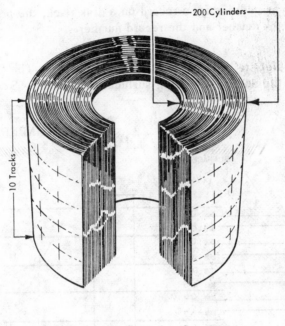

Figure 1-19 Cylinder Concept

Each 2316 disk pack has 200 cylinders which is equal to the number of positions to which the access mechanism can move. Each cylinder has ten tracks, which is equal to the number of recording surfaces. Thus, a cylinder has a maximum capacity of 36,250 bytes (3,625 bytes per track, 10 tracks per cylinder). A pack has a maximum capacity of 7.25 million bytes (36,250 bytes per cylinder, 200 cylinders per pack).

RECORDS

Each track can hold a maximum of 3,625 characters. Of course, every record which is recorded on the disk is not 3,625 characters long. Therefore, more than one record can be recorded on a track. These records are separated by a gap similar in function to the inter-block-gap on tape. One method of referencing a particular record on a track is by a "record number". The first record on a track is called record "0". Record zero is used for a special purpose by Logical IOCS. The first user record is normally record "1".

In order to develop an address for a record on a disk pack, the program specifies the cylinder number, the track number and the record number.

The track number refers to the number of the disk surface. The first recording surface is called track 0, the second recording surface track 1, etc. See the illustration below.

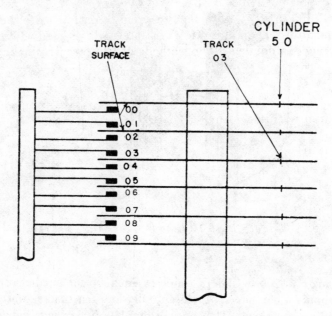

Figure 1-20 Data Record Recorded on Disk

In the example above, if data is recorded beginning on cylinder 50, track 3, one could specify the address of "RECORD2" by indicating that it resides on cylinder 50, track 3, record 2.

DISK LABELS

Whenever Logical IOCS is used, labels must be used for disk files. The labels provide the pertinent information about the disk file. They give the file a name, a creation and an expiration date, the beginning cylinder and track, and the ending cylinder and track (called EXTENTS) and other necessary data.

DISK AND TAPE PROCESSING

Tape and disk processing is handled with macros much in the same manner as cards and the printer. A DTF is written for each file to be processed and then imperative macros (such as GET and PUT) are issued to actually read or write the data. All tape processing is sequential. There are, however, three primary methods of file organization when using direct access devices. The methods of file organization include:

1. Sequential file processing

2. Direct access file processing

3. Indexed sequential file processing

Sequential file processing and indexed sequential file processing are explained in subsequent chapters of this text.

MAGNETIC TAPE SEQUENTIAL PROCESSING
SEQUENTIAL UPDATING

INTRODUCTION

As discussed in Chapter 1, magnetic tape can be used to store large amounts of data to be processed in a sequential manner. Magnetic tape is commonly used to store sequential master files. A MASTER FILE is a file consisting of records which contain up-to-date information relating the status of a system of which a master record is a part. For example, in a customer sales system, the master file could contain a record for each customer reflecting year-to-date sales.

MASTER FILE UPDATING

Once a master file has been created, it is periodically necessary to update this file with current information so that the file always contains the most recent data. Typically, file updating procedures take three forms: additions, deletions, and changes.

An ADDITION takes place when a new record is added to an already established master file. For example, in a customer sales system, if a new customer is acquired, it would be necessary to add a record to the master file reflecting the acquisition of the new customer.

A DELETION becomes necessary when data currently stored on the master file is to be removed. For example, if a customer is lost, that is, the customer no longer purchases from the company, it would be necessary to delete the corresponding master record from the file.

A CHANGE must be made to the master file whenever the data on the master file no longer contains accurate, up-to-date information. For example, in a customer sales system, when a new sale is made, the sales amount must be added to the sales amount in the master record to reflect a sale to the customer.

SEQUENTIAL FILE UPDATE

SEQUENTIAL UPDATING involves the reading of a sequential master file, the reading of a sorted sequential transaction file and the creation of a new, updated master file. Normally, an exception report which lists transaction errors such as invalid transaction codes is also created.

A system flowchart of a sequential file update is shown in Figure 2-1.

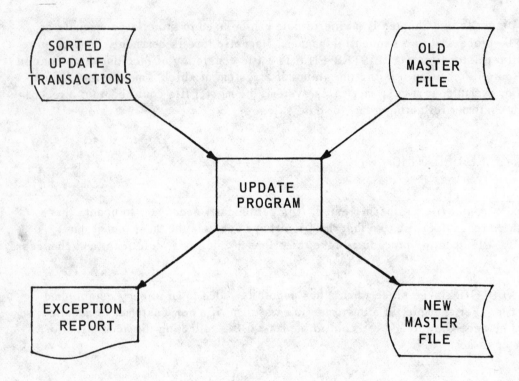

Figure 2-1 System flowchart of sequential update

SAMPLE PROBLEM

The program presented in this chapter illustrates a technique to sequentially update a master file stored on magnetic tape with sorted transaction records stored on punched cards. The master file contains the year-to-date sales amounts for customers. This master file is to be updated with the new sales figures for the month. In addition, the update program will add customers or delete customers from the master file as needed. An error listing will also be produced which contains a list of any transaction records with errors such as invalid transaction codes or invalid data in numeric fields.

The format of the master and transaction files is illustrated below.

MASTER FILE

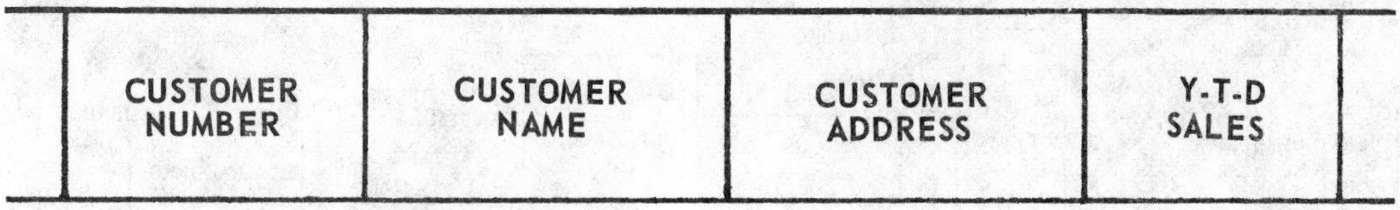

CUSTOMER NUMBER	CUSTOMER NAME	CUSTOMER ADDRESS	Y-T-D SALES

Figure 2-2 Master file record format

A logical record in the master file will occupy 59 positions on the tape. Sixty-one records will be blocked to form a physical record, or block. The year-to-date amount field will be stored in packed-decimal format.

TRANSACTION FILE

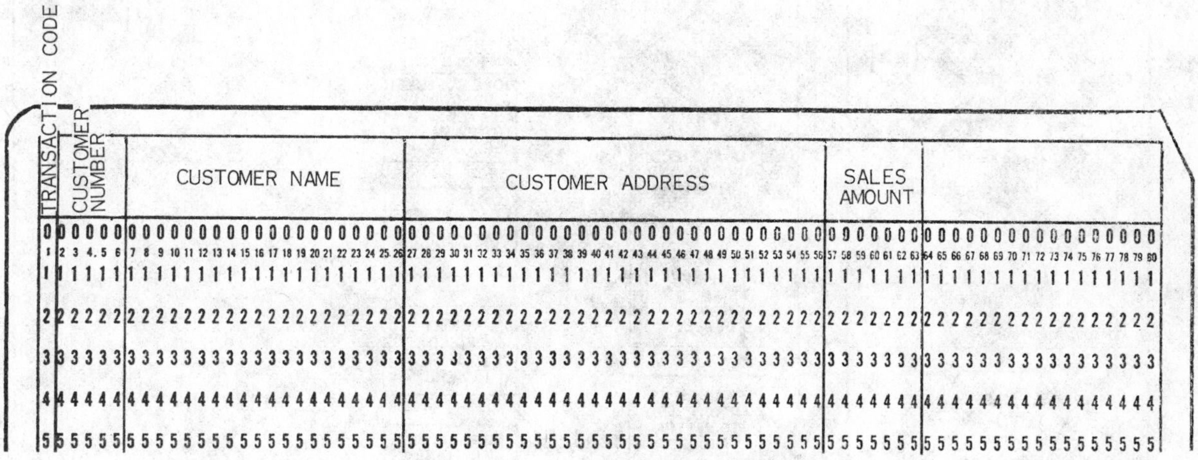

Figure 2-3 Transaction file record format

The transaction file contains a transaction code. A "1", indicates that the transaction record is an addition; a "2" indicates a deletion and a "3" indicates a change.

The flowchart logic for a file updating procedure is illustrated on the following pages. The basic logic requires the following basic steps: (1) a transaction record is read (2) a master record is read (3) the customer number of the master record and the transaction are compared to determine if the master record is equal to, less than, or greater than the transaction record (4) the required processing is performed based upon the comparison.

The logic of this file updating procedure should be analyzed carefully and thoroughly understood prior to reviewing the coding for the problem explained on subsequent pages of this chapter.

2.3

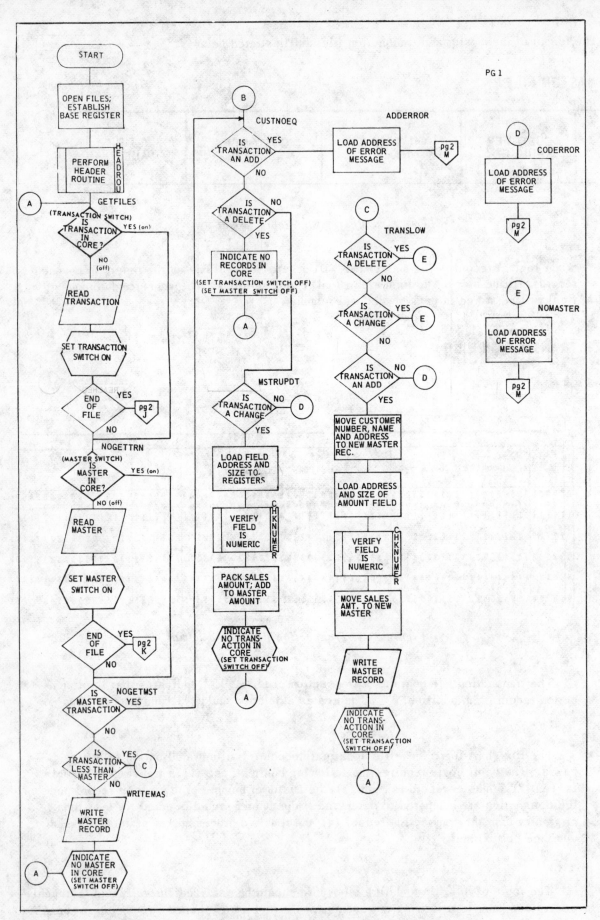

Figure 2-4 Sequential update program flowchart - Part 1 of 2

2.4

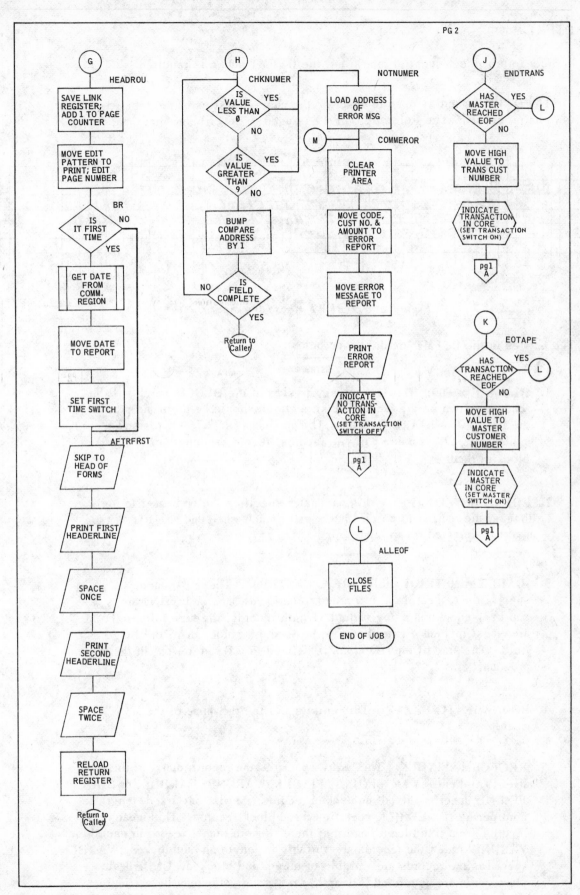

Figure 2-5 Sequential update program flowchart - Part 2 of 2

DTFMT Macro

In order to process sequential tape files, the DTFMT macro is required.

The DTFMT macro is used to describe the characteristics of the tape file which is to be processed. The following DTFMT is used to describe an input master file.

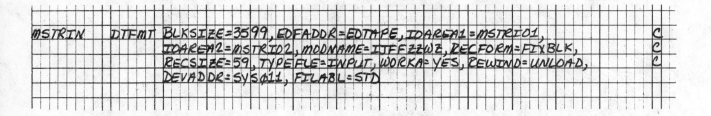

Figure 2-6 DTFMT macro for input master file

The entries in the DTFMT are described below.

1. BLKSIZE = 3599: This entry gives the size of the BLOCK which will be read or written on the tape. The size stated should be the same size as the IOAREA or IOAREA's used. The maximum is 32,767 bytes and the minimum is 12. If using variable records, record the length of the largest block of records.

2. EOFADDR = EOTAPE: This parameter specifies the end-of-file routine, that is, the routine to which LIOCS will branch when end-of-file (a tape mark) is detected on an input tape.

3. IOAREA1 = MSTRIO1 and IOAREA2 = MSTRIO2: These parameters specify the names of the I/O areas to be used. One or two I/O areas can be used. When using variable length records, the size of the I/O area must include 4 extra bytes to be used as a block or record length field. The size of the I/O areas is defined in a DS statement in the program.

4. MODNAME = IJFFZZWZ: This entry specifies the name of the I/O module.

5. RECFORM = FIXBLK: This entry specifies the record format of the tape file. Valid entries are FIXUNB, FIXBLK, VARUNB, VARBLK, or UNDEF. FIXUNB specifies fixed-unblocked records, that is, one fixed-length record per block. FIXBLK specifies fixed block records. This means the records are a fixed length and that there is more than 1 record in each block. VARUNB states the records are variable in length and unblocked. VARBLK specifies the records are variable in length and blocked. UNDEF states the records are undefined in length, that is, any size may be written or read. In this case, the RECSIZE parameter is used to define the length of the record.

6. RECSIZE = 59: If RECFORM = FIXBLK, this parameter specifies the size of each individual record within the block. If RECFORM = UNDEF, this parameter specifies a register which can be used to specify the length of the record read or written. The format to be used for stating the register number when using undefined records is RECSIZE = (r), where r is a register number from 2 through 12. For OUTPUT, the program must place the length of the record to be written in the register——this operand is required for output files. For INPUT, if the register is specified, Logical IOCS will place the length of the record read in the register and the program can refer to this length to determine its processing.

7. TYPEFLE = INPUT: This parameter specifies the use of the tape file. It may be an INPUT file, an OUTPUT file or a WORK file. An input file and output file mean the file is either being read as input or written as output. A WORK file is one which can be used as both input and output within the same program. It is normally used to pass information from one part of the program to another. Special macros for input and output are used with work files. For more information see IBM SRL C24-5037, Supervisor and Input/ Output Macros.

8. WORKA = YES: This operand is used if a work area is to be used with the tape file. If one is not used, this parameter is omitted. It should be noted that if two I/O areas are being used, either the WORKA = YES or the IOREG = (r) parameters must be specified, but not both.

9. REWIND = UNLOAD: This operand is used to state what the disposition of the tape will be when the file is CLOSED. If this operand is not stated, the tape will REWIND when the file is closed. The valid entries for this keyword are UNLOAD, which causes the tape to be rewound and unloaded or NORWD, which will cause the tape to be positioned where it was when the close is issued. This entry may be used if multiple files are on the same tape.

10. DEVADDR = SYS011: This entry specifies what "SYS" number will be used for this file. The "SYS" number is related to a particular tape drive by the use of an assign ("ASSGN") card in the job control statements of the program. The SYS number can vary from 000 to 244.

11. FILABL = STD: FILABL is the keyword which is used to specify what type of labels will be used on the tape. STD specifies standard labels; other entries could be NSTD for user labels or NO for no labels.

The output file is described in the following DTFMT.

```
MSTROUT  DTFMT BLKSIZE=3599, IOAREA1=MSTRIO3, IOAREA2=MSTRIO4,      C
               MODNAME=IJFFZZWZ, RECFORM=FIXBLK, RECSIZE=59,        C
               DEVADDR=SYS010, TYPEFLE=OUTPUT, WORKA=YES, REWIND=UNLOAD,  C
               FILABL=STD
```

Figure 2-7 DTFMT macro for output master file

The unique entries for the output file are described below.

1. DEVADDR = SYS010: This entry specifies what "SYS" number will be used for this output file. The "SYS" number used must be a different number from that used for the input file because the input file will be on a different tape drive than the output file.

2. TYPEFLE = OUTPUT: This entry specifies that the file defined by the DTFMT will be an OUTPUT file.

Note also the absence of the EOFADDR operand. An output file does not specify an end-of-file address.

READING THE INPUT FILES

The first step in this program, as in most programs, is to establish a base register and open the files. The files to be opened are the old master (MSTRIN), the new master (MSTROUT), the update transaction file (TRANSIN), and the printer file (PRTFLE).

```
BALR    BASEREG, 0              ESTABLISH BASE REGISTER
USING   *, BASEREG
SPACE
OPEN    MSTRIN, MSTROUT, TRANSIN, PRTFLE    OPEN FILES
SPACE
BAL     HEADREG, HEADROU        GO TO HEADER ROUTINE
SPACE
```

Figure 2-8 Routine to establish base register, open files and print header

The OPEN macro is issued before the actual processing of the file begins. In addition to preparing the file for processing, it checks the labels on the tape volume to ensure that the proper tape is being used. The tape label information is supplied to the OPEN routines by the Job Control TLBL card.(see appendices for an example of the TLBL card).

After the files are opened, the header for the first page of the exception report is printed.

The basic logic in a sequential update is to compare a transaction record with a master record, that is, compare the controlling field in these records (in the sample program, this field is the customer number), and process the records dependent upon a high, low or equal condition. If an unequal condition occurs, normally either the transaction record or the master record will be processed but not both. Thus, after an unequal condition, it is necessary to read only the type of record which was processed because the record not processed is still in core ready to be processed. Therefore, switches are established which indicate whether or not a transaction or master record should be read.

Thus, at the GETFILES routine illustrated below, the first test is to determine if a transaction is already in core. The first time, of course, a record will not be in core so a GET is issued to read the transaction file and a switch is set to indicate an unprocessed transaction in core.

```
GETFILES EQU   *
         TM    SWITCH,X'01'        IS UPDATE TRANSACTION IN CORE
         BO    NOGETTRN           YES, BYPASS GET OF UPDATE TRANS
         GET   TRANSIN,TRANWORK   NO, READ TRANSACTION FILE
         SPACE
         OI    SWITCH,X'01'       INDICATE TRANS IN CORE
         SPACE
NOGETTRN EQU   *
         TM    SWITCH,X'02'        IS MASTER RECORD IN CORE
         BO    NOGETMST           YES, BYPASS GET OF MASTER RECORD
         GET   MSTRIN,MSTRWORK    NO, READ OLD MASTER FILE
         SPACE
         OI    SWITCH,X'02'       INDICATE MASTER IN CORE
         SPACE
NOGETMST EQU   *
```

Figure 2-9 Routine to read transaction file and master file

A similar test is performed for the master file records. The first time, an unprocessed master record will not be in core, so a master record is read and the switch is set to indicate the record is in core storage.

In order to read a tape input file, the GET macro is used.

The format of the GET macro used for tape input files is identical to that used with card files. The first operand is the name of the file as defined by the DTF. The second operand, if used, is the name of the work area into which the logical record will be moved for processing.

COMPARING MASTER AND TRANSACTION

The next step is to determine whether the customer number in the transaction
record is equal to, less than, or greater than the customer number in the master record.

```
NOGETMST  EQU   *
          CLC   CUSTNOTW(5),CUSTNOMW    ARE CUSTOMER NUMBERS EQUAL
          BE    CUSTNOEQ                YES, GO TO EQUAL ROUTINE
          BL    TRANSLOW                IF LOW, GO TO LOW ROUTINE
          SPACE 2
```

Figure 2-10 Routine to compare customer numbers

TRANSACTION HIGH

When the customer number in the master record is lower than the customer number
in the transaction record, it indicates that there is no updating to be performed on the
master record. This is because all the remaining records on the transaction file are
sorted in an ascending sequence and therefore, there will never be an equal condition
between the current master record and a transaction record. Thus, the master record
is written onto the new master file without being changed.

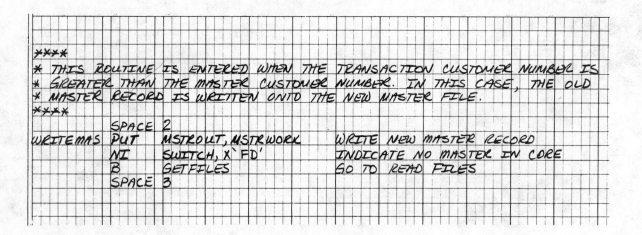

```
****
*  THIS ROUTINE IS ENTERED WHEN THE TRANSACTION CUSTOMER NUMBER IS
*  GREATER THAN THE MASTER CUSTOMER NUMBER. IN THIS CASE, THE OLD
*  MASTER RECORD IS WRITTEN ONTO THE NEW MASTER FILE.
****
          SPACE 2
WRITEMAS  PUT   MSTROUT,MSTRWORK        WRITE NEW MASTER RECORD
          NI    SWITCH,X'FD'            INDICATE NO MASTER IN CORE
          B     GETFILES               GO TO READ FILES
          SPACE 3
```

Figure 2-11 Transaction high routine

The PUT macro is used to write a tape output record. The first operand is the
name of the file as defined by the DTF. The second operand if used is the name of
the work area.

After the record is written on the new file, a switch which indicates than an unprocessed master record is in core is turned off. This is performed by use of the NI (AND
IMMEDIATE) INSTRUCTION. Because the master record in core has been processed
by being written on the new master file, the master switch is turned off. Turning this
switch off allows another master record to be read. See the flowchart in Figure 2-3.

At the GETFILES routine, a test is first made to determine if a transaction record is in core storage. Since the switch was set when the transaction record was read, and the switch was never turned off, a branch around the GET for the transaction file will take place. Next, when a check is made for an unprocessed master record, the switch is off because it was turned off in the WRITEMAS routine. Therefore, a master record will be read.

AND IMMEDIATE Instruction

In the sample problem two programmed switches are used. One switch, a transaction switch, is turned ON to bypass the reading of a transaction record, and is turned OFF when a transaction record is to be read.

A master switch is also required. The master switch is turned ON to bypass the reading of a master record and turned OFF when a master record is to be read.

One byte of storage referenced by the symbolic name SWITCH is used for both the transaction and master switches. Bit 7 is used as the transaction switch. Bit 6 is used as the master switch. At the beginning of the execution of the program, the bits in the byte used for the switches will be set to zero.

The following example explains the use of the master switch. When bit 6 is ON, the switch is considered ON. When bit 6 is OFF, the switch is considered OFF. The same concept is applied to the transaction switch.

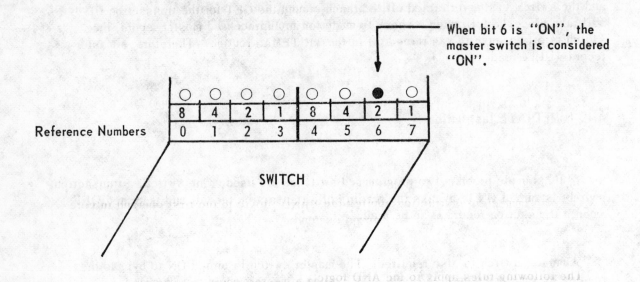

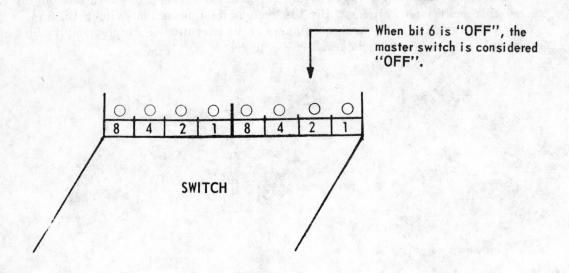

Figure 2-12 Use of master switch

Note that by using this technique a single byte can be used for eight different switches.

In the text INTRODUCTION TO COMPUTER PROGRAMMING, SYSTEM/360 ASSEMBLER LANGUAGE, it was explained that the OR IMMEDIATE instruction can be used to turn a bit ON, that is, change its value from 0 to 1. The AND IMMEDIATE instruction can be used to turn a bit OFF, that is, change its value from 1 to 0. Thus the OR IMMEDIATE and the AND IMMEDIATE instructions can be used to turn switches ... is an explanation of the AND IMMEDIATE instruction.

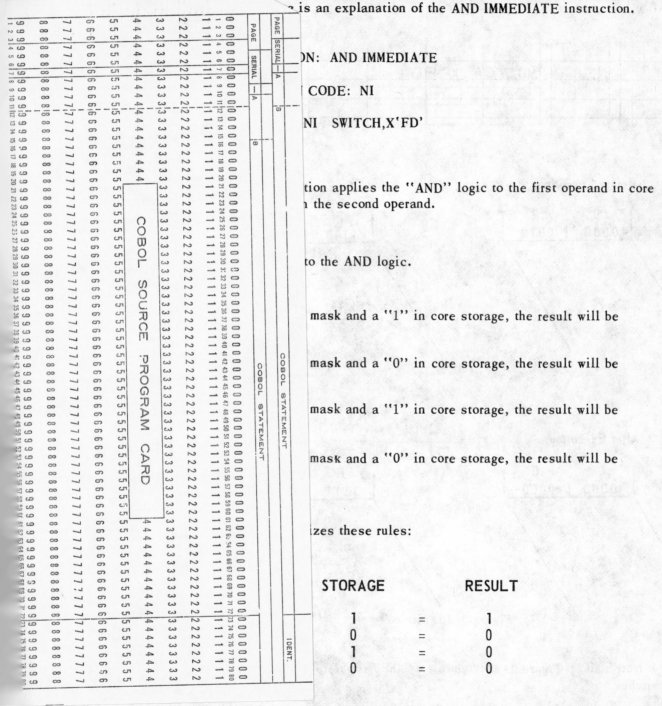

ON: AND IMMEDIATE

CODE: NI

NI   SWITCH,X'FD'

...tion applies the "AND" logic to the first operand in core ... the second operand.

...to the AND logic.

...mask and a "1" in core storage, the result will be

...mask and a "0" in core storage, the result will be

...mask and a "1" in core storage, the result will be

...mask and a "0" in core storage, the result will be

...zes these rules:

	STORAGE		RESULT
1	1	=	1
1	0	=	0
0	1	=	0
0	0	=	0

To summarize, a "1" in the mask leaves core storage the same; a "0" in the mask always gives a "0" in core storage.

The following example illustrates the use of the And Immediate instruction to turn the master switch off. The master switch uses bit 6 of the byte referenced by SWITCH.

EXAMPLE

Before Execution:

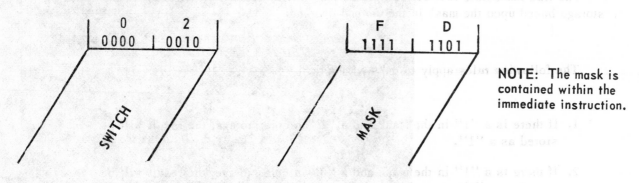

NOTE: The mask is contained within the immediate instruction.

After Execution:

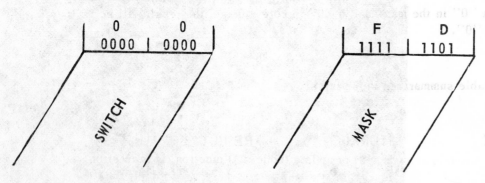

Figure 2-13 Example of And Immediate instruction

Note that after the execution of the And Immediate instruction, bit 6 of the first operand has been set to 0 because bit 6 in the immediate mask was 0. Thus, when using the And Immediate instruction to turn off a bit, the mask must contain a 0 for the bit or bits to be turned off and a "1" in the other bits so that core storage will not be altered.

TRANSACTION LOW

When the transaction record is low, it indicates that the transaction is not to be used to delete or change a master record because there is not a master record which will match the transaction record. This is because all the remaining master records on the old master file will be higher in sequence than the transaction record. Therefore, the only valid function the transaction can perform is an add function, that is, inserting a new master record between two existing master records.

```
****
*  THE FOLLOWING ROUTINE IS ENTERED WHEN THE TRANSACTION RECORD
*  IS LOWER THAN THE MASTER RECORD
****
          SPACE 2
TRANSLOW  EQU    *
          CLI    TRCODETW,C'2'      IS IT A DELETE TRANSACTION
          BE     NOMASTER           YES, GO TO ERROR ROUTINE
          CLI    TRCODETW,C'3'      IS IT AN UPDATE TRANSACTION
          BE     NOMASTER           YES, GO TO ERROR ROUTINE
          CLI    TRCODETW,C'1'      IS IT AN ADD TRANSACTION
          BNE    CODERROR           NO, GO TO CODE TYPE ERROR ROUTINE
          SPACE
          MVC    CUSTNONM(5),CUSTNOTW   MOVE CUST NO TO NEW MASTER REC
          MVC    CUSTNANM(20),CUSTNATW  MOVE CUST NAME TO NEW MASTER REC
          MVC    CUSTADNM(30),CUSTADTW  MOVE CUST ADDRESS TO NEW MASTER
          LA     COMPREG,SALESTW    LOAD ADDRESS OF SALES FIELD
          LA     BCTREG,7           LOAD SIZE OF AMOUNT FIELD
          BAL    LINKREG1,CHKNUMER  GO TO VERIFY FIELD IS NUMERIC
          PACK   SALESNM(4),SALESTW(7)  PACK NEW SALES AMT TO NEW MASTER
          PUT    MSTROUT,NEWMAST    WRITE NEW MASTER RECORD
          NI     SWITCH,X'FE'       INDICATE NO TRANSACTION IN CORE
          B      GETFILES           GO TO READ NEXT TRANSACTION RECORD
```

Figure 2-14 Transaction low routine

Thus, when the transaction is low, the transaction code must be checked to ensure that it indicates an add function (in the sample program, the code to add a record is a "1"). If it indicates a delete (code = 2) or update (code = 3) function, it is in error because it is attempting to delete or change a non-existent master record. If the transaction code indicates that a delete or a change is to be done, the error routine NOMASTER is entered to print the appropriate "no master" error message on the exception report. If the transaction code is invalid, that is, it does not indicate an add, delete or change, a branch is taken to the routine to issue the "invalid code" message.

If the transaction code indicates the record is an add transaction, the fields are moved from the transaction fields to the add work area. When the moves are complete, the added master record is written on the new master file. The switch which indicates an unprocessed transaction record is in core is then turned off. This is because the transaction has been processed by adding it to the master file. A return is then made to the GETFILES routine.

At the GETFILES routine, a transaction record is read because the switch was turned off in the TRANSLOW routine.

A master record is not read, however, because the switch indicating an unprocessed master in core has not been turned off.

TRANSACTION EQUAL TO MASTER

When the customer number on the transaction file is equal to the customer number on the master file, it indicates that either a change to the master record or a deletion of the master record is to take place. An addition of a master record cannot occur because a master record is already on the master file.

```
****
*  THIS ROUTINE IS ENTERED WHEN THE CUSTOMER NUMBERS ARE EQUAL. IF
*  THE TRANSACTION IS AN ADD TRANSACTION, IT IS AN ERROR BECAUSE
*  AN ADD CANNOT OCCUR FOR A RECORD ALREADY ON THE FILE. IF IT IS A
*  DELETE TRANSACTION, A NEW MASTER RECORD WILL BE READ BUT THE OLD
*  MASTER RECORD IS NOT WRITTEN ON THE NEW FILE. IF THE TRANSACTION
*  IS AN UPDATE TO THE SALES AMOUNT, THE NEW AMOUNT IS ADDED TO THE
*  OLD AMOUNT.
****
           SPACE 2
CUSTNOEQ   EQU    *
           CLI    TRCODETW,C'1'           IS IT AN ADD RECORD
           BE     ADDERROR                YES, GO TO ERROR ROUTINE
           SPACE
           CLI    TRCODETW,C'2'           IS IT A DELETE TRANSACTION
           BNE    MSTRUPDT                NO, GO TO CHECK IF IT IS AN UPDATE
           SPACE
           NI     SWITCH,X'FC'            SET SWITCH TO INDICATE NO RECORDS
*                                         IN CORE
           B      GETFILES                GO TO READ BOTH FILES
           SPACE 2
MSTRUPDT   EQU    *
           CLI    TRCODETW,C'3'           IS IT AN AMOUNT UPDATE
           BNE    CODERROR                NO, THE TRANS CODE IS IN ERROR
           LA     COMPREG,SALESTW         LOAD ADDRESS OF AMOUNT FIELD
           LA     BCTREG,7                LOAD SIZE OF FIELD
           BAL    LINKREG1,CHKNUMER       GO TO VERIFY FIELD IS NUMERIC
           SPACE
           PACK   SALESTW+3(4),SALESTW    PACK SALES AMOUNT
           AP     SALESMW(4),SALESTW+3(4) ADD TO MASTER AMOUNT
           NI     SWITCH,X'FE'            INDICATE NO TRANS RECORD IN CORE
           B      GETFILES                GO TO READ TRANSACTION RECORD
```

Figure 2-15 Transaction equal routine

Thus, the first check made on the transaction record is to determine if the transaction code indicates an add function. If so, a branch is made to the ADDERROR routine which prints the appropriate "duplicate record" message.

A check is then made to determine if the transaction is a delete transaction, that is, its purpose is to delete the corresponding master record from the master file. If not, further checks are made on the transaction code at MSTRUPDT. If it is a delete transaction, the switches are set to indicate neither a master record nor a transaction record is unprocessed in core. Thus, when the GETFILES routine is entered, both a transaction record and a master record will be read. This deletes the old master record from the new master file because the old master record is never written to the new master file before another old master record is read. Thus, the deleted record is never written on the new master file. The transaction record has been processed, so a new transaction record must also be read.

If the purpose of the transaction record is not to delete the master, a check is made at MSTRUPDT to ensure the transaction code is equal to 3 (change). If not, the CODERROR routine is entered to print the "invalid transaction code" message on the error listing. If it is a valid change transaction, the amount field in the transaction is checked to verify it contains numeric information and it is then packed and added to the sales field in the master record. The switch which indicates an unprocessed transaction in core is turned off so that a new transaction record will be read. The indicator for the master record, however, is left on. This is so that more than one transaction record can update a master record. If the next transaction record is high, the master record will be written by the WRITEMAS routine and the next master record will be read. If the next transaction is equal, it will also update the master record. The transaction record will never be lower because the transactions are sorted in ascending sequence.

END-OF-FILE

When two files are being read, one file will reach the end of its data before the other file. The transaction file will reach end-of-file first if the last transaction record is less than or equal to the last record on the master file. The master file will reach end-of-file first if its last record is less than the last record on the transaction file. The end-of-file routines for each file are similar and are illustrated below.

```
****
* THIS ROUTINE IS ENTERED AT END OF FILE FOR THE TRANSACTIONS.
****
         SPACE 2
ENDTRANS EQU   *
         CLC   CUSTNOMW,HIGHVALU     HAS MASTER FILE REACHED EOF
         BE    ALLEOF                YES, GO TO COMPLETE PROGRAM
         SPACE
         MVC   CUSTNOTW,HIGHVALU     MOVE HIGH VALUES TO TRANS CUST NO
         OI    SWITCH,X'01'          INDICATE TRANS RECORD IN CORE
         B     GETFILES              GO TO READ MASTER FILE
         SPACE 3
****
* THIS ROUTINE IS ENTERED WHEN END OF FILE IS REACHED FOR THE
* MASTER FILE
****
         SPACE 2
EOTAPE   EQU   *
         CLC   CUSTNOTW,HIGHVALU     HAS TRANS REACHED END OF FILE
         BE    ALLEOF                YES, GO TO COMPLETE PROGRAM
         SPACE
         MVC   CUSTNOMW,HIGHVALU     NO, MOVE HIGH VALUES TO CUST NO
         OI    SWITCH,X'02'          INDICATE MASTER IN CORE
         B     GETFILES              GO TO READ TRANSACTION FILE
         SPACE 3
****
* THIS ROUTINE IS ENTERED WHEN BOTH FILES ARE COMPLETED
****
         SPACE 2
ALLEOF   CLOSE MSTRIN,MSTROUT,TRANSIN,PRTFLE   CLOSE FILES
         EOJ                         END OF JOB
```

Figure 2-16 End-of-file routines

The ENDTRANS routine is entered when the transaction file reaches end-of-file. It first checks if the master file has reached end-of-file. If so, the update processing has been completed and the job can be completed. If not, it moves the constant labelled HIGHVALU to the customer number field in the transaction record work area. HIGHVALU is defined as DC 5X'FF'. Thus, five bytes containing the value X'FF' are moved to the transaction customer number field. When a customer number from a master record is compared to the customer number in the transaction record work area, the master file will always be low (ie. transaction record is high). Therefore, the transaction high routine (WRITEMAS) will always be entered and the old master record will be written on the new master file with no changes. This is the desired result because there are no more transaction records to update or change the master file. The switch is also set to indicate a transaction record is in core storage so that the transaction file will not be read again. The transaction end-of-file routine then branches to the GETFILES routine to read the remainder of the old master records.

2.19

The EOTAPE routine is entered when the old master reaches end-of-file. It checks if the transaction file has reached end-of-file. It does this by comparing the customer number in the transaction record work area to the HIGHVALU constant. If the customer number in the transaction record work area contains all X'FF', then the ENDTRANS routine has been entered previously and therefore the transaction file has reached end-of-file. If this has happened, the EOTAPE routine goes to the ALLEOF routine to complete the program. If not, this routine moves 5 bytes containing X'FF' to the customer number in the master record work area. Placing this value in the customer number area of the master record will make the customer number in any transaction records read lower than the master records. Thus, after end-of-file is reached on the master file, the transaction low routine (TRANSLOW) will always be entered when a transaction record is read. This is the desired routine because there cannot be a match between a transaction record and a master record because there are no more master records. Therefore, the transaction record must either be an addition to the master file or it is in error. The switch is also set to indicate a master record is in core so that the master file will not be read again. The master end-of-file routine then branches to the GETFILES routine to read the remainder of the transaction records.

When both files are completed, the ALLEOF routine is entered to close the files and go to end-of-job.

MASTER FILE CREATION

In the previous explanation of the sequential update logic, it was assumed that the master file had been created and stored on magnetic tape. In actual practice, the master file must be created before it is updated.

In order to create the master file, data which will comprise the master file is normally recorded on punched cards and a program is written to transfer the information contained on the punched card to magnetic tape. In many applications the program used to create the master file is the same program used to update the file. This is accomplished by having a "first-time" routine, that is, a master creation routine, in the update program.

The "first-time" routine, which is executed when there is no master file, reads the card file and writes the new master file on magnetic tape, thus performing a function similar to the addition routine in the update program. The addition routine writes a record on the new master file when one did not exist previously. Thus, with minor modification to the program, the addition routine can be used to create the master file.

In order to incorporate a "first-time" routine into an update program, there must be an external indicator available for the program to test indicating whether or not it is the first time. Again, it should be noted that when it is the first time, the program will be used to create the master file. One method to set an external indicator is through the use of the UPSI switch. The UPSI switch is a single byte in the Communication Region of the Supervisor. At the beginning of each job, the bits are all set to zero. However, by using a job control card, the bits in the UPSI byte can be set to 1. Thus, each bit in the byte can be used as a switch in a manner similar to the switch used in the update logic. The use of the UPSI job control card is illustrated in the appendices.

In the sample program, bit 0 of the UPSI byte is to be used to indicate whether or not the master file has been created. If the bit is equal to 1, it indicates that there is no master file and that it must be created by the program using the first-time routine. If the bit is equal to 0, it indicates there is a master file and that the normal update processing should be done. Thus, when the master file is to be created, the UPSI job control card must be used to set bit 0 equal to 1. At the conclusion of the job, the DOS Job Control routines will reset bit 0 equal to 0.

FIRST-TIME ROUTINE

The first-time routine must first test the UPSI byte to determine if there is an old master. The address of the UPSI byte is determined by the address of the Communication Region. The following example illustrates the testing of the UPSI byte.

EXAMPLE

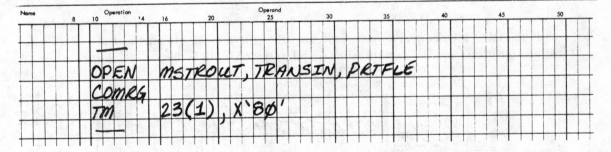

Figure 2-17 Routine to open files and test UPSI bit

As shown above, the address of the Communication Region is returned in Register 1 by the COMRG macro. The displacement of the UPSI byte in the Communication Region is +23 bytes. Thus, the Test Under Mask instruction tests bit 0 of the UPSI byte. Note in the example above that the output file (MSTROUT), the transaction file (TRANSIN), and the print file (PRTFLE) are opened but the old master file (MSTRIN) is not. The old master file cannot be opened until it is determined that there is an old master file.

If bit 0 is equal to 1, it indicates that there is no master file and that it must be created. Since the Addition Routine is to be used to create the master file, some indication must be set in the program so that the Add Routine will always be entered. This can be accomplished by the end-of-file routine for the old master file (EOTAPE). Thus, as shown in the following example, when bit 0 of the UPSI byte is equal to 1, the EOTAPE routine should be entered.

EXAMPLE

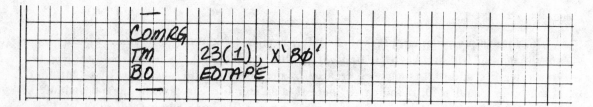

```
        COMRG
        TM      23(1), X'80'
        BO      EOTAPE
```

Figure 2-18 Branch to EOTAPE routine if UPSI bit equals 1

The EOTAPE routine, as shown in Figure 2-16, sets a switch indicating a master record is in core storage and also moves 5 bytes containing X'FF' to the customer number field in the old master record work area. Although there is no master record, this routine will accomplish what is necessary for the first-time creation routine because it insures that the old master file will not be read (this is necessary because there is no old master file) and that the TRANSLOW routine (ie. the Add Routine) will always be entered because the transaction customer number will always be less than the old master customer number. Thus, when the GETFILES routine is entered, only the transaction file will be read and only the TRANSLOW routine will be entered. This is the desired result to create the master file the first time. It should also be noted that the type code in the transaction record must be equal to 1 (Add) or the transaction record is invalid.

If the UPSI bit is equal to 0, it indicates that there is an old master file. Thus, the old master file is opened and the normal update processing is begun, as shown below.

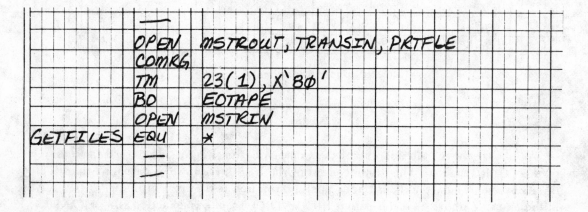

```
            OPEN    MSTROUT, TRANSIN, PRTFLE
            COMRG
            TM      23(1), X'80'
            BO      EOTAPE
            OPEN    MSTRIN
GETFILES    EQU     *
```

Figure 2-19 "First-time" test routine

2.22

SAMPLE PROGRAM

The following pages contain the documentation for the sample file updating problem, including the format of the input, the format of the output, and the program listing.

INPUT

The input to the sample program is a sorted transaction file and the old master file. The transaction file is on cards and the master file is on tape. The record layouts for the two files are illustrated below.

Transaction Records

FIELD	FIELD NAME	FORMAT	POSITION	NO OF DIGITS	LENGTH
Transaction Code	TRCODETW	N - Z	1	1	1
Customer Number	CUSTNOTW	N - Z	2 - 6	5	5
Customer Name	CUSTNATW	AN	7 - 26	20	20
Customer Address	CUSTADTW	AN	27 - 56	30	30
Sales Amount	SALESTW	N - Z	57 - 63	7	7

Master Records

FIELD	FIELD NAME	FORMAT	POSITION	NO OF DIGITS	LENGTH
Customer Number	CUSTNOMW	N - Z	1 - 5	5	5
Customer Name	CUSTNAMW	AN	6 - 25	20	20
Customer Address	CUSTADMW	AN	26 - 55	30	30
Sales Amount	SALESMW	N - P	56 - 59	7	4

LEGEND: N - Z — Numeric, zoned - decimal   AN — Alpha - numeric

N - P — Numeric, packed - decimal

OUTPUT

The output consists of the updated master file with the same record layout as shown above and an error listing.

The format of the error listing is shown below.

	0	1	2	3	4	5	6	7

```
           XX/XX/XX              UPDATE EXCEPTION REPORT                    PAGE XXX

        CODE     CUST NO.   AMOUNT              ERROR

            X        XXXXX   XXXXX.XX   XXXXXXXXXXXXXXXXXXXXXXXXXXXXXXXXXXXXXXXXXXXXXXX
            X        XXXXX   XXXXX.XX   XXXXXXXXXXXXXXXXXXXXXXXXXXXXXXXXXXXXXXXXXXXXXXXX
```

PROGRAM

The following is the listing of the program which sequentially updates the customer sales master file. Note in the segment of the sample program shown on page 2.29 that the DTF's are written at the end of the program rather than as the first entries in the program as illustrated in the programs in the text INTRODUCTION TO COMPUTER PROGRAMMING IBM SYSTEM/360 ASSEMBLER LANGUAGE. This technique allows the DTF to be addressable by using a base register and displacement and in some applications this is desirable. In the sample program, either technique could be used. Note also that the END instruction at statement 558 (page 2.29) does not have an operand. Whenever the operand is omitted on the END statement, the first instruction which will be executed when the program is loaded is the instruction associated with the value 000000 in the location counter. Thus, the first instruction to be executed in the sample program would be the BALR BASEREG,0 instruction at statement 25 (page 2.25). This is the desired beginning point. Thus, when the beginning point is to be the first instruction in the program, the END instruction does not require an operand.

Statement 395 (page 2.28) illustrates the use of the LTORG instruction. The LTORG instruction is used to ensure the addressability of all literals in the program and should be used, as shown in the sample program, whenever large I/O areas are used. A more detailed explanation of the LTORG instruction is contained in Chapter 3.

```
  LOC  OBJECT CODE    ADDR1 ADDR2  STMT   SOURCE STATEMENT                                         DOS CL3-5 09/11/70
  000000                             2 SEQUPDAT START 0                                                      SQUP0020
                                     3        PRINT NOGEN


                                     5 ****                                                                  SQUP0040
                                     6 * THIS PROGRAM UPDATES THE SALES MASTER FILE TO REFLECT MONTHLY SALES SQUP0050
                                     7 * AND GIVE NEW YEAR-TO-DATE SALES FIGURES. THE OLD MASTER AND SORTED  SQUP0060
                                     8 * UPDATE TRANSACTIONS ARE INPUT TO THE PROGRAM. THE OUTPUT OF THE     SQUP0070
                                     9 * PROGRAM IS AN UPDATED MASTER FILE AND AN ERROR EXCEPTION REPORT.    SQUP0080
                                    10 *                                                                     SQUP0090
                                    11 * THREE TYPES OF TRANSACTIONS CAN BE PROCESSED: 1) ADDITIONS-CODE 1;  SQUP0100
                                    12 * 2) DELETIONS - CODE 2; 3) SALES UPDATE- CODE 3.                     SQUP0110
                                    13 *                                                                     SQUP0120
                                    14 * REGISTER USAGE IS AS FOLLOWS                                        SQUP0130
                                    15 *                                                                     SQUP0140
  00000C                            17 BASEREG  EQU    12                                                    SQUP0160
  00000E                            18 HEADREG  EQU    14                                                    SQUP0170
  00000A                            19 LINKREG1 EQU    10                                                    SQUP0180
  000009                            20 COMPREG  EQU    9                                                     SQUP0190
  000007                            21 BCTREG   EQU    7                                                     SQUP0200
  000008                            22 MOVEREG  EQU    8                                                     SQUP0210
                                    23 *                                                                     SQUP0220


  000000 05C0                       25        BALR   BASEREG,0        ESTABLISH BASE REGISTER               SQUP0240
  000002                            26        USING  *,BASEREG                                               SQUP0250

                                    28        OPEN   MSTROUT,TRANSIN,PRTFLE   OPEN FILES                     SQUP0270

  00001A 45E0 C1B8        001BA     39        BAL    HEADREG,HEADROU   GO TO HEADER ROUTINE                 SQUP0290

                                    41        COMRG                    GET COMM REGION ADDRESS              SQUP0292

  000024 9180 1017  00017           46        TM     23(1),X'80'       IS UPSI SWITCH ON                    SQUP0294
  000028 4710 C24A        0024C     47        BO     EOTAPE            YES, GO TO MASTER EOF ROUTINE        SQUP0295
                                    48        OPEN   MSTRIN            NO, OPEN OLD MASTER FILE             SQUP0296

  00003A                            57 GETFILES EQU   *                                                      SQUP0310
  00003A 9101 C31D  0031F           58        TM     SWITCH,X'01'      IS UPDATE TRANSACTION IN CORE        SQUP0320
  00003E 4710 C054        00056     59        BO     NOGETTRN          YES, BYPASS GET OF UPDATE TRANS      SQUP0330
                                    60        GET    TRANSIN,TRANWORK  NO, READ TRANSACTION FILE            SQUP0340

  000052 9601 C31D  0031F           67        OI     SWITCH,X'01'      INDICATE TRANS IN CORE               SQUP0360

  000056                            69 NOGETTRN EQU   *                                                      SQUP0380
  000056 9102 C31D  0031F           70        TM     SWITCH,X'02'      IS MASTER RECORD IN CORE             SQUP0390
  00005A 4710 C070        00072     71        BO     NOGETMST          YES, BYPASS GET OF MASTER RECORD     SQUP0400
                                    72        GET    MSTRIN,MSTRWORK   NO, READ OLD MASTER FILE             SQUP0410

  00006E 9602 C31D  0031F           79        OI     SWITCH,X'02'      INDICATE  MASTER IN CORE             SQUP0430

  000072                            81 NOGETMST EQU   *                                                      SQUP0450
  000072 D504 C293 C2E2 00295 002E4 82        CLC    CUSTNOTW(5),CUSTNOMW  ARE CUSTOMER NUMBERS EQUAL       SQUP0460
  000078 4780 C096        00098     83        BE     CUSTNOEQ          YES, GO TO EQUAL ROUTINE             SQUP0470
  00007C 4740 C0D6        000D8     84        BL     TRANSLOW          IF LOW, GO TO LOW ROUTINE            SQUP0480

                                    86 ****                                                                  SQUP0500
                                    87 * THIS ROUTINE IS ENTERED WHEN THE TRANSACTION CUSTOMER NUMBER IS     SQUP0510
                                    88 * GREATER THAN THE MASTER CUSTOMER NUMBER. IN THIS CASE, THE          SQUP0520
                                    89 * OLD MASTER RECORD IS WRITTEN ONTO THE NEW MASTER FILE.              SQUP0530
                                    90 ****                                                                  SQUP0540

  000090 94FD C31D  0031F           92 WRITEMAS PUT   MSTROUT,MSTRWORK   WRITE NEW MASTER RECORD             SQUP0560
                                    98        NI     SWITCH,X'FD'      TURN OFF IN CORE SWITCH              SQUP0570
  000094 47F0 C038        0003A     99        B      GETFILES          GO TO READ FILES                     SQUP0580


                                   101 ****                                                                  SQUP0600
                                   102 * THIS ROUTINE IS ENTERED WHEN THE CUSTOMER NUMBERS ARE EQUAL. IF     SQUP0610
                                   103 * THE TRANSACTION IS ADD TRANSACTION, IT IS AN ERROR BECAUSE AN ADD   SQUP0620
                                   104 * CANNOT OCCUR FOR A RECORD ALREADY ON THE FILE. IF IT IS A DELETE    SQUP0630
                                   105 * TRANSACTION, A NEW MASTER RECORD IS READ BUT THE OLD MASTER RECORD  SQUP0640
                                   106 * IS NOT WRITTEN ON THE NEW FILE. IF THE TRANSACTION IS AN UPDATE TO  SQUP0650
                                   107 * THE SALES AMOUNT, THE ADDITION IS DONE.                             SQUP0660
                                   108 ****                                                                  SQUP0670

  000098                           110 CUSTNOEQ EQU   *                                                      SQUP0690
  000098 95F1 C292  00294          111        CLI    TRCODETW,C'1'     IS IT AN ADD RECORD                  SQUP0700
  00009C 4780 C12A        0012C    112        BE     ADDERROR          YES, GO TO ERROR ROUTINE            SQUP0710

  0000A0 95F2 C292  00294          114        CLI    TRCODETW,C'2'     IS IT A DELETE TRANSACTION           SQUP0730
  0000A4 4770 C0AE        000B0    115        BNE    MSTRUPDT          NO, GO TO CHECK IF IT IS AN UPDATE   SQUP0740

  0000A8 94FC C31D  0031F          117        NI     SWITCH,X'FC'      SET SWITCH TO INDICATE NO RECORDS    SQUP0760
                                   118 *                                 IN CORE                            SQUP0770
  0000AC 47F0 C038        0003A    119        B      GETFILES          GO TO READ FILES                     SQUP0780
```

LOC   OBJECT CODE   ADDR1 ADDR2 STMT SOURCE STATEMENT   DOS CL3-5 09/11/70

```
                                    121 MSTRUPDT EQU  *                                        SQUP0800
0000B0 95F3 C292      00294         122          CLI  TRCODETW,C'3'      IS IT AN AMOUNT UPDATE  SQUP0810
0000B4 4770 C132            00134   123          BNE  CODERROR           NO, THE TRANS CODE IS IN ERROR  SQUP0820
0000B8 4190 C2CA            002CC   124          LA   COMPREG,SALESTW    LOAD FIELD ADDRESS      SQUP0830
0000BC 4170 0007            00007   125          LA   BCTREG,7           LOAD FIELD SIZE         SQUP0840
0000C0 45A0 C196            00198   126          BAL  LINKREG1,CHKNUMER  GO TO VERIFY FIELD IS NUMERIC  SQUP0850

0000C4 F236 C2CD C2CA 002CF 002CC  128          PACK SALESTW+3(4),SALESTW  PACK SALES AMOUNT    SQUP0870
0000CA FA33 C319 C2CD 0031B 002CF  129          AP   SALESMW(4),SALESTW+3(4)  ADD TO MASTER AMOUNT  SQUP0875
0000D0 94FE C31D      0031F         130          NI   SWITCH,X'FE'       INDICATE NO TRANSACTION RECORD  SQUP0880
0000D4 47F0 C038            0003A   131          B    GETFILES           GO TO READ TRANSACTION FILE  SQUP0890


                                    133 ****                                                    SQUP0910
                                    134 * THE FOLLOWING ROUTINE IS ENTERED WHEN THE TRANSACTION FILE IS  SQUP0920
                                    135 * LOWER THAN THE MASTER RECORD                         SQUP0930
                                    136 ****                                                    SQUP0940


0000D8                              138 TRANSLOW EQU  *                                         SQUP0960
0000D8 95F2 C292      00294         139          CLI  TRCODETW,C'2'      IS IT A DELETE         SQUP0970
0000DC 4780 C13A            0013C   140          BE   NOMASTER           YES, GO TO ERROR ROUTINE  SQUP0980
0000E0 95F3 C292      00294         141          CLI  TRCODETW,C'3'      IS IT AN UPDATE        SQUP0990
0000E4 4780 C13A            0013C   142          BE   NOMASTER           YES, GO TO ERROR ROUTINE  SQUP1000
0000E8 95F1 C292      00294         143          CLI  TRCODETW,C'1'      IS IT AN ADD           SQUP1010
0000EC 4770 C132            00134   144          BNE  CODERROR           NO, GO TO CODE TYPE ERROR  SQUP1020

0000F0 D204 C31E C293 00320 00295  146          MVC  CUSTNONM(5),CUSTNOTW  MOVE CUSTOMER NUMBER TO NEW REC  SQUP1040
0000F6 D213 C323 C298 00325 0029A  147          MVC  CUSTNANM(20),CUSTNATW  MOVE CUSTOMER NAME TO NEW REC  SQUP1050
0000FC D21D C337 C2AC 00339 002AC  148          MVC  CUSTADNM(30),CUSTADTW  MOVE CUSTOMER ADDRESS TO NEW REC  SQUP1060
000102 4190 C2CA            002CC   149          LA   COMPREG,SALESTW    LOAD ADDRESS OF SALES FIELD  SQUP1070
000106 4170 0007            00007   150          LA   BCTREG,L'SALESTW   LOAD SIZE OF FIELD     SQUP1080
00010A 45A0 C196            00198   151          BAL  LINKREG1,CHKNUMER  GO TO VERIFY FIELD IS NUMERIC  SQUP1090
00010E F236 C355 C2CA 00357 002CC  152          PACK SALESNM(4),SALESTW(7)  PACK NEW SALES FIGURE  SQUP1100
                                    153          PUT  MSTROUT,NEWMAST    WRITE NEW MASTER RECORD  SQUP1110
000124 94FE C31D      0031F         159          NI   SWITCH,X'FE'       INDICATE NO TRANSACTION RECORD  SQUP1120
000128 47F0 C038            0003A   160          B    GETFILES           GO TO READ NEXT TRANS RECORD  SQUP1130


                                    162 ****                                                    SQUP1150
                                    163 * THIS ROUTINE IS ENTERED WHEN A RECORD HAS AN ADD TYPE CODE AND  SQUP1160
                                    164 * THERE IS ALREADY A RECORD ON THE FILE                SQUP1170
                                    165 ****                                                    SQUP1180


00012C                              167 ADDERROR EQU  *                                         SQUP1200
00012C 4180 C449            0044B   168          LA   MOVEREG,ADDMSG     LOAD ADDRESS OF ERROR MSG  SQUP1210
000130 47F0 C142            00144   169          B    COMMEROR           GO TO THE COMMON ERROR ROUTINE  SQUP1220


                                    171 ****                                                    SQUP1240
                                    172 * THIS ROUTINE IS ENTERED WHEN THE TRANS CONTAINS AN INVALID TYPE CODE  SQUP1250
                                    173 ****                                                    SQUP1260


000134                              175 CODERROR EQU  *                                         SQUP1280
000134 4180 C478            0047A   176          LA   MOVEREG,CODEMSG    LOAD ADDRESS OF ERROR MSG  SQUP1290
000138 47F0 C142            00144   177          B    COMMEROR           GO TO COMMON ERROR ROUTINE  SQUP1300


                                    179 ****                                                    SQUP1320
                                    180 * THIS ROUTINE IS ENTERED WHEN NO MASTER EXISTS FOR THE TRANSACTION  SQUP1330
                                    181 ****                                                    SQUP1340


00013C                              183 NOMASTER EQU  *                                         SQUP1360
00013C 4180 C4A7            004A9   184          LA   MOVEREG,MASTMSG    LOAD ADDRESS OF ERROR MSG  SQUP1370
000140 47F0 C142            00144   185          B    COMMEROR           GO TO COMMON ERROR ROUTINE  SQUP1380


                                    187 ****                                                    SQUP1400
                                    188 * THIS ROUTINE IS ENTERED FOR ALL ERRORS               SQUP1410
                                    189 ****                                                    SQUP1420


000144                              191 COMMEROR EQU  *                                         SQUP1440
000144 9240 C3F9      003FB         192          MVI  REPORT,C' '        CLEAR PRINTER AREA     SQUP1450
000148 D24E C3FA C3F9 003FC 003FB  193          MVC  REPORT+1(79),REPORT                       SQUP1460
00014E D200 C3FD C292 003FF 00294  194          MVC  CODER(1),TRCODETW  MOVE CODE TO REPORT    SQUP1470
000154 D204 C404 C293 00406 00295  195          MVC  CUSTNOR(5),CUSTNOTW  MOVE CUSTOMER NO TO REPORT  SQUP1480
00015A D204 C40D C2CA 0040F 002CC  196          MVC  AMOUNTR(5),SALESTW  MOVE AMOUNT           SQUP1490
000160 D201 C413 C2CF 00415 002D1  197          MVC  AMOUNTR+6(2),SALESTW+5                    SQUP1500
000166 9248 C412      00414         198          MVI  AMOUNTR+5,C'.'                           SQUP1510
00016A D22E C41A 8000 0041C 00000  199          MVC  ERRR(47),0(MOVEREG)  MOVE ERROR MSG TO REPORT  SQUP1520
                                    200          PUT  PRTFLE,REPORT      WRITE REPORT           SQUP1530
                                    206          PRTOV PRTFLE,12,HEADROU                        SQUP1540
000190 94FE C31D      0031F         212          NI   SWITCH,X'FE'       INDICATE NO TRANSACTION  SQUP1550
000194 47F0 C038            0003A   213          B    GETFILES           GO READ NEXT RECORD    SQUP1560
```

2.26

    LOC   OBJECT CODE   ADDR1 ADDR2 STMT   SOURCE STATEMENT   FDOS CL3-6 09/30/70

```
                                       215 ****                                              SQUP1580
                                       216 * THIS ROUTINE IS ENTERED TO CHECK FOR NUMERIC DATA   SQUP1590
                                       217 ****                                              SQUP1600

000198                                 219 CHKNUMER EQU  *                                   SQUP1620
000198 95F0 9000       00000           220          CLI  0(COMPREG),C'0'   IS VALUE LESS THAN ZERO   SQUP1630
00019C 4740 C1B0             001B2     221          BL   NOTNUMER          YES, GO TO ERROR         SQUP1640
0001A0 95F9 9000       00000           222          CLI  0(COMPREG),C'9'   IS VALUE GREATER THAN NINE SQUP1650
0001A4 4720 C1B0             001B2     223          BH   NOTNUMER          YES, GO TO ERROR         SQUP1660
0001A8 4199 0001       00001           224          LA   COMPREG,1(COMPREG) BUMP ADDRESS BY 1      SQUP1670
0001AC 4670 C196             00198     225          BCT  BCTREG,CHKNUMER    GO TO CHECK NEXT DIGIT   SQUP1680
0001B0 07FA                            226          BR   LINKREG1          IF FALL THRU, FIELD IS OK SQUP1690

0001B2                                 228 NOTNUMER EQU  *                                   SQUP1710
0001B2 4180 C4DA             004DC     229          LA   MOVEREG,NUMMSG     LOAD ADDRESS OF ERROR MSG SQUP1720
0001B6 47F0 C142             00144     230          B    COMMEROR          GO TO COMMON ERROR ROUTINE SQUP1730


                                       232 ****                                              SQUP1750
                                       233 * THIS ROUTINE IS ENTERED TO PRINT THE REPORT HEADING   SQUP1760
                                       234 ****                                              SQUP1770


0001BA                                 236 HEADROU  EQU  *                                   SQUP1790
0001BA 50E0 C50A             0050C     237          ST   HEADREG,SAVEHEAD   SAVE LINK REGISTER       SQUP1800
0001BE FA10 C512 C55A 00514 0055C      238          AP   PGCNT,=P'1'       UPDATE PAGE COUNT        SQUP1810
0001C4 D203 C3A8 C50E 003AA 00510      239          MVC  PGNO(4),PGEDIT     MOVE EDIT PATTERN FOR PAGE SQUP1820
0001CA DE03 C3A8 C512 003AA 00514      240          ED   PGNO(4),PGCNT      EDIT PAGE NO             SQUP1830
0001D0 9140 C321       00323           241 BR       TM   SWITCH,X'40'       IS IT FIRST TIME         SQUP1840
0001D4 4710 C1E6             001E8     242          BO   AFTRFRST          NO BYPASS DATE ROUTINE   SQUP1850
                                       243          COMRG                                      SQUP1860
0001DE D207 C35F 1000 00361 00000      247          MVC  HDATE(8),0(1)      MOVE DATE TO HEADER      SQUP1870
0001E4 9640 C321       00323           248          OI   SWITCH,X'40'       SET BRANCH TO UNCONDITIONAL SQUP1880

                                       250 AFTRFRST CNTRL PRTFLE,SK,1        SKIP TO HEAD OF FORMS    SQUP1900
                                       256          PUT  PRTFLE,HEADER1     PRINT FIRST LINE         SQUP1910

                                       263          CNTRL PRTFLE,SP,1       SPACE ONCE               SQUP1930

                                       270          PUT  PRTFLE,HEADER2     PRINT SECOND LINE        SQUP1950

                                       277          CNTRL PRTFLE,SP,2       SPACE TWICE              SQUP1970

000232 58E0 C50A             0050C     284          L    HEADREG,SAVEHEAD   RELOAD REGISTER          SQUP1990
000236 07FE                            285          BR   HEADREG           RETURN TO CALLER         SQUP2000


                                       287 ****                                              SQUP2020
                                       288 * THIS ROUTINE IS ENTERED AT END OF FILE FOR THE TRANSACTIONS SQUP2030
                                       289 ****                                              SQUP2040


000238                                 291 ENDTRANS EQU  *                                   SQUP2060
000238 D504 C2E6 C514 002E8 00516      292          CLC  CUSTNOMW,HIGHVALU  HAS MASTER FILE REACHED EOF SQUP2070
00023E 4780 C266             00268     293          BE   ALLEOF            YES, GO TO COMPLETE PROGRAM SQUP2080

000242 D204 C297 C514 00299 00516      295          MVC  CUSTNOTW,HIGHVALU  MOVE HIGH VALUES TO TRANS CUST NO SQUP2100
000248 9601 C321       00323           296          OI   SWITCH,X'01'       INDICATE TRANS IN CORE   SQUP2110
00024C 47F0 C038             0003A     297          B    GETFILES          GO TO READ MASTER FILE   SQUP2120


                                       299 ****                                              SQUP2140
                                       300 * THIS ROUTINE IS ENTERED WHEN END OF FILE IS REACHED FOR THE MASTER SQUP2150
                                       301 * FILE                                             SQUP2160
                                       302 ****                                              SQUP2170


000250                                 304 EOTAPE   EQU  *                                   SQUP2190
000250 D504 C297 C514 00299 00516      305          CLC  CUSTNOTW,HIGHVALU  HAS TRANS REACHED END OF FILE SQUP2200
000256 4780 C266             00268     306          BE   ALLEOF            YES, GO TO COMPLETE PROGRAM SQUP2210

00025A D204 C2E6 C514 002E8 00516      308          MVC  CUSTNOMW,HIGHVALU  NO, MOVE HIGH VALUES TO MSTR CUST NO SQUP2230
000260 9602 C321       00323           309          OI   SWITCH,X'02'       INDICATE MASTER IN CORE  SQUP2240
000264 47F0 C038             0003A     310          B    GETFILES                                   SQUP2245


                                       312 ****                                              SQUP2260
                                       313 * THIS ROUTINE IS ENTERED WHEN BOTH FILES ARE COMPLETED   SQUP2270
                                       314 ****                                              SQUP2280


000268                                 316 ALLEOF   EQU  *                                   SQUP2300
000268 9180 1017       00017           317          TM   23(1),X'80'        WAS THERE AN OLD MASTER  SQUP2303
00026C 4710 C27E             00280     318          BO   NOCLOSE           NO, DO NOT CLOSE THE OLD MASTER SQUP2305
                                       319          CLOSE MSTRIN            CLOSE THE OLD MASTER FILE SQUP2306
                                       327 NOCLOSE  CLOSE MSTROUT,TRANSIN,PRTFLE  CLOSE THE FILES   SQUP2308
                                       337          EOJ                    END OF JOB               SQUP2310
```

```
                                      341 ****                                     SQUP2330
                                      342 * CONSTANTS, WORK AREAS, ETC.            SQUP2340
                                      343 ****                                     SQUP2350

000294                                345 TRANWORK DS    OCL80                     SQUP2370
000294                                346 TRCODETW DS    CL1                       SQUP2380
000295                                347 CUSTNOTW DS    CL5                       SQUP2390
00029A                                348 CUSTNATW DS    CL20                      SQUP2400
0002AE                                349 CUSTACTW DS    CL30                      SQUP2410
0002CC                                350 SALESTW  DS    CL7                       SQUP2420
0002D3                                351          DS    CL17                      SQUP2430


0002E4                                353 MSTRWORK DS    OCL59                     SQUP2450
0002E4                                354 CUSTNOMW DS    CL5                       SQUP2460
0002E9                                355 CUSTNAMW DS    CL20                      SQUP2470
0002FD                                356 CUSTADMW DS    CL30                      SQUP2480
00031B                                357 SALESMW  DS    CL4                       SQUP2490


00031F 00                             359 SWITCH   DC    X'00'                     SQUP2510
000320                                360 NEWMAST  DS    OCL59                     SQUP2520
000320                                361 CUSTNONM DS    CL5                       SQUP2530
000325                                362 CUSTNANM DS    CL20                      SQUP2540
000339                                363 CUSTADNM DS    CL30                      SQUP2550
000357                                364 SALESNM  DS    CL4                       SQUP2560


00035B                                366 HEADER1  DS    OCL80                     SQUP2580
00035B 4040                           367          DC    CL2' '                    SQUP2590
00035D                                368 HDATE    DS    CL8                       SQUP2600
000365 4040404040404040               369          DC    CL17' '                   SQUP2610
000376 E4D7C4C1E3C540C5               370          DC    C'UPDATE EXCEPTION REPORT' SQUP2620
00038D 4040404040404040               371          DC    CL21' '                   SQUP2630
0003A2 D7C1C7C5                       372          DC    C'PAGE'                    SQUP2640
0003A6                                373 PGNO     DS    CL4                       SQUP2650
0003AA 40                             374          DC    CL1' '                    SQUP2660
0003AB                                375 HEADER2  DS    OCL80                     SQUP2670
0003AB 4040C3D6C4C54040               376          DC    C' CODE    CUST NO.    AMOUNT          ERROR' SQUP2680
0003D9 4040404040404040               377          DC    CL34' '                   SQUP2690
0003FB                                378 REPORT   DS    OCL80                     SQUP2700
0003FB                                379          DS    CL4                       SQUP2710
0003FF                                380 CODER    DS    CL1                       SQUP2720
000400                                381          DS    CL6                       SQUP2730
000406                                382 CUSTNOR  DS    CL5                       SQUP2740
00040B                                383          DS    CL4                       SQUP2750
00040F                                384 AMOUNTR  DS    CL8                       SQUP2760
000417                                385          DS    CL5                       SQUP2770
00041C                                386 ERRR     DS    CL47                      SQUP2780
00044B C1C4C4C9E3C9D6D5               387 ADDMSG   DC    CL47'ADDITION OF DUPLICATE RECORD ATTEMPTED' SQUP2790
00047A C9D5E5C1D3C9C440               388 CODEMSG  DC    CL47'INVALID TYPE CODE'   SQUP2800
0004A9 D5D640D4C1E3C3C8               389 MASTMSG  DC    CL47'NO MATCHING MASTER RECORD' SQUP2810
0004D8 D5D6D560D5E4D4C5               390 NUMMSG   DC    CL47'NON-NUMERIC VALUE IN NUMERIC FIELD' SQUP2820
000508                                391 SAVEHEAD DS    F                         SQUP2830
00050C 40202020                       392 PGEDIT   DC    X'40202020'               SQUP2840
000510 000C                           393 PGCNT    DC    PL2'0'                    SQUP2850
000512 FFFFFFFFFF                     394 HIGHVALU DC    5X'FF'                    SQUP2860
000518                                395          LTORG                           SQUP2870
000518 5B5BC2D6D7C5D540               396                =C'$$BOPEN '
000520 5B5BC2C3D3D6E2C5               397                =C'$$BCLOSE'
000528 00000588                       398                =A(TRANSIN)
00052C 00000294                       399                =A(TRANWORK)
000530 000005C0                       400                =A(MSTRIN)
000534 000002E4                       401                =A(MSTRWORK)
000538 00000630                       402                =A(MSTROUT)
00053C 00000320                       403                =A(NEWMAST)
000540 00000558                       404                =A(PRTFLE)
000544 000003FB                       405                =A(REPORT)
000548 000001BA                       406                =A(HEADROU)
00054C 0000035B                       407                =A(HEADER1)
000550 000003AB                       408                =A(HEADER2)
000554 1C                             409                =P'1'
```

2.28

LOC   OBJECT CODE   ADDR1 ADDR2 STMT   SOURCE STATEMENT   DOS CL3-5 09/11/70

```
                                    411 ****                                          SQUP2890
                                    412 * PRINTER FILE DEFINITION                     SQUP2900
                                    413 ****                                          SQUP2910

                                    415 PRTFLE   DTFPR DEVADDR=SYSLST,IOAREA1=PRTIO1,IOAREA2=PRTIO2,   CSQUP2930
                                                 BLKSIZE=80,CONTROL=YES,DEVICE=1403,MODNAME=IJDFCPIW,  CSQUP2940
                                                 PRINTOV=YES,RECFORM=FIXUNB,WORKA=YES                  SQUP2950


                                    437 ****                                          SQUP2970
                                    438 * UPDATE TRANSACTION FILE                     SQUP2980
                                    439 ****                                          SQUP2990

                                    441 TRANSIN  DTFCD BLKSIZE=80,EOFADDR=ENDTRANS,IOAREA1=TRANSIO1,   CSQUP3010
                                                 IOAREA2=TRANSIO2,MODNAME=IJCFZIB3,RECFORM=FIXUNB,     CSQUP3020
                                                 TYPEFLE=INPUT,DEVICE=2501,DEVADDR=SYSRDR,WORKA=YES    SQUP3030


                                    462 ****                                          SQUP3060
                                    463 * OLD MASTER FILE                             SQUP3070
                                    464 ****                                          SQUP3080

                                    466 MSTRIN   DTFMT BLKSIZE=3599,EOFADDR=EOTAPE,IOAREA1=MSTRIO1,    CSQUP3100
                                                 IOAREA2=MSTRIO2,MODNAME=IJFFZZWZ,RECFORM=FIXBLK,      CSQUP3110
                                                 RECSIZE=59,TYPEFLE=INPUT,WORKA=YES,REWIND=UNLOAD,     CSQUP3120
                                                 DEVADDR=SYS011,FILABL=STD                             SQUP3130


                                    505 ****                                          SQUP3150
                                    506 * NEW MASTER FILE                             SQUP3160
                                    507 ****                                          SQUP3170

                                    509 MSTROUT  DTFMT BLKSIZE=3599,IOAREA1=MSTRIO3,IOAREA2=MSTRIO4,   CSQUP3190
                                                 MODNAME=IJFFZZWZ,RECFORM=FIXBLK,RECSIZE=59,           CSQUP3200
                                                 TYPEFLE=OUTPUT,WORKA=YES,REWIND=UNLOAD,DEVADDR=SYS010, CSQUP3210
                                                 FILABL=STD                                           SQUP3215
                                    545 ****                                          SQUP3220
                                    546 * I/O AREAS                                   SQUP3230
                                    547 ****                                          SQUP3240

000698                              549 PRTIO1   DS    CL80                           SQUP3260
0006E8                              550 PRTIO2   DS    CL80                           SQUP3270
000738                              551 TRANSIO1 DS    CL80                           SQUD3280
000788                              552 TRANSIO2 DS    CL80                           SQUD3290
0007D8                              553 MSTRIO1  DS    CL3599                         SQUP3300
0015E7                              554 MSTRIO2  DS    CL3599                         SQUP3310
0023F6                              555 MSTRIO3  DS    CL3607                         SQUP3320
00320D                              556 MSTRIO4  DS    CL3607                         SQUP3330

                                    558          END                                 SQUP3350
```

PROGRAMMING ASSIGNMENT

INSTRUCTIONS

A salesman master file is to be created and updated. The format of the master file is illustrated below. This master file is to be stored on magnetic tape.

FIELD	FORMAT	POSITION	NO OF DIGITS	LENGTH
Department Number	N-P	1-2	2	2
Salesman Number	N-P	3-4	3	2
Salesman Name	AN	5-24	20	20
Year-To-Date Sales	N-P	25-28	7	4
Months Employed	N-P	29-30	3	2

LEGEND   N-P — Numeric, pack-decimal   AN — Alpha-numeric

The salesman master file is created or updated from sales transaction cards. The format of the cards is illustrated below.

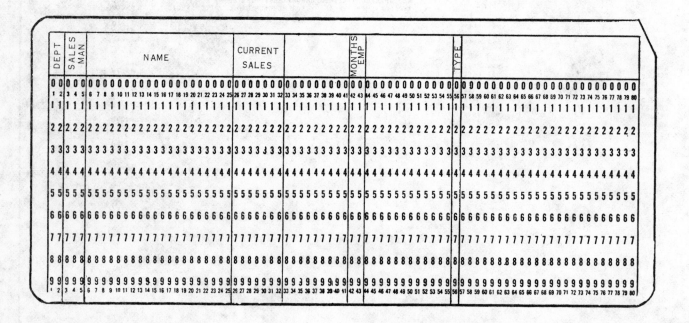

In the transaction cards, the "type" field (card column 56) may contain the following values:

1 = add or load   3 = change
2 = delete

A single program should be written that will initially load the master file and will also update the file after it has been loaded. Processing should take place as follows:

1. The UPSI switch should be used to determine if the "first-time" routine in the program should be used. If bit 0 is equal to 1, it indicates there is no master and if bit 0 is equal to 0, it indicates there is a master. If there is not a master, the new master must be created.

2. If a master exists, an addition (type = 1), a deletion (type = 2), or a change (type = 3) must be processed. An addition takes place when a new salesman is to be added to the master file. A deletion takes place when a salesman's number is to be removed from the master file. A change occurs when the Year-To-Date Sales Field is to be updated by the Current Sales Field in the Transaction record.

3. All numeric fields in the transaction card must be numeric.

4. The Months Employed Field in the master record must be updated by 1 each time the master is updated.

5. An exception report is to be created which identifies each transaction record with an error and the type of error must also be specified. The programmer is to design the format of this exception report.

CHAPTER 3

SEQUENTIAL ACCESS METHOD

DIRECT ACCESS DEVICES

INTRODUCTION

As illustrated in Chapter 2, magnetic tape files utilize the sequential access method. Direct access devices can also use the sequential access method to process records.

The program presented in this chapter illustrates the use of magnetic tape and the sequential access method for direct access devices. The program reads a card file and a tape input file and creates a sequential disk output file.

The record format of the two input files and the output file is identical. The card format is illustrated below.

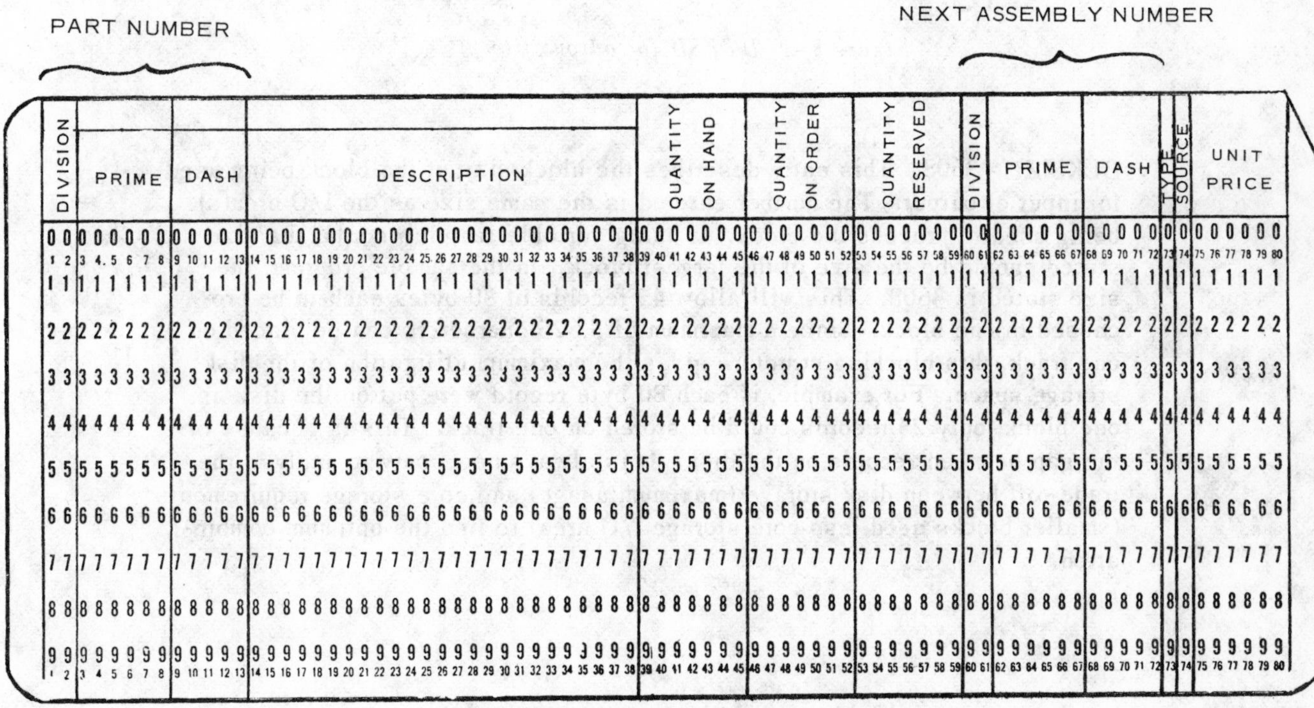

Figure 3-1 Card format

The record length of the records is, as shown, 80 bytes. The tape input file contains 4 records per block. Thus, the block size is 320 bytes. The disk output file contains 45 records per block. Thus, the block size is 3600 bytes.

DTFSD

When processing a disk file in a sequential manner, the file must be defined by a DTFSD. The DTFSD supplies all the definitions needed for the sequential disk file. The following example illustrates the entries for a DTFSD followed by an explanation of the entries.

```
****
* SEQUENTIAL DISK DTF
****


SEQDISK   DTFSD BLKSIZE=3608,IOAREA1=DISKIO1,IOAREA2=DISKIO2,
                DEVADDR=SYSOO4,DEVICE=2311,
                MODNAME=IJGFOZZZ,RECFORM=FIXBLK,RECSIZE=80,
                TYPEFLE=OUTPUT,VERIFY=YES,WORKA=YES
```

Figure 3 - 2 DTFSD for output file

1. BLKSIZE = 3608: This entry describes the block size of the block being used for input or output. The number entered is the same size as the I/O area(s) being used to process the block. If using variable length records, the size stated should be the size of the largest block. In the sample program, the size stated is 3608. This will allow 45 records of 80 bytes each to be processed in one block. Since a maximum of 3,625 characters can be placed on one track, this blocking structure gives the maximum utilization of the disk storage space. For example, if each 80 byte record were put on the disk as one block, only 25 records could be stored on one track. This is because of the gap between records on the disk. It is always necessary to analyze the trade - off between disk storage (maximum usage) and core storage requirements (smaller blocks need less core storage I/O area) to find the optimum combination.

The extra 8 bytes in the number stated are a requirement of all sequential disk OUTPUT files. This area (first 8 bytes in I/O area) is used as a count area by Logical IOCS. The count area is used by Logical IOCS to locate and retrieve records on a disk file. The count area contains the cylinder number, track number, record number, key length and data length of the record. When using variable-length records, the size of the I/O area must include 4 bytes for the block size.

2. IOAREA1 = DISKIO1 and IOAREA2 = DISKIO2: These entries specify the names of the I/O areas to be used for this file. Each I/O area will have a length as stated in the BLKSIZE keyword. The I/O areas must begin on a half-word boundary.

3. DEVADDR = SYS004: This entry indicates which SYS number will be used for the file.

4. DEVICE = 2311: This operand states which direct-access device is to be used with this file. The valid entries are 2311, 2314, or 2321 (data cell). If this operand is omitted, the 2311 device is assumed.

5. MODNAME = IJGFOZZZ: This entry specifies the name of the I/O module which will be used to process the file.

6. RECFORM = FIXBLK: This entry states the type of record and blocking structure to be used. Valid entries are FIXUNB (fixed-unblocked), FIXBLK (fixed-blocked), VARUNB (variable-unblocked), VARBLK (variable-blocked), or UNDEF (undefined).

7. RECSIZE = 80: This operand states the record size if FIXBLK records are being used. For undefined records, it states a register to be used for record sizes.

8. TYPEFLE = OUTPUT: This entry specifies what type of file this DTF is defining. The valid entries are INPUT, OUTPUT and WORK. (For more detailed information on work files, see IBM SRL C24-5037, Supervisor & I/O Macros.)

9. VERIFY = YES: This entry is applicable to output files only. If used, it tells logical IOCS to verify the parity of each record that it writes.

10. WORKA = YES: This entry is specified if a work area is going to be used with the GET and PUT macros for this file.

If two I/O areas are used, either the WORKA = YES or IOREG = (r) operands must be stated.

In order to write on a direct access device using the sequential access method, a PUT macro is used. Its format is identical to that used with cards, the printer, and tape.

```
PUT     SEQDISK,ALLWORK     PUT CARD ONTO DISK
B       CARDAGIN            GO TO READ ANOTHER CARD
```

Figure 3-3 Example of PUT macro for sequential disk

The name SEQDISK is the name specified in the DTFSD. The name specified in the second operand, ALLWORK, is the name of a work area. When a work area is used, the WORKA=YES operand must be included in the DTFSD macro.

LTORG

As has been pointed out, the System/360 uses a base register plus displacement addressing technique. Although the base register can address any addressable location in the 360, the displacement from the address in the base register is limited in size because of the format of the machine language instructions.

RX Format:

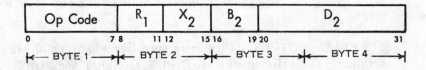

Figure 3-4 Example of RX instruction format

Note in the sample RX instruction format shown above that the displacement occupies 12 bits (20-31). The maximum value which can be specified in these 12 bits is FFF (hexadecimal) or 4095 (decimal). Therefore, the maximum displacement which may be specified in the instruction is 4,096 bytes (one greater then the machine language instruction). It should be recalled that addresses are obtained by adding the value in the base register plus the displacement. Thus, any location more than 4,096 bytes away from the value in the base register will not be addressable.

Various techniques exist in the System/360 addressing scheme to override this problem and these will be discussed in ensuing chapters. One technique, however, is illustrated in the sample program presented in this chapter.

One method of introducing data into a program is the use of a LITERAL. As has been shown in previous sample programs, the LITERAL is introduced by using an equal sign and the constant in the second operand of an instruction.

When an instruction identifying a literal is assembled, the data specified in the second operand of the instruction is placed in a LITERAL POOL. This literal pool contains all literals introduced within the program. When the assembly is complete, the literal pool is brought together and placed at the end of the assembly. The displacement to the various literals is then computed by the assembler and the base register plus displacement is placed in the machine language instruction.

The following example illustrates the literal pool at the end of the assembly.

```
0000D4 FD52 421F 40F8 00289 00162      77        DP      DIVFIELD,QUANTITY+1(3)
0000DA F921 4222 42AA 0028C 00314      78        CP      DIVFIELD+3(3),=P'000'
0000E0 4770 40A4            0010E       79        BNE     ERROR
0000E4 F342 417F 421F 001E9 00289      80        UNPK    UNITCOST(5),DIVFIELD(3)
0000EA 96F0 4183           001ED       81        OI      UNITCOST+4,X'F0'
                                                   •
                                                   •
                                                   •
000289 00000000000C                    138 DIVFIELD DC    PL6'0'
00028F                                 139 ENDMSG  DS      CL90'END OF JOB'
000068                                 140         END     BEGIN
0002F0 5B5BC2D6D7C5D540                141                 =C'$$BOPEN '
0002F8 5B5BC2C4E4D4D740                142                 =CL8'$$BDUMP'
000300 5B5BC2C3D3D6E2C5                143                 =C'$$BCLOSE'
000308 00000038                        144                 =A(PRINTER)
00030C 00000000                        145                 =A(CARDFLE)
000310 F0F0F0F0                        146                 =C'0000'
000314 000C                            147                 =P'000'
```

Figure 3-5 Example of assembly without LTORG instruction

Note in the example that the literal pool is placed at the end of the assembly and that the references to the values in the pool are by base register plus displacement. For example, in statement 78, the literal P'000' generates a statement in the literal pool at statement 147. It is addressed by referencing base register 4 plus a displacement of 2AA.

As has been noted, the literal pool is at the end of the assembly. In many instances that is perfectly all right. However, in the sample program for this chapter, if the literals were to be at the end of the assembly, they would be unaddressable. This is due to the fact that the I/O areas alone have a size greater than 4096 bytes. Note in the DTFSD illustrated in Figure 3-2 that the block size is specified as 3608. As two I/O areas are used, 7216 bytes are required for just the output areas. Thus, if the literals were at the end of the assembly, they would be unaddressable.

In order to correct this situation, the LTORG instruction is used. The LTORG instruction causes all literals which have been used up to the point of the LTORG statement to be assembled into the program at that point.

The following segment of a program illustrates the use of a LTORG statement within a program.

```
00002A 4570 C0CA                   000CC    32        BAL     LINKREG1,CHKALL
00002E 47F0 C018                   0001A    33        B       CARDAGIN
000032 FA20 C2CC C302  002CE 00304 34        AP      CARDCNT(3),=P'1'
                                            35        PUT     SEQDISK,ALLWORK
                                                •
                                                •
                                                •

0002D8                                      197       LTORG
0002D8 5B5BC2D6D7C5D540                      198               =C'$$BOPEN '
0002E0 5B5BC2C3D3D6E2C5                      199               =C'$$BCLOSE'
0002E8 00000308                             200               =A(CARDFLE)
0002EC 00000528                             201               =A(ALLWORK)
0002F0 00000370                             202               =A(SEQDISK)
0002F4 00000000                             203               =A(TAPEFLE)
0002F8 00000340                             204               =A(PRTFLE)
0002FC 00000256                             205               =A(TOTMSG)
000300 000001BE                             206               =A(BADMSG)
000304 1C                                   207               =P'1'
```

Figure 3-6 Example of assembly with LTORG instruction

Thus, with the use of the LTORG instruction, the programmer can insure that all literals used in the program are addressable.

INVENTORY SYSTEM

The sample program presented in this chapter is the first of a series of four programs presented to illustrate a "typical" inventory system. Although most inventory systems in use are much more complex than the one presented here, the concepts presented are intended to illustrate basic programming methods and techniques useful in a wide variety of applications.

The system flowchart is illustrated below.

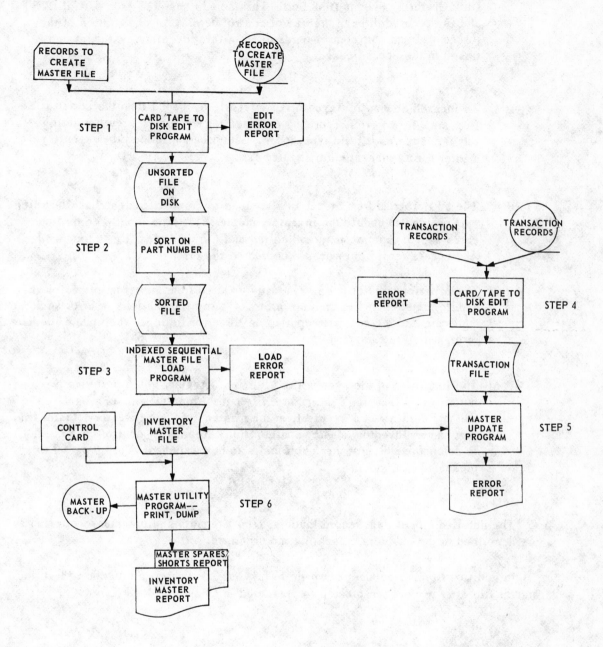

Figure 3-7 Inventory system flowchart

The inventory system can be segmented into steps, as explained below.

STEP 1: Unsorted records from cards and tape are read and edited and a sequential
         file is created. The records in step 1 are used to load the indexed
         sequential inventory master file. An error report is created which
         indicates edit errors, such as non-numeric fields. The program to
         create this sequential file is explained in this chapter.

STEP 2: The file created in step 1 is sorted on part number through the use of the Disk Operating System Disk Sort. This sort is supplied as a part of DOS and is executed through the use of control cards. An explanation of the job control and sort control cards used in this inventory system is contained in the appendices.

STEP 3: An Indexed Sequential inventory master file is loaded from the sorted file from step 2. An error report is generated for any errors occuring during loading, such as invalid type codes. The program to load the inventory master file is presented in Chapter 4.

STEP 4: The edit program from Step 1 is also used to create a transaction file which will be used to update the inventory master file. The input records from cards and/or tape are read and edited and a transaction file is produced. Any update record in error is recorded on the error report.

STEP 5: The inventory master file is randomly updated from the transactions on the update transaction file created in Step 4. Any transactions in error such as duplicate add records, are reported on the error listing. The update program is presented in Chapter 6.

STEP 6: The final step of the system is a "utility" program which performs two functions: "Dumping" the master file onto a tape for use as a back-up file and creating two reports from the master file——an Inventory Master Report and an Inventory Master Spares/Shorts Report. A control card is read to determine which of the functions is to be performed. This program is presented in Chapter 8.

The detailed processing, record layouts, report formats and program requirements are described in the chapters presenting the programs.

In addition to the programs shown in the systems flowchart, a program to list the master file after it has been created is presented in Chapters 5 and 7.

SAMPLE PROGRAM

The sample program reads both tape and card input files and creates a sequential disk output file which, after being sorted, is input to create the indexed sequential master file. The program is also used to create a transaction file which is used to update the inventory master file. See step 1 and step 4 of the systems flowchart.

As each card or tape record is read, an "editing" process is performed to insure that the input records contain valid data. Each numeric field in the input is checked to insure that it contains either all blanks (in which case, zeros are moved to the output field) or all numeric data. If the field contains invalid data, an error message is issued and the record is not included on the output file.

INPUT

The chart below summarizes the format of the record layout and includes the field
name, the field format (zoned-decimal numeric and zoned-decimal alphanumeric), the
position of each field in the record, the number of digits in the field, and the length
of each field in bytes.

FIELD	FIELD NAME	FORMAT	POSITION	NO OF DIGITS	LENGTH
Part Number					
Division Number	DIV	N-Z	1-2	2	2
Prime Number	PRIME	N-Z	3-8	6	6
Dash Number	DASH	N-Z	9-13	5	5
Description	NAME	AN	14-38	25	25
Qty on Hand	QTYOH	N-Z	39-45	7	7
Qty on Order	QTYOO	N-Z	46-52	7	7
Qty Reserved	QTYRSV	N-Z	53-59	7	7
Part Number-NA					
Division-NA	NADIV	N-Z	60-61	2	2
Prime-NA	NAPRIME	N-Z	62-67	6	6
Dash-NA	NADASH	N-Z	68-72	5	5
Type	TYPE	N-Z	73	1	1
Source	SOURCE	N-Z	74	1	1
Unit Price	UNITPRCE	N-Z	75-80	6	6

LEGEND: N-Z – Numeric, zoned-decimal   AN – Alpha-numeric

The fields are defined as follows:

1. Part Number: The part number consists of a division number, a prime number, and
a dash number. The part number identifies each part in an inventory.

   A. Division Number (DIV): The division number portion of the part number
   identifies the division of the plant in which the part is manufactured.

   B. Prime Number (PRIME): The prime number portion of the part number is the
   number given to each part type which is in the inventory. It uniquely identifies
   the type of part.

   C. Dash Number (DASH): The dash number portion of the part number can be
   used for various functions in a manufacturing environment. It may be a work
   order number, a purchase order number, a cycle control number, an assembly
   number, etc. For example, all dash 00001 parts may go into the first finished
   product, all dash 00002 parts may go into the second finished product, etc.

2. Description (NAME): The description field contains a description of the part.

3. Quantity on Hand (QTYOH): The quantity on hand field specifies how many parts are in stock——that is, how many parts have been manufactured or purchased and are currently held in a storage area.

4. Quantity on Order (QTYOO): The quantity on order field specifies how many parts are on order. The parts on order may be either parts which are currently being manufactured in the plant or parts which have been ordered from an outside "vendor".

5. Quantity Reserved (QYTRSV): This field contains the number of parts which have been reserved for use in other assemblies, the number of parts needed to keep a fixed number of parts on hand, etc. For example, the part may be a screw. If 10 screws are needed for assemblying a handle and 5 handles are being built, then 50 screws would be put on reserve so that they would be available for use. If there are more parts on hand and on order than are reserved, then there are "spares" of the part, that is, there are more parts than are needed. If there are more parts on reserve than on hand and on order, a "shortage" exists, that is, there are not enough parts to fill the needs. In this case, more parts must be put on order.

6. Part Number - Next Assembly: This field contains the part number of the next assembly part. The next assembly is the part into which the part described in the record will go. Thus, if the part in the record is a screw, and it goes into a handle, the part number of the handle is the next assembly number.

   A. Division Number - Next Assembly (NADIV): The division number of the part number for next assembly.

   B. Prime Number - Next Assembly (NAPRIME): The prime number of the part for next assembly.

   C. Dash Number - Next Assembly (NADASH): The dash number of the part for next assembly.

7. Type (TYPE): The type field specifies the function of the record. The codes for the type field are:

> 1 = Add Record
>
> 2 = Delete Record
>
> 3 = Change Quantity on Hand
>
> 4 = Change Quantity on Order
>
> 5 = Change Quantity Reserved
>
> 6 = Change Next Assembly Part Number
>
> 7 = Change Source
>
> 8 = New Load
>
> 9 = Change Unit Price

When the program is used in Step 1 of the inventory system, that is, to create the sequential file which is used to load the inventory master, the type field should be equal to "8", which indicates a "new load" (ie. a master record). When used in Step 4, that is, when the program is used to create the transaction file which is used to update the inventory master file, any of the codes except "8" are valid.

8. Source (SOURCE): The source field indicates whether the part is a manufactured part (source = 1) or a purchased part (source = 2).

9. Unit Price (UNITPRCE): The unit price indicates the price for one item.

OUTPUT

All numeric fields in the input records must contain numeric data or be blank. The type field must contain a value of 1-9. An error report is generated for each record which is in error.

The format of the report is illustrated below.

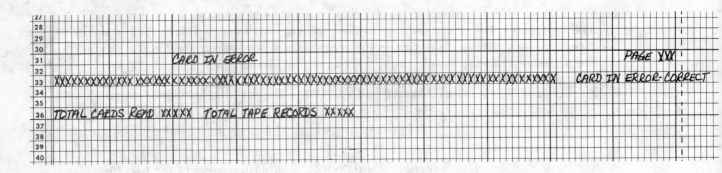

It should be noted in the program listings shown on the following pages that when the various fields are checked for numeric values, a branch and link instruction (statements 34 and 56) is used to go to the CHKALL subroutine. This subroutine verifies that numeric fields contain either blanks, in which case zeros are substituted, or numeric data. If the fields contain valid data, the subroutine returns via a B 4(0,LINKREG1) instruction (statement 156). This instruction will bypass the branch instructions at statements 35 and 57 and allow the record to be written on the disk. If any of the fields are invalid, a return is made via the instruction BR LINKREG1 (statement 195). This causes the next input record to be read without writing the record in error. This technique can be used by subroutines to return to different routines in a program dependent upon conditions found in the subroutine.

PROGRAM

The following is the program to read a card file and a tape file to create a sequential
disk output file and an error exception report.

```
            CARD/TAPE TO DISK                                                                PAGE   1

     LOC  OBJECT CODE    ADDR1 ADDR2  STMT  SOURCE STATEMENT                          DOS CL3-5 08/26/70

    00C000                             2 CREATE   START 0                                     TPDK0020
                                       3          PRINT NOGEN                                 TPDK0030


                                       5 ****                                                 TPDK0050
                                       6 * THIS PROGRAM CREATES A SEQUENTIAL DISK FILE FROM BOTH CARDS AND  TPDK0060
                                       7 * TAPES SUBMITTED FROM VARIOUS DIVISIONS. THIS DISK FILE IS USED   TPDK0070
                                       8 * AS INPUT TO A SORT TO CREATE A FILE TO LOAD THE MASTER FILE.     TPDK0080
                                       9 ****                                                 TPDK0090

    000000 05C0                        11          BALR BASEREG,0            ESTABLISH BASE REGISTER        TPDK0110
    000002                             12          USING *,BASEREG                            TPDK0120

                                       14          OPEN TAPEFLE,CARDFLE,PRTFLE,SEQDISK  OPEN FILES          TPDK0140
    00001E 45E0 C1EC           001EE   25          BAL  14,HEADROU            GO TO HEADING ROUTINE         TPDK0145

    000022                             27 CARDAGIN EQU  *                                     TPDK0160
                                       28          GET  CARDFLE,ALLWORK      READ A CARD                    TPDK0170
    000032 4570 C0D2           000D4   34          BAL  LINKREG1,CHKALL      GO TO CHECK NUMERIC FIELDS     TPDK0180
    000036 47F0 C020           00022   35          B    CARDAGIN            IF RETURN HERE, FIELD WAS IN ERROR  TPDK0190
    00003A FA20 C34E C40A  00350 0040C 36          AP   CARDCNT(3),=P'1'     INCREMENT CARD COUNTER BY 1   TPDK0200
                                       37          PUT  SEQDISK,ALLWORK      PUT CARD ONTO DISK            TPDK0210
    000050 47F0 C020           00022   43          B    CARDAGIN            GO TO READ ANOTHER CARD        TPDK0220


                                       45 ****                                                 TPDK0240
                                       46 * THIS ROUTINE IS ENTERED WHEN ALL CARDS HAVE BEEN READ.          TPDK0250
                                       47 ****                                                 TPDK0260

    000054                             49 EOCARD   EQU  *                                     TPDK0410
                                       50          GET  TAPEFLE,ALLWORK      READ A TAPE RECORD            TPDK0290
    000064 4570 C0D2           000D4   56          BAL  LINKREG1,CHKALL      GO TO CHECK NUMERIC FIELDS    TPDK0300
    000068 47F0 C052           00054   57          B    EOCARD             IF RETURN HERE, ERROR ON CARD   TPDK0310
    00006C FA20 C351 C40A  00353 0040C 58          AP   TAPECNT(3),=P'1'     INCREMENT TAPE COUNTER BY 1   TPDK0320
                                       59          PUT  SEQDISK,ALLWORK      WRITE DISK RECORD             TPDK0330
    000082 47F0 C052           00054   65          B    EOCARD             GO READ ANOTHER TAPE RECORD     TPDK0340


                                       67 ****                                                 TPDK0360
                                       68 * THIS ROUTINE IS ENTERED WHEN ALL OF THE TAPE FILE AND ALL OF THE  TPDK0370
                                       69 * CARDS HAVE BEEN READ. IT PRINTS THE TOTALS AND CLOSES THE FILES.  TPDK0380
                                       70 ****                                                 TPDK0390

    000086                             72 EOTAPE   EQU  *                                     TPDK0280
    000086 D205 C2E6 C2B6  002E8 002B8 73          MVC  TOTMSG+16(6),EDPTTRN1  MOVE EDIT PATTERN FOR OUTPUT TPDK0420
    00008C D205 C300 C2B6  00302 002B8 74          MVC  TOTMSG+42(6),EDPTTRN1  MOVE EDIT PATTERN          TPDK0430
    000092 DE05 C300 C351  00302 00353 75          ED   TOTMSG+42(6),TAPECNT  EDIT TAPE COUNT             TPDK0440
    000098 DE05 C2E6 C34E  002E8 00350 76          ED   TOTMSG+16(6),CARDCNT  EDIT CARD COUNT             TPDK0450
                                       77          CNTRL PRTFLE,SK,1          SKIP TO HEAD OF FORMS        TPDK0460
                                       83          PUT  PRTFLE,TOTMSG         PRINT END MESSAGE            TPDK0470
                                       89          CLOSE CARDFLE,PRTFLE,SEQDISK   CLOSE FILES              TPDK0480
                                       99          EOJ                       END OF JOB                   TPDK0490
    0000D4                            102 CHKALL   EQU  *                                     TPDK0500
    0000D4 4150 000D           0000D  103          LA   BCTREG,13            LOAD FIELD SIZE - DIV,PRIME,DASH TPDK0510
    0000D8 4140 C69E           006A0  104          LA   FIELDREG,ALLWORK     LOAD ADDRESS OF FIELD        TPDK0520
    0000DC 4560 C192           00194  105          BAL  LINKREG2,CHKNUMER     GO TO CHECK NUMERIC         TPDK0530
    0000E0 D506 C6C4 C2C9  006C6 002CB 106         CLC  QTYOH,BLANKS         IS QTY FIELD BLANK           TPDK0540
    0000E6 47F0 C0F2           00100  107          BNE  CHKQTYOH            NO, GO TO VERIFY NUMERIC       TPDK0550
    0000EA D206 C6C4 C2BC  006C6 002BE 108         MVC  QTYOH,ZEROS         MOVE ZEROS TO FIELD           TPDK0560
    0000F0 47F0 C0FE           00100  109          B    DCNEXT1             GO TO CHECK NEXT FIELD         TPDK0570
    0000F4                            110 CHKQTYOH EQU  *                                     TPDK0580
    0000F4 4150 0007           00007  111          LA   BCTREG,7            LOAD SIZE - QTY ON HAND        TPDK0590
    0000F8 4140 C6C4           006C6  112          LA   FIELDREG,QTYOH       LOAD ADDRESS OF FIELD        TPDK0600
    0000FC 4560 C192           00194  113          BAL  LINKREG2,CHKNUMER     GO TO VERIFY NUMERIC        TPDK0610
    000100                            114 DONEXT1  EQU  *                                     TPDK0620
    000100 D506 C6CB C2C9  006CD 002CB 115         CLC  QTYOO,BLANKS         IS QTY ON ORDER BLANK        TPDK0630
    000106 4770 C112           00114  116          BNE  CHKQTYOO            NO, GO TO CHECK FOR NUMERIC    TPDK0640
    00010A D206 C6CB C2BC  006CD 002BE 117         MVC  QTYOO,ZEROS         MOVE ZEROS TO FIELD           TPDK0650
    000110 47F0 C11E           00120  118          B    DONEXT2             GO TO CHECK NEXT FIELD         TPDK0660
    000114                            119 CHKQTYOO EQU  *                                     TPDK0670
    000114 4150 0007           00007  120          LA   BCTREG,7            LOAD FIELD SIZE               TPDK0680
    000118 4140 C6CB           006CD  121          LA   FIELDREG,QTYOO       LOAD QTY ON ORDER ADDRESS    TPDK0690
    00011C 4560 C192           00194  122          BAL  LINKREG2,CHKNUMER    GO TO VERIFY FIELD NUMERIC   TPDK0700
    000120                            123 DONEXT2  EQU  *                                     TPDK0710
    000120 D506 C6D2 C2C9  006D4 002CB 124         CLC  QTYRSV,BLANKS        IS FIELD BLANK               TPDK0720
    000126 4770 C132           00134  125          BNE  CHKQTYRS            NO, GO TO CHECK FIELD          TPDK0730
    00012A D206 C6D2 C2BC  006D4 002BE 126         MVC  QTYRSV,ZEROS         MOVE ZEROS TO FIELD          TPDK0740
    000130 47F0 C13E           00140  127          B    DONEXT3             GO TO CHECK NEXT FIELD         TPDK0750
    000134                            128 CHKQTYRS EQU  *                                     TPDK0760
    000134 4150 0007           00007  129          LA   BCTREG,7            LOAD FIELD SIZE - QTY RESERVED  TPDK0770
    000138 4140 C6D2           006D4  130          LA   FIELDREG,QTYRSV      LOA D ADDRESS OF FIELD       TPDK0780
    00013C 4560 C192           00194  131          BAL  LINKREG2,CHKNUMER    GO TO VERIFY NUMERIC         TPDK0790
    000140                            132 DONEXT3  EQU  *                                     TPDK0800
    000140 D50C C6D9 C2C9  006DB 002CB 133         CLC  NADIV(13),BLANKS     IS NEXT ASSEMBLY BLANK       TPDK0810
    000146 4770 C152           00154  134          BNE  CHKNA               NO, GO TO VERIFY NUMERIC       TPDK0820
    00014A D20C C6D9 C2BC  006DB 002BE 135         MVC  NADIV(13),ZEROS      MOVE ZEROS TO NEXT ASSEMBLY  TPDK0830
    000150 47F0 C15E           00160  136          B    DONEXT4             GO TO CHECK NEXT FIELD         TPDK0840
    000154                            137 CHKNA    EQU  *                                     TPDK0850
    000154 4150 000D           0000D  138          LA   BCTREG,13           LOAD FIELD SIZE               TPDK0860
```

3.13

LOC   OBJECT CODE   ADDR1 ADDR2 STMT   SOURCE STATEMENT   DOS CL3-5 08/26/70

```
000158 4140 C6D9          006DB  139          LA    FIELDREG,NADIV        LOAD ADDRESS OF FIELD         TPDK0870
00015C 4560 C192          00194  140          BAL   LINKREG2,CHKNUMER        GO TO VERIFY NUMERIC       TPDK0880
000160                           141  DONEXT4 EQU   *                                                   TPDK0890
000160 D505 C6E8 C2C9 006EA 002CB 142         CLC   UNITPRCE,BLANKS       IS UNIT PRICE BLANK           TPDK0900
000166 4770 C172          00174  143          BNE   CHKUNIT               NO, GO TO VERIFY NUMERIC      TPDK0910
00016A D205 C6EB C2BC 006EA 002BE 144         MVC   UNITPRCE,ZEROS        YES, MOVE ZEROS TO FIELD      TPDK0920
000170 47F0 C17E          00180  145          B     DONEXT5                                             TPDK0930
000174                           146  CHKUNIT EQU   *                                                   TPDK0940
000174 4150 0006          00006  147          LA    BCTREG,6              LOAD SIZE OF UNIT PRICE       TPDK0950
000178 4140 C6E8          006EA  148          LA    FIELDREG,UNITPRCE     LOAD ADDRESS OF UNIT PRICE    TPDK0960
00017C 4560 C192          00194  149          BAL   LINKREG2,CHKNUMER        GO TO VERIFY NUMERIC       TPDK0970

000180                           151  DONEXT5 EQU   *                                                   TPDK0990
000180 95F1 C6E6          006E8  152          CLI   TYPE,X'F1'            IS TYPE LESS THAN 1           TPDK1000
000184 4740 C1C4          001C6  153          BL    BADDATA               YES, GO TO INVALID ROUTINE    TPDK1010
000188 95F9 C6E6          006E8  154          CLI   TYPE,C'9'             IS TYPE GREATER THAN 9        TPDK1020
00018C 4720 C1C4          001C6  155          BH    BADDATA               YES, GO TO ERROR ROUTINE      TPDK1030
000190 47F0 7004          00004  156          B     4(0,LINKREG1)        NO, RETURN TO CALLER          TPDK1040


                                 158  ****                                                              TPDK1060
                                 159  * THIS ROUTINE IS ENTERED TO CHECK FIELDS TO SEE IF THEY CONTAIN  TPDK1070
                                 160  * NUMERIC DATA                                                    TPDK1080
                                 161  ****                                                              TPDK1090


000194                           163  CHKNUMER EQU  *                                                   TPDK1110
000194 0650                      164          BCTR  BCTREG,0              DECREMENT BY 1                TPDK1120
000196                           165  CHKNUMB EQU   *                                                   TPDK1130
000196 95F0 4000          00000  166          CLI   0(FIELDREG),X'F0'     IS FIELD LESS THAN 0          TPDK1140
00019A 4740 C1C4          001C6  167          BL    BADDATA               YES, GO TO ERROR ROUTINE      TPDK1150
00019E 95F9 4000          00000  168          CLI   0(FIELDREG),C'9'      IS FIELD GREATER THAN 9       TPDK1160
0001A2 4720 C1C4          001C6  169          BH    BADDATA               YES, GO TO ERROR ROUTINE      TPDK1170
0001A6 4144 0001          00001  170          LA    FIELDREG,1(FIELDREG)   BUMP ADDRESS FIELD BY 1      TPDK1180
0001AA 4650 C194          00196  171          BCT   BCTREG,CHKNUMB        GO TO CHECK NEXT FIELD        TPDK1190
0001AE 95F0 4000          00000  172          CLI   0(FIELDREG),X'F0'     IS IT LESS THAN ZERO          TPDK1200
0001B2 4740 C1BE          001C0  173          BL    CHKNEG                YES, GO TO CHECK NEGATIVE NUMBER TPDK1210
0001B6 95F9 4000          00000  174          CLI   0(FIELDREG),X'F9'     IS IT GREATER THAN 9          TPDK1220
0001BA 4720 C1C4          001C6  175          BH    BADDATA               YES, IT IS IN ERROR           TPDK1230
0001BE 07F6                      176          BR    LINKREG2              RETURN TO CALLER              TPDK1240

0001C0                           178  CHKNEG  EQU   *                                                   TPDK1260
0001C0 91D0 4000          00000  179          TM    0(FIELDREG),X'D0'     IS IT A NEGATIVE SIGN         TPDK1270
0001C4 0716                      180          BCR   1,LINKREG2            YES, RETURN TO CALLER         TPDK1280
0001C6                           181  BADDATA EQU   *                                                   TPDK1290
0001C6 D24F C23E C69E 00240 006A0 182         MVC   BADMSG(80),ALLWORK    MOVE WORK AREA TO MESSAGE     TPDK1300
                                 183          PUT   PRTFLE,BADMSG         PRINT ERROR MESAAGE           TPDK1310
                                 189          PRTOV PRTFLE,12,HEADROU     AT HEADER OVERFLOW,GO TO NEW PG TPDK1315
0001EC 07F7                      195          BR    LINKREG1              RETURN TO CALLER              TPDK1320


                                 197  ****                                                              TPDK1321
                                 198  * THIS ROUTINE IS ENTERED TO PRINT A HEADER                       TPDK1322
                                 199  ****                                                              TPDK1323


0001EE                           201  HEADROU EQU   *                                                   TPDK1324
0001EE 50E0 C23A          0023C  202          ST    14,SAVE14             SAVE REGISTER                 TPDK1325
0001F2 FA10 C3D0 C40A 003D2 0040C 203         AP    PGCNT,=P'1'           ADD 1 TO PAGE COUNTER         TPDK1326
0001F8 D203 C3B4 C3D2 003B6 003D4 204         MVC   HEADPG+4(4),PGEDIT    MOVE EDIT WORD TO REPORT AREA TPDK1327
0001FE DE03 C3B4 C3D0 003B6 003D2 205         ED    HEADPG+4(4),PGCNT     EDIT PAGE NO                  TPDK1328
000204 D203 C3B0 C3CC 003B2 003CE 206         MVC   HEADPG(4),PAGECON     MOVE CONTANT TO REPORT        TPDK1329
                                 207          CNTRL PRTFLE,SK,1           SKIP TO HEAD OF FORMS         TPDK1330
                                 213          PUT   PRTFLE,HEADER         PRINT HEADER                  TPDK1331
                                 219          CNTRL PRTFLE,SP,2           SPACE TWICE                   TPDK1332
000236 58E0 C23A          0023C  225          L     14,SAVE14             LOAD RETURN ADDRESS           TPDK1333
00023A 07FE                      226          BR    14                    RETURN TO CALLER              TPDK1334
```

3.14

LOC   OBJECT CODE   ADDR1 ADDR2 STMT   SOURCE STATEMENT   DOS CL3-5 08/26/70

```
                                228 ****                                              TPDK1340
                                229 * CONSTANTS, EQUATES, ETC.                        TPDK1350
                                230 ****                                              TPDK1360

00023C                          232 SAVE14   DS   F
000240                          233 BADMSG   DS   OCL120
000240                          234          DS   CL80                               TPDK1380
000290 404040C3C1D9C440         235          DC   CL40'    CARD IN ERROR-CORRECT'     TPDK1390
0002B8 402020202020             236 EDPTTRN1 DC   X'402020202020'                     TPDK1400
000007                          237 LINKREG1 EQU  7                                   TPDK1410
000006                          238 LINKREG2 EQU  6                                   TPDK1420
000005                          239 BCTREG   EQU  5                                   TPDK1430
000004                          240 FIELDREG EQU  4                                   TPDK1440
0002BE F0F0F0F0F0F0F0F0         241 ZEROS    DC   13C'0'                              TPDK1450
0002CB 404040404040404040       242 BLANKS   DC   CL13' '                            TPDK1460
0002D8 E3D6E3C1D340C3C1         243 TOTMSG   DC   CL120'TOTAL CARDS READ       TOTAL TAPE RECORDS' TPDK1470
00000C                          244 BASEREG  EQU  12                                  TPDK1480
000350 00000C                   245 CARDCNT  DC   PL3'0'                              TPDK1490
000353 00000C                   246 TAPECNT  DC   PL3'0'                              TPDK1500
000356 4040404040404040         247 HEADER   DC   CL120'                  CARD IN ERROR' TPDK1510
0003B2                          248 HEADPG   EQU  HEADER+92                            TPDK1511
0003CE D7C1C7C5                 249 PAGECON  DC   C'PAGE'                             TPDK1512
0003D2 000C                     250 PGCNT    DC   X'000C'                             TPDK1513
0003D4 40202021                 251 PGEDIT   DC   X'40202021'                         TPDK1514
0003D8                          252          LTORG                                    TPDK1515
0003D8 5B5BC2D6D7C5D540         253          =C'$$BOPEN '                             TPDK1520
0003E0 5B5BC2C3D3D6E2C5         254          =C'$$BCLOSE'
0003E8 00000410                 255          =A(CARDFLE)
0003EC 000006A0                 256          =A(ALLWORK)
0003F0 00000478                 257          =A(SEQDISK)
0003F4 0000051B                 258          =A(TAPEFLE)
0003F8 00000448                 259          =A(PRTFLE)
0003FC 000002D8                 260          =A(TOTMSG)
000400 00000240                 261          =A(BADMSG)
000404 000001EE                 262          =A(HEADROU)
000408 00000356                 263          =A(HEADER)
00040C 1C                       264          =P'1'

                                266 ****                                              TPDK1540
                                267 * CARDFILE DTF                                    TPDK1550
                                268 ****                                              TPDK1560

                                270 CARDFLE  DTFCD BLKSIZE=80,RECFORM=FIXUNB,IOAREA1=CARDIN1,TYPEFLE=INPUT,CTPDK1580
                                             DEVADDR=SYSIPT,DEVICE=2501,EOFADDR=EOCARD,            CTPDK1590
                                             MODNAME=IJCFZIB3,IOAREA2=CARDIN2,WORKA=YES            TPDK1600

                                291 ****                                              TPDK1620
                                292 * PRINTER DTF                                     TPDK1630
                                293 ****                                              TPDK1640

                                295 PRTFLE   DTFPR BLKSIZE=120,RECFORM=FIXUNB,IOAREA1=PRTIO,DEVADDR=SYSLST,CTPDK1660
                                             DEVICE=1403,MODNAME=IJDFCPZW,WORKA=YES,CONTROL=YES,   CTPDK1670
                                             PRINTOV=YES                                           TPDK1671

                                317 ****                                              TPDK1690
                                318 * SEQUENTIAL DISK DTF                             TPDK1700
                                319 ****                                              TPDK1710

                                321 SEQDISK  DTFSD BLKSIZE=3608,IOAREA1=DISKIO1,IOAREA2=DISKIO2,  CTPDK1730
                                             DEVADDR=SYS004,DEVICE=2311,                           CTPDK1740
                                             MODNAME=IJGFOZZZ,RECFORM=FIXBLK,RECSIZE=80,           CTPDK1750
                                             TYPEFLE=OUTPUT,VERIFY=YES,WORKA=YES                   TPDK1760

                                372 ****                                              TPDK1780
                                373 * TAPE FILE DTF                                   TPDK1790
                                374 ****                                              TPDK1800

                                376 TAPEFLE  DTFMT BLKSIZE=320,DEVADDR=SYS010,EOFADDR=EOTAPE,FILABL=STD, CTPDK1820
                                             IOAREA1=TAPEIO1,IOAREA2=TAPEIO2,MODNAME=IJFFZZWZ,     CTPDK1830
                                             READ=FORWARD,RECFORM=FIXBLK,RECSIZE=80,REWIND=UNLOAD, CTPDK1840
                                             TYPEFLE=INPUT,WORKA=YES                               TPDK1850
```

LOC   OBJECT CODE   ADDR1 ADDR2 STMT   SOURCE STATEMENT   DOS CL3-5 08/26/70

```
                                 415 ****                                       TPDK1870
                                 416 * I/O AREAS AND WORK AREAS                 TPDK1880
                                 417 ****                                       TPDK1890

000588                           419 CARDIN1  DS   CL80                         TPDK1910
0005D8                           420 CARDIN2  DS   CL80                         TPDK1920
000628                           421 PRTIO    DS   CL120                        TPDK1930
0006A0                           422 ALLWORK  DS   OCL80                        TPDK1940
0006A0                           423 DIV      DS   CL2                          TPDK1950
0006A2                           424 PRIME    DS   CL6                          TPDK1960
0006A8                           425 DASH     DS   CL5                          TPDK1970
0006AD                           426 NAME     DS   CL25                         TPDK1980
0006C6                           427 QTYOH    DS   CL7                          TPDK1990
0006CD                           428 QTYOD    DS   CL7                          TPDK2000
0006D4                           429 QTYRSV   DS   CL7                          TPDK2010
0006DB                           430 NADIV    DS   CL2                          TPDK2020
0006DD                           431 NAPRIME  DS   CL6                          TPDK2030
0006E3                           432 NADASH   DS   CL5                          TPDK2040
0006E8                           433 TYPE     DS   CL1                          TPDK2050
0006E9                           434 SOURCE   DS   CL1                          TPDK2060
0006EA                           435 UNITPRCE DS   CL6                          TPDK2070
0006F0                           436 TAPEIO1  DS   CL320                        TPDK2080
000830                           437 TAPEIO2  DS   CL320                        TPDK2090
000970                           438 DISKIO1  DS   CL3608  - 45 RECORDS;EACH RECORD 80 BYTES  TPDK2100
001788                           439 DISKIO2  DS   CL3608                       TPDK2110
                                 440          END                              TPDK2120
```

3.16

CHAPTER 3

PROGRAMMING ASSIGNMENT

...gnments in the next six chapters consist of a series of pro-
...es Commission System. The first program to be written is
...k file from input data cards. This sequential disk file will
...to create an indexed sequential master file (Chapter 4).

...be used to create a transaction file that will be used as the input
...sequential file (Chapter 6). Thus, the program in this assignment
...e program used in Step 1 and Step 4 of the Inventory System ex—

...ted below, a sequential disk file is to be created. The
...Illustrated below.

The sequential disk output file should consist of records containing the same fields as the input cards. The record layout is to be determined by the programmer. The output file should be blocked. The blocking factor should be determined by the programmer.

The program should incorporate checking features to insure that the Department Field, the Salesman Field, the Current Sales, the Commission Rate and the Current Sales Returns are numeric.

The type field must contain the values 1-7 to indicate the following.

    1 — LOAD
    2 — NAME CHANGE
    3 — Y-T-D Sales UPDATE
    4 — COMMISSION RATE CHANGE
    5 — Y-T-D Sales Return UPDATE
    6 — ADDITION
    7 — DELETION

An error report should be generated indicating any errors in punching in the numeric fields, and any invalid codes. The format of the report is to be designed by the programmer.

It should be noted the sequential output file created in this program must be sorted on department number and salesman number. This may be accomplished by sorting the cards prior to loading the file on the disk, or by use of the DOS Disk Sort after the file has been loaded on the disk.

CHAPTER 4

INDEXED SEQUENTIAL ACCESS METHOD

As discussed in Chapter 1, the 3 types of file organization methods which are commonly used with disk storage devices are sequential, indexed sequential and direct access. This chapter explains the second of these methods—the INDEXED SEQUENTIAL ACCESS METHOD (ISAM).

Sequential processing, as has been shown, involves processing records one after another. Due to the addressing scheme used on direct access devices, another type of processing called RANDOM PROCESSING is possible. Random processing is a means by which non-sequential records may be read, written, and processed. Devices such as card readers and tape drives cannot process records randomly because there is no way, for example, to read the fourth record in an input stream and then read the first record because the first record must be read first, followed by the second, third, fourth, etc.

Direct access devices, however, offer the opportunity to read the fourth record in a file and then the first record in a file because the only thing governing which record is read is the record address which is presented to the channel.

The Indexed Sequential Access Method allows BOTH sequential and random access to a file.

FILE STRUCTURE

The records of an indexed sequential file are organized on the basis of a collating sequence determined by a specific control field or key within the record. An indexed sequential file exists in space allocated on the disk called PRIME data areas, OVER-FLOW areas, and INDEX areas.

When an index sequential file is initially established on the disk, all data records are loaded into an area called the PRIME DATA AREA. The data in this area is available to be processed by both sequential and random access methods. After the file is established, the user can ADD records without reorganizing the entire file as in sequential file organization.

A new record added to an indexed sequential file is placed into a location on a track determined by the value of a "key" or control field in each record. To handle additions an OVERFLOW AREA exists.

Two types of overflow areas may be used either separately or together--the cylinder overflow area and the independent overflow area. A CYLINDER OVERFLOW AREA is a track or tracks located on each cylinder within the prime data area extents. The number of tracks used for the overflow area is specified in the DTF for indexed sequential files (DTFIS). The INDEPENDENT OVERFLOW AREA is a separate area outside the extents for the prime data area and is used strictly as an overflow area.

The following diagram illustrates the concept of the prime data area, the cylinder overflow area, and the independent overflow area as they appear on the disk.

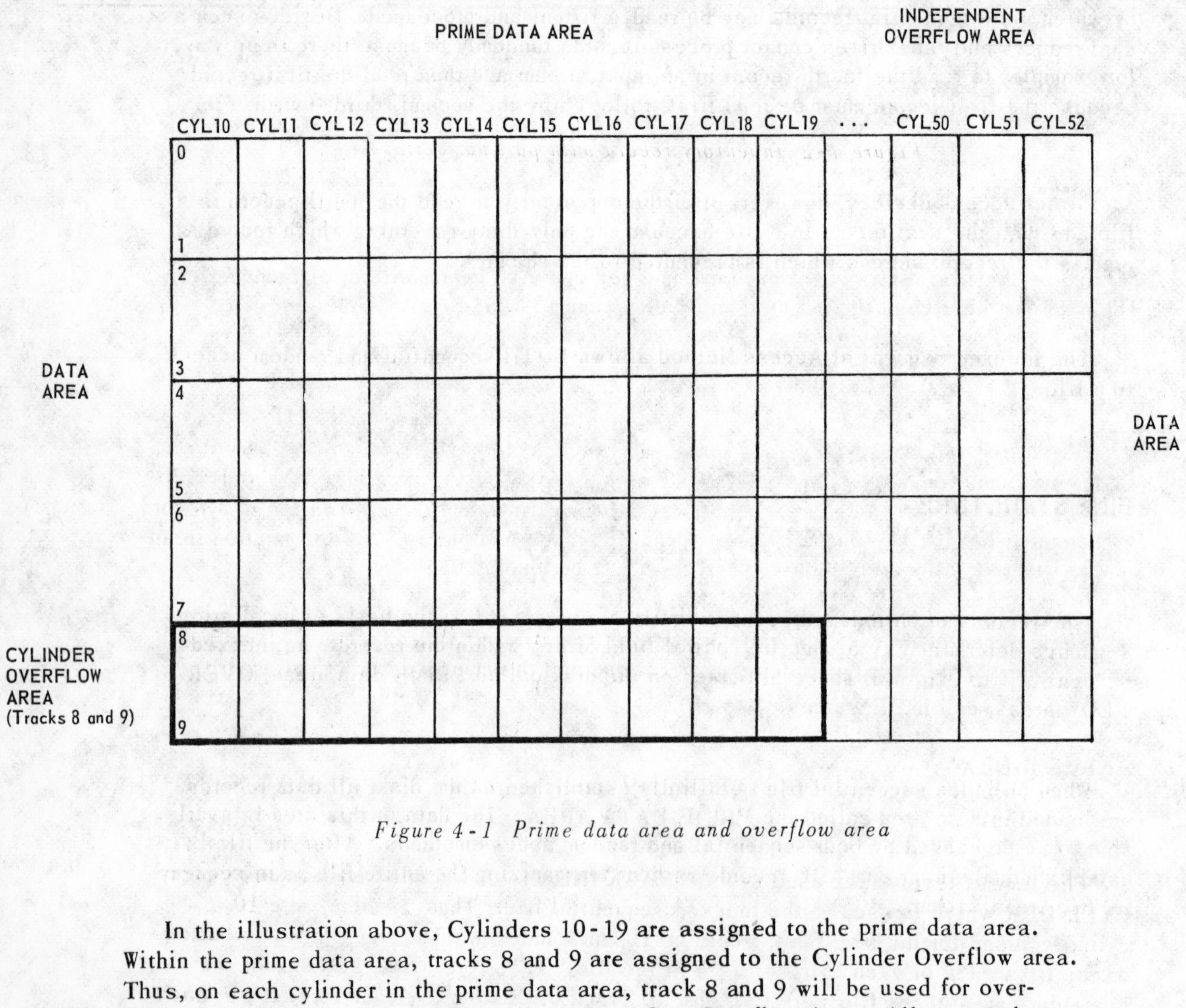

Figure 4-1 Prime data area and overflow area

In the illustration above, Cylinders 10-19 are assigned to the prime data area. Within the prime data area, tracks 8 and 9 are assigned to the Cylinder Overflow area. Thus, on each cylinder in the prime data area, track 8 and 9 will be used for overflow. Cylinders 50-52 are used as the Independent Overflow Area. All ten tracks (0-9) will be used for the Independent Overflow area.

KEYS AND INDEXES

The indexed sequential access method allows both sequential and random access to data through the use of KEYS and INDEXES. A KEY is a means by which a record may be identified. The KEY is normally a part of the record which will uniquely identify the record. For example, an inventory file may be composed of a series of individual records, with each record representing a part which is manufactured or purchased by the company. Each inventory record contains a unique part-number. Thus, the part number acts as the key to the record and always uniquely identifies the record.

80 Bytes

13A12345B234 HAMMER 001257 000050 00000611A23456 F235681001256

PART NUMBER=KEY

Figure 4-2 Inventory record with part number as key

It should be noted that the key could be anywhere within the record--it does not have to be the first digits in the record. The key can also be numeric or alphanumeric. The minimum key length is one byte and the maximum is 255 bytes. Within one file, all keys must have the same length. Duplicate keys can never be used on an indexed sequential file.

In addition to keys, the Indexed Sequential Access Method utilizes INDEXES. An INDEX is a pointer which is used by ISAM to point to the disk location of a record within the file. Thus, by assigning a particular cylinder, track and record location to a record and associating the key of the record with that address and placing this information in an index, any record for which the key is known can be located and processed.

Three types of indexes are used by ISAM, a track index, a cylinder index, and a master index. The first two indexes are required and the master index is optional.

TRACK INDEX

The lowest level index used is the TRACK INDEX. A track index is built on every CYLINDER which is used in the indexed sequential file. Thus, if there were 10 cylinders used for the file, there would be 10 track indexes. The track index is built on the first track of each cylinder used in the file. Therefore, if the extents for the prime data area of the file were Cylinder 10 Track 0, through Cylinder 19 Track 9, each cylinder (10, 11, 12, etc.) would have a track index on its track 0. The track index always is contained on the cylinder for which it is the index and it contains index entries for only the cylinder on which it resides. See Figure 4-1.

The format of the track index and a schematic of the data records as they are stored on disk is illustrated below. Note that the track index consists of a series of entries for the prime data area and the overflow area for each track, with each of these entries containing a KEY entry and a DATA entry.

TRACK INDEX

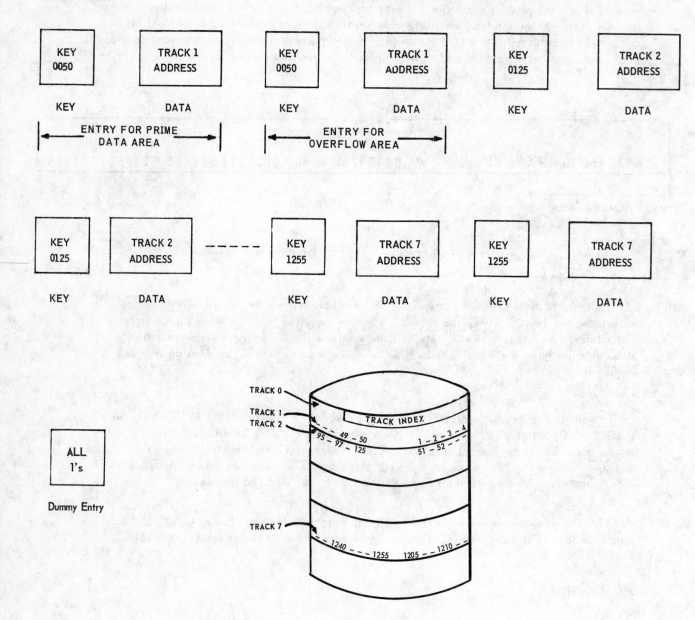

Figure 4-3 Track Index

The track index consists of two parts: (1) For the prime data area, the KEY entry in the track index specifies the HIGHEST KEY of a record on that track and the DATA entry specifies the ADDRESS of the LOWEST RECORD on that track; (2) For the overflow area, the KEY entry specifies the HIGHEST KEY associated with that track and the DATA entry specifies the address of the LOWEST RECORD in the overflow area. If no overflow entry has been made, the second entry is the same as the first entry.

4.4

The DATA entry labelled **TRACK1 ADDRESS** uses a cylinder number and a track number to specify the address of the lowest record on a track. For example, in the illustration above, the basic entries in the **TRACK1 ADDRESS** would include "cylinder 10" (where cylinder 10 is the cylinder for which the track index is used) and "track 1". Since the first record on the track is always the lowest, this **TRACK1 ADDRESS** entry would effectively "point" to the lowest record on track 1.

Thus, in the previous example, it can be seen that the track index resides on Track 0 of a cylinder and the data area begins on Track 1. The highest key on Track 1 is 0050 and this is indicated by the key entry in the prime data area for Track 1. The overflow entry for Track 1 is the same as the prime data entry which indicates that no records have been placed in the overflow area. Similarly, the highest key on Track 2 is 0125 and the highest key on Track 7 is 1255.

As can be seen from the example, the keys are in ascending order. It is, therefore, one of the requirements of an indexed sequential file that all records which are used to build the file be sorted by key so that the incoming keys are in ascending order.

Note, that when a record is to be found, the index can be searched to find a key higher than the given key. When the higher key is found, its associated track address points to the track which contains the record having the given key. See the illustration below.

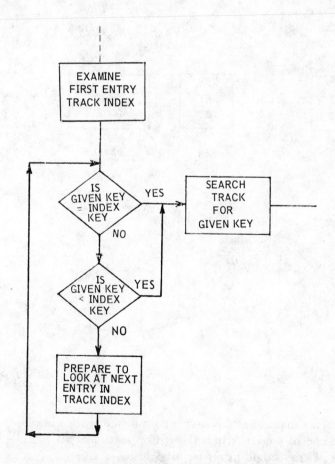

Figure 4-4 Logic for finding key in track index

The example in figure 4.5 illustrates the steps which occur in retrieving a record from an indexed sequential file.

In the example below, the record to be found has a key of 0095. Since the highest key on track 1 is 0050, the next entry in the index is checked. It shows that the highest key on track 2 is 0125. Therefore, the desired record resides on track 2. The track is then read for the proper key and the record can then be retrieved.

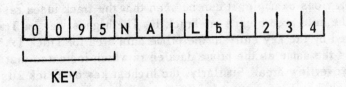

KEY

TRACK INDEX

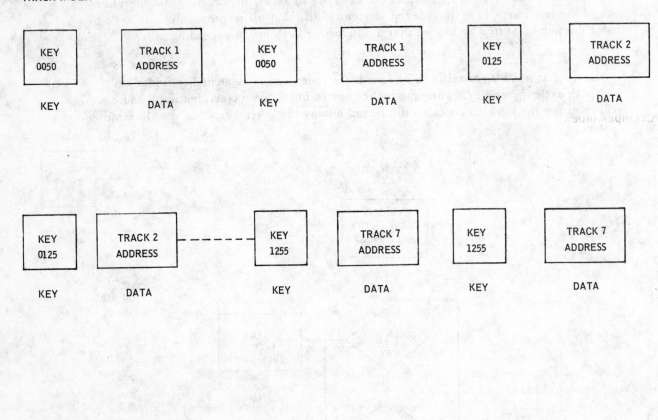

Figure 4-5 Record and Track Index

Note in the example that the last record in the track index is a dummy record which indicates the end of the track index––it is a record of all 1 bits. Therefore, to avoid any problems, a key should never be all 1 bits.

Note also that track 7 is the last entry in the index when the file is organized––this is because of the cylinder overflow feature.

CYLINDER INDEX

The CYLINDER INDEX is the intermediate index used by the Indexed Sequential Access Method. It has a function similar to that of the track index, except that it points to the cylinders in the file rather than the tracks within the cylinder. The cylinder index is built on a separate area of the disk from the prime data and overflow areas. Job control is used to specify the cylinder(s) to be used for the cylinder index. The cylinder index cannot be on the same cylinder as the prime data record area and it must be located on one or more consecutive cylinders.

The cylinder index has one entry in it for each cylinder in the prime data area of the file. Thus, if there were 100 cylinders for the prime data area, there would be 100 entries in the cylinder index. The format of the cylinder index is similar to the format of the track index but there is only one entry for each cylinder. The following diagram illustrates the entries in the cylinder index.

CYLINDER INDEX

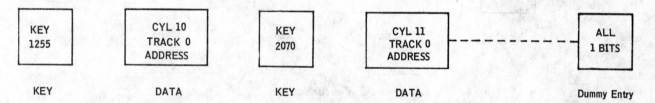

Figure 4-6 Cylinder Index

The entries in the cylinder index consist of the HIGHEST KEY OF A RECORD on the entire cylinder and the ADDRESS OF THE TRACK INDEX for that cylinder. The key area contains the highest key associated with the given cylinder. The data area contains the address of the associated track index. Thus, in the example, the highest key on cylinder 10 is 1255 and the address of the track index is cylinder 10, track 0. The track index for cylinder 10 is contained in Figure 4-3. The highest key on cylinder 11 is 2070 and the address of the track index is cylinder 11, track 0. This example assumes the prime data area begins on cylinder 10.

To retrieve record 95 the cylinder index is searched using the same logic as illustrated in Figure 4-4. In the example, record 95 would be compared to the first KEY entry in the cylinder index. Since record 95 is less than 1255, the associated track index whose address is specified in the DATA portion of the first entry is searched in the manner shown previously. In this example, the track index would be found on cylinder 10, track 0.

MASTER INDEX

The master index is an optional index which can be used if desired by the programmer. It contains the track address of each track in the cylinder index and the highest key referenced by the corresponding track. Its use is not recommended unless the cylinder index is more than four tracks. This is because it is more efficient, time-wise, to search a 4 track cylinder index than it is to search a master index and then the 4 track cylinder index.

The master index is built within the extents specified by the job control EXTENT statement. The master index must immediately precede the cylinder index on the disk volume. It may be more than one cylinder long.

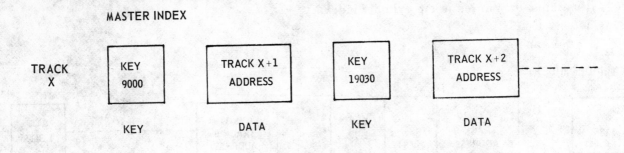

Figure 4-7 Master Index

In the example, the master index is located on track X. The data portion of the master index contains the address of the first track of the cylinder index, which must immediately follow the master index. Thus, in the example, it is assumed the master index takes one track and, since the cylinder index must immediately follow the master index, the first track of the cylinder index would be track (X + 1).

Thus, by using these indexes, the indexed sequential access method can randomly retrieve any record for which the key is known. It can also process the records sequentially by beginning anywhere in the file (determined by key) and sequentially process the records by just reading the prime data and overflow areas. This flexibility of indexed sequential files makes it an extremely useful tool in many applications requiring diversified usage of the data on the file.

SAMPLE PROGRAM

The sample program presented in this chapter illustrates an application in which an inventory master file is being created. The input to the program is the sorted output of the file created in the sample program in Chapter 3. The input fields are the same as the output fields of Chapter 3. The file has been sorted on the key (positions 1 - 13) of the record.

The output file is the master inventory file. It is an indexed sequential file. Its record layout is illustrated below.

FIELD	FIELD NAME	FORMAT	POSITION	NO. OF DIGITS	LENGTH
Part Number					
Division Number	MSTRDIV	N - B	1	2	1
Prime Number	MSTRPRME	N - B	2 - 4	6	3
Dash Number	MSTRDASH	N - B	5 - 7	5	3
Description	MSTRNAME	AN	8 - 32	25	25
Qty on Hand	MSTRQOH	N - B	33 - 35	7	3
Qty on Order	MSTRQOO	N - B	36 - 38	7	3
Qty Reserved	MSTRQRSV	N - B	39 - 41	7	3
Part Number - NA					
Division - NA	MASYDIV	N - B	42	2	1
Prime - NA	MASYPRME	N - B	43 - 45	6	3
Dash - NA	MASYDASH	N - B	46 - 48	5	3
Type	MSTRTYPE	N - Z	49	1	1
Source	MSTRSRCE	N - Z	50	1	1
Unit Price	MSTRUNIT	N - B	51 - 53	6	3
Filler	MSTRXTRA	AN	54 - 55	2	2

LEGEND: N - B – Numeric, Binary   N - Z – Numeric, Zoned Decimal
AN – Alpha - numeric

Figure 4 - 8 Inventory master record layout

Note in the record layout above that most of the numeric values in the inventory master record are stored in a binary format. The use of binary numbers and the technique to convert zoned decimal numbers to a binary format are explained later in the chapter.

The record length of the master record is 55 bytes. The blocking factor is 65; therefore, there are 3575 bytes per block. Notice that two bytes of filler have been reserved in the master record. This is done in case another field must be added to the record and is normally a good practice.

LOAD MACROS

In order to "load" an indexed sequential file, that is, create it from sequential data, four macros are used. They are DTFIS, SETFL, WRITE, and ENDFL.

DTFIS

The DTFIS macro (Define The File Indexed Sequential) is used to define the file which will be created. The following is an example of the entries in a DTFIS macro.

```
INVMSTR  DTFIS  DSKXTNT=3,IOROUT=LOAD,KEYLEN=7,NRECDS=65,RECFORM=FIXBLK,C
                RECSIZE=55,CYLOFL=2,DEVICE=2311,HINDEX=2311,            C
                IOAREAL=MASTERIO,KEYLOC=1,MODNAME=IJHZLZZZ,             C
                VERIFY=YES,WORKL=LOADWORK,MSTIND=YES
```

Figure 4-9 DTFIS for load function

INVMSTR is the name given to the DTF and wherever the file is referenced in the program, it is referenced by that name.

1. DSKXTNT=3: This entry in the DTF states how many disk extents, that is, how many different areas, are going to be used for this file. Disk extents are required for the following types of areas: indexes (cylinder and master), prime data areas, and independent overflow areas. For the file in the sample problem, three extents are necessary: one for the master index and cylinder index, one for the single prime data area, and one for the independent overflow area. It should be noted that the minimum is two (one for the cylinder index and one for the prime data area). The maximum is determined by the user because the prime data areas do not have to be consecutive on any disk volume nor do they have to be contained on a single volume. The cylinder and master indexes, however, must reside on a single volume and are considered as one extent.

2. IOROUT = LOAD: The IOROUT operand specifies what type of I/O function is going to be performed. The LOAD entry specifies that the file is to be loaded.

3. KEYLEN = 7: This operand must be included to specify the length of the key to be used by the records on the file. The minimum key length is 1 byte and the maximum is 255 bytes. In the sample program, a key 7 bytes long will be used.

4. NRECDS = 65: This entry specifies the number of records in a block for this file. This value, called the "blocking factor", is necessary only when the records are to be fixed-blocked records. When the records are fixed-unblocked, this value is assumed to be one.

5. **RECFORM = FIXBLK:** This entry specifies the type of records to be used in the file. FIXBLK states that the records will be fixed-blocked—that is, they will be a fixed length and blocked. The other valid entry is FIXUNB, which specifies the records will be fixed length and unblocked. It should be noted that only fixed length records can be used with indexed sequential files. Variable length and undefined length records cannot be used.

6. **RECSIZE = 55:** This operand must be included to specify the number of bytes in a logical record. In the sample program there are 55 bytes in each record.

7. **CYLOFL = 2:** This operand must be included if a cylinder overflow area is to be used for the file. It states how many tracks are to be allocated for cylinder overflow. In the sample program, two tracks are to be used for cylinder overflow. Thus, on each cylinder within the prime data extents, two tracks will be reserved for overflow. The determination of the number of tracks used for cylinder overflow is governed by the size and use of the file. Cylinder overflow tracks take space away from the prime data tracks. Thus, when more tracks are used for cylinder overflow, more space must be allocated for the prime data area. The alternative to the cylinder overflow area is the independent overflow area. When using the independent overflow area, less space must be allocated for the prime data area and space on the disk volume can be saved. The "trade-off", however, is in retrieval and adding speed. It takes more time, because of disk arm movements, to retrieve a record from or add a record to the independent overflow area than it does the cylinder overflow area. Thus, when determining the number of tracks to be used for cylinder overflow, one must consider both the disk space requirements and the time it takes to add and retrieve records.

8. **DEVICE = 2311:** This entry is used to specify the type of unit that contains the prime data area or overflow areas of the file.

9. **HINDEX = 2311:** This entry specifies the unit containing the highest index used for the file (that is, the master index if one is used or the cylinder index).

10. **IOAREAL = MASTERIO:** This operand must be included when a file is to be loaded. "MASTERIO" is the name of the output area which is used for loading records onto the file. When loading records, "MASTERIO" (normally defined by a DS statement) must have a length equal to: (8 + key length + (record length x blocking factor) for fixed blocked records and (8 + key length + record length) for unblocked records. The eight bytes are used for the count field by ISAM. Thus, in the sample program, "MASTERIO" is 3590 bytes long. This is calculated by: $8 + 7 + (55 \times 65) = 3590$.

11. **KEYLOC = 1:** This operand is used to specify at which byte in the record the key starts. In the sample program, the key starts in the first byte of the record; thus the entry is 1. It should be noted that the key can start anywhere in the record but must consist of consecutive bytes. Thus, in the program illustrated, the key starts in byte 1 and continues through byte 7 (KEYLEN = 7).

12. MODNAME = IJHZLZZZ: This operand specifies the name of the I/O module
    to be used to load the indexed sequential file. A complete discussion of the
    MODNAME operand is included in the appendices.

13. VERIFY = YES: This operand is included if the user wishes to check the
    parity of the disk records after they are written. It is normally a good idea
    to use the VERIFY = YES parameter to insure that data written on the disk
    is correct.

14. WORKL = LOADWORK: This operand must be included whenever a file is
    loaded. It specifies the name of the work area (in the sample program the
    name is "LOADWORK") in which the program must supply the data records
    which are to be loaded. The WORKL work area must be large enough to con-
    tain the data record if the records are blocked or the key and data if the
    records are unblocked. In the sample program, the records are blocked;
    therefore, LOADWORK is 55 bytes long, which is the length of a data record.
    If the records were unblocked, the work area would have to be 62 bytes long
    (7 + 55).

15. MSTIND = YES: This parameter states that a master index will be used for
    the file being created. If it is desired to use a master index, this entry is
    required. If not, the entry is omitted from the DTF.

SETFL

The SETFL macro is used by ISAM to set up the file so that the load function can
be performed. It preformats all the necessary tracks for the track indexes and prepares
all the necessary index entries.

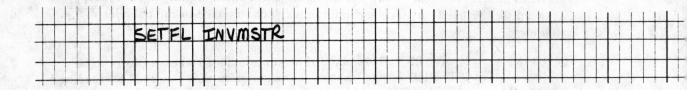

Figure 4-10 SETFL Macro

The one operand used with the SETFL macro is the name of the DTF. In the sample
program, the name of the DTF is INVMSTR.

This macro must be issued whenever a load is to be performed but it is only issued
once for each file that is to be loaded.

The WRITE macro is issued in the program whenever it is desired to load a new data record onto the file. A sample statement is illustrated below.

Figure 4-11 WRITE Macro for loading file

The WRITE macro contains two operands. The first operand is the name of the DTF. In the sample program, the name is INVMSTR. The second operand is the keyword NEWKEY. This operand is required on every write instruction used to load a new file.

The problem program must move the desired data record to be written to the work area (specified in the WORKL operand of the DTF) prior to issuing the WRITE macro. For blocked records, as in the sample program, the data portion of the record (which includes the key) must be moved to the work area. For unblocked records, the data portion of the record (including key) and the key must be moved to the work area.

For blocked records, just the data record is moved to the work area. The key is included in the data record. In the example below, the data records are to be blocked and only the data record is moved to the work area.

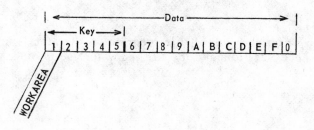

Figure 4-12 Blocked record in load work area

For unblocked records, the key must be moved to the first portion of the work area and the data portion (including the key in the data) is moved to the data portion of the work area.

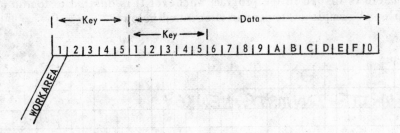

Figure 4-13 Unblocked record in load work area

ENDFL

The ENDFL macro is issued after all records have been loaded onto the file by means of the WRITE macro.

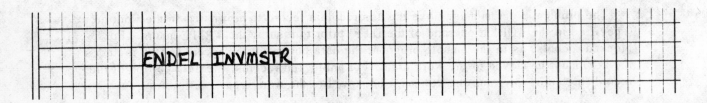

Figure 4-14 ENDFL Macro

The format for the ENDFL macro is shown in Figure 4-14. The name of the DTF is the only operand used with the ENDFL macro.

The ENDFL macro writes the end-of-file record after the last data records and performs other functions necessary to make the file ready for use in other programs.

As with all files using logical IOCS, indexed sequential files must be OPENed and CLOSEd. The OPEN macro must be issued prior to any other macros for the indexed sequential files. The OPEN macro checks the disk labels and insures that all requirements for the Index Sequential files have been met (for a further discussion of label and disk requirements, see the appendices).

The CLOSE macro is issued after all processing of the indexed sequential file has been completed. It deactivates the file that was previously activated by an OPEN macro.

Thus, the sequence of events necessary to load an indexed sequential file are shown in Figure 4-15.

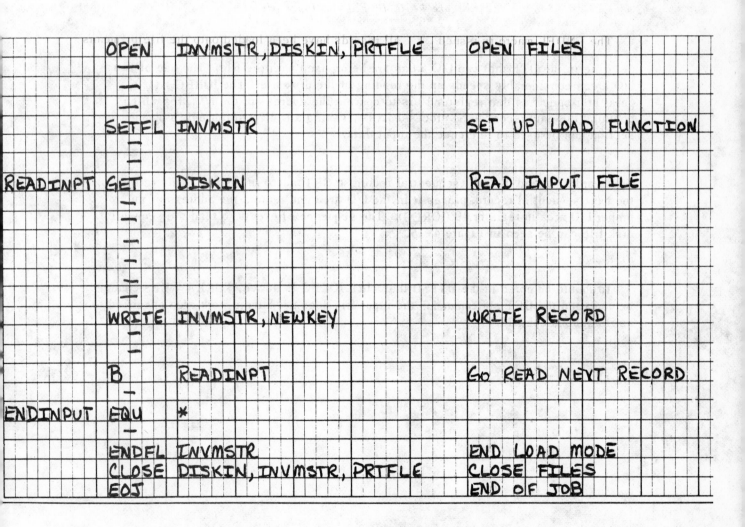

```
            OPEN    INVMSTR,DISKIN,PRTFLE        OPEN FILES

            SETFL   INVMSTR                      SET UP LOAD FUNCTION

READINPT    GET     DISKIN                       READ INPUT FILE



            WRITE   INVMSTR,NEWKEY               WRITE RECORD

            B       READINPT                     GO READ NEXT RECORD
ENDINPUT    EQU     *
            ENDFL   INVMSTR                      END LOAD MODE
            CLOSE   DISKIN,INVMSTR,PRTFLE        CLOSE FILES
            EOJ                                  END OF JOB
```

Figure 4-15 Typical sequence to load Indexed Sequential file

SEQUENTIAL DISK INPUT

In order to read a sequential disk file, the file must be defined by a DTFSD. The following example illustrates the DTFSD used in the sample program.

```
DISKIN      DTFSD BLKSIZE=3600, EOFADDR=ENDINPUT, IOAREA1=DISKIN1,      C
                  IOAREA2=DISKIN2, DEVADDR=SYS006, DEVICE=2311, IOREG=(10),  C
                  MODNAME=IJGFIZZZ, RECFORM=FIXBLK, RECSIZE=80,        C
                  TYPEFLE=INPUT
DISKIN1     DS    CL3600
DISKIN2     DS    CL3600
```

Figure 4-16 DTFSD for input file

Note in the DTF that two I/O areas are being used with the file. The use of two I/O areas considerably speeds up the reading of the disk file. The IOREG = (10) parameter specifies that register 10 is to contain the address of the I/O area which contains the data record to be processed. By issuing a USING statement, a dummy section can be used to reference the input data.

In order to read the next sequential record, a GET macro is issued. This retrieves the next sequential record, places it in the I/O area and returns the address of the proper I/O area in register 10 (IOREG). The sequence of events to read the sequential disk file can be seen in Figure 4-15.

It should be noted in the DTFSD that when IOREG is stated, WORKA = YES cannot be used and the GET statement for the input file does not have a work area specified as its second operand.

4.16

DEFINE STORAGE

As has been previously shown, the Define Storage statement can be used to reserve storage for I/O areas, save areas and other necessary storage areas. Figure 4-17 shows the DS instruction necessary to reserve a fullword (4 bytes) on a fullword boundary.

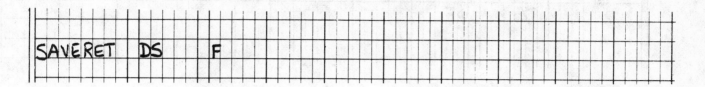

Figure 4-17 Define Storage instruction to reserve a fullword

In addition to a fullword, the DS instruction can be used to reserve a doubleword on a doubleword boundary. A doubleword is 8 consecutive bytes. A doubleword boundary is any address in memory whose hexadecimal address ends in the numbers 0 or 8. The DS statement in Figure 4-18 reserves a doubleword of storage on a doubleword boundary.

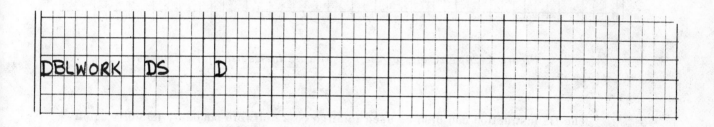

Figure 4-18 Define Storage instruction to reserve a doubleword

The label DBLWORK refers to a doubleword aligned on a doubleword boundary. It should be noted that the instruction DS CL8 would reserve 8 bytes (a doubleword) but the start of this 8 byte field would not necessarily be on a doubleword boundary.

Alignment can also be forced by use of the DS statement but without reserving any core storage. The DS instruction in Figure 4-19 would force alignment of the next labelled statement on a fullword boundary.

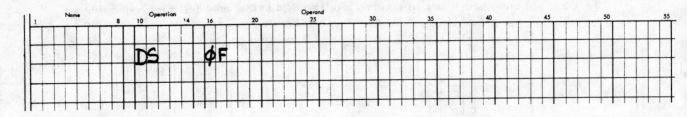

Figure 4-19 Define Storage instruction to align on a fullword boundary

Thus, in Figure 4-20, NAME1 would begin on a fullword boundary and would reserve 6 bytes of storage.

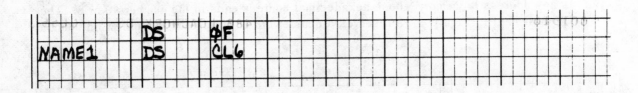

Figure 4-20 Example of the use of a DS instruction for alignment

The DS instruction can also be used to align on a halfword boundary (DS 0H) and a doubleword boundary (DS 0D).

A-TYPE ADDRESS CONSTANTS

It was stated previously that the base register plus displacement addressing concept was valid as long as the displacement is 4096 bytes or less. One method of obtaining the address of any label anywhere in the program is by using an address constant. An address constant is established by using a Define Constant statement as shown in Figure 4-21.

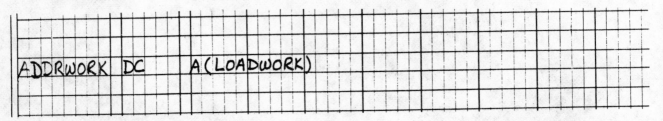

Figure 4-21 A-type Address Constant

Note that, unlike other DC instructions, the address constant DC instruction uses parentheses around the constant rather than apostrophes.

This DC instruction will construct a fullword on a fullword boundary which contains the location counter value of LOADWORK. Thus in Figure 4-22 it can be seen that the location counter value of LOADWORK is stored in a fullword and that this value can be referenced by the name ADDRWORK.

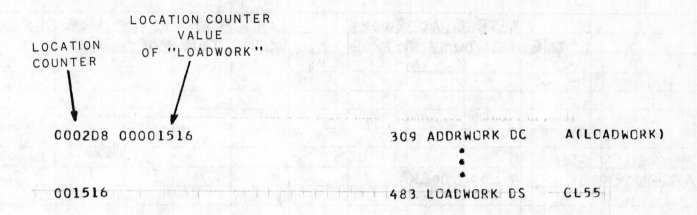

Figure 4-22 Location counter value in an A-type address constant

When the program is link-edited, this "adcon" will be resolved so that it contains the actual core storage address of LOADWORK. Thus, in the program, the address at ADDRWORK can be loaded into a register and LOADWORK can then be referenced in instructions through the use of the loaded register.

In the sample program, the work area for loading the file is unaddressable because it is defined following some large I/O areas. Therefore, an address constant for the work area is established and this address is loaded into a register. A dummy section is then used to reference the work area. The following section of coding illustrates the use of an address constant and a dummy section.

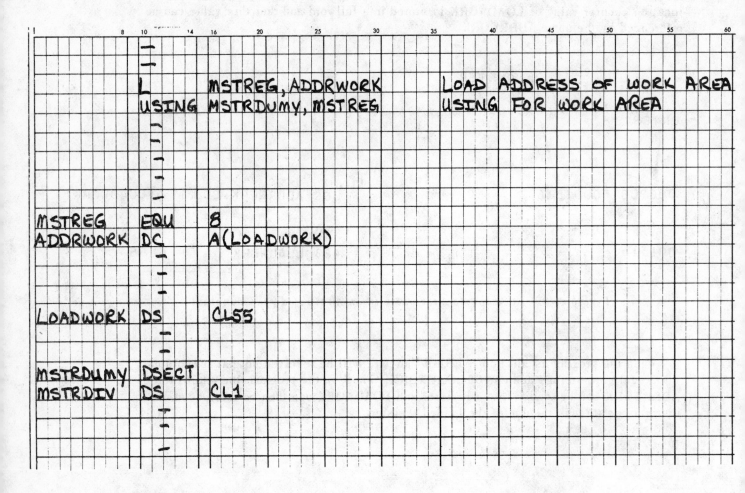

Figure 4-23 *Example of the use of an A-type address constant*

BINARY NUMBERS

As has been previously shown, numeric values on the System/360 can be represented in three different formats: zoned decimal, packed decimal, and binary. Thus the number 28 may be represented in core storage as:

F2F8 – Zoned decimal

028F – Packed decimal

00011100 (Hex 1C) – Binary

When a numeric value is input from a punched card, it is normally represented in a zoned decimal format. Before being printed on the printer, values must be stored in core in the zoned decimal format. When using tape or disk as auxiliary storage, however, there are no requirements that zoned decimal be used. In fact, there are advantages to using packed decimal and binary representation on tape and disk.

The primary advantage in using packed or binary representation on disk and tape is that considerable storage space may be saved. Figure 4-24 shows the relationship of the number of bytes needed to store numbers in the three formats.

Numerical Value	ZONED DEC		PACKED DEC		BINARY		
	Rep	Bytes	Rep	Bytes	Hex	Rep	Bytes
9	F9	1	9F	1	09	0000 1001	1
99	F9 F9	2	09 9F	2	63	0110 0011	1
999	F9 F9 F9	3	99 9F	2	03 E7	0000 0011 1110 0111	2
9999	F9 F9 F9 F9	4	09 99 9F	3	27 0F	0010 0111 0000 1111	2
99999	F9 F9 F9 F9 F9	5	99 99 9F	3	01 86 9F	0000 0001 1000 0110 1001 1111	3
999999	F9 F9 F9 F9 F9 F9	6	09 99 99 9F	4	0F 42 3F	0000 1111 0100 0010 0011 1111	3
9999999	F9 F9 F9 F9 F9 F9 F9	7	99 99 99 9F	4	98 96 7F	1001 1000 1001 0110 0111 1111	3

Figure 4-24 Required storage for zoned-decimal, packed and binary formats

As can be seen from the table, binary representation takes less space to store data than either packed decimal or zoned decimal and packed decimal takes less than zoned decimal. Although one byte may seem insignificant, it can be quite meaningful when a complete file is considered. In the sample program, for example, there are ten numeric fields which can be represented in any of the three formats. Figure 4-25 shows the storage requirements for each of the ten fields in the three different formats.

STORAGE REQUIREMENTS

Field	# of Numeric digits	Zoned Decimal	Packed Decimal	Binary
Division Number	2	2	2	1
Prime Number	6	6	4	3
Dash Number	5	5	3	3
Qty on Hand	7	7	4	3
Qty on Order	7	7	4	3
Qty Reserved	7	7	4	3
Division-N.A.	2	2	2	1
Prime-N.A.	6	6	4	3
Dash-N.A.	5	5	3	3
Unit Price	6	6	4	3
	53	53	34	26

Figure 4-25 Master Record storage requirements

It can be seen from Figure 4-25 that in one record on the inventory file from the sample program, 19 bytes can be saved if packed decimal is used instead of zoned decimal and 27 bytes can be saved if binary is used instead of zoned decimal. Note also that eight bytes can be saved if binary is used instead of packed decimal. If an inventory file of 10,000 parts is needed, 190,000 bytes can be saved if packed decimal is used and 270,000 bytes can be saved if binary is used.

Therefore, a strong argument can be made for using binary representation on auxiliary storage. In order to use binary, however, it is necessary that the input data, which normally is received in a zoned decimal format, be converted to a binary representation. This is accomplished by using the convert to binary instruction.

CONVERT TO BINARY Instruction

The convert to binary instruction is used to convert packed decimal numeric data to binary data.

> INSTRUCTION: CONVERT TO BINARY
>
> OPERATION CODE: CVB
>
> EXAMPLE: CVB 6,DBLWORK

The convert to binary instruction causes the data stored in packed decimal format in the doubleword referenced by the second operand (DBLWORK) to be converted to a binary representation and stored in the register specified in the first operand (6). The register can be any of the general purpose registers. The second operand must be a doubleword on a doubleword boundary and contain the number to be converted. This number must be stored in the packed decimal format.

The following examples illustrate the sequence of events to be followed to convert zoned decimal numeric data to binary and store it in an output record:

EXAMPLE

STEP 1: PACK the field to be converted to binary (INPTPRME).

```
PACK   DBLWORK(8),INPTPRME(6)
```

Before Execution:

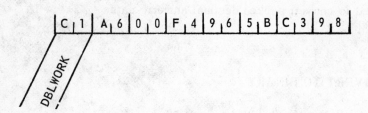

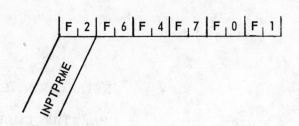

After Execution:

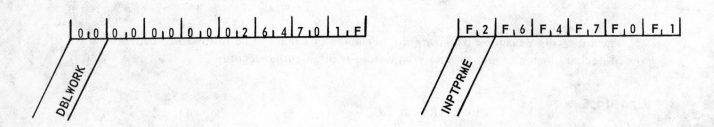

Figure 4-26 Pack instruction to pack data in doubleword

Note that DBLWORK is a doubleword (8 bytes) and that it must be on a doubleword boundary. Thus, it is defined as:

DBLWORK   DS D

Note also that the PACK instruction sets the high-order bits in DBLWORK to zero.

STEP 2: Use the CVB instruction to convert the data stored in DBLWORK to binary.

Before Execution:

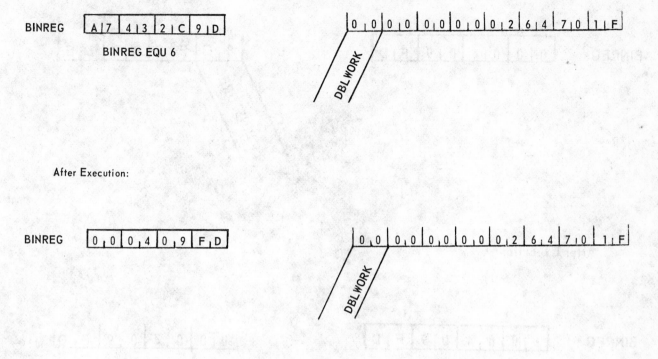

BINREG | A|7 | 4|3 | 2|C | 9|D |

BINREG EQU 6

| 0 |0 |0 |0 |0 |0 |0 |0 |0 |0 |2 |6 |4 |7 |0 |1 |F |

DBLWORK

After Execution:

BINREG | 0 |0 |0 |4 |0 |9 |F |D |

| 0 |0 |0 |0 |0 |0 |0 |0 |0 |2 |6 |4 |7 |0 |1 |F |

DBLWORK

*Figure 4-27 Convert to Binary instruction to convert from packed
decimal to binary*

Note that after the execution of the CVB instruction, the value in BINREG (register 6) is the binary representation of the decimal number 264701.

The decimal number 264701 represented in pure binary notation in a fullword is:

0000 0000 0000 0100 0000 1001 1111 1101

When represented in hexadecimal form the format is:

0000 0000 0000 0100 0000 1001 1111 1101
0   0   0   4   0   9   F D

STEP 3: Store the result in a fullword in core storage.

ST   BINREG, BINSTORE

Before Execution:

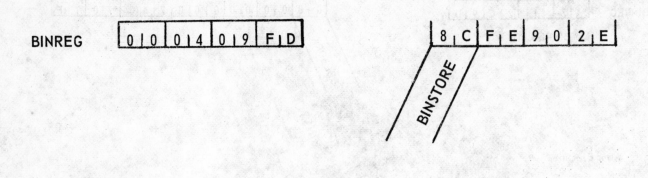

BINREG

After Execution:

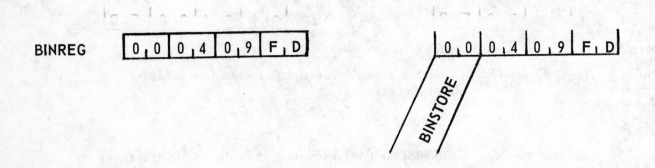

BINREG

Figure 4-28 Store instruction to store converted data

After the register is stored in core storage, the fullword BINSTORE defined as BINSTORE DS F contains the number 264701 in binary form.

STEP 4: Move the result to the field in the master record.

4.26

Before Execution:

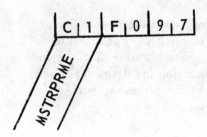

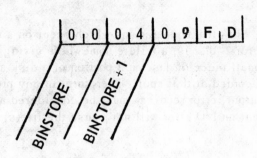

After Execution:

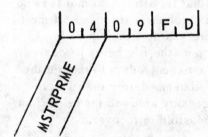

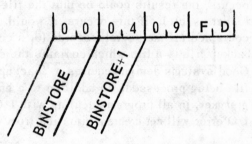

Figure 4-29 Move instruction to move binary data to master record

Since it is known the highest value **INPTPRME** could have is 999999, and that any six digit figure will fit in 3 bytes when it is in binary form, a three byte area (**MSTRPRME**) was reserved for the prime number of the part number, and the number was moved from the store area (**BINSTORE**) to the output area.

As can be observed from the above example, four instructions, two separate work areas and one register were needed to convert the number from zoned decimal to binary and move it to the output area. If the data were to be stored in packed decimal format, one pack instruction is the only instruction necessary. Since more instructions and storage areas are used for binary, the program will require more core than one which does not use binary data and it will have a longer execution time. Thus, the "trade-off" is the saving of auxiliary storage and a larger and slower program versus a faster and smaller program with more auxiliary storage being used. It is up to the analyst or programmer to determine the exact requirements and priorities of the system being written and then take the most useful and economical alternatives.

INDEXED SEQUENTIAL ERROR RECOVERY

In all I/O operations which occur on a computer there exists the possibility of an error——that is, a failure somewhere giving invalid data or results. For example, a small piece of dust on a portion of a disk may make it impossible to read the records recorded at that spot. Therefore, in any program or application involving input and output, error recovery must be considered and analyzed by the programmer to be sure that an I/O error will not cause the file(s) being processed to be no longer usable.

For example, if the program is a card-to-print program and a card has a nick in it so that the card reader cannot read it, the effect is merely a card read "failure". To continue the operation the card can be duplicated and re-read and the program can continue.

If the program, however, is an update of an indexed sequential file and a disk error occurs, the results could be that the file is destroyed (that is, altered so that it is no longer usable). If this occurs, it would create a serious problem, particularly if the file contained all the payroll records for a company and there was no "backup" file. (A backup file is a file which contains the same information as the file being processed.) Good systems design requires a "backup" file or at least enough data to restore the file being processed. In addition to a backup file it is also mandatory that the programmer, in all programs dealing with I/O, take the necessary steps to insure that an I/O error will not create a situation from which it is impossible to recover.

The Indexed Sequential Access Method gives the programmer a great deal of latitude when dealing with I/O errors which have occurred when indexed sequential files are being processed. Therefore, it is important to be aware of the error recovery procedures available under ISAM.

STATUS OR CONDITION CODE INDICATION

The DTF macro instruction, when expanded by the assembler, provides a 1-byte field where all status codes are placed after the execution of each imperative macro instruction pertaining to the defined file. The problem program must check this byte to find the status of the file after each imperative macro. This byte in the DTF field can be referenced in the program by the name filenameC, where filename is the name of the DTF. Thus, in the sample program, the byte can be referenced by the name INVMSTRC. The eight bits in this byte are each used as a switch or indicator and when the bit is on (that is, the bit is = "1") it indicates an error condition. Figure 4-30 shows the use of each bit in the byte filenameC for the load function.

Bit	Cause	Explanation
0	DASD error	Any uncorrectable DASD error has occurred (except wrong length record).
1	Wrong length record	A wrong length record has been detected during an I/O operation.
2	Prime data area full	The next to the last track of the prime data area has been filled during the load or extension of the data file. The problem programmer should issue the ENDFL macro, then do a load extend on the file with new extents given.
3	Cylinder Index area full	The Cylinder Index area is not large enough to contain all the entries needed to index each cylinder specified for the prime data area. This condition can occur during the execution of the SETFL. The user must extend the upper limit of the cylinder index by using a new extent card.
4	Master Index full	The Master Index area is not large enough to contain all the entries needed to index each track of the Cylinder Index. This condition can occur during SETFL. The user must extend the upper limit, if he is creating the file, by using an extent card. Or, he must reorganize the data file and assign a larger area.
5	Duplicate record	The record being loaded is a duplicate of the previous record.
6	Sequence check	The record being loaded is not in the sequential order required for loading.
7	Prime data area overflow	There is not enough space in the prime data area to write an EOF record. This condition can occur during the execution of the ENDFL macro.

Figure 4-30 FilenameC status indicators

In the sample program, the following error procedures were determined to be necessary to insure the integrity of the file.

X'80' — Uncorrectable DASD error: A message will be printed indicating an uncorrectable error and that the job will be cancelled. The error byte will then be displayed and the job cancelled.

X'40' — Wrong length record error: The record in error will be printed with a message showing the error byte.

X'20' — Prime data area full: A message will be printed indicating an uncorrectable error and then the job will be cancelled.

X'10' — Cylinder Index full: A message will be printed indicating an uncorrectable error and that the job will be cancelled. The error byte will be displayed and the job cancelled.

X'08' — Master Index full: A message will be printed indicating an uncorrectable error and that the job will be cancelled. The error byte will then be displayed and the job cancelled.

X'04' — Duplicate record: The record in error will be printed with a message showing the error byte.

X'02' — Sequence check: The record in error will be printed with a message showing the error byte.

X'01' — Prime data area overflow: A message will be printed indicating an uncorrectable error and that the job will be cancelled. The error byte will then be displayed and the job cancelled.

Any combination of X'40', X'04', or X'02' errors totaling 5 will also cause the job to be cancelled.

When the job is cancelled, the error(s) will have to be corrected and the job re-run. For those errors occurring which do not cause the job to be cancelled, the invalid records will have to be corrected.

The status byte, as has been mentioned, can be addressed by the name filenameC (in the sample program, INVMSTRC). ISAM also provides addressability of the status byte by returning the address of the DTF in register 1 after each imperative macro. Thus, the two instructions shown in Figure 4-31 are identical.

Name		Operation		Operand							

```
          WRITE  INVMSTR,NEWKEY
          TM     INVMSTRC,X'04'



          WRITE  INVMSTR,NEWKEY
          TM     30(1),X'04'
```

Figure 4-31 Two methods to test FilenameC indicators

TRANSLATE Instruction

INSTRUCTION: TRANSLATE

OPERATION CODE: TR

EXAMPLE: TR ERRBYTE1(2),TRTBL

The TRANSLATE instruction uses an "input" field (the first operand) and a table in core storage (the second operand). The translate instruction considers each byte in the input field to be a binary value and adds that value to the address specified in the second operand. The input byte is then replaced by the byte in the table at the address generated by the above calculation.

4.30

Assume an application existed where each blank in a field is to be replaced by a zero. This might be true if numeric fields were punched on a card but were not "zero-filled". A table would be constructed as shown in Figure 4-32.

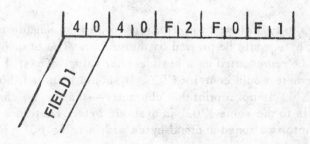

```
            0  1  2  3  4  5  6  7  8  9  A  B  C  D  E  F
TRTABLE  DC  X'00 01 02 03 04 05 06 07 08 09 0A 0B 0C 0D 0E 0F'   +X'00'
         DC  X'10 11 12 13 14 15 16 17 18 19 1A 1B 1C 1D 1E 1F'   +X'10'    (X'40')
         DC  X'20 21 22 23 24 25 26 27 28 29 2A 2B 2C 2D 2E 2F'   +X'20'
         DC  X'30 31 32 33 34 35 36 37 38 39 3A 3B 3C 3D 3E 3F'   +X'30'
         DC  X'F0 41 42 43 44 45 46 47 48 49 4A 4B 4C 4D 4E 4F'   +X'40'
         DC  X'50 51 52 53 54 55 56 57 58 59 5A 5B 5C 5D 5E 5F'   +X'50'
         DC  X'60 61 62 63 64 65 66 67 68 69 6A 6B 6C 6D 6E 6F'   +X'60'
         DC  X'70 71 72 73 74 75 76 77 78 79 7A 7B 7C 7D 7E 7F'   +X'70'
         DC  X'80 81 82 83 84 85 86 87 88 89 8A 8B 8C 8D 8E 8F'   +X'80'
         DC  X'90 91 92 93 94 95 96 97 98 99 9A 9B 9C 9D 9E 9F'   +X'90'
         DC  X'A0 A1 A2 A3 A4 A5 A6 A7 A8 A9 AA AB AC AD AE AF'   +X'A0'
         DC  X'B0 B1 B2 B3 B4 B5 B6 B7 B8 B9 BA BB BC BD BE BF'   +X'B0'
         DC  X'C0 C1 C2 C3 C4 C5 C6 C7 C8 C9 CA CB CC CD CE CF'   +X'C0'
         DC  X'D0 D1 D2 D3 D4 D5 D6 D7 D8 D9 DA DB DC DD DE DF'   +X'D0'
         DC  X'E0 E1 E2 E3 E4 E5 E6 E7 E8 E9 EA EB EC ED EE EF'   +X'E0'
         DC  X'F0 F1 F2 F3 F4 F5 F6 F7 F8 F9 FA FB FC FD FE FF'   +X'F0'
```

Figure 4-32 Translate table to convert blanks to zeros

This table consists of all possible bit configurations that can be stored in core beginning with X'00' and continuing through X'FF'. The only bit configuration which must be altered is X'40', which is the EBCDIC bit configuration of a blank. It should be changed to a X'F0' which is the EBCDIC representation of a zero; therefore, the entry at X'40' in the table is equal to X'F0'.

The "input" field consists of the following characters (hex representation).

```
| 4 0 | 4 0 | F 2 | F 0 | F 1 |
```

FIELD1

To convert the first two bytes of FIELD1, which contain X'40' (blanks), the translate instruction could be used in conjunction with the table illustrated in Figure 4-32.

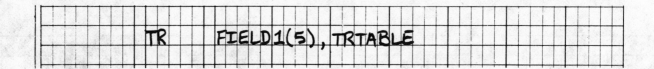

Before Execution:

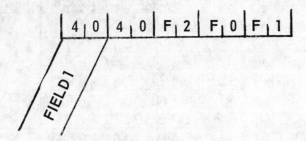

The translate table does not change during the translate instruction.

After Execution:

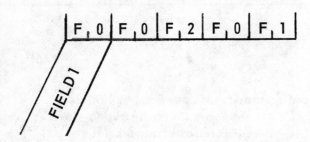

Figure 4-33 Translate instruction to convert blanks to zeros

Note that the leading blanks in FIELD1 were changed to zoned-decimal zeros. This was accomplished in the following manner: The hex '40', which represents a blank, was added to the address of TRTABLE. The byte at TRTABLE + X'40' was moved to the byte in FIELD1. At TRTABLE + X'40' in the table is X'F0'. This X'F0' was moved to the byte in FIELD1. Note that for the X'F2' in FIELD1, the corresponding value in the table is X'F2' so that essentially no change took place.

In the procedures to be followed for error recovery in the sample program, it was stated that the error byte would be printed on the printer. The error byte is a single byte whose contents can be represented as a hexadecimal value. Thus, if the error were a sequence error, the byte would contain X'02'. It should be noted, however, that the hexadecimal value X'02' is not a printable character——that is, no character or special character corresponds to the value X'02' in a single byte. Therefore, the single byte must be translated into two zoned decimal bytes with a value F0F2 in order to be printed.

The following sequence of instructions illustrates the steps necessary for the conversion.

STEP 1: The field ERRBYTE1 is set to zero.

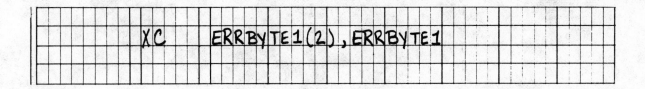

Before Execution:

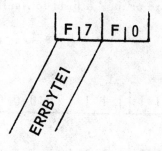

After Execution:

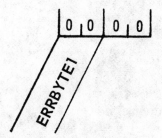

Figure 4-34 Exclusive or instruction to zero field

4.33

The EXCLUSIVE OR instruction can be used to set a field to hex zeros by "exclusive or'ing" the field to itself. To review, the Exclusive Or logic is:

First Operand	Second Operand		Result
1	1	=	0
1	0	=	1
0	1	=	1
0	0	=	0

Figure 4-35 Exclusive or logic

Thus, the effect when "exclusive or'ing" a field to itself is to zero the field.

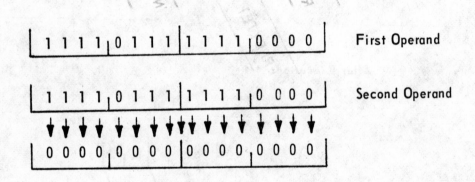

Figure 4-36 Effect of exclusive or'ing a field to itself

STEP 2: The status byte is moved to the ERRBYTE1 field using the Move With Offset Instruction.

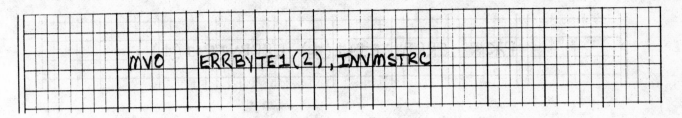

Before Execution:

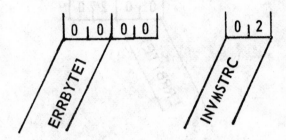

After Execution:

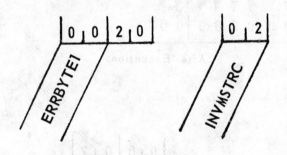

Figure 4-37 Move with offset instruction

The error byte is moved to the error byte area in the print area and is separated into two bytes. It should be recalled that when the Move With Offset instruction is executed the data referenced in the second operand is placed to the left of and adjacent to the low-order four bits of the data referenced in the first operand.

4.35

STEP 3: The second byte is reversed using the Pack instruction.

```
PACK    ERRBYTE1+1(1),ERRBYTE+1(1)
```

Before Execution:

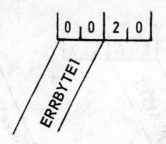

After Execution:

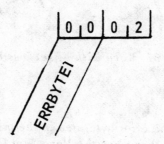

Figure 4-38 Pack instruction

The error byte has now been set up so that the high-order 4 bits of each byte contain hex zero. This is necessary because the translate table is established for only the value 00 through 0F.

4.36

STEP 4: The two error bytes are translated.

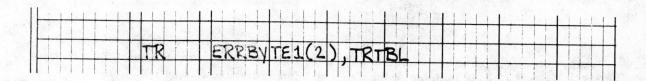

Before Execution:

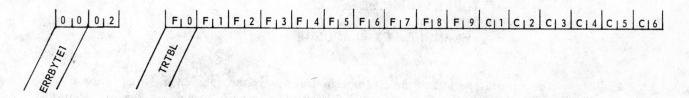

After Execution:

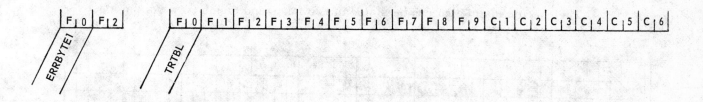

Figure 4-39 Translate instruction to translate error byte to zoned decimal

The values in ERRBYTE1 and ERRBYTE1+1 were each added to the address of TRTBL and the byte at the resultant address in the table replaced the byte in the "input" field. It should be noted that after Steps 1, 2 and 3 shown above, the high-order four bits in the two bytes of the input field (ERRBYTE1 and ERRBYTE1+1) were hexadecimal 0. This was done so that the translate table need only be constructed for the values 00-0F. If these bits were not zero, the table would have to be built for values 00-FF. Thus, by ensuring that the high-order four bits of each byte were zero, only a 16 byte translate table was built and 240 bytes of core storage were saved.

EXECUTE Instruction

The EXECUTE instruction is used to execute a single instruction which is not in the normal sequence of instructions. It can be thought of as a branch and link instruction to execute a single instruction for which no address linkage is required.

INSTRUCTION: EXECUTE

OPERATION CODE: EX

EXAMPLE: EX 0,ADDERR

The second operand of the Execute Instruction is the name of the instruction to be executed (the "subject instruction"). The first operand is a register number. When the number specified is zero, it has no effect on the instruction (ADDERR) being executed.

The execute instruction can be stated in two forms and thus has two distinct uses.

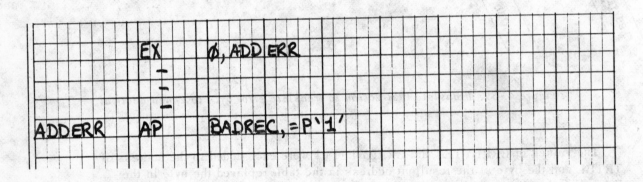

Figure 4-40 Execute instruction to execute an Add Packed instruction

In Figure 4-40, the Execute Instruction is used to execute the Add Packed Instruction with the label ADDERR. Thus, when the Execute Instruction is performed, 1 will be added to BADREC.

The normal use of the Execute Instruction with a zero first operand is to save core in the program. If a six-byte instruction, such as the Add Packed Instruction in the example, is to be performed more than once in the program, core storage can be saved by using the Execute Instruction.

Note in the table below that if a 6 byte instruction is used 3 times it will require 18 bytes of storage. If the Execute instruction is used with the instruction, only 14 bytes are required.

TIMES USED	NO EXECUTE	EXECUTE
1	6	6
2	12	10
3	18	14

Figure 4-41 Core savings using execute instruction

It can be seen from the table that if the same six-byte instruction is to be executed more than once in the program, core storage can be saved by using the Execute Instruction.

The second use of the Execute Instruction allows the "subject instruction" to be altered by the execute and then performed. When the register specified in the first operand is other than zero, bits 8-15 of the subject are OR'ed by bits 24-31 of the register specified in the first operand. Figure 4-42 shows an example of this.

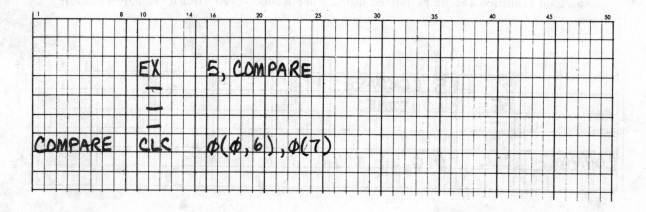

4.39

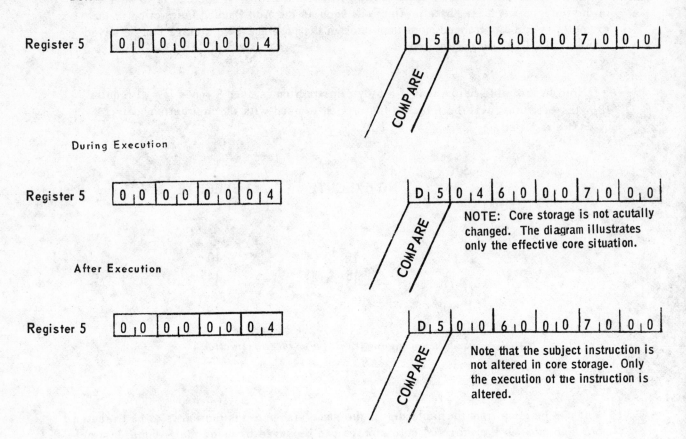

Figure 4-42 Execute instruction to modify and execute CLC instruction

The effect of the Execute Instruction as illustrated is to compare the field located at the address in register 7 with the field located at the address in register 6. The compare is for 5 bytes. The condition code indicating high, low or equal is set in the same manner as if the compare were in-line. Thus, after the Execute Instruction, a branch on condition can be performed in the same manner used after a compare instruction.

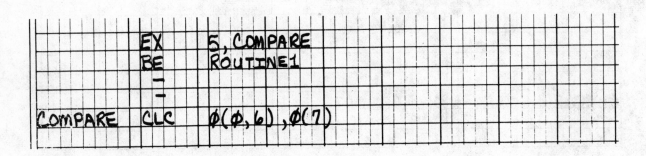

Figure 4-43 Use of branch equal instruction after execute instruction

Any instruction, with the exception of another Execute Instruction, can be used as the "subject instruction". If the subject instruction is a branch, it will take place as if it were in the normal sequence of instructions.

INSTRUCTION MODIFICATION

Dependent upon situations arising during program execution, it may be advantageous to alter an instruction during execution. Altering a branch instruction is a common technique.

The instruction BC 0,CANCEL is known as a NO-OP because it will cause no operation to take place. The branch on condition instruction tests the condition code and branches or doesn't branch dependent upon that condition code. When no condition code is being tested, no branch can take place. Thus, the effect of the NO-OP is to fall through and execute the next instruction following it.

The machine language format of the BC 0,CANCEL instruction is $\boxed{4\,7\,|\,0\,|\,0\,|\,C\,2\,|\,C\,2}$ where C 2 C 2 is the base register + displacement address of CANCEL. The mask to test the condition code is in bits 8-11 of the instruction. In the example, the condition code being tested for is 0, that is, no condition code is being tested. The table in Figure 4-44 illustrates the masks in the BC instruction to test condition codes after compare instructions (for a complete listing see the appendix).

Mask To Test	Meaning	Mnemonic
2	A > B	BH
4	A < B	BL
8	A = B	BE
13(D)	A not > B	BNH
11(B)	A not < B	BNL
7	A not = B	BNE
15(F)	UNconditional Branch	B

Figure 4-44 Branch on condition instruction masks

Thus, the instruction BC 4,GOTO means if, after a compare instruction, it is determined that the first operand (A) is less than the second operand (B), branch to GOTO.

In order to change the NO-OP instruction to a meaningful branch, the mask in bits 8-11 can be "OR'ed" to whatever mask is desired (as illustrated in Figure 4-45).

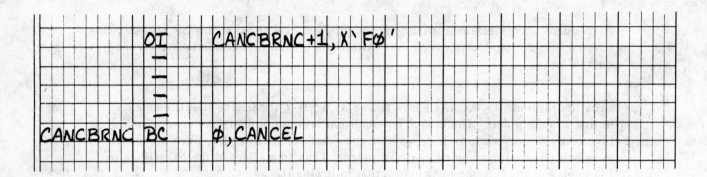

Before Execution:

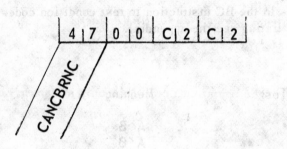

After Execution:

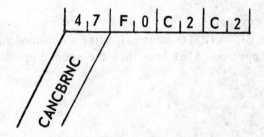

Figure 4-45 Example of instruction modification using OI instruction

Note that the branch instruction has been changed from a NO-OP to a branch unconditional instruction.

It should be noted that any instruction in core could be changed to any valid format at any time during the execution of the program.

DUMP Macro

The DUMP macro can be utilized in a program at any point the programmer wishes to cancel the job and get a core dump.

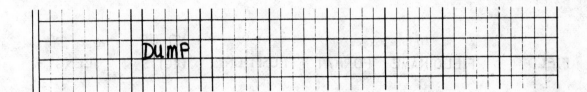

Figure 4-46 DUMP Macro

The word DUMP in the operation field is the only statement needed for the DUMP macro.

SAMPLE PROGRAM

The sample program in this chapter loads the indexed sequential master file from sorted sequential transactions.

The input file record layout is illustrated below.

FIELD	FIELD NAME	FORMAT	POSITION	NO. OF DIGITS	LENGTH
Part Number					
Division Number	INPTDIV	N-Z	1-2	2	2
Prime Number	INPTPRME	N-Z	3-8	6	6
Dash Number	INPTDASH	N-Z	9-13	5	5
Description	INPTNAME	AN	14-38	25	25
Qty on Hand	INPTQOH	N-Z	39-45	7	7
Qty on Order	INPTQOO	N-Z	46-52	7	7
Qty Reserved	INPTQRSV	N-Z	53-59	7	7
Part Number - NA					
Division - NA	IASYDIV	N-Z	60-61	2	2
Prime - NA	IASYPRME	N-Z	62-67	6	6
Dash - NA	IASYDASH	N-Z	68-72	5	5
Type	INPTTYPE	N-Z	73	1	1
Source	INPTSRCE	N-Z	74	1	1
Unit Price	INPTUNIT	N-Z	75-80	6	6

LEGEND: N-Z – Numeric, zoned-decimal   AN – Alpha-numeric

In the input record, the Type indicates the function of the record. When creating the master file, the Type must be equal to 8 (new load transaction). The Source indicates whether the part is a manufactured part (code = 1) or a purchased part (code = 2).

The output record layout is illustrated below.

FIELD	FIELD NAME	FORMAT	POSITION	NO. OF DIGITS	LENGTH
Part Number					
Division Number	MSTRDIV	N - B	1	2	1
Prime Number	MSTRPRME	N - B	2 - 4	6	3
Dash Number	MSTRDASH	N - B	5 - 7	5	3
Description	MSTRNAME	AN	8 - 32	25	25
Qty on Hand	MSTRQOH	N - B	33 - 35	7	3
Qty on Order	MSTRQOO	N - B	36 - 38	7	3
Qty Reserved	MSTRQRSV	N - B	39 - 41	7	3
Part Number - NA					
Division - NA	MASYDIV	N - B	42	2	1
Prime - NA	MASYPRME	N - B	43 - 45	6	3
Dash - NA	MASYDASH	N - B	46 - 48	5	3
Type	MSTRTYPE	N - Z	49	1	1
Source	MSTRSRCE	N - Z	50	1	1
Unit Price	MSTRUNIT	N - B	51 - 53	6	3
Filler	MSTRXTRA	AN	54 - 55	2	2

LEGEND: N - B — Numeric, Binary   N - Z — Numeric, Zoned Decimal
           AN — Alpha - numeric

In the master record, the type field is used to indicate whether a record is an active record (type = 1) or a deleted record (type = 2).

A report is created in the program which lists all transactions which are in error. The format of the report is shown below.

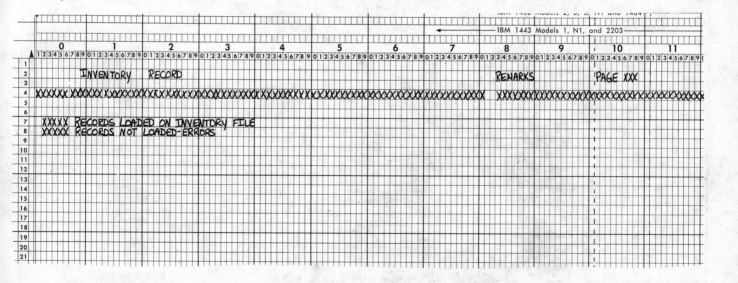

4.45

PROGRAM

The following is the listing of the program used to load the indexed sequential inventory master file.

```
CREATE MASTER FILE FROM SORTED INPUT                                            PAGE   1

  LOC  OBJECT CODE   ADDR1 ADDR2 STMT  SOURCE STATEMENT                      DOS CL3-5 08/26/70

  000000                             2 BLDMASTR START 0                                   LOAD0020
                                     3        PRINT NOGEN


                                     5 ****                                               LOAD0040
                                     6 * THIS PROGRAM BUILDS THE INDEXED SEQUENTIAL MASTER FILE FROM  LOAD0050
                                     7 * SORTED INPUT ON THE DISK.                         LOAD0060
                                     8 * THIS PROGRAM READS THE DISK AND VERIFIES THAT THE KEYS ARE  IN  LOAD0070
                                     9 * SEQUENCE AND THAT IT IS A LOAD TYPE CARD.  IT THEN LOADS THE  LOAD0080
                                    10 * RECORD INTO THE MASTER FILE.  IF THE KEY IS OUT OF SEQUENCE OR IF  LOAD0090
                                    11 * THE TYPE IS INCORRECT, THE APPROPRIATE MESSAGE IS PRINTED ON THE  LOAD0100
                                    12 * PRINTER.                                          LOAD0110
                                    13 ****                                                LOAD0120

  000000 05C0                      15        BALR  BASEREG,0        ESTABLISH A BASE REGISTER    LOAD0140
  000002                           16        USING *,BASEREG        USING FOR BASE REGISTER     LOAD0150
                                    17        OPEN  INVMSTR,DISKIN,PRTFLE      OPEN FILES           LOAD0160


  00001A 5880 C2C6          002C8  28        L     MSTREG,ADDRWORK   LOAD ADDRESS OF WORK AREA    LOAD0180
  000000                           29        USING MSTRDUMY,MSTREG   USING FOR MASTER DUMMY SECTION  LOAD0190
  000000                           30        USING INPTDUMY,INPUTREG  USING FOR INPUT DUMMY SECTION  LOAD0200

  00001E 45E0 C1EA          001EC  32        BAL   RETREG,HEADRTN    GO TO PRINT HEADING FOR REPORT  LOAD0220
                                    33        SETFL INVMSTR          READY FILE TO BE LOADED      LOAD0230

  00002E 9110 C5E4   005E4  001D6  40        TM    INVMSTRC,X'10'    IS CYLINDER INDEX AREA LARGE ENOUGH  LOAD0250
  000032 4710 C1D4          001D6  41        BO    BADMAST           NO GO TO NOTIFY AND CANCEL JOB  LOAD0260
  000036 9108 C5E4   005E6         42        TM    INVMSTRC,X'08'    IS MASTER INDEX LARGE ENOUGH  LOAD0270
  00003A 4710 C1D4          001D6  43        BO    BADMAST           NO, GO TO INDICATE AND CANCEL JOB  LOAD0280


                                    45 READINPT GET   DISKIN          READ THE SEQ DISK INPUT FILE  LOAD0300
  00004A 95F8 A048   00048         51        CLI   INPTTYPE,C'8'     IS IT A LOAD TYPE RECORD     LOAD0320
  00004E 4770 C192          00194  52        BNE   TYPERROR          NO, GO TO PRINT ERROR MESSAGE  LOAD0330


                                    54 ****                                                LOAD0350
                                    55 * IT IS NOW ESTABLISHED THAT THE RECORD JUST READ IS A VALID RECORD.  LOAD0360
                                    56 *        ALL VALUES MUST BE READIED FOR THE MASTER FILE FORMAT  LOAD0370
                                    57 ****                                                LOAD0380


  000052 F271 C2BE A000 002C0 00000  59      PACK  DBLWORK(8),INPTDIV(2)  PACK DIVISION NUMBER    LOAD0400
  000058 4590 C188          0018A  60        BAL   LINKREG,CONVERT    GO TO CONVERT TO BINARY     LOAD0410
  00005C 4590 C188          0018A  61        BAL   LINKREG,CONVERT    GO TO CONVERT VALUE TO BINARY  LOAD0420
  000060 D200 8000 C2CD 00000 002CF 62       MVC   MSTRDIV(1),BINSTORE+3  MOVE DIVISION TO OUTPUT  LOAD0430

  000066 F275 C2BE A002 002C0 00002 64       PACK  DBLWORK(8),INPTPRME(6)  PACK PRIME NUMBER      LOAD0450
  00006C 4590 C188          0018A  65        BAL   LINKREG,CONVERT    GO TO CONVERT VALUE TO BINARY  LOAD0460
  000070 D202 8001 C2CB 00001 002CD 66       MVC   MSTRPRME(3),BINSTORE+1  MOVE PRIME NUMBER TO OUTPUT  LOAD0470

  000076 F274 C2BE A008 002C0 00008 68       PACK  DBLWORK(8),INPTDASH(5)  PACK DASH NUMBER       LOAD0490
  00007C 4590 C188          0018A  69        BAL   LINKREG,CONVERT    GO TO CONVERT DASH NUMBER TO BINARY  LOAD0500
  000080 D202 8004 C2CB 00004 002CD 70       MVC   MSTRDASH(3),BINSTORE+1  STORE THE DASH NO IN OUTPUT  LOAD0510

  000086 D218 8007 A00D 00007 0000D 72       MVC   MSTRNAME(25),INPTNAME   MOVE NAME TO OUTPUT     LOAD0530

  00008C F276 C2BE A026 002C0 00026 74       PACK  DBLWORK(8),INPTQOH(7)  PACK QUANTITY TO HAND   LOAD0550
  000092 4590 C188          0018A  75        BAL   LINKREG,CONVERT    GO TO CONVERT QTY ON HAND TO BINARY  LOAD0560
  000096 D202 8020 C2CB 00020 002CD 76       MVC   MSTRQOH(3),BINSTORE+1  MOVE QOH TO OUTPUT       LOAD0570

  00009C F276 C2BE A02D 002C0 0002D 78       PACK  DBLWORK(8),INPTQOO(7)  PACK QUANTITY ON ORDER  LOAD0590
  0000A2 4590 C188          0018A  79        BAL   LINKREG,CONVERT    CONVERT QTY ON ORDER TO BINARY  LOAD0600
  0000A6 D202 8023 C2CB 00023 002CD 80       MVC   MSTRQOO(3),BINSTORE+1  MOVE QTY ON ORDER TO OUTPUT  LOAD0610

  0000AC F276 C2BE A034 002C0 00034 82       PACK  DBLWORK(8),INPTQRSV(7)  PACK QUANTITY RESERVED  LOAD0630
  0000B2 4590 C188          0018A  83        BAL   LINKREG,CONVERT    CONVERT QTY RESERVED TO BINARY  LOAD0640
  0000B6 D202 8026 C2CB 00026 002CD 84       MVC   MSTRQRSV(3),BINSTORE+1  MOVE QTY RESERVED TO OUTPUT  LOAD0650

  0000BC F275 C2BE A04A 002C0 0004A 86       PACK  DBLWORK(8),INPTUNIT  PACK UNIT PRICE           LOAD0670
  0000C2 4590 C188          0018A  87        BAL   LINKREG,CONVERT    CONVERT UNIT PRICE TO BINARY  LOAD0680
  0000C6 D202 8032 C2CB 00032 002CD 88       MVC   MSTRUNIT(3),BINSTORE+1  MOVE UNIT PRICE TO MASTER  LOAD0690

  0000CC F271 C2BE A03B 002C0 0003B 90       PACK  DBLWORK(8),IASYDIV(2)  PACK DIVISION- NEXT ASSEMBLY  LOAD0710
  0000D2 4590 C188          0018A  91        BAL   LINKREG,CONVERT    CONVERT DIVISION TO BINARY   LOAD0720
  0000D6 D200 8029 C2CD 00029 002CF 92       MVC   MASYDIV(1),BINSTORE+3  MOVE DIVISION TO OUTPUT  LOAD0730

  0000DC F275 C2BE A03D 002C0 0003D 94       PACK  DBLWORK(8),IASYPRME(6)  PACK PRIME-NEXT ASSEMBLY  LOAD0750
  0000E2 4590 C188          0018A  95        BAL   LINKREG,CONVERT    GO TO CONVERT PRIME TO BINARY  LOAD0760
  0000E6 D202 802A C2CB 0002A 002CD 96       MVC   MASYPRME(3),BINSTORE+1  MOVE PRIME TO OUTPUT    LOAD0770

  0000EC F274 C2BE A043 002C0 00043 98       PACK  DBLWORK(8),IASYDASH(5)  PACK DASH/NEXT ASSEMBLY  LOAD0790
  0000F2 4590 C188          0018A  99        BAL   LINKREG,CONVERT    CONVERT DASH TO BINARY       LOAD0800
  0000F6 D202 802D C2CB 0002D 002CD 100      MVC   MASYDASH(3),BINSTORE+1  MOVE DASH TO OUTPUT     LOAD0810

  0000FC 92F1 8030   00030         102       MVI   MSTRTYPE,C'1'      SET TYPE CODE TO ACTIVE RECORD  LOAD0830
  000100 D200 8031 A049 00031 00049 103      MVC   MSTRSRCE(1),INPTSRCE  MOVE SOURCE TO OUTPUT     LOAD0840
```

4.46

```
 000106 D201 8035 C39A 00035 0039C  104          MVC    MSTRXTRA(2),BLANKS  MOVE FILLER BLANKS TO OUTPUT       LOAD0850


                                    106  ****                                                                  LOAD0870
                                    107  * AT THIS POINT, THE MASTER RECORD IS READY TO BE WRITTEN TO THE      LOAD0880
                                    108  * DISK FILE.                                                          LOAD0890
                                    109  ****                                                                  LOAD0900


                                    111          WRITE  INVMSTR,NEWKEY      WRITE MASTER RECORD                LOAD0920
 000118 91FF C5E4      005E6        117          TM     INVMSTRC,X'FF'  ANY ERROR CONDITIONS                  LOAD0940
 00011C 4780 C146            00148  118          BZ     WRITEOK            NO, GO TO CONTINUE                  LOAD0950
 000120 9180 C5E4      005E6        119          TM     INVMSTRC,X'80'     WASIT AN UNRECOVERABLE ERROR       LOAD0960
 000124 4710 C1D4            001D6  120          BO     BADMAST            YES, GO TO CANCEL JOB               LOAD0970
 000128 9120 C5E4      005E6        121          TM     INVMSTRC,X'20'     IS PRIME AREA TOO FULL             LOAD0980
 00012C 4710 C1D4            001D6  122          BO     BADMAST            YES, GO TO CANCEL JOB               LOAD0990
 000130 9140 C5E4      005E6        123          TM     INVMSTRC,X'40'     IT IT WRONG LENGTH                 LOAD1000
 000134 4710 C1AE            001B0  124          BO     CHKERROR           YES, GO TO PRINT ERROR AND CONTINUE LOAD1010
 000138 9104 C5E4      005E6        125          TM     INVMSTRC,X'04'     WAS IT A DUPLICATE RECORD          LOAD1020
 00013C 4710 C1AE            001B0  126          BO     CHKERROR           YES, GO TO PRIT ERROR AND GO ON     LOAD1030
 000140 9102 C5E4      005E6        127          TM     INVMSTRC,X'02'     WAS IT OUT OF SEQUENCE             LOAD1040
 000144 4710 C1AE            001B0  128          BO     CHKERROR           YES$ TO TO CONTINUE                LOAD1050
 000148                             129 WRITEOK  EQU    *                                                     LOAD1060
 000148 FA20 C2CF C536 002D1 0053F  130          AP     GOODREC,=P'1'      INCREMENT GOOD REORD COUNTER       LOAD1070
 00014E 47F0 C03C            0003E  131          B      READINPT           GO TO READ NEXT RECORD             LOAD1080


 000152 9240 C4D0      004D2        133          MVI    PRIO1+80,X'40'     CLEAR PRINTER AREA                 LOAD1100
 000156 D226 C4D1 C4D0 004D3 004D2  134          MVC    PRIO1+81(39),PRIO1+80                                 LOAD1110

 00015C                             136 PRINTALL EQU    *                                                     LOAD1130
 00015C D24F C480 A000 00482 00000  137          MVC    PRIO1(80),INPTDUMY  MOVE THE INPUT MSG TO THE PRINTER  LOAD1140
                                    138          PUT    PRTFLE             PRINT LINE                         LOAD1150

                                    144          PRTOV  PRTFLE,12,HEADRTN  IF OVERFLOW, GO TO HEADER ROUTINE  LOAD1170
 00017E 955C C2CE      002D0        151          CLI    ERCNT,X'5C'        IS COUNTER = 5                     LOAD1190
 000182 4780 C1E2            001E4  152          BE     DONE               YES, GO TO CANCEL PROGRAM          LOAD1200
 000186 47F0 C03C            0003E  153          B      READINPT           GO TO READ NEXT RECORD             LOAD1210


                                    155  ****                                                                 LOAD1230
                                    156  * THIS ROUTINE IS ENTERED TO CONVERT PACKED DATA TO BINARY           LOAD1240
                                    157  ****                                                                 LOAD1250


 00018A                             159 CONVERT  EQU    *                                                     LOAD1270
 00018A 4F60 C2BE            002C0  160          CVB    BINREG,DBLWORK     CONVERT DATA TO BINARY             LOAD1280
 00018E 5060 C2CA            002CC  161          ST     BINREG,BINSTORE    STORE RESULTS IN CORE              LOAD1290
 000192 07F9                        162          BR     LINKREG            RETURN TO CALLER                   LOAD1300


                                    164  ****                                                                 LOAD1320
                                    165  * THIS ROUTINE IS ENTERED WHEN THE TYPE CODE IS NOT CORRECT          LOAD1330
                                    166  ****                                                                 LOAD1340


 000194                             168 TYPERROR EQU    *                                                     LOAD1360
 000194 D227 C4D0 C322 004D2 00324  169          MVC    PRIO1+80(40),TYPEMSG  MOVE MESSAGE TO OUTPUT          LOAD1370
 00019A 4400 C4F8            004FA  170          EX     0,ADDERR           INCREMENT AN ERROR COUNTER         LOAD1380
 00019E 47F0 C15A            0015C  171          B      PRINTALL           GO TO PRINT IT                     LOAD1390


                                    173  ****                                                                 LOAD1410
                                    174  * THIS ROUTINE IS ENTERED WHEN THE KEY IS OUT OF SEQUENCE            LOAD1420
                                    175  ****                                                                 LOAD1430


 0001A2                             177 KEYERROR EQU    *                                                     LOAD1450
 0001A2 D227 C4D0 C34A 004D2 0034C  178          MVC    PRIO1+80(40),KEYMSG  MOVE MESSAGE TO OUTPUT           LOAD1460
 0001A8 4400 C4F8            004FA  179          EX     0,ADDERR           INCREMENT AN ERROR COUNTER         LOAD1470
 0001AC 47F0 C15A            0015C  180          B      PRINTALL           GO TO PRINT MESSAGE                LOAD1480


                                    182  ****                                                                 LOAD1500
                                    183  * THIS ROUTINE IS ENTERED WHEN AN ERROR IS ENCOUNTERED               LOAD1510
                                    184  * DURING THE WRITE. THE STATUS BYTE IS DISPLAYED AND PGM CONTINUES   LOAD1520
                                    185  ****                                                                 LOAD1530


 0001B0                             187 CHKERROR EQU    *                                                     LOAD1550
 0001B0 4400 C4F8            004FA  188          EX     0,ADDERR           INCREMENT AN ERROR COUNTER         LOAD1560
 0001B4 D701 C387 C387 00389 00389 189          XC     ERRBYTE1(2),ERRBYTE1  ZERO ERROR BYTE                 LOAD1570
 0001BA F110 C387 C5E4 00389 005E6 190          MVO    ERRBYTE1(2),INVMSTRC  MOVE ERROR BYTE TO MSG AREA     LOAD1580
 0001C0 F200 C388 C388 0038A 0038A 191          PACK   ERRBYTE1+1(1),ERRBYTE1+1(1)  PACK BYTE                LOAD1590
```

```
    LOC   OBJECT CODE     ADDR1 ADDR2  STMT  SOURCE STATEMENT                                              DOS CL3-5 08/26/70

  0001C6 DC01 C387 C39E   00389 003A0   192       TR    ERRBYTE1(2),TRTBL      TRANSLATE THE TWO ERROR BYTES        LOAD1600
  0001CC D227 C4D0 C372   004D2 00374   193       MVC   PRIO1+80(40),DISKMSG  MOVE MESSAGE TO PRINTER              LOAD1610
  0001D2 47F0 C15A              0015C   194       B     PRINTALL              GO TO PRINT ERROR MESSAGE            LOAD1620
  0001D6                                195 BADMAST EQU  *                                                         LOAD1630
  0001D6 D200 A000 C2D2   00000 002C4   196       MVC   INPTDUMY,LASTMSG      MOVE ERROR MESSASE TO DUMMY AREA     LOAD1640
  0001DC 925C C2CE              002D0   197       MVI   ERCNT,X'5C'           MOVE ERR COUNT TO END                LOAD1650
  0001E0 47F0 C15A              0015C   198       B     PRINTALL              GO TO PRINT MESSAGE                  LOAD1660
  0001E4                                199 DONE  EQU   *                                                          LOAD1670
  0001E4 96F0 C281           00283      200       OI    CANCBRNC+1,X'F0'      SET INSTRUCTION TO UNCONDITIONAL BR  LOAD1680
  0001E8 47F0 C29A              0029C   201       B     ALLDONE               GO TO END THE PROGRAM                LOAD1690


                                       203 ****                                                                   LOAD1710
                                       204 * THIS ROUTINE IS ENTERED TO PLACE A HEADING ON THE                    LOAD1720
                                       205 * RPINTED REDPRT                                                       LOAD1730
                                       206 ****                                                                   LOAD1740


  0001EC                                208 HEADRTN EQU  *                                                         LOAD1760
  0001EC 50E0 C3AE              003B0   209       ST    RETREG,SAVERET        SAVE RETURN REGISTER                 LOAD1770
                                       210       CNTRL PRTFLE,SK,1           GO TO HEAD OF FORMS                  LOAD1790

  0001FE FA10 C3B2 C536   00384 00538   217       AP    PAGENO(2),=P'1'       INCREMENT PAGE NO                    LOAD1810
  000204 D203 C420 C384   00422 003B6   218       MVC   PAGE(4),PAGEPTRN      MOVE EDIT PATTERN                    LOAD1820
  00020A DE03 C420 C3B2   00422 003B4   219       ED    PAGE(4),PAGENO        EDIT PAGE NUMBER                     LOAD1830
  000210 D277 C480 C3B8   004B2 003BA   220       MVC   PRIO1(120),HEADMSG    MOVE MESSAGE TO OUTPUT               LOAD1840
                                       221       PUT   PRTFLE                PRINT HEADER                         LOAD1850
                                       226       CNTRL PRTFLE,SP,2           SPACE TWICE                          LOAD1860
  000230 58E0 C3AE              003B0   232       L     RETREG,SAVERET        RELOAD REGISTER                      LOAD1870
  000234 07FE                           233       BR    RETREG                RETURN TO CALLER                     LOAD1880


                                       235 ****                                                                   LOAD1900
                                       236 * THIS ROUTINE IS ENTERED WHEN THE END OF THE INPUT FILE               LOAD1910
                                       237 * IS REACHED                                                           LOAD1920
                                       238 ****                                                                   LOAD1930


  000236                                240 ENDINPUT EQU  *                                                        LOAD1950
  000236 D205 C430 C477   00432 00479   241       MVC   ENDMSG1(6),PTTRN1     MOVE EDIT PATTERN                    LOAD1960
  00023C DE05 C430 C2CF   00432 002D1   242       ED    ENDMSG1(6),GOODREC    EDIT NUMBER OF GOOD RECORDS          LOAD1970
  000242 9240 C480              00482   243       MVI   PRIO1,X'40'           CLEAR PRINT I/O AREA                 LOAD1980
  000246 D276 C481 C480   00483 00482   244       MVC   PRIO1+1(119),PRIO1                                        LOAD1990
  00024C D226 C480 C430   00482 00432   245       MVC   PRIO1(39),ENDMSG1     MOVE MESSAGE TO PRINTER I/O          LOAD2000
                                       246       PUT   PRTFLE                PRINT MESSAGE                        LOAD2010
  00025E D205 C457 C477   00459 00479   251       MVC   ENDMSG2(6),PTTRN1     MOVE EDIT PATTERN                    LOAD2020
  000264 DE05 C457 C47D   00459 0047F   252       ED    ENDMSG2(6),BADREC     EDIT NUMBER OF BAD RECORDS           LOAD2030
  00026A D226 C480 C457   00482 00459   253       MVC   PRIO1(39),ENDMSG2     MOVE MESSAGE TO PRINTER I/O          LOAD2040
                                       254       PUT   PRTFLE                PRINT MESSAGE                        LOAD2050

                                       260       ENDFL INVMSTR              END THE LOAD OPERATION               LOAD2070
                                       272 ALLDONE CLOSE DISKIN,INVMSTR,PRTFLE  CLOSE FILES                        LOAD2080
  0002B2 4700 C2B6              002B9   282 CANCBRNC BC  0,CANCEL             IF ON, GO TO CANCEL JOB              LOAD2090
                                       283       EOJ   NORMAL END OF JOB                                          LOAD2100
                                       286 CANCEL DUMP                        IF ABNORMAL, GET CORE DUMP           LOAD2110
```

4.48

```
      LOC   OBJECT CODE    ADDR1 ADDR2  STMT   SOURCE STATEMENT                              DOS CL3-5 08/26/70

                                         291 * CONSTANTS,EUQATES, AND PRINTER I/O AREA              LOAD2130
                                         292 ****                                                   LOAD2140

      00000C                             294 BASEREG  EQU   12                                      LOAD2160
      000008                             295 MSTREG   EQU   8                                        LOAD2170
      00000A                             296 INPUTREG EQU   10                                       LOAD2180
      00000E                             297 RETREG   EQU   14                                       LOAD2190
      000009                             298 LINKREG  EQU   9                                        LOAD2200
      0002C0                             299 DBLWORK  DS    D                                         LOAD2210
      0002C8 00001506                    300 ADDRWORK DC    A(LOADWORK)                              LOAD2220
      0002CC                             301 BINSTORE DS    F                                         LOAD2230
      0002D0 0C                          302 ERCNT    DC    PL1'0'                                   LOAD2240
      0002D1 00000C                      303 GOODREC  DC    PL3'0'                                   LOAD2250
      000006                             304 BINREG   EQU   6                                         LOAD2260
      0002D4 E4D5C3D6D9D9C5C3            305 LASTMSG  DC    CL80'UNCORRECTABLE ERROR ON DISK - JOB CANCELLED'   LOAD2270
      000324 4040E3E8D7C540D6            306 TYPEMSG  DC    CL40'  TYPE OF INPUT INVALID-RECORD NOT LOADED'     LOAD2280
      00034C 4040D2C5E840D6E4            307 KEYMSG   DC    CL40'  KEY OUT OF SEQUENCE-RECORD NOT LOADED'       LOAD2290
      000374 4040C4C9E2D240C5            308 DISKMSG  DC    CL40'  DISK ERROR- STATUS   - NOT LOADED'          LOAD2300
      00039C 4040                        309 BLANKS   DC    C'  '                                    LOAD2310
      000389                             310 ERRBYTE1 EQU   DISKMSG+21                               LOAD2320
      00038A                             311 ERRBYTE2 EQU   DISKMSG+22                               LOAD2330
      00039E 0000                        312 HEXZERO  DC    X'0000'                                  LOAD2340
      0003A0 F0F1F2F3F4F5F6F7            313 TRTHL    DC    X'F0F1F2F3F4F5F6F7F8F9C1C2C3C4C5C6'      LOAD2350
      0003B0                             314 SAVERLT  DS    F                                         LOAD2360
      0003B4 000C                        315 PAGENO   DC    PL2'0'                                   LOAD2370
      0003B6 40202020                    316 PAGEPTRN DC    X'40202020'                              CLOAD2380
                                         317 HEADMSG  DC    CL120'        INVENTORY      RECORD      CLOAD2390
      0003BA 4040404040404040                                                REMARKS         PAGE'  LOAD2400
      000422                             318 PAGE     EQU   HEADMSG+104                              LOAD2410
      000432 4040404040404049            319 ENDMSG1  DC    C'     RECORDS LOADED ON INVENTORY FILE' LOAD2420
      000459 4040404040404049            320 ENDMSG2  DC    C'     RECORDS NOT LOADED-ERRORS'        LOAD2430
      000479 402020202120                321 PTTRN1   DC    X'402020202120'                          LOAD2440
      00047F 00000C                      322 BADREC   DC    PL3'0'                                   LOAD2450
      000482                             323 PRIO1    DS    CL120                                     LOAD2460
      0004FA                             324          DS    0H                                        LOAD2470
      0004FA FA20 C47D C536 0047F 00538  325 ADDERR   AP    BADREC,=P'1'          GENERAL ERROR COUNT INCREMENT   LOAD2480
      000500                             326          LTORG                                           LOAD2490
      000500 5B5BC2D6D7C5D540            327                =C'$$BOPEN '
      000508 5B5BC2E2C5E3C6D3            328                =C'$$BSETFL'
      000510 5B5BC2C5D5C4C6D3            329                =C'$$BENDFL'
      000518 5B5BC2C3D3D6E2C5            330                =C'$$BCLOSE'
      000520 5B5BC2C4E4D4D740            331                =CL8'$$BDUMP'
      000528 000005C8                    332                =A(INVMSTR)
      00052C 00000540                    333                =A(DISKIN)
      000530 000006D0                    334                =A(PRTFLE)
      000534 000001EC                    335                =A(HEADRTN1)
      000538 1C                          336                =P'1'
```

```
                            338 ****                                                          LOAD2510
                            339 * DEFINITION OF SEQUENTIAL DISK INPUT FILE                    LOAD2520
                            340 ****                                                          LOAD2530

                            342 DISKIN   DTFSD BLKSIZE=3600,EOFADDR=ENDINPUT,IOAREA1=DISKIN1,  CLOAD2550
                                               IOAREA2=DISKIN2,DEVADDR=SYS006,DEVICE=2311,IOREG=(10),  CLOAD2560
                                               MODNAME=IJGFIZZZ,RECFORM=FIXBLK,RECSIZE=80,     CLOAD2570
                                               TYPEFLE=INPUT                                   LOAD2580


                            388 ****                                                          LOAD2600
                            389 * DEFINITION OF INVENTORY MASTER FILE                         LOAD2610
                            390 ****                                                          LOAD2620

                            392 INVMSTR  DTFIS DSKXTNT=3,IOROUT=LOAD,KEYLEN=7,NRECDS=65,RECFORM=FIXBLK,CLOAD2640
                                               RECSIZE=55,CYLOFL=2,DEVICE=2311,HINDEX=2311,    CLOAD2650
                                               IOAREAL=MASTERIO,KEYLOC=1,MODNAME=IJHZLZZZ,     CLOAD2660
                                               VERIFY=YES,WORKL=LOADWORK,MSTIND=YES            LOAD2670


                            438 ****                                                          LOAD2690
                            439 * DEFINITION OF PRINTER FILE                                  LOAD2700
                            440 ****                                                          LOAD2710

                            442 PRTFLE   DTFPR BLKSIZE=120,IOAREA1=PRIO1,DEVADDR=SYSLST,DEVICE=1403,  CLOAD2730
                                               MODNAME=IJDFCPZZ,CONTROL=YES,PRINTOV=YES,RECFORM=FIXUNB  LOAD2740
```

```
    LOC   OBJECT CODE    ADDR1 ADDR2 STMT    SOURCE STATEMENT                                    DOS CL3-5 08/26/70

                                      465 ****                                                           LOAD2780
                                      466 * I/O AREAS                                                    LOAD2790
                                      467 ****                                                           LOAD2800

   000700                             469 MASTERIO DS   OCL3590                                          LOAD2820
   000700                             470 DSKCOUNT DS   CL8                                              LOAD2830
   000708                             471 DSKEY    DS   CL7                                              LOAD2840
   00070F                             472 DISKDATA DS   CL3575                                           LOAD2850
   001506                             473 LOADWORK DS   CL55                                             LOAD2860
   00153D                             474 DISKIN1  DS   CL3600                                           LOAD2870
   00234D                             475 DISKIN2  DS   CL3600                                           LOAD2880

   000000                             477 MSTRDUMY DSECT                                                 LOAD2900
   000000                             478 MSTRDIV  DS   CL1                                              LOAD2910
   000001                             479 MSTRPRME DS   CL3                                              LOAD2920
   000004                             480 MSTRDASH DS   CL3                                              LOAD2930
   000007                             481 MSTRNAME DS   CL25                                             LOAD2940
   000020                             482 MSTRQOH  DS   CL3                                              LOAD2950
   000023                             483 MSTRQOO  DS   CL3                                              LOAD2960
   000026                             484 MSTRQRSV DS   CL3                                              LOAD2970
   000029                             485 MSTRASSY DS   OCL7                                             LOAD2980
   000029                             486 MASYDIV  DS   CL1                                              LOAD2990
   00002A                             487 MASYPRME DS   CL3                                              LOAD3000
   00002D                             488 MASYDASH DS   CL3                                              LOAD3010
   000030                             489 MSTRTYPE DS   CL1                                              LOAD3020
   000031                             490 MSTRSRCE DS   CL1                                              LOAD3030
   000032                             491 MSTRUNIT DS   CL3                                              LOAD3040
   000035                             492 MSTRXTRA DS   CL2                                              LOAD3050

   000000                             494 INPTDUMY DSECT                                                 LOAD3070
   000000                             495 INPTDIV  DS   CL2                                              LOAD3080
   000002                             496 INPTPRME DS   CL6                                              LOAD3090
   000008                             497 INPTDASH DS   CL5                                              LOAD3100
   00000D                             498 INPTNAME DS   CL25                                             LOAD3110
   000026                             499 INPTQOH  DS   CL7                                              LOAD3120
   00002D                             500 INPTQOO  DS   CL7                                              LOAD3130
   000034                             501 INPTQRSV DS   CL7                                              LOAD3140
   00003B                             502 INPTASSY DS   OCL13                                            LOAD3150
   00003B                             503 IASYDIV  DS   CL2                                              LOAD3160
   00003D                             504 IASYPRME DS   CL6                                              LOAD3170
   000043                             505 IASYDASH DS   CL5                                              LOAD3180
   000048                             506 INPTTYPE DS   CL1                                              LOAD3190
   000049                             507 INPTSRCE DS   CL1                                              LOAD3200
   00004A                             508 INPTUNIT DS   CL6                                              LOAD3210
                                      509         END                                                   LOAD3220
```

CHAPTER 4

PROGRAMMING ASSIGNMENT

INSTRUCTIONS

This program uses the sorted sequential disk file as input (Chapter 3) to create an indexed sequential sales master file. The input record format was to be determined by the programmer in Chapter 3. The record format for the master file is also to be determined by the programmer. It should contain the following fields:

1 — Department Number
2 — Salesman Number
3 — Salesman Name
4 — Y-T-D Sales
5 — Y-T-D Sales Returns
6 — Commission Rate
7 — Type Field (active or deleted record)
   NOTE: an active record will contain a "1" code. A deleted record a "2".

The Department Number and Salesman Number are to be used as the "Key" for the records on the indexed sequential file.

When the file is loaded, the Current Sales in the transaction record is to become the Y-T-D Sales in the master record and the Current Sales Returns in the transaction record is to become the Y-T-D Sales Returns in the master records. (See Chapter 3 Programming Assignment).

In addition, the value in the type field in the transaction record must be a "1" (new load).

All numeric fields in the master record are to be binary in format.

CHAPTER 5

INDEXED SEQUENTIAL ACCESS METHOD

SEQUENTIAL RETRIEVAL

INTRODUCTION

After a master file, such as the inventory master file, has been created, it is normally desirable to have a report listing its contents. The sample program presented in this chapter reads the master file and prints a list containing all the master records. The format of the report is illustrated in Figure 5-1.

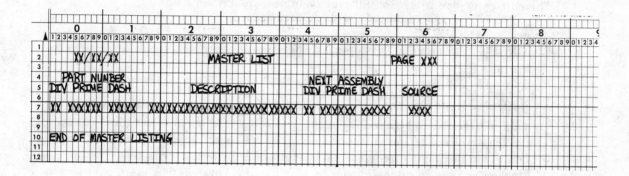

Figure 5-1 Format of master list report

In order to create the report, the master file must be retrieved sequentially.

SEQUENTIAL PROCESSING – INDEXED SEQUENTIAL FILES

As noted previously, indexed sequential files can be processed either randomly or in a sequential manner. Sequential processing can be used either to retrieve records from an indexed sequential file for use, for example, in a printed report, or to update (change) records currently in the file. Sequential processing is accomplished with a series of macros. The five macros used with sequential processing are DTFIS, SETL, GET, PUT, and ESETL.

In the sample problem presented in this chapter, the inventory master file will be retrieved sequentially to create a printed report. The indexed sequential inventory master file must be defined by a DTFIS macro.

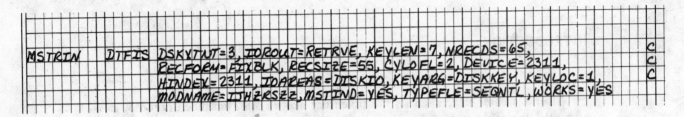

Figure 5-2 DTFIS for sequential retrieval

The entries unique to sequential processing are described below.

1. IOROUT = RETRVE: This operand specifies that records are to be retrieved from the file.

2. IOAREAS = DISKIO: This entry specifies the name of the I/O area defined by a DS instruction to be used for sequential retrieval. When using blocked records, the length of the I/O area must be equal to the record length x the blocking factor. In the sample program, this length is 3575 bytes (55 x 65). For unblocked records, the length must be equal to the key length + the record length + 10 bytes. The 10 bytes are used for a sequence link field associated with the overflow areas (see Chapter 6).

3. KEYARG = DISKKEY: This operand specifies the name of the area defined by a DS instruction which will contain the beginning key if sequential retrieval is to begin by key.

4. TYPEFLE = SEQNTL: This operand specifies that sequential retrieval will be performed on the file defined by the DTF.

5. WORKS = YES: This operand specifies that a work area will be used in the GET and PUT macros used with this file.

Unlike sequential processing when using sequential files, sequential processing when using indexed sequential files can begin at any point in the file. This is because, using the indexes, ISAM is able to locate any record in the file by key. Therefore, before sequential processing can begin, the SETL macro (Set Limits) must be issued to determine a starting point for sequential retrieval. Four different methods of stating the first record to be processed can be used: the ID of the record (that is, the cylinder, track and record address) can be given, the key of the record can be given, the first record in the file can be used, or a partial key can be given to begin processing at a group of related records.

To begin processing at the first record in a file, the SETL macro would be used as illustrated in Figure 5-3.

EXAMPLE

Figure 5-3 SETL for beginning of the file

The filename (as specified in the DTF) is the first operand and the keyword BOF (Beginning Of File) is specified in the second operand. When BOF is the second operand, sequential processing begins with the first record in the file.

To begin processing at a record with a specific key, the SETL macro would be used as shown below.

EXAMPLE

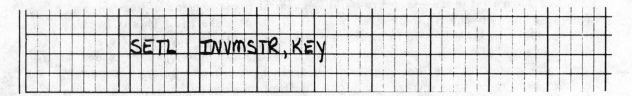

```
            SETL   INVMSTR,KEY
```

Figure 5-4 SETL for beginning at a key

The first operand is the name of the file and the second operand must be the word KEY. When processing is to begin with a record with a specific key, the desired key must be moved to the field specified in the KEYARG operand of the DTF before the SETL macro is issued. It should be noted that the key specified in the field must be in the same format as the key on the file. Thus, if the key on the file is in binary format, as in the sample problems, then the value in the KEYARG field must be binary also.

To begin processing with a record located at a specific cylinder, track and record location, the SETL macro would be used as shown in Figure 5-5.

EXAMPLE

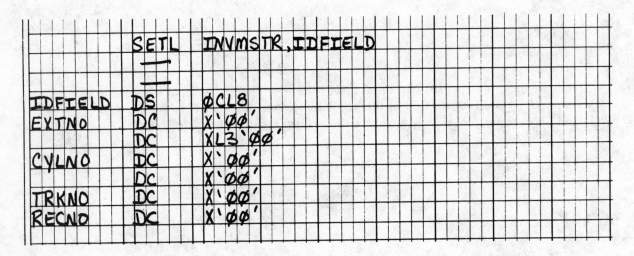

```
            SETL   INVMSTR,IDFIELD


IDFIELD     DS     ØCL8
EXTNO       DC     X'ØØ'
            DC     XL3'ØØ'
CYLNO       DC     X'ØØ'
            DC     X'ØØ'
TRKNO       DC     X'ØØ'
RECNO       DC     X'ØØ'
```

Figure 5-5 SETL for beginning at record ID

The first operand in the SETL macro is the name of the DTF. The second operand is the name of an 8-byte field which will contain the disk address of the record. As noted previously, the location of a record on disk storage can be determined by specifying the cylinder number, track number and record number where the record resides. The 8-byte field is used to supply ISAM with this information so that processing may begin at the specified disk location.

For a 2311 disk, the cylinder number (0-199) is specified in byte 4 of the field (bytes are numbered 0-7). The track number (0-9) is specified in byte 6 and the record number (1-254) is specified in byte 7. All values must be binary values. It should be noted that the record number specified is the physical record number, not the logical record number. Thus, if there are five logical records per block, and the sixth logical record is to be the beginning point, the record number specified in the ID field should be 2. The extent number (2-245) refers to the sequence number which appears in each EXTENT card used for indexed sequential files. Prime data extent sequence numbers begin with 2 (0 is used for the master index and 1 is used for the cylinder index). Thus, by using the sequence number and EXTENT cards, Logical IOCS can determine which device the file is on.

If processing is to begin at the start of a group of related records, the GKEY operand can be used with the SETL macro.

EXAMPLE

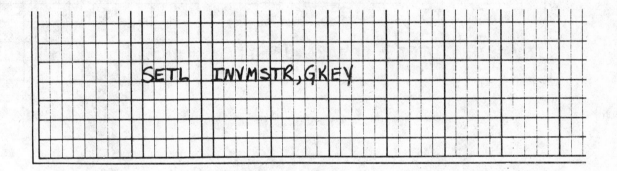

Figure 5-6 SETL for beginning at a generic key

The first operand is the name of the file and the second operand is the keyword GKEY. The use of the GKEY operand allows processing to begin with records having identical data in the high-order bytes of their keys.

In the inventory master file, the division number is the high-order byte in the key. The GKEY option can be used to begin sequential processing for a given division number. The desired division number should be moved to the high-order byte in the KEYARG field. The low-order bytes of the KEYARG field must be lower than any key on the file (that is, in the sample problem, the low-order bytes should be binary zeros). When the SETL macro is executed, the block of data which contains the first record of the desired division will be made available for reading.

For example, if it was desired to begin processing with division 10, the following steps would be taken.

EXAMPLE

STEP 1: Zero the KEYARG field.

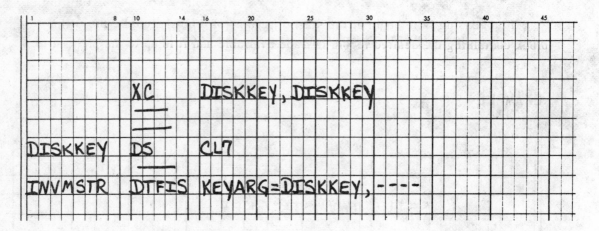

Figure 5-7 Exclusive Or to zero key field

STEP 2: Move the desired division to the high-order portion of the key.

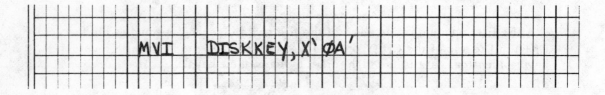

Figure 5-8 Moving first byte of key to key area

Note that the value moved to the key area is a binary value because the key on the file is in binary.

STEP 3: Issue the SETL macro.

Figure 5-9 SETL to begin at division 10

After the SETL macro is executed, the block which contains the first record in division 10 will be available for reading and processing.

It should be noted that if the records are unblocked, the first logical record with the desired high-order value will be available but if the records are blocked, the block containing the desired record is made available and it is up to the program to find the desired record in the block.

It should also be noted that if the requested key group is not on the file, no indication will be returned by the SETL macro unless the requested high-order value is greater than the highest key on the file, which will result in an error indication of X'10' (no record found) in the filenameC indicator byte. Thus if division 10 was requested but only divisions 9 and 11 were on the file, the block which should contain division 10 (that is, the block which contains the last division 9 record and the first division 11 record) would be made available. Therefore, it is required that the problem program determine that the correct key group has been retrieved.

GET Macro

After the beginning point for sequential retrieval has been determined by the SETL macro, the GET macro is used to read the records.

EXAMPLE

Figure 5-10 GET Macro to read inventory file

As with the GET macros used for sequential retrieval with card files, the first operand is the name of the file as defined by the DTF and the second operand, if used, is the name of the work area into which the logical record will be moved. If a work area is used in sequential retrieval of an indexed sequential file, then the WORKS = YES operand must be specified in the DTFIS.

After the record has been retrieved from the file, it can be used for any purpose desired. If it is to be updated, any field except the key can be changed.

ESETL Macro

The ESETL macro is issued when sequential retrieval for the file has been completed. It ends the sequential retrieval mode initiated by the SETL macro.

EXAMPLE

Figure 5-11 ESETL Macro to end sequential retrieval

The only operand of the ESETL macro is the name of the file.

ERROR INDICATOR

As with all Indexed Sequential files, indicators are made available for the problem program to check in the FilenameC byte in the DTF. The indicators applicable to sequential retrieval are listed below.

X'80' - An uncorrectable DASD error has occurred.

X'40' - A wrong length record has been detected during an I/O operation.

X'20' - End-of-file has been encountered during the sequential retrieval.

X'10' - The record specified in the SETL macro using KEY or GKEY has not been found.

X'08' - The ID specified in the SETL macro is outside the prime data file limits.

X'01' - The record being processed is an overflow record.

Figure 5-12 FilenameC Error Indicators

These indicators are tested after the SETL, GET or PUT macros. Note that the X'20' indicator must be tested for end-of-file. The DTFIS does not have an EOFADDR operand like the sequential processing DTF's.

CARRIAGE CONTROL CHARACTER

In the sample programs presented previously, printer spacing has been accomplished using the CNTRL macro. Another method can be used to accomplish the same task. This involves the use of a CARRIAGE CONTROL CHARACTER. A Carriage Control Character is a single character located in the first byte of a printer record which indicates to the printer what spacing or skipping action to take before or after a line is printed.

Two types of carriage control characters can be used on the System/360. The first is an ASA (American Standards Association) control character. The characters comprising the ASA set of control characters for the printer are illustrated below.

CODE	ACTION
blank	Space one line before printing
0	Space two lines before printing
—	Space three lines before printing
+	Suppress space before printing
1	Skip to channel 1 before printing
2	Skip to channel 2 before printing
3	Skip to channel 3 before printing
4	Skip to channel 4 before printing
5	Skip to channel 5 before printing
6	Skip to channel 6 before printing
7	Skip to channel 7 before printing
8	Skip to channel 8 before printing
9	Skip to channel 9 before printing
A	Skip to channel 10 before printing
B	Skip to channel 11 before printing
C	Skip to channel 12 before printing

Figure 5-13 ASA Control Characters

Thus, if an ASA carriage control character is used, and the first character in the record is a 1, the printer will skip to channel 1 (head of forms) before the line is printed.

The second type of control character is a hexadecimal character which is peculiar to the System/360. A complete list of these control characters may be found in the IBM SRL C24-5037, SUPERVISOR AND INPUT/OUTPUT MACROS.

5.9

In the sample program presented in this chapter, ASA control characters are to be used. Thus, the printer file is defined by the DTFPR as illustrated in Figure 5-14.

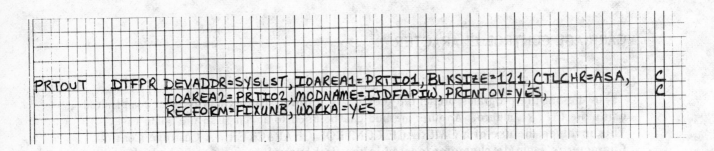

```
PRTOUT    DTFPR DEVADDR=SYSLST,IOAREA1=PRTIO1,BLKSIZE=121,CTLCHR=ASA,    C
                IOAREA2=PRTIO2,MODNAME=IJDFAPIW,PRINTOV=YES,             C
                RECFORM=FIXUNB,WORKA=YES
```

Figure 5-14 DTFPR used for ASA Carriage Control

The unique operands for the use of a carriage control character are described below.

1. BLKSIZE = 121: This entry specifies there will be 121 characters in the printer record. The carriage control character will be the first character in the record and will <u>not</u> be printed. Thus, 120 characters will be printed on the printer.

2. CTLCHR = ASA: This operand states that ASA control characters will be used for carriage control. The other valid operand is CTLCHR = YES. This specifies that System/360 control characters will be used. When this operand is used, the CONTROL = YES operand cannot be used. Thus, printer spacing can be handled by a control character or by the CNTRL macro but not by both.

3. MODNAME = IJDFAPIW: An I/O module must be used which will process carriage control characters. A complete listing of module names is contained in the appendices.

When using carriage control characters, there is no change in the PUT macro used with the file. The only requirement is that the first byte of the I/O area (or the work area, if one is used) must contain a valid control character. This control character may be altered at any time in the program dependent upon spacing requirements.

INSERT CHARACTER Instruction

In the sample program, the division number is a one byte binary number. In order to convert the division number to a zoned-decimal number, the Convert to Decimal instruction is used. Before the Convert to Decimal instruction can be executed, however, the data to be converted must be stored in a register. One method previously shown to place data in a register is the load instruction. However, when only one byte is to be placed in a register, such as the division number in the sample program, the Insert Character instruction can be used. The operation of this instruction is explained below. In addition, the Store Character instruction which can be used to store a single byte from a register into core storage is explained.

INSTRUCTION: INSERT CHARACTER

OPERATION CODE: IC

EXAMPLE: IC CVDREG,MSTRDIV

The Insert Character instruction inserts the single character located at the address specified in the second operand into the low-order 8 bits of the register specified in the first operand. The remaining bits in the register remain unchanged. The following example illustrates the use of the Insert Character instruction.

EXAMPLE

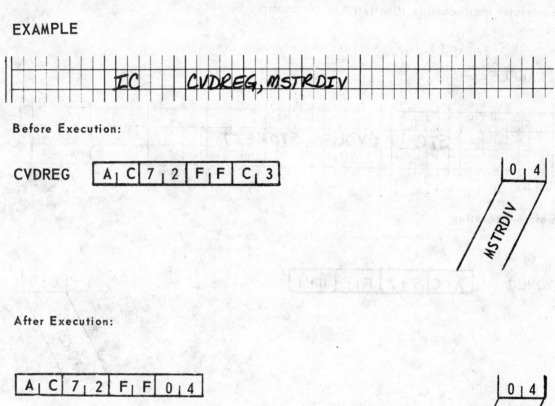

Figure 5-15 Example of Insert Character instruction

Note that after the execution of the Insert Character instruction the low-order byte of the register is changed but the remaining bytes are unchanged.

STORE CHARACTER Instruction

The Store Character instruction can be used to store the low-order byte (8 bits) of a register in core storage.

INSTRUCTION: STORE CHARACTER

OPERATION CODE: STC

EXAMPLE: STC CVDREG,STOREIT

The low-order byte in the register specified in the first operand is stored in core storage at the address specified in the second operand. The use of the Store Character instruction is illustrated in the example below.

EXAMPLE

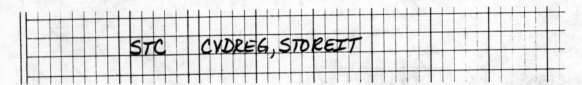

Before Execution:

CVDREG

| A | C | 7 | 2 | F | F | 0 | 4 |

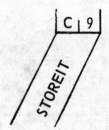

After Execution:

CVDREG

| A | C | 7 | 2 | F | F | 0 | 4 |

Figure 5-16 Example of Store Character instruction

Note that only the low-order byte of the register is stored when the Store Character instruction is used. It should also be noted that there are no boundary alignment requirements with the Insert Character and Store Character instructions.

CONVERT TO DECIMAL Instruction

Before data which is stored in a binary format can be printed, it must be converted from a binary format to a zoned-decimal format. Thus, in the sample program, all the numeric fields stored in a binary format must be changed to zoned-decimal before being printed. The Convert to Decimal instruction is used to convert the data from binary to packed-decimal format and its use is explained below.

INSTRUCTION: CONVERT TO DECIMAL

OPERATION CODE: CVD

EXAMPLE: CVD CVDREG,DBLWORD

The Convert to Decimal instruction converts the binary data contained in the register specified in the first operand to packed decimal data and stores it in the doubleword specified in the second operand. The following example illustrates the use of the Convert to Decimal instruction.

EXAMPLE

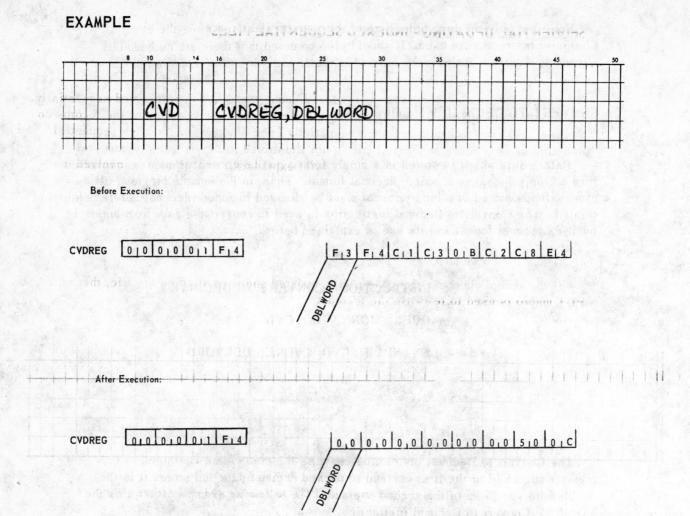

Before Execution:

CVDREG | 0 0 0 0 0 1 F 4 | F 3 F 4 C 1 C 3 0 B C 2 C 8 E 4 | DBLWORD

After Execution:

CVDREG | 0 0 0 0 0 1 F 4 | 0 0 0 0 0 0 0 0 0 0 0 0 0 5 0 0 C | DBLWORD

Figure 5-17 Example of Convert to Decimal instruction

Note that the binary value in CVDREG (01F4) is converted to its decimal equivalent (500) and stored in packed decimal format in the doubleword DBLWORD. The second operand must be a doubleword on a doubleword boundary. Thus, the second operand is defined as DBLWORD DS D. Note also that the unused high-order bytes of the doubleword are set to zero.

It should also be noted that the sign in the converted number is a "C", not an "F". Therefore, if the converted number is not to be edited on a printed report, the sign must be OR'ed to an "F" for proper printing.

5.14

SEQUENTIAL UPDATING - INDEXED SEQUENTIAL FILES

As has been noted previously, an indexed sequential file can be updated sequentially. Sequential updating of an indexed sequential file involves the changing of the records on the file. Additions cannot be made sequentially (see Chapter 6). Although sequential updating of an indexed sequential file is not illustrated in the sample program presented in this chapter, the following is a brief explanation of the process involved in sequential updating.

PUT Macro

If the records being retrieved are to be updated and re-written on the file, the PUT macro is used to re-write the records.

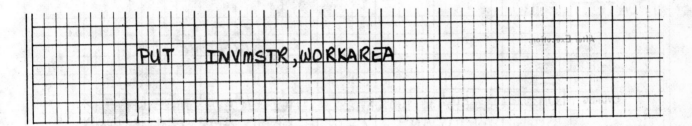

Figure 5-18 Example of PUT to rewrite updated record

The first operand of the PUT macro is the name of the file as defined in the DTF and the second operand, if used, is the name of the work area which contains the record to be re-written.

It should be noted that when a record is retrieved sequentially from an indexed sequential file, updated, and then re-written on the file, the same record which was retrieved by the GET is written into the same location it came from. However, the possibility exists that a record retrieved by a GET macro would not have to be updated. Therefore, it is not necessary to issue a PUT macro because the record still exists on the file in its original form. Thus, the determination of whether a block of records needs to be re-written is made by the routine called by the GET macro, not the routine called by the PUT macro. The PUT routine merely sets a switch to indicate that a write is necessary. When the GET routine is ready to read another block of records, it first determines whether a write is necessary (ie, has a PUT macro been issued for the block of records in core). If a write is necessary, the GET routine re-writes the block it previously retrieved before retrieving the next block. If a PUT macro has not been issued, it reads the next block of data. A "typical" update routine using sequential retrieval is shown in the following example.

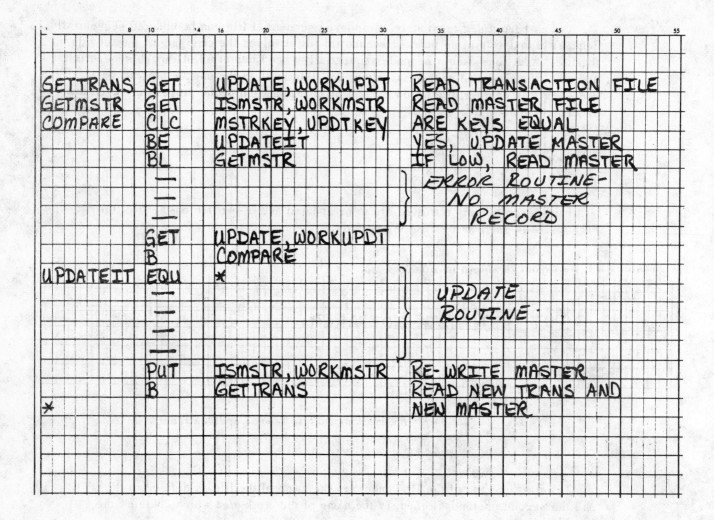

```
GETTRANS  GET      UPDATE, WORKUPDT      READ TRANSACTION FILE
GETMSTR   GET      ISMSTR, WORKMSTR      READ MASTER FILE
COMPARE   CLC      MSTRKEY, UPDTKEY      ARE KEYS EQUAL
          BE       UPDATEIT             YES, UPDATE MASTER
          BL       GETMSTR              IF LOW, READ MASTER
          —                          } ERROR ROUTINE-
          —                             NO MASTER
          —                               RECORD
          GET      UPDATE, WORKUPDT
          B        COMPARE
UPDATEIT  EQU      *
          —                          } UPDATE
          —                             ROUTINE
          —
          —
          PUT      ISMSTR, WORKMSTR      RE-WRITE MASTER
          B        GETTRANS             READ NEW TRANS AND
*                                       NEW MASTER
```

Figure 5-19 Typical routine to sequentially update an indexed sequential file

In the example illustrated above, if there is not a match on the master record, a PUT is not issued. If a block of master records are read and there is no corresponding transaction record, then all the records in the block will remain as they are and there is no need to re-write the block. However, if one of the master records was updated and a PUT macro was issued, then before a new block of records is read by the GET routine, the block containing the updated record is re-written.

If records are to be retrieved sequentially, but no update is to occur, then only the GET macro is used and no re-writing of records takes place.

SAMPLE PROGRAM

INPUT

The input to the sample program is the inventory master file built in Chapter 4. (See page 4.45.)

OUTPUT

The output of the sample program is a printed report listing the parts on the master file. Its layout is shown in Figure 5-20.

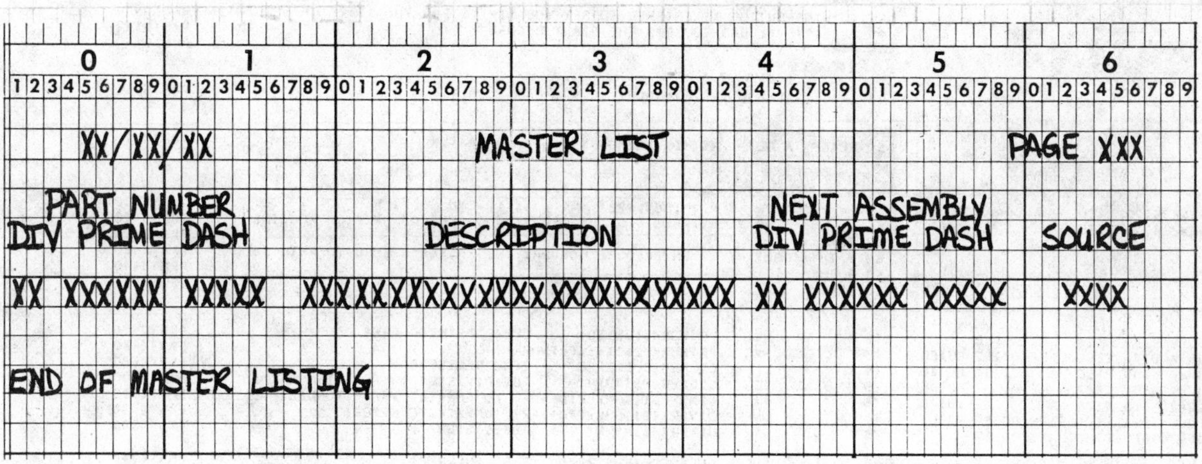

Figure 5-20 Report layout

PROGRAM

The following is a listing of the program to sequentially retrieve the inventory master file and create a printed report.

```
  000000                              2 PRTMASTR START 0                                                PRNT0020
                                      3         PRINT NOGEN


                                      5 ****                                                            PRNT0040
                                      6 * THIS PROGRAM IS USED TO PRINT THE MASTER FILE AFTER IT HAS BEEN  PRNT0050
                                      7 * CREATED. IT MERELY GIVES A COMPLETE LISTING OF ALL PARTS IN THE  PRNT0060
                                      8 * MASTER FILE.                                                  PRNT0070
                                                                                                        PRNT0080
                                      9 *                                                               PRNT0090
                                     10 * REGISTER USAGE IS AS FOLLOWS                                  PRNT0100
                                     11 *
  00000C                             13 BASEREG  EQU   12                                               PRNT0120
  00000E                             14 LINKRG14 EQU   14                                               PRNT0130
  00000B                             15 LINKREG1 EQU   11                                               PRNT0140
  00000A                             16 CVDREG   EQU   10                                               PRNT0150


                                     18 ****                                                            PRNT0170
                                     19 * THIS ROUTINE ESTABLISHES A BASE REGISTER, OPENS THE FILES, AND  PRNT0180
                                     20 * PRINTS THE FIRST PAGE HEADER.                                 PRNT0190
                                     21 ****                                                            PRNT0200

  000000 05C0                        23         BALR  BASEREG,0          ESTABLISH BASE REGISTER         PRNT0220
  000002                             24         USING *,BASFREG                                         PRNT0230

                                     26         OPEN  MSTRIN,PRTOUT      OPEN FILES                      PRNT0250

                                     36         COMRG                    GET COMM REGION ADDRESS         PRNT0270
  00001C D207 C267 1000 00269 00000  40         MVC   DATEHDR(8),0(1)    MOVE DATE TO HEADER             PRNT0280
  000022 45E0 C130           00132   41         BAL   LINKRG14,HEADROU   PRINT HEADER ROUTINE            PRNT0290


                                     43 ****                                                            PRNT0310
                                     44 * THIS ROUTINE IS ENTERED TO SET THE LIMITS FOR THE START OF SEQUENTIAL PRNT0320
                                     45 * RETRIEVAL AND TO READ THE FIRST RECORD                        PRNT0330
                                     46 ****                                                            PRNT0340

                                     48         SETL  MSTRIN,BOF         SET LIMITS                      PRNT0360


                                     58 READMSTR GET   MSTRIN,MSTRWORK   READ MASTER                     PRNT0380

  00004E 9120 C4D4           004D6   65         TM    MSTRINC,X'20'      IS IT END OF FILE               PRNT0400
  000052 4710 C180           00182   66         BO    MSTREND            YES, GO TO END OF FILE ROUTINE  PRNT0410
                                     67 ****                                                            PRNT0420
                                     68 * THIS ROUTINE IS ENTERED TO CONVERT THE MASTER RECORD TO PRINTABLE  PRNT0430
                                     69 * FORM                                                          PRNT0440
                                     70 ****                                                            PRNT0450


  000056 9240 C1EA           001EC   72         MVI   PRTWORK+1,X'40'    CLEAR PRINTER AREA              PRNT0470
  00005A D276 C1EB C1EA 001EC 001EC  73         MVC   PRTWORK+2(119),PRTWORK+1                          PRNT0480
  000060 58A0 C45E           00460   74         L     CVDREG,FULLZERO    ZERO REGISTER                   PRNT0490
  000064 43A0 C182           001B4   75         IC    CVDREG,MSTRDIV     PUT DIVISION IN REGISTER        PRNT0500
  000068 45B0 C12A           0012C   76         BAL   LINKREG1,CONVERTD+4 GO TO CONVERT VALUE TO DECIMAL PRNT0510
  00006C F311 C1EA C3D4 001EC 003D6 77         UNPK  DIVPRT(2),DBLWORD+6(2)  UNPACK TO REPORT           PRNT0520
  000072 96F0 C1EB           001ED   78         OI    DIVPRT+1,X'F0'     RESET SIGN                      PRNT0530

  000076 D203 C3D6 C45E 003D8 00460  80         MVC   FULLWORD,FULLZERO   ZERO FULLWORD                  PRNT0550
  00007C D202 C3D7 C1B3 003D9 001B5  81         MVC   FULLWORD+1(3),MSTRPRME MOVE PRIME TO WORK AREA    PRNT0560
  000082 45B0 C126           00128   82         BAL   LINKREG1,CONVERTD   GO TO CONVERT VALUE TO DECIMAL PRNT0570
  000086 F353 C1ED C3D2 001EF 003D4 83         UNPK  PRMEPRT(6),DBLWORD+4(4)  UNPACK TO REPORT          PRNT0580
  00008C 96F0 C1F2           001F4   84         OI    PRMEPRT+5,X'F0'    RESET SIGN                      PRNT0590

  000090 D202 C3D7 C1B6 003D9 001B8  86         MVC   FULLWORD+1(3),MSTRDASH MOVE DASH TO WORK AREA     PRNT0610
  000096 45B0 C126           00128   87         BAL   LINKREG1,CONVERTD   GO TO CONVERT TO DECIMAL       PRNT0620
  00009A F342 C1F4 C3D3 001F6 003D5 88         UNPK  DASHPRT(5),DBLWORD+5(3) UNPACK TO REPORT           PRNT0630
  0000A0 96F0 C1F8           001FA   89         OI    DASHPRT+4,X'F0'    RESET SIGN                      PRNT0640

  0000A4 D218 C1FB C1B9 001FD 001BB  91         MVC   DESCPRT(25),MSTRNAME MOVE DESCRIPTION TO REPORT    PRNT0660

  0000AA 58A0 C45E           00460   93         L     CVDREG,FULLZERO    ZERO REGISTER                   PRNT0680
  0000AE 43A0 C1DB           001DD   94         IC    CVDREG,MASYDIV     PUT DIVISION IN REGISTER        PRNT0690
  0000B2 45B0 C12A           0012C   95         BAL   LINKREG1,CONVERTD+4 GO TO CONVERT TO DECIMAL       PRNT0700
  0000B6 F311 C215 C3D4 00217 003D6 96         UNPK  NADIVPRT(2),DBLWORD+6(2) UNPACK TO REPORT          PRNT0710
  0000BC 96F0 C216           00218   97         OI    NADIVPRT+1,X'F0'   RESET SIGN                      PRNT0720

  0000C0 D202 C3D7 C1DC 003D9 001DE  99         MVC   FULLWORD+1(3),MASYPRME  MOVE PRIME TO WORK AREA    PRNT0740
  0000C6 45B0 C126           00128  100         BAL   LINKREG1,CONVERTD   GO TO CONVERT TO DECIMAL       PRNT0750
  0000CA F353 C21B C3D2 0021A 003D4 101         UNPK  NAPRMPRT(6),DBLWORD+4(4) UNPACK TO REPORT          PRNT0760
  0000D0 96F0 C21D           0021F  102         OI    NAPRMPRT+5,X'F0'   RESET SIGN                      PRNT0770

  0000D4 D202 C3D7 C1DF 003D9 001E1 104         MVC   FULLWORD+1(3),MASYDASH MOVE DASH TO WORK AREA     PRNT0790
  0000DA 45B0 C126           00128  105         BAL   LINKREG1,CONVERTD   GO TO CONVERT TO DECIMAL       PRNT0800
  0000DE F342 C21F C3D3 00221 003D5 106         UNPK  NADASPRT(5),DBLWORD+5(3) UNPACK TO REPORT          PRNT0810
  0000E4 96F0 C223           00225  107         OI    NADASPRT+4,X'F0'   RESET SIGN                      PRNT0820
```

```
 LOC   OBJECT CODE    ADDR1 ADDR2  STMT   SOURCE STATEMENT                                       DOS CL3-5 08/26/70
0000E8 95F1 C1E3      001E5         109        CLI    MSTRSRCE,C'1'       IS IT A MANUFACTURED PART    PRNT0840
0000EC 4770 C0F8            000FA   110        BNE    VENDPART            NO, GO TO VENDOR ROUTINE     PRNT0850
0000F0 D203 C227 C48E 00229 00490   111        MVC    SRCEPRT(4),=C'MANU' YES, MOVE MANU TO REPORT     PRNT0860
0000F6 47F0 C0FE            00100   112        B      PUTPRT              GO TO PRINT RECORD           PRNT0870

0000FA                              114 VENDPART EQU   *
0000FA D203 C227 C492 00229 00494   115        MVC    SRCEPRT(4),=C'VEND' MOVE VENDOR TO REPORT        PRNT0890
                                                                                                       PRNT0900

000110 9240 C1E9      001EB         117 PUTPRT  PUT    PRTOUT,PRTWORK      WRITE PRINT LINE             PRNT0920
                                    123        MVI    SKIP,X'40'          MOVE CC CHARACTER TO WORK AREA  PRNT0930
                                    124        PRTOV  PRTOUT,12,HEADROU   IF, PAGE OVERFLOW, GO TO HEADER ROUT  PRNT0940
000124 47F0 C03C            0003E   130        B      READMSTR            GO READ NEXT RECORD          PRNT0950


                                    132 ****                                                            PRNT0970
                                    133 * THIS ROUTINE IS ENTERED TO CONVERT BINARY DATA TO PACKED DECIMAL  PRNT0980
                                    134 * DATA.                                                         PRNT0990
                                    135 ****                                                            PRNT1000


000128                              137 CONVERTD EQU   *
000128 58A0 C3D6            003D8   138        L      CVDREG,FULLWORD     LOAD BINARY DATA TO REGISTER  PRNT1020
00012C 4EA0 C3CE            003D0   139        CVD    CVDREG,DBLWORD      CONVERT TO PACKED DECIMAL    PRNT1030
000130 07FB                         140        BR     LINKREG1            RETURN TO CALLER             PRNT1040
                                                                                                       PRNT1050


                                    142 ****                                                            PRNT1070
                                    143 * THIS ROUTINE IS ENTERED TO PRINT THE REPORT HEADINGS.         PRNT1080
                                    144 ****                                                            PRNT1090


000132                              146 HEADROU  EQU   *
000132 50E0 C3DA            003DC   147        ST     LINKRG14,SAVE14     SAVE LINK REGISTER           PRNT1110
000136 FA10 C3DE C4B2 003E0 004B4   148        AP     PGCNT,=P'1'         INCREMENT PAGE COUNT         PRNT1120
00013C D203 C2A0 C3E0 002A2 003E2   149        MVC    PGNOHDR-1(4),PGEDIT MOVE EDIT PATTERN TO HEADER  PRNT1130
000142 DE03 C2A0 C3DF 002A2 003E0   150        ED     PGNOHDR-1(4),PGCNT  EDIT PAGE NUMBER             PRNT1140
                                    151        PUT    PRTOUT,HEAD1        PRINT HEADER 1               PRNT1150
                                                                                                       PRNT1160
                                    158        PUT    PRTOUT,HEAD2        PRINTER HEADER 2             PRNT1180

                                    165        PUT    PRTOUT,HEAD3        PRINT HEADER 3               PRNT1200

000178 92F0 C1E9      001EB         172        MVI    SKIP,C'0'           MOVE CONTROL CHARACTER FOR FIRST  PRNT1220
                                    173 *                                 LINE OF REPORT AFTER HEADING PRNT1230
00017C 58E0 C3DA            003DC   174        L      LINKRG14,SAVE14     RELOAD RETURN REGISTER       PRNT1240
000180 07FE                         175        BR     LINKRG14            RETURN TO CALLER             PRNT1250


                                    177 ****                                                            PRNT1270
                                    178 * THIS ROUTINE IS ENTERED WHEN END-OF-FILE IS REACHED ON THE   PRNT1280
                                    179 * MASTER FILE                                                   PRNT1290
                                    180 ****                                                            PRNT1300


000182                              182 MSTREND  EQU   *
                                    183        PUT    PRTOUT,ENDMSG       PRINT END MESSAGE            PRNT1320
                                    189        ESETL  MSTRIN                                           PRNT1330
                                                                                                       PRNT1340
                                    195        CLOSE  MSTRIN,PRTOUT       CLOSE FILES                  PRNT1360

                                    205        EOJ    END OF JOB                                       PRNT1380
```

```
LOC   OBJECT CODE    ADDR1 ADDR2 STMT   SOURCE STATEMENT                                              DOS CL3-5 08/26/70

                                 209 ****                                                             PRNT1400
                                 210 * CONSTANTS, WORK AREA, ETC.                                     PRNT1410
                                 211 ****                                                             PRNT1420

      0001B4                     213 MSTRWORK DS    OCL55                                             PRNT1440
      0001B4                     214 MSTRDIV  DS    CL1                                               PRNT1450
      0001B5                     215 MSTRPRME DS    CL3                                               PRNT1460
      0001B8                     216 MSTRDASH DS    CL3                                               PRNT1470
      0001BB                     217 MSTRNAME DS    CL25                                              PRNT1480
      0001BB                     218          DS    CL9                                               PRNT1490
      0001D4                     219 MSTRASSY DS    OCL7                                              PRNT1500
      0001DD                     220 MASYDIV  DS    CL1                                               PRNT1510
      0001DD                     221 MASYPRME DS    CL3                                               PRNT1520
      0001DE                     222 MASYDASH DS    CL3                                               PRNT1530
      0001E1                     223          DS    CL1                                               PRNT1540
      0001E4                     224 MSTRSRCE DS    CL1                                               PRNT1550
      0001E5                     225          DS    CL5                                               PRNT1560
      0001E6

      0001EB                     227 PRTWORK  DS    OCL121                                            PRNT1580
      0001EB                     228 SKIP     DS    CL1                                               PRNT1590
      0001EC                     229 DIVPRT   DS    CL2                                               PRNT1600
      0001EE                     230          DS    CL1                                               PRNT1610
      0001EF                     231 PRMEPRT  DS    CL6                                               PRNT1620
      0001F5                     232          DS    CL1                                               PRNT1630
      0001F6                     233 DASHPRT  DS    CL5                                               PRNT1640
      0001FB                     234          DS    CL2                                               PRNT1650
      0001FD                     235 DESCPRT  DS    CL25                                              PRNT1660
      000216                     236          DS    CL1                                               PRNT1670
      000217                     237 NADIVPRT DS    CL2                                               PRNT1680
      000219                     238          DS    CL1                                               PRNT1690
      00021A                     239 NAPRMPRT DS    CL6                                               PRNT1700
      000220                     240          DS    CL1                                               PRNT1710
      000221                     241 NADASPRT DS    CL5                                               PRNT1720
      000226                     242          DS    CL3                                               PRNT1730
      000229                     243 SRCEPRT  DS    CL4                                               PRNT1740
      00022D                     244          DS    CL55                                              PRNT1750

      000264                     246 HEAD1    DS    OCL121                                            PRNT1770
      000264 F1                  247          DC    C'1'                                              PRNT1780
      000265 40404040            248          DC    CL4' '                                            PRNT1790
      000269                     249 DATEHDR  DS    CL8                                               PRNT1800
      000271 4040404040404040    250          DC    C'          MASTER LIST            PAGE '         PRNT1810
      0002A3                     251 PGNOHDR  DS    CL3                                               PRNT1820
      0002A6 4040404040404040    252          DC    CL55' '                                          PRNT1830

      0002DD                     254 HEAD2    DS    OCL121                                            PRNT1850
      0002DD F0                  255          DC    C'0'                                              PRNT1860
      0002DE 4040                256          DC    CL2' '                                            PRNT1870
      0002E0 D7C1D9E340D5E4D4    257          DC    C'PART NUMBER'                                    PRNT1880
      0002EB 4040404040404040    258          DC    CL31' '                                          PRNT1890
      00030A D5C5E7E340C1E2E2    259          DC    C'NEXT ASSEMBLY'                                  PRNT1900
      000317 4040404040404040    260          DC    CL63' '                                          PRNT1910
      000356                     261 HEAD3    DS    OCL121                                            PRNT1920
      000356 40                  262          DC    C' '                                              PRNT1930
                                 263          DC    C'DIV PRIME DASH         DESCRIPTION        DIV PRIME D PRNT1940
      000357 C4C9E540D7D9C9D4                       ASH    SOURCE'                                    PRNT1950
      000399 4040404040404040    264          DC    CL54' '                                          PRNT1960

      0003D0                     266 DBLWORD  DS    D                                                 PRNT1980
      0003D8                     267 FULLWORD DS    F                                                 PRNT1990
      0003DC                     268 SAVE14   DS    F                                                 PRNT2000
      0003E0 000C                269 PGCNT    DC    PL2'0'                                            PRNT2010
      0003E2 40202020            270 PGEDIT   DC    X'40202020'                                       PRNT2020

      0003E6                     272 ENDMSG   DS    OCL121                                            PRNT2040
      0003E6 60                  273          DC    C'-'                                              PRNT2050
      0003E7 C5D5C440D6C640D4    274          DC    CL120'END OF MASTER LISTING'                      PRNT2060

      00045F 00                  276 FULLZERO DC    F'0'                                              PRNT2080
      000460 00000000            277 DISKKEY  DS    CL7                                               PRNT2090
      000464                     278          LTORG                                                   PRNT2100
      000470                     279               =C'$$BOPEN '
      000470 5B5BC2D6D7C5D540    280               =C'$$BSETL '
      000478 5B5BC2E2C5E3D340    281               =C'$$BCLOSE'
      000480 5B5BC2C3D3D6E2C5    282               =A(MSTRIN)
      000488 000004B8            283               =A(MSTRWORK)
      00048C 000001B4            284               =C'MANU'
      000490 D4C1D5E4            285               =C'VEND'
      000494 E5C5D5C4            286               =A(PRTOUT)
      000498 000005E0            287               =A(PRTWORK)
      00049C 000001EB            288               =A(HEADROU)
      0004A0 00000132            289               =A(HEAD1)
      0004A4 00000264            290               =A(HEAD2)
      0004A8 000002DD            291               =A(HEAD3)
      0004AC 00000356            292               =A(ENDMSG)
      0004B0 000003E6            293               =P'1'
      0004B4 1C
```

5.20

```
      LOC  OBJECT CODE    ADDR1 ADDR2  STMT   SOURCE STATEMENT                                      DOS CL3-5 08/26/70

                                        295 ****                                                              PRNT2120
                                        296 * MASTER INPUT FILE DEFINITION                                    PRNT2130
                                        297 ****                                                              PRNT2140

                                        299 MSTRIN    DTFIS DSKXTNT=3,IOROUT=RETRVE,KEYLEN=7,NRECDS=65, .     CPRNT2160
                                                      RECFORM=FIXBLK,RECSIZE=55,CYLOFL=2,DEVICE=2311,         CPRNT2170
                                                      HINDEX=2311,IOAREAS=DISKIO,KEYARG=DISKKEY,KEYLOC=1,     CPRNT2180
                                                      MODNAME=IJHZRSZZ,MSTIND=YES,TYPEFLE=SEQNTL,WORKS=YES    PRNT2190


                                        374 ****                                                              PRNT2210
                                        375 * PRINTER FILE DEFINITION                                         PRNT2220
                                        376 ****                                                              PRNT2230

                                        378 PRTOUT    DTFPR DEVADDR=SYSLST,IOAREA1=PRTIO1,BLKSIZE=121,CTLCHR=ASA,  CPRNT2250
                                                      IOAREA2=PRTIO2,MODNAME=IJDFAPIW,PRINTOV=YES,            CPRNT2260
                                                      RECFORM=FIXUNB,WORKA=YES                                PRNT2270


                                        400 ****                                                              PRNT2290
                                        401 * I/O AREAS                                                       PRNT2300
                                        402 ****                                                              PRNT2310

    000610                              404 DISKIO    DS    CL3575                                            PRNT2330
    001407                              405 PRTIO1    DS    CL121                                             PRNT2340
    001480                              406 PRTIO2    DS    CL121                                             PRNT2350
                                        407           END                                                    PRNT2360
```

CHAPTER 5

PROGRAMMING ASSIGNMENT

INSTRUCTIONS

The master file created in the student programming assignment in Chapter 4 is to be used as input to create a Salesman Commission Rate Report. The report should contain:

1. Department Number
2. Salesman Number
3. Salesman Name
4. Commission Rate

The format of the report is to be designed by the programmer. The Report is sequential listing of all salesman contained on the master file.

CHAPTER 6

INDEXED SEQUENTIAL ACCESS METHOD

RANDOM UPDATING

INTRODUCTION

As was mentioned in Chapter 2, when a master file is created, it is normally necessary to update the file so that the master contains accurate, up-to-date information. The Indexed Sequential Access Method allows both sequential and random access to a file. Therefore, when using an indexed sequential master file, updating can take place both sequentially and randomly.

RANDOM FILE UPDATE

A RANDOM update takes place when a transaction is read and the corresponding master record for that transaction is randomly retrieved from the master file. When a random update is used, it must be possible to randomly retrieve any record on the master file. Random updating can only be performed on a direct access storage device.

A new master file is not created when random updating is used. Thus, a deletion does not eliminate the record from the file as with a sequential update. Instead, in random updating, the deleted record is 'flagged'' to indicate that the record is to be considered deleted upon subsequent processing runs. A deletion is flagged by recording some type of code on the master record. For example, in the sample program at the end of the chapter, a master record that is effectively deleted from the file is identified by a '2' in the type field of the master record. This code thus indicates that the record is considered deleted even though it is still physically part of the master file.

It must also be possible to add records to the file so that new information can be added to the file. The basic logic of the random update is shown in the flowchart illustrated below.

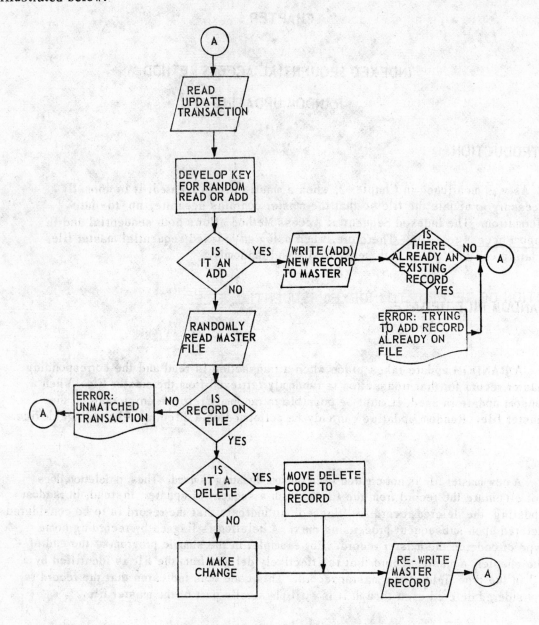

Figure 6-1 Basic logic of a random update

Note that, although the results of the random update are the same as those of the sequential update, the techniques are quite different.

The choice of a sequential or random update is normally made by determining the type of file in use (sequential, indexed sequential, or direct access) and the amount of update activity which will be done against the master file. A sequential file cannot be conveniently updated by any method except the sequential method. A direct access file is normally updated randomly.

An indexed sequential file, however, can be easily updated using a sequential or random technique because records can be processed either sequentially or randomly. Therefore, when using an indexed sequential file, the decision to update randomly or sequentially is normally determined by how much update activity there will be against the master file. Although sequential updating is, when compared on a record to record basis, faster than random updating, it takes a high volume of update activity to make the sequential method faster on an overall run basis. This is because when the sequential method is used, all of the records on the master file must be read and compared to the update transactions. Thus, if the master file consisted of 10,000 records, 10,000 GET's must be issued to read the master records. If only 100 update transactions are being processed against a master file containing 10,000 records, random processing would be faster because, even though random retrieval is slower than sequential retrieval, only 100 master records would have to be retrieved as opposed to 10,000 with sequential updating. It should be noted that when using a sequential update with an indexed sequential file, a new master is not created (this can only be done with a LOAD routine). Instead, the record to be updated is re-written on the file after being changed.

ADDITION OF RECORDS TO INDEXED SEQUENTIAL FILES

As stated previously, one of the functions to be performed by an update program is the addition of records to the master file. Records to be added to the master file have keys which normally place them somewhere between the first and last record on the master file; however, the additions may fall behind the last record on the master file (that is, the key of the record to be added is greater than any key on the master file).

If ALL the records to be added to the master file have keys greater than the highest key on the file, the update records can be LOADED onto the file by making the proper entries in the EXTENT card in job control and specifying IOROUT = LOAD in the DTFIS. This situation would normally occur when the file is being extended because a new group of part numbers, etc. were being added to the file. This is not the normal situation when performing an addition, deletion, and change type update to a file.

When making additions to the file where the key of the new record is unknown before processing, the ADD function of ISAM is utilized. This allows records to be added anywhere in the file.

The method of adding records to an existing indexed sequential file is illustrated in the following examples. These examples illustrate the contents of the cylinder index, the track index, the prime data area and the overflow area, when the file is initially loaded and after records have been added to the file.

EXAMPLE

STEP 1: The file is loaded by specifying the load function as shown in Chapter 4. The results are:

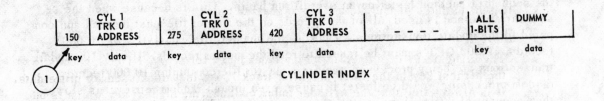

CYLINDER INDEX

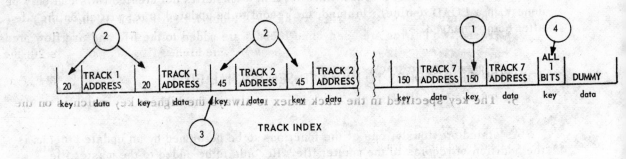

TRACK INDEX

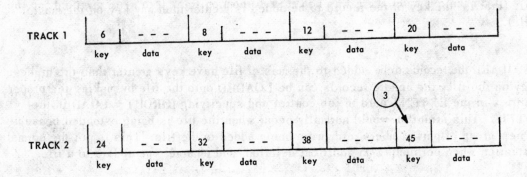

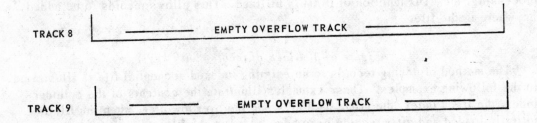

Figure 6 - 2 Indexes and data area — file is loaded

6.4

The file was created with CYLOFL = 2; therefore, tracks 8 and 9 are the overflow tracks for each cylinder in the prime data area. Note in the example problem that only the first two tracks of the prime data area are shown. This is for illustration purposes and the complete file would be processed in the same manner as shown for these two tracks.

Important features of the file as it is organized are:

1. The highest key contained in the cylinder index for cylinder 1 corresponds to the highest key in the track index for track 7, the last track used for prime data. It is always true that the cylinder index contains the highest key which is on the corresponding cylinder. In the example the highest key on cylinder 1 is 150. Note the entries in the cylinder index and the track index.

2. There are always two entries in the track index for each track on the cylinder. These two entries are used when records are added to the file and overflow areas are used, as will be shown. In the example the highest key on track 1 is 20; the highest key on track 2 is 45.

3. The key specified in the track index is always the highest key which is on the associated track.

4. The end of the track index is specified by a key of all 1-bits. It is possible to have data following the track index on track 0 if there is room on the track to write a block of data. When this is done, track 0 is called a SHARED TRACK. In the example, there was not enough room on track 0 to write a record, so the data begins on track 1.

It should also be noted that if the records being used for the file are blocked, the key used for the block and in the indexes is the highest key in the block. Thus, if the block of records appeared as illustrated below, the key for the block would be 125.

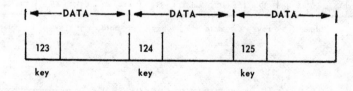

Figure 6-3 Block of records with keys

STEP 2: A record with a key of 18 is added to the file.

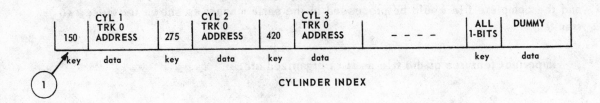

	CYL 1 TRK 0 ADDRESS		CYL 2 TRK 0 ADDRESS		CYL 3 TRK 0 ADDRESS		– – – –	ALL 1-BITS	DUMMY
150		275		420					
key	data	key	data	key	data			key	data

CYLINDER INDEX

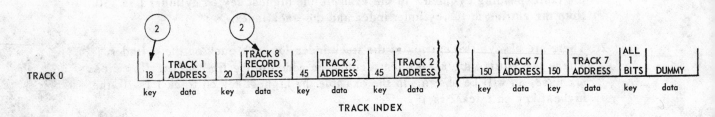

TRACK 0

18	TRACK 1 ADDRESS	20	TRACK 8 RECORD 1 ADDRESS	45	TRACK 2 ADDRESS	45	TRACK 2 ADDRESS	150	TRACK 7 ADDRESS	150	TRACK 7 ADDRESS	ALL 1 BITS	DUMMY
key	data	key	data	key	data	key	data	key	data	key	data	key	data

TRACK INDEX

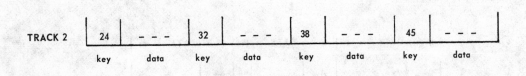

TRACK 1

6	– – –	8	– – –	12	– – –	18	– – –
key	data	key	data	key	data	key	data

TRACK 2

24	– – –	32	– – –	38	– – –	45	– – –
key	data	key	data	key	data	key	data

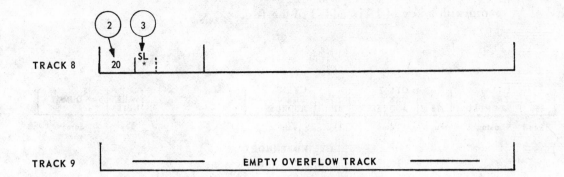

TRACK 8

TRACK 9 EMPTY OVERFLOW TRACK

Figure 6-4 Indexes and data area — record with key of 18 is added

After a record with a key = 18 has been added to the file, note the following:

1. The entries in the cylinder index have not been altered because the highest key on the cylinder has not been altered.

2. Record 18* was inserted between record 12 and record 20. ISAM always inserts a new record where it belongs on the prime data area to keep the key in ascending sequence. When record 18 was inserted, no room remained on the track for record 20, so it was moved to the overflow area. The track index reflects this move by altering its entries as shown. The first entry in the track index for track 1 contains the highest key on the track. This is key 18 because it became the highest key on the track. The second entry contains the highest key from track 1 which is in the overflow area. In the example, the key is 20. The data portion of the second entry for track 1 contains the track and record address of the record which would immediately follow the highest key on the track. In the example, this is record 20.

3. The sequence link field (S.L.) is established by ISAM for every record which goes into the overflow area. The sequence link field is used to link the records in the overflow area. The * indicates that there are no other records in the overflow area from track 1.

---

* *When referencing the records in this example, a record with a key = 18 will be called record 18, etc.*

STEP 3: A record with a key of 15 is added to the file.

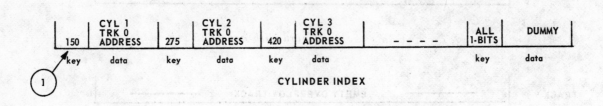

CYLINDER INDEX

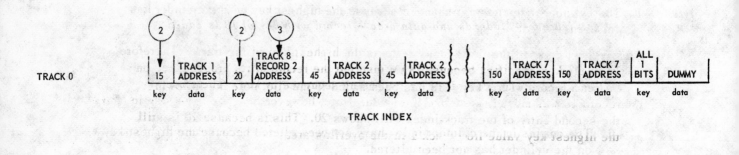

TRACK INDEX

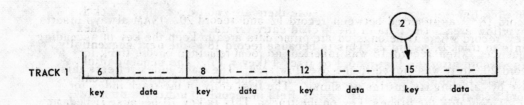

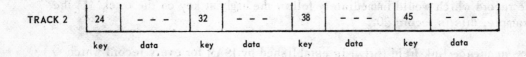

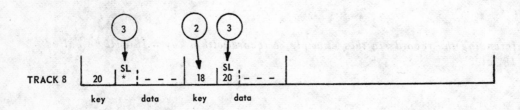

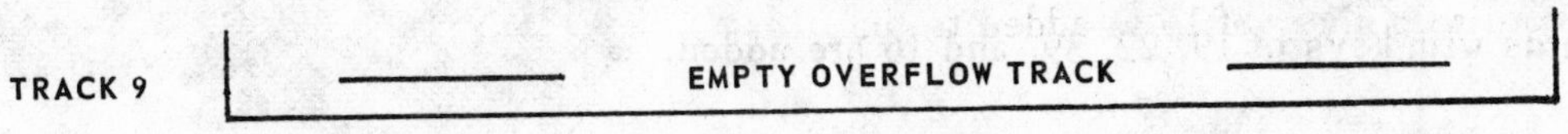

Figure 6-5 Indexes and data area — record with key of 15 is added.

After a record with a key of 15 has been added, note the following:

1. The cylinder index has not changed because the highest key on the cylinder has not been altered.

2. The first entry in the track index reflects the highest key on the track. Therefore, 15 is the key specified because ISAM inserted the record in its proper place on the track to keep the records in an ascending sequence by key. Therefore, record 18 was moved to the overflow area. Note, however, that the key value in the second entry of the track index still shows 20. This is because 20 is still the highest key value from track 1 in the overflow area.

3. The sequence link field is now used because there are two records from track 1 in the overflow area. The data in the second entry for track 1 in the track index now points to track 8, record 2. This is because record 18 is the next sequentially ascending record after the last record on track 1 (key = 15). The sequence link field in record 18 points to record 20 because it is the next sequentially ascending record from track 1. The sequence link field in record 20 indicates no more records are in the overflow area from track 1.

STEP 4: Records with keys of 19, 22, 39, and 16 are added.

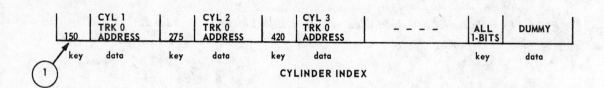

CYLINDER INDEX

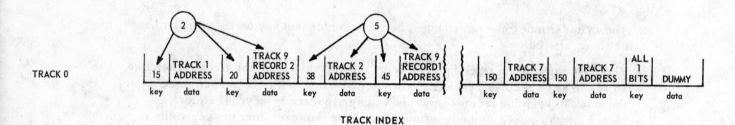

TRACK INDEX

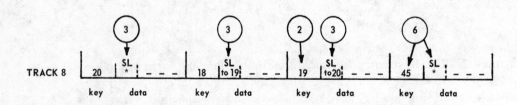

6.10

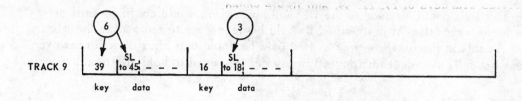

Figure 6-6 Indexes and data area — records with key of 19, 22, 39 and 16 are added

After the above records have been added, note the following:

1. The cylinder index has not been altered.

2. The key entries for track 1 in the track index are still the same. The highest key on the track is 15 and the highest key in the overflow area from track 1 is 20. Note, however, that the address in the second data entry for track 1 in the track index has changed. It now points to record 16. Record 16 was added directly to the overflow area because its key was higher than the highest key located on track 1 (15).

3. The sequence link fields in the overflow records for track 1 all point to the next sequentially ascending record from track 1. Thus, 16 points to 18, 18 points to 19 and 19 points to 20. Note that the sequence link field in record 18 was altered to point to record 19 when record 19 was added. Record 20 indicates no more linkages. Even though there are higher keys in the overflow area (39 and 45), they are not from track 1 in the prime data area and thus are not linked with record 20.

4. Record 22 was added to track 2. It was added to track 2 even though its key was lower than the previous low key (24) because it was higher than the highest key on track 1. Records are always added in this manner. The highest key on a track when a file is loaded remains the highest key when other processing is done against the file.

5. The entries in the track index have been modified to reflect the addition of records to track 2. The first entry for track 2 indicates that the highest key on track 2 is 38. This is because record 22 was added. The second key entry for track 2 indicates that 45 is the highest key associated with the track. The data for the second entry points to record 39 which is the next sequentially ascending record in the overflow area after the last record on track 2 (38).

6. Record 45 was moved to the overflow area when record 22 was added. Record 39 was added directly to the overflow area because its key was greater than the highest key in the prime data area. Its sequence link field points to record 45 because record 45 is the next sequentially ascending record from track 2.

More additions could be made to the file and processing would continue until the overflow areas were full. At that point, it would be necessary to reorganize the file to eliminate records in the overflow areas. It should be noted that after the cylinder overflow areas are full, an independent overflow area can be used to hold additional records.

All records in both the cylinder and independent overflow areas are unblocked even though the file may be blocked in the prime data areas.

RANDOM RETRIEVAL

Random retrieval and updating normally involves the retrieving of a master record from a file (based on a given key from the corresponding transaction record), updating the master record and re-writing the updated master record on the master file. When an indexed sequential file is randomly retrieved, a search of the indexes precedes the actual retrieval of the desired record. The search of the indexes locates the exact disk location of the record and the record is then read into core storage. If it was desired to retrieve the record with a key of 19 from the previous example, the following routine would be followed (this assumes no master index):

1. The cylinder index is read and it is determined record 19 resides on cylinder 1. This is because the highest key on cylinder 1 is 150.

2. The track index is read and searched to find what track record 19 is on. It is found that the highest key associated with track 1 is 20 but that the highest key on track 1 in the prime data area is 15. Therefore, record 19, if it is on the file, must be in the overflow area.

3. The address of the first sequentially ascending record in the overflow area is obtained from the second data entry in the track index for track 1. This address is track 9, record 2.

4. The record at track 9, record 2 is read and the key is 16. However, the sequence link field points to another record, so that record is read. The key for the record is 18 but the sequence link field points to the next record from track 1. This record is record 19, so it is returned to core storage in the I/O area or work area for random retrieval. The program can then process the record.

It should be noted that, had record 19 not been on the file, the next record would have been record 20. Since 20 is greater than 19 and the records are in ascending order, an indication would have been supplied by ISAM to the user in the filenameC indicator byte that the record was not on the file.

In the sample program developed in this chapter to update the inventory master file, it was determined that random updating would be the most efficient method. Therefore, the file must be defined to allow both additions and random retrieval. This is done in the DTFIS.

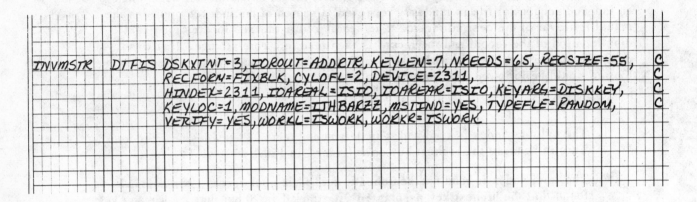

Figure 6-7 DTFIS for additions and random retrieval

The entries unique in the DTFIS for adding and random retrieval using an indexed sequential file are:

1. IOROUT = ADDRTR: This entry must be given to specify that both ADDing and ReTRieving will be done using the defined file. If just adding were to be performed, the entry after the equal sign is ADD and if just retrieving were to be performed, the entry RETRVE is required after the equal sign.

2. IOAREAL = ISIO: This entry must be included whenever records are added to an indexed sequential file. ISIO is the name given to the area defined by a DS statement. The length of ISIO for blocked records must be 8 + keylength + (record length times blocking factor). Thus, the length of ISIO for the sample program is 3590 bytes: 8 + 7 + (55 x 65).

3. IOAREAR = ISIO: This entry must be included whenever records are retrieved randomly from an indexed sequential file. ISIO is the name given to the area defined by a DS statement. The length of ISIO for blocked records must be the record length times blocking factor. Thus, the minimum length of ISIO for the sample program is 3575:(55 x 65). It should be noted that the same I/O area is being used for adding records and retrieving records. This presents no problem because records will not be added at the same time they are being ____ ____. This technique saves the core storage required for a

is entry is required if random processing is to be
entries are SEQNTL if sequential processing is to
random and sequential processing is to be done.

entry is required when adding records. The name
given to the area defined by a DS statement. For
must be large enough to contain one logical record.
must be large enough to contain one logical record and

entry is required if a work area is used to randomly
The name ISWORK must be the same as that used by
efines the work area. The area must be large enough
ord.

an indexed sequential file, two imperative macros are

to add the record to the file.

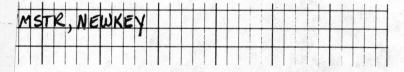

MSTR, NEWKEY

re 6-8   WRITE Macro to add records

The first operand is the name of the file as defined in the DTF. The second operand is the keyword NEWKEY and must be included as shown.

Before the write macro is issued, the record to be added must be moved to the area defined in the WORKL operand of the DTF. For blocked records, the data record must be moved to the work area. For unblocked records, the key and the data must be moved to the work area. The key is moved to the high-order position in the work area and the data record follows the key.

When the write macro is issued, the record is added to the file in the manner shown in the previous example.

WAITF Macro

The WAITF macro is issued to insure that the transfer of a record has been completed.

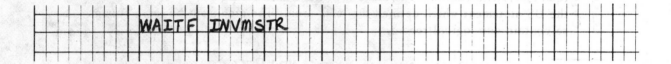

Figure 6-9 WAITF Macro used after WRITE Macro

The WAITF macro requires the name of the file as defined in the DTF as the only operand. This macro must be issued before another record is added to the file. When the WAITF macro is issued, the program does not regain control until the transfer of data is complete.

The following example illustrates a "typical" sequence of instructions to add records to an indexed sequential file.

EXAMPLE

```
                        IBM System/360 Assembler Coding Form

          OPEN   INVMSTR,PRTFLE,DISKIN

GETINPUT  GET    DISKIN                    READ TRANSACTION FILE
                        - DETERMINE THAT UPDATE IS AN ADD TYPE-

                        - BUILD RECORD TO BE ADDED FROM INPUT RECORD-

          MVC    DISKEY,INPUTKEY           MOVE KEY TO 'KEYARG' FIELD FROM DTF

          WRITE  INVMSTR,NEWKEY            WRITE NEW RECORD
          WAITF  INVMSTR                   WAIT FOR I/O COMPLETION


          B      GETINPUT                  GO READ NEXT RECORD


INVMSTR   DTFIS  KEYARG=DISKEY, - - - -
```

Figure 6-10 *Typical sequence of instructions for adding a record*

Note in the example above that the key for the new record, as determined from the transaction record, is moved to the "KEYARG" field before the WRITE macro. The WAITF macro must be issued after the WRITE macro to ensure that the record has been added properly.

IMPERATIVE MACROS – RANDOM RETRIEVAL AND UPDATE

When records are randomly retrieved, updated and re-written, three macro instructions are used: READ, WRITE and WAITF.

READ Macro

The READ macro is used to randomly retrieve a record.

Figure 6-11 READ Macro for random retrieval

Two operands are required with the read to randomly retrieve records. The first is the name of the file as defined in the DTF. The second is the keyword KEY and it must be included as shown. Prior to the issuing of the READ macro, the key of the record to be retrieved must be moved to the disk key area named in the KEYARG operand of the DTFIS. When the READ macro is issued, the indexes are searched as shown in the previous example. When the record is found, it is moved to the I/O area specified in the DTF operand IOAREAR. If the records are blocked, the requested record is made available for processing in the work area (if WORKR is specified) or by loading the address of the record in the I/O area into the register specified in the IOREG operand of the DTF.

The WRITE macro is used to rewrite a previously retrieved record.

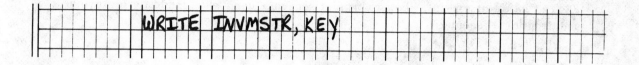

Figure 6-12 WRITE Macro to rewrite an updated record

Two operands are required with the WRITE macro. The first is the name of the file as defined in the DTFIS statement. The second operand is the keyword KEY and must be included as shown.

The WRITE command rewrites the record previously retrieved by the READ command. The record is written from the work area if one is defined or from the I/O area.

Between the random read and the random write, the record can be updated. Any field EXCEPT THE KEY can be altered in any manner desired. The key cannot be changed because it would cause the file's indexes to be incorrect. The indexes are not altered by a random update (a read followed by a write).

When randomly processing and updating, each record retrieved should be rewritten before any other processing is done to the file. If records are added between a read and a write, a lost record or a duplicate key may result on the file.

WAITF Macro

The WAITF macro is issued after a read macro for random retrieval and after a write macro. The format is the same as shown for the add macros.

The following example shows a typical sequence used when randomly retrieving and updating a record.

EXAMPLE

```
Name      Operation  Operand                       Comments
          -
          -
          OPEN      INVMSTR,DISKIN             OPEN FILES
          -
          -
GETINPUT  GET       DISKIN                     READ UPDATE FILE
          -
          -                  - DETERMINE UPDATE TYPE AND EXTRACT
          -                    KEY FROM UPDATE TRANSACTION -
          -
          MVC       DISKEY,INPUTKEY            MOVE KEY TO 'KEYARG' FIELD FROM DTF
          -
          READ      INVMSTR,KEY                READ MASTER RECORD
          WAITF     INVMSTR                    WAIT FOR I/O COMPLETION
          -
          -                  - UPDATE RECORD AS REQUIRED -
          -
          WRITE     INVMSTR,KEY                WRITE UPDATED MASTER RECORD
          WAITF     INVMSTR                    WAIT FOR I/O COMPLETION
          -
          B         GETINPUT                   GO READ NEXT RECORD
          -
          -
INVMSTR   DTFIS     KEYARG=DISKEY,----
```

Figure 6-13 Typical sequence of instructions for randomly retrieving and updating a record

in Chapter 4, the error status of the file is indicated
in filenameC (INVMSTRC in the sample program).
he status byte is posted as a result of the WAITF
be tested after the WAITF macro. The following
as a result of an add function or a random retrieval

Explanation

table DASD error has occurred (except wrong length record).

th record has been detected during an I/O operation.

lition has been encountered during execution of the sequential retrieval function.

be retrieved has not been found in the data file. This applies to Random (RANSEQ)
SEQNTL (RANSEQ) when KEY is specified.

ed to the SETL in SEQNTL (RANSEQ) is outside the prime data file limits.

be added to the file has a duplicate record key of another record in the file.

rea in a cylinder is full, and no independent overflow area has been specified, or
t overflow area is full, and the addition cannot be made. The user should assign
t overflow area or extend the limit.

ng processed in one of the retrieval functions (RANDOM/SEQNTL) is an overflow

FilenameC status indicators

procedures are taken when an error occurs:

ne program is cancelled with a message to

the program is cancelled with a message to
message is issued to the printer and the next
dom write, the program is cancelled with a

is written on the printer indicating the update
cannot be done because there is no master record.

X'04' – Duplicate record - If the duplicate record is a deleted record, the new
record is re-written on the file. If not, an error message is written on
the printer indicating a duplicate record when an add is attempted.

X'02' – Overflow areas full - The program is cancelled with a message to the
printer.

X'01' – Overflow record - No action is taken when this indication is given.

BINARY ARITHMETIC

One of the functions of a file update is to change various fields in the record. These changes could include adding or subtracting a value from a field in the master record. For example, in an inventory application, if parts in an inventory file are put on order, the quantity on order field in the record must be incremented to show the new quantity on order. If an order is cancelled, the quantity on order field must be decremented by the number of parts cancelled. If, as in the sample programs, the fields contain binary values, the arithmetic for the fields should be done in binary.

To facilitate binary arithmetic operations, a series of binary instructions exist which enable the programmer to add, subtract, multiply and divide in binary.

Before examining the binary arithmetic instructions, however, it is necessary to understand how the System/360 accomplishes binary arithmetic so that the results can be properly interpreted. This, in turn, requires a knowledge of complement numbers.

COMPLEMENT NUMBERS

A COMPLEMENT NUMBER is defined as that quantity which, when added to a number, would result in a zero answer and a "carry out" of the high-order position. For example, when the quantity 367 is added to 633, the answer is 000 with a carry out of the high-order position.

$$\begin{array}{r} 633 \\ + \ 367 \\ \hline \text{"1" } 000 \end{array}$$

Figure 6-15 Addition with carry-out in high-order position

Thus, 367 is said to be the COMPLEMENT of 633. Notice that the example given is in the decimal number system. Thus, the complement number is called the "tens" complement, because the decimal number system has a base 10. Every number in the decimal number system except zero has a "tens" complement. For example, the "tens" complement of 99 is 1.

In order to calculate the "tens" complement of a number, the following procedure is used:

STEP 1: Subtract the number from all 9's (which is the highest digit value of the numbering system).

Given: Number = 5462

$$\begin{array}{r} 9999 \\ - 5462 \\ \hline 4537 \end{array}$$

Figure 6-16 Subtraction of a number from the highest value in the number base

STEP 2: Add 1 to the low-order position of the result of the subtraction.

$$\begin{array}{r} 4537 \\ + \quad 1 \\ \hline 4538 \end{array} = \text{"tens" complement of 5462}$$

Figure 6-17 Addition of 1 to get tens complement

In order to check the result, the number (5462) and its "tens" complement (4538) can be added to verify that the definition of a complement number is satisfied.

$$\begin{array}{r} 5462 \\ + 4538 \\ \hline \text{"1"}0000 \end{array}$$

Figure 6-18 Verification of tens complement

As can be seen, the answer is zero with a carry out of the high-order position.

This technique of determining a complement number can be applied to a number in any number system. Thus, if it is desired to find the complement of the number 6AC in the hexadecimal number system, the following procedure is used.

STEP 1: Subtract the number from all F's (which is the highest digit value of the numbering system).

$$\begin{array}{r} FFF \\ 6AC \\ \hline 953 \end{array}$$

Figure 6-19 Subtraction of number from highest value in number base

STEP 2: Add 1 to the low-order position of the result of the subtraction.

$$\begin{array}{r} 953 \\ +\quad 1 \\ \hline 954 \end{array}$$

Figure 6-20 Addition of 1 to get sixteens complement

Thus 954 is the "sixteens" complement of 6AC. Verification shows this is true.

$$\begin{array}{r} 954 \\ +6AC \\ \hline \text{"1"}000 \end{array}$$

Figure 6-21 Verification of sixteens complement

As with all numbering systems, a complement can be found for binary numbers in the binary number system.

Thus, if it was desired to find the complement of the binary number 10010010, the following procedure could be used:

STEP 1: Subtract the number from all 1's (the highest digit value of the numbering system).

$$
\begin{array}{r}
11111111 \\
10010010 \\
\hline
01101101
\end{array}
$$

Figure 6-22 Subtraction of number from highest value in number base

STEP 2: Add 1 to the low-order position of the result of the subtraction.

$$
\begin{array}{r}
01101101 \\
1 \\
\hline
01101110
\end{array} = \text{``Two's'' complement of} \\
10010010
$$

Figure 6-23 Addition of 1 to get two's complement

Again, to verify the result, the two numbers are added.

$$
\begin{array}{r}
10010010 \\
+ 01101110 \\
\hline
\text{``1''} \ 00000000
\end{array}
$$

Figure 6-24 Verification of two's complement

Another method to find the "two's" complement of a binary number is to "invert" each binary digit and add 1. Thus, using the previous example, the "two's" complement could have been found by the following method.

STEP 1: "Invert" or switch each binary digit.

$$10010010$$
$$\text{Inverted}$$
$$\overline{}$$
$$01101101 \text{ - Note that each binary digit has been switched from 0 to 1 or from 1 to 0.}$$

Figure 6-25 Inverting binary number

STEP 2: Add 1 to the result.

$$\begin{array}{r} 01101101 \\ + 1 \\ \hline 01101110 \end{array} = \text{"Two's" complement of 10010010}$$

Figure 6-26 Addition of 1 to get two's complement

Note that the results are the same as the previous example.

The understanding of complement numbers is necessary because the System/360, as do most computers, performs subtraction by means of COMPLEMENT ADDITION. This means that, instead of subtracting a number, the computer derives the correct result by adding the complement of a number. For example, the computer is given the instruction to subtract decimal 472 from 873. The "normal" way of doing this problem is

$$
\begin{array}{r}
873 \\
-\ 472 \\
\hline
401
\end{array}
$$

Figure 6-27 "Normal" method of subtraction

The computer does it in the following manner:

STEP 1: Obtain the complement of the subtrahend (472).

$$
\begin{array}{r}
999 \\
-\ 472 \\
\hline
527 \\
+\quad 1 \\
\hline
528 = \text{complement of } 472
\end{array}
$$

Figure 6-28 Obtain complement of 472

STEP 2: Add the complement of the subtrahend to the minuend (873).

$$
\begin{array}{r}
873 \\
528 \\
\hline
\text{"1" } 401
\end{array}
$$

Figure 6-29 Addition of complement of subtrahend to minuend

Note that the correct answer is obtained and a carry out of the high-order position results.

Complement addition will always result in the same answer as subtraction.

The result of complement addition, however, may result in an answer in one of two forms: true or complement. When complement addition was performed in the previous example, the answer was a "true" answer, that is, the result was the same as if subtraction were performed. The computer could tell the result was a true result because there was a carry out of the high-order position. Whenever, after using complement addition, there is a carry out of the high-order position, the answer is a true result. Whenever there is not a carry out of the high-order position, the answer is in complement form and must be RE-COMPLEMENTED before the true answer is obtained. The following example illustrates the re-complementing technique. When the instruction is to subtract 873 from 472, the following steps are taken:

STEP 1: Obtain the complement of the subtrahend (873).

$$
\begin{array}{r}
999 \\
873 \\
\hline
126 \\
+\quad 1 \\
\hline
127 = \text{complement of 873}
\end{array}
$$

Figure 6-30 Obtain complement of 873

STEP 2: Add the complement of the subtrahend to the minuend.

$$
\begin{array}{r}
472 \\
127 \\
\hline
599
\end{array}
$$

Figure 6-31 Addition of complement of subtrahend to minuend

Note that there is no carry out of the high-order position. This indicates that the answer is in complement form and that re-complementing must take place before a true answer is obtained.

STEP 3: Re-complement the answer.

$$
\begin{array}{r}
999 \\
\underline{599} \\
400 \\
+\ \underline{1} \\
401
\end{array}
$$

Figure 6-32 Re-complement answer

Notice that the answer obtained from re-complementing is now the true answer to the problem. The sign, however, is incorrect—it should be negative. Therefore, whenever re-complementing occurs, the sign on the answer obtained must be switched.

STEP 4: Switch sign.

$$401 \longrightarrow -401$$

Figure 6-33 Switch sign of result

The answer now obtained is the same answer that would have been obtained had subtraction been performed as follows:

$$
\begin{array}{r}
472 \\
-\ 873 \\
\hline
-\ 401
\end{array}
$$

Figure 6-34 "Normal" method of subtraction

As has been shown with decimal numbers, complement addition can be performed on binary numbers. The following example illustrates the steps the System/360 would take to subtract the binary value 01100011 from 00010011.

STEP 1: Obtain complement of subtrahend (01100011).

$$
\begin{array}{r}
01100011 \\
\text{Invert} \\
10011100 \\
+\qquad\quad 1 \\
\hline
10011101
\end{array}
$$

Figure 6-35 Obtain complement of subtrahend

STEP 2: Add complement of subtrahend to minuend.

$$
\begin{array}{rl}
00010011 & \text{(minuend)} \\
+\ 10011101 & \text{(complement of subtrahend)} \\
\hline
10110000 &
\end{array}
$$

Figure 6-36 Addition of complement of subtrahend to minuend

Note that there was no high-order carry out; therefore, the result must be re-complemented and the sign changed.

STEP 3: Re-complement the answer and change the sign to obtain the true answer.

$$+ 1011\ 0000$$

Invert

$$\begin{array}{r} 0100\ 1111 \\ +\qquad\qquad 1 \\ \hline -\ 0101\ 0000 \end{array}$$ —— true answer

Figure 6-37 Recomplement the answer and switch signs

BINARY DATA

When performing decimal arithmetic using the add packed, subtract packed, etc. instructions, it will be recalled that the operands could vary from 1 to 16 bytes each and that the length was determined implicitly from the lengths of the fields or explicitly from lengths specified in the instruction. When using the binary arithmetic instructions, however, the lengths of the operands are fixed——that is, the operands are either registers (4 bytes in length), halfwords (2 bytes in length) or fullwords (4 bytes in length). Thus, the binary arithmetic instructions are referred to as fixed-length arithmetic instructions.

Data in registers, halfwords or fullwords to be used in fixed-length arithmetic operations is in binary form. Thus, the number +100 represented in a halfword appears as follows:

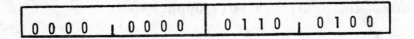

Figure 6-38 Decimal +100 in binary form in a halfword

Whenever halfwords, fullwords or registers contain data to be used in arithmetic operations, the high-order bit (bit 0) contains the "sign" of the number. Positive numbers contain a 0 in the sign bit position and negative numbers contain a 1 in the sign bit position.

POSITIVE binary numbers are represented in their TRUE form while NEGATIVE numbers are represented in their complement form. Thus, the number −100 would be represented by its complement form as shown below.

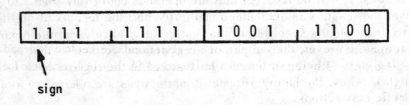

Figure 6-39 Decimal −100 in binary form in a halfword

Note that the high-order bit (bit 0) is a 1. This indicates that the number is negative, that is, it is represented in its complement form. Thus, the high-order bit is not truly a sign but rather an indication that the number is in true form (bit 0 = 0) or in complement form (bit 0 = 1). It is important to remember when performing fixed-length arithmetic that positive numbers are represented in their true form and negative numbers are represented in their complement form.

As has been stated, fixed-length arithmetic uses registers, fullwords and halfwords. A halfword is 2 bytes in length (16 bits) and a fullword is 4 bytes in length (32 bits). Halfwords and fullwords are located in core storage on halfword or fullword boundaries. When fixed-length arithmetic is performed, the halfword or fullword must contain the value to be acted upon as a positive binary number in true form or a negative binary number in complement form.

FIXED-LENGTH ADD INSTRUCTIONS

Three add instructions are normally used in fixed-length arithmetic operations: ADD FULLWORD, ADD REGISTERS, and ADD HALFWORD.

ADD HALFWORD Instruction

The ADD HALFWORD instruction is used to add a value in a halfword in core storage to a value in a register.

> INSTRUCTION: ADD HALFWORD
>
> OPERATION CODE: AH
>
> EXAMPLE: AH 6,HALFCON

The first operand is any general purpose register and the second operand is a halfword in core storage. The result of the add is stored in the register specified in the first operand.

The following example illustrates the use of the add halfword instruction to add the decimal value 200 + 100.

EXAMPLE

6.33

Before Execution:

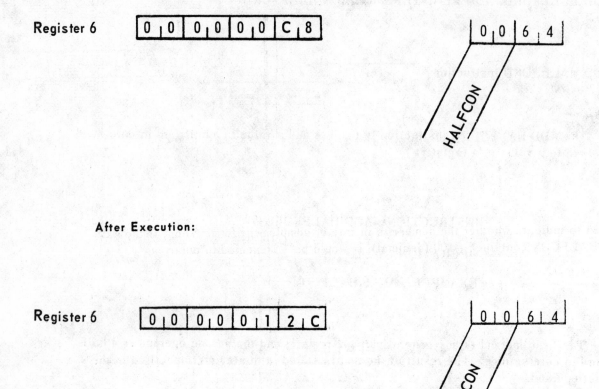

Register 6 | 0 0 0 0 0 0 C 8 |

0 0 6 4

HALFCON

After Execution:

Register 6 | 0 0 0 0 0 1 2 C |

0 0 6 4

HALFCON

Note: The contents of the register are illustrated in hexadecimal form.

Figure 6-40 Example of Add Halfword instruction

Note that the value in the halfword HALFCON is added to the value in register 6 and the answer (decimal 300) is stored in register 6.

When using halfwords, the System/360 internally expands the halfword to a fullword before executing the add instruction. Thus, in the previous example, the value in HALFCON would have been expanded to a fullword. Note that the high-order bit is propogated throughout the high-order bits of the fullword (in this case, zero).

Figure 6-41 Expansion of a halfword to a fullword

In the halfword, as with all operands in fixed-length arithmetic, the high-order bit is used to indicate whether the number is in true or complement form. Thus, if the halfword HALFCON contained −100 (decimal), it would be represented in binary as

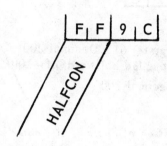

Figure 6-42 Decimal −100 in a halfword

This is the complement of decimal 100 with the high-order bit = 1. When the half-word is expanded to a fullword before addition, the high-order bit is propogated throughout the fullword. Thus the expansion takes place as follows:

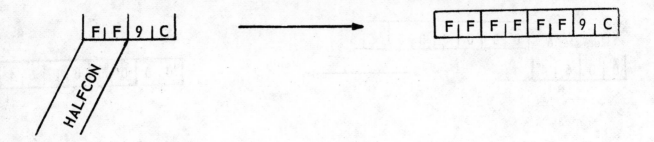

Figure 6-43 *Expansion of a halfword to a fullword*

Note that the high-order bit of the halfword is in the high-order bits of the fullword.

The addition would take place as follows:

```
    0 0 0 0 0 0 C 8   (Register 6) = Decimal 200
    F F F F F F 9 C   (Expanded halfword) of –100)
"1" 0 0 0 0 0 0 6 4   = Decimal 100
```

Figure 6-44 *Addition of decimal 200 and decimal -100*

Since the instruction was add, the answer obtained is a true answer. The answer is decimal 100, which one would expect (200 - 100 = 100).

If the value in HALFCON was decimal −300, the add halfword instruction would take place in the following steps:

STEP 1: Expand HALFCON to fullword.

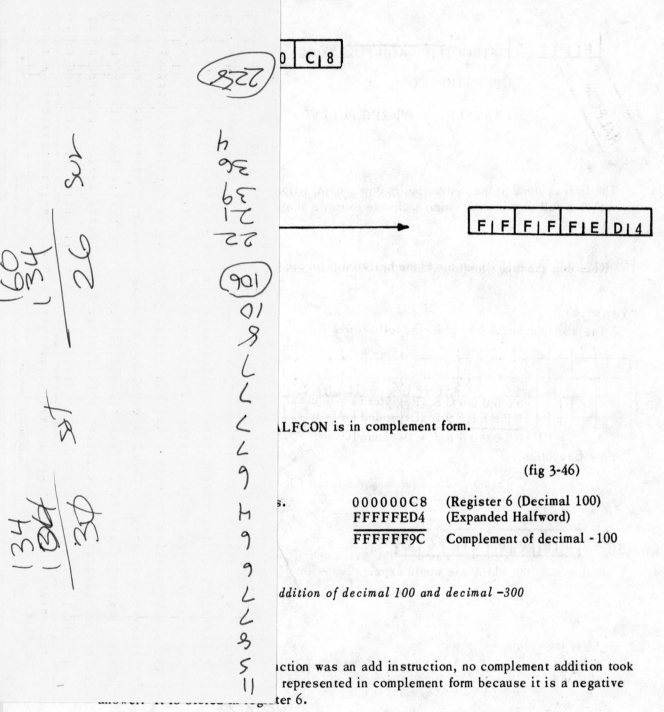

HALFCON is in complement form.

(fig 3-46)

000000C8 (Register 6 (Decimal 100)
FFFFFED4 (Expanded Halfword)
FFFFFF9C Complement of decimal - 100

addition of decimal 100 and decimal −300

ction was an add instruction, no complement addition took represented in complement form because it is a negative ter 6.

ADD FULLWORD Instruction

The ADD FULLWORD instruction is used to add a fullword in core storage to a value in a register.

> INSTRUCTION: ADD FULLWORD
>
> OPERATION CODE: A
>
> EXAMPLE: A BINREG,FULLWORK

The first operand of the instruction is any general purpose register and the second operand is a fullword in core storage. In the example above BINREG is equated to Register 5.

The following example illustrates the add fullword instruction.

EXAMPLE

Before Execution:

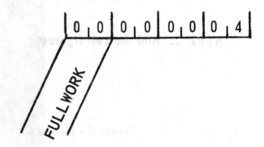

BINREG | 0 | 0 | 0 | 0 | 0 | 0 | 6 | 0 |

After Execution:

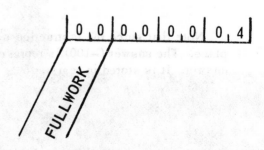

BINREG | 0 | 0 | 0 | 0 | 0 | 0 | 6 | 4 |

Figure 6-46 Example of Add Fullword instruction

Note that the value in FULLWORK is added to the value in BINREG and the result is stored in the register (BINREG). If the value in FULLWORK or BINREG is a negative value, it would be represented in its complement form with the high-order bit = 1.

ADD REGISTER Instruction

The ADD REGISTER instruction is used to add the contents of one register to the contents of a second register.

INSTRUCTION: ADD REGISTER

OPERATION CODE: AR

EXAMPLE: AR 5,2

The first and second operands are any general register 0-15. The value in the register specified in the second operand is added to the value in the register specified in the first operand and the result is stored in the register specified in the first operand.

The following example illustrates the use of the Add Register instruction.

EXAMPLE

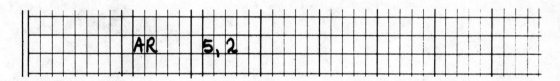

Before Execution:

Register 5  Register 2

| 0 | 0 | 0 | 0 | 0 | 1 | F | 4 |

| 0 | 0 | 0 | 0 | 0 | 0 | 6 | 4 |

After Execution:

Register 5 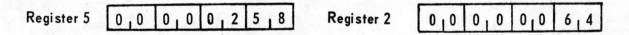 Register 2

| 0 | 0 | 0 | 0 | 0 | 2 | 5 | 8 |

| 0 | 0 | 0 | 0 | 0 | 0 | 6 | 4 |

Figure 6-47 Example of Add Register instruction

Note that the answer is stored in the first operand (register 5) and the second operand (register 2) is undisturbed.

FIXED-LENGTH SUBTRACTION INSTRUCTIONS

As with the add instructions, there are three primary subtract instructions in fixed-length arithmetic: SUBTRACT FULLWORD, SUBTRACT REGISTERS, and SUBTRACT HALFWORD.

SUBTRACT HALFWORD Instruction

The SUBTRACT HALFWORD instruction is used to subtract a value in a halfword in core storage from a value in a register.

INSTRUCTION: SUBTRACT HALFWORD

OPERATION CODE: SH

EXAMPLE: SH 6,HALFCON

The first operand is any general purpose register 0-15. The second operand is a halfword in core storage. The answer is stored in the register specified in the first operand.

6.40

The following illustrates the use of the Subtract Halfword instruction:

EXAMPLE

Before Execution:

Register 6 | 0,0 | 0,0 | 0,0 | C,8 |

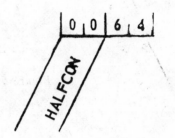

After Execution:

Register 6 | 0,0 | 0,0 | 0,0 | 6,4 |

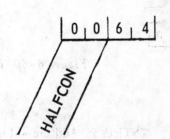

Figure 6-48   Example of Subtract Halfword instruction

Notice that the value in the halfword HALFCON is subtracted from the value in register 6 and the answer is stored in register 6.

It should be recalled that all subtraction on the System/360 is done by complement addition. Therefore, the following steps would be taken by the computer to solve the above problem.

STEP 1: Expand the halfword to a fullword.

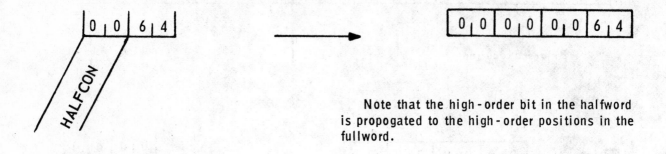

Note that the high-order bit in the halfword is propogated to the high-order positions in the fullword.

Figure 6-49 Example of expansion of a halfword to a fullword

STEP 2: Take the complement of the subtrahend.

| 0 | 0 | 0 | 0 | 0 | 0 | 6 | 4 |

→

| F | F | F | F | F | F | 9 | C |

Figure 6-50 Example of taking the complement of the subtrahend

STEP 3: Add the subtrahend and minuend.

```
      0 0 0 0 0 0 C 8    Minuend
   + F F F F F F 9 C    Subtrahend
"1" 0 0 0 0 0 0 6 4
```

Figure 6-51 Example of adding the subtrahend and the minuend

Note that since there was a carryout of the high-order position, the answer is the true answer. Therefore, recomplementing was not necessary.

SUBTRACT FULLWORD Instruction

The SUBTRACT FULLWORD instruction is used to subtract a value in a fullword in core storage from a value in a register.

INSTRUCTION: SUBTRACT FULLWORD

OPERATION CODE: S

EXAMPLE: S 6,FULL

The first operand is any general register 0-15 and the second operand is a fullword in core storage. The following example illustrates the use of the Subtract Fullword instruction.

EXAMPLE

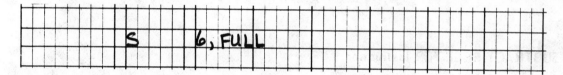

Before Execution:

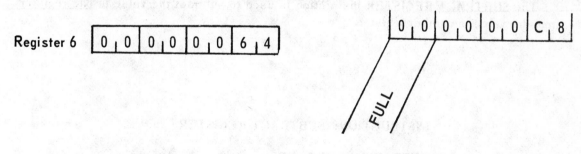

After Execution:

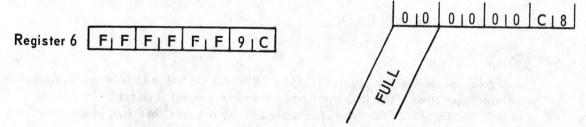

Figure 6-52 Example of the Subtract Fullword instruction

Notice that the answer is a negative number (because high-order bit = 1) and thus is the complement of the true answer. The answer will stay in register 6 as shown. In order to find the true answer, however, one must re-complement the answer and change the sign.

6.43

The following example shows the result being recomplemented to obtain the true answer.

| F | F | F | F | F | F | 9 | C |

COMPLEMENT ⟶

| 0 | 0 | 0 | 0 | 0 | 0 | 6 | 4 |

Figure 6-53 Example of result being recomplemented to find true answer

Note that the answer is X'64' which is decimal 100. When the sign is changed, the answer becomes −100, which is the expected result.

SUBTRACT REGISTER Instruction

The SUBTRACT REGISTER instruction is used to subtract the value in one register from the value in another register.

INSTRUCTION: SUBTRACT REGISTER

OPERATION CODE: SR

EXAMPLE: SR 5,6

The second operand is any general register 0-15 and the value in it is the subtrahend of the subtract operation. The first operand is also any general register 0-15 and the value in it is the minuend. The answer is stored in the register specified in the first operand. The use of the subtract register instruction is illustrated below.

6.44

EXAMPLE

Before Execution:

Register 5 `0 0 0 0 0 1 A F`   Register 6 `0 0 0 0 0 0 A C`

After Execution:

Register 5 `0 0 0 0 0 1 0 3`   Register 6 `0 0 0 0 0 0 A C`

Figure 6-54 Example of Subtract Register instruction

Note that the answer is stored in the register specified in the first operand (register 5) and the second register (register 6) is undisturbed.

A common technique used to "zero" a register, that is, make the value in a register equal to zero, is to use the subtract register to subtract the value in a register from itself. Thus, the instruction SR 7,7 would subtract the value in register 7 from itself, thus resulting in a zero value in register 7.

CONDITION CODES AFTER ARITHMETIC OPERATIONS

After an arithmetic operation has been performed, one of four possibilities exists——— the result of the calculation was zero, the result was less than zero, the result was greater than zero, or an overflow occurred (that is, the result has exceeded the maximum value that could be contained in the result field). These conditions are available to test after the arithmetic operation has been completed. The masks to be used for testing the results of the fixed-length instructions just discussed are shown below.

Instruction	Mask	8	4	2	1
Add Halfword		Zero	< Zero	> Zero	Overflow
Add Fullword		Zero	< Zero	> Zero	Overflow
Add Register		Zero	< Zero	> Zero	Overflow
Subtract Halfword		Zero	< Zero	> Zero	Overflow
Subtract Fullword		Zero	< Zero	> Zero	Overflow
Subtract Register		Zero	< Zero	> Zero	Overflow

Figure 6-55 Condition code settings after fixed-length arithmetic instructions

In the sample program, as has been mentioned, the various fields in the master record are updated from update transactions. Although the numeric fields in the update transactions were checked in the card-to-disk program presented in Chapter 3 to verify they contained numeric information, there could be no check on them to be sure the values they contained were correct. It is known, however, that any change to any field in the master record could not result in a negative value. For example, there can be zero parts on order or there can be one or more parts on order but there cannot be less than zero parts on order. Therefore, if any update transaction causes the quantity on order to go below zero, it must be in error. This situation can be tested as shown in the following example:

EXAMPLE

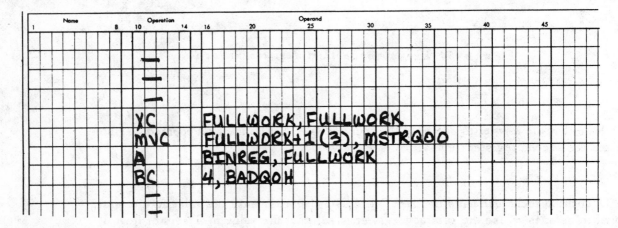

Figure 6-56 Example of using the condition code after an arithmetic instruction

The routine above moves the quantity on order (MSTRQOO) from the master file record to a fullword work area and adds it to the update quantity, which is contained in "BINREG". If the result is negative, the BC 4,BADQOH instruction will branch to a routine which will issue an error message and process the next update transaction.

LOAD INSTRUCTIONS

As was shown previously, the LOAD FULLWORD instruction loads a fullword from core storage into a register and the LOAD ADDRESS instruction loads the address of the second operand into the register specified in the first operand. Several other load instructions are also used in business applications.

LOAD HALFWORD Instruction

The LOAD HALFWORD instruction loads a halfword from core storage into a register.

> INSTRUCTION: LOAD HALFWORD
>
> OPERATION CODE: LH
>
> EXAMPLE: LH 8,HALFCON

The Load Halfword instruction loads the halfword specified in the second operand into the register specified in the first operand. Before it is loaded, however, the half-word is expanded to a fullword as in the halfword arithmetic instructions. The high-order bit of the half-word is propogated through the high-order bits of the fullword. Thus, if the high-order bit of the halfword is equal to 1, the bit will be propogated throughout the high-order bits of the fullword and the value will be considered to be in complement form.

LOAD AND TEST REGISTER Instruction

The LOAD AND TEST REGISTER instruction loads a value contained in one register into another register and sets a condition code depending upon the value loaded.

> INSTRUCTION: LOAD AND TEST REGISTER
>
> OPERATION CODE: LTR
>
> EXAMPLE: LTR 7,9

The value in the register specified in the second operand is loaded into the first operand and the condition code is set to indicate whether the value loaded is equal to zero, greater than zero, or less than zero. The masks to test the condition code are:

Instruction	Mask	8	4	2	1
Load and Test Register		Zero	< Zero	> Zero	Not used

Figure 6-57 Condition code settings after Load and Test Register instruction

A common technique to test the sign of a value in a register is to use the Load and Test Register instruction. The following example shows this technique.

EXAMPLE

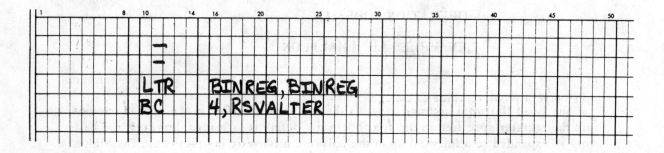

```
LTR     BINREG,BINREG
BC      4,RSVALTER
```

Before Execution:

BINREG | 0 | 0 | 0 | 0 | 0 | 1 | 6 | C |

After Execution:

BINREG | 0 | 0 | 0 | 0 | 0 | 1 | 6 | C |

Figure 6-58 Example of using Load and Test Register instruction

Note that the value in the register BINREG was loaded back into BINREG. Thus, the contents of BINREG were not altered. The only result of the instruction was that the condition code was set to indicate that the value in BINREG is greater than zero. Thus, the branch to "RSVALTER" will not take place because the condition tested for was a negative value.

LOAD NEGATIVE REGISTER Instruction

CTION: LOAD NEGATIVE REGISTER

TION CODE: LNR

LE: LNR 8,11

the absolute value of the second operand is loaded into the
operand. Thus, if a positive value is in the register
nd, its complement is loaded into the register specified
cond operand is negative, that is, already in its complement
nd the value is loaded from the register specified in the
r specified in the first operand.

lustrates the use of the Load Negative Register instruction
a negative value in the same register.

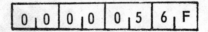

fore Execution:

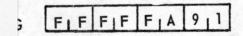

fter Execution:

| F | F | F | F | F | A | 9 | 1 |

Figure 6-59 Example of Load Negative Register instruction

Note that after the instruction has been executed, the value in BINREG has been changed from a positive number to a negative number (in two's complement form).

LOAD POSITIVE REGISTER Instruction

INSTRUCTION: LOAD POSITIVE REGISTER

OPERATION CODE: LPR

EXAMPLE: LPR 6,10

The Load Positive Register instruction loads the absolute value of the number in the register specified in the second operand into the register specified in the first operand. If the value in the register in the second operand is positive, no change occurs when the value is loaded. If the value is negative, it is complemented before being loaded into the register specified in the first operand.

LOAD COMPLEMENT REGISTER Instruction

INSTRUCTION: LOAD COMPLEMENT REGISTER

OPERATION CODE: LCR

EXAMPLE: LCR 7,6

The Load Complement Register instruction complements the value in the register specified in the second operand and loads it into the register specified in the first operand.

The Load Complement Register instruction can be used to switch signs in a register if the same register is used in both operands. The following example illustrates the use of the LCR instruction with the same register specified in the first and second operands.

EXAMPLE

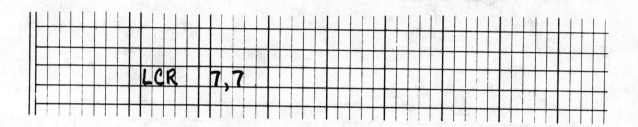

Before Execution:

Register 7 | 0 | 0 | 0 | 0 | 6 | F | A | B |

After Execution:

Register 7 | F | F | F | F | 9 | 0 | 5 | 5 |

Figure 6-60 Example of Load Complement Register instruction

Note that the positive value in register 7 has been changed to the negative value in two's complement form.

BRANCH ON CONDITION Instruction

The Branch on Condition instruction, as has been shown, is normally executed after the condition code has been set by an arithmetic, compare, or test instruction. The "branch to" operand is normally a label specified in the program.

EXAMPLE

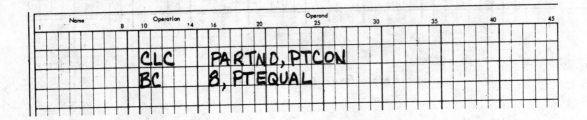

Figure 6-61 Example of Branch on Condition instruction

The example above shows a branch on equal condition instruction. If the condition code reflected an equal condition, a branch would be performed to PTEQUAL.

Another method of stating the second operand is to use the value in the location counter and a displacement to derive a "branch to" address.

EXAMPLE

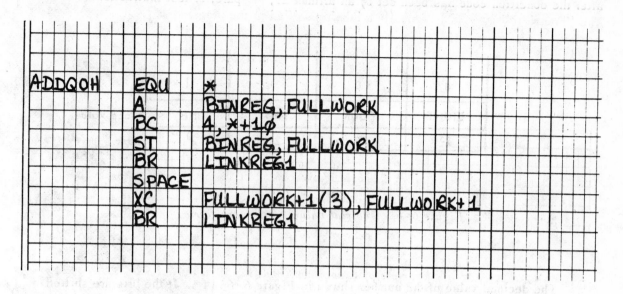

*Figure 6-62 Example of the use of the * operand*

In the example above, the add instruction sets the condition code. If the result is less than zero, a branch is desired around the next two instructions. The BC 4,*+10 instruction will branch to the XC FULLWORK+1(3),FULLWORK+1 instruction. This is calculated as shown:

$$
\begin{array}{llr}
\text{BC} & 4,*+10 & = \quad 4 \text{ bytes} \\
\text{ST} & \text{BINREG,FULLWORK} & = \quad 4 \text{ bytes} \\
\text{BR} & \text{LINKREG1} & = \quad \underline{2 \text{ bytes}} \\
& & 10 \text{ bytes}
\end{array}
$$

Therefore, the *+10 address is the next byte following the first **BR LINKREG1** instruction.

This technique is commonly used when it is desired to bypass several instructions dependent upon a condition. The programmer must be careful, however, when using this technique. The displacement in the second operand may become incorrect if another instruction is inserted between the branch instruction and the "branch to" instruction. The use of the * operand should therefore be limited to small displacements and portions of the program where change is unlikely.

SHIFT INSTRUCTIONS

In the binary number system, each position in the number is a multiple of two.

0	0	1	1	
EIGHT	FOUR	TWO	ONE	Place Value
2^3	2^2	2^1	2^0	Base

Figure 6-63 Decimal value 3 in binary format

The decimal value of the number shown in Figure 6-63 is 3. If the bits are shifted one position to the left, the decimal value becomes 6.

0	1	1	0	
EIGHT	FOUR	TWO	ONE	Place Value
2^3	2^2	2^1	2^0	Base

Figure 6-64 Decimal value 6 in binary format

Thus, by shifting the bits to the left, the decimal value of the number can be multiplied by 2, 4, 8, etc. That is, to multiply the value in a register by 2, the bits in the register would be shifted one position to the left; to multiply by 4, the bits would be shifted two positions to the left, etc.

To divide the value in a register by 2, the bits in a register could be shifted one position to the right.

A set of instructions called shift instructions are available to move bits left or right in a register.

SHIFT LEFT SINGLE LOGICAL Instruction

The SHIFT LEFT SINGLE LOGICAL instruction moves all 32 bits in a register to the left.

INSTRUCTION: SHIFT LEFT SINGLE LOGICAL

OPERATION CODE: SLL

EXAMPLE: SLL INDEXREG,2

The first operand specifies the register to be shifted and the second operand specifies the number of bit positions to shift.

The following example illustrates the use of the shift left single logical instruction to multiply the contents of a register by 4.

EXAMPLE

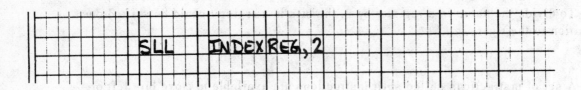

Before Execution:

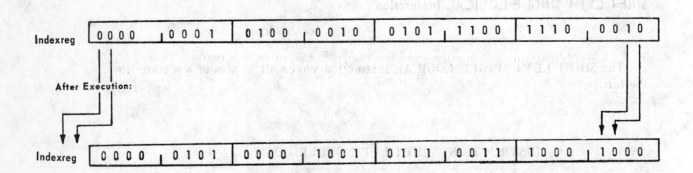

Figure 6-65 Example of Shift Left Single Logical instruction

Note that after the execution of the shift left single logical instruction all bits in the register have been shifted two positions to the left. The effect of the instruction in the example is to multiply the value in INDEXREG by 4.

SHIFT RIGHT SINGLE LOGICAL Instruction

The SHIFT RIGHT SINGLE LOGICAL instruction moves all 32 bits in a register to the right.

INSTRUCTION: SHIFT RIGHT SINGLE LOGICAL

OPERATION CODE: SRL

EXAMPLE: SRL 5,1

The first operand specifies the register to be shifted and the second operand specifies the number of bit positions to be shifted. The following example illustrates the use of the shift right single logical instruction to divide the value in a register by 2.

EXAMPLE

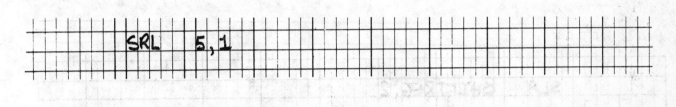

Figure 6-66 Example of Shift Right Single Logical instruction

Note that after the execution of the shift right single logical instruction all bits in the register have been shifted one position to the right. The effect of the instruction in the example is to divide the value in register 5 by 2.

SHIFT LEFT SINGLE Instruction

The SHIFT LEFT SINGLE instruction is an algebraic left shift of the data in a register. That is, the sign bit, which is the high-order bit in the register, is not disturbed by an algebraic shift. Thus, the shift left single instruction shifts bits 1-31 to the left and leaves bit 0 (high-order bit) undisturbed.

INSTRUCTION: SHIFT LEFT SINGLE

OPERATION CODE: SLA

EXAMPLE: SLA SHIFTREG,2

The first operand of the instruction specifies the register and the second operand specifies the number of bit positions to shift. The following example shows how a shift can be accomplished with the sign bit remaining the same.

EXAMPLE

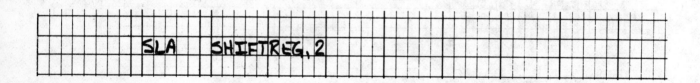

Before Execution:

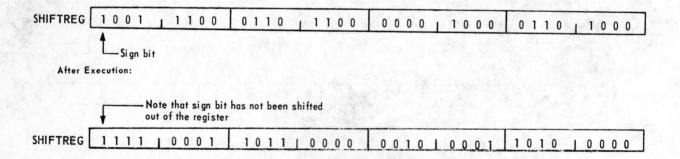

Figure 6-67 Example of Shift Left Single Algebraic instruction

The effect of the instruction in the example is to multiply the negative number in SHIFTREG by 4.

SHIFT RIGHT SINGLE Instruction

The SHIFT RIGHT SINGLE instruction is an algebraic right shift of the data in a register.

INSTRUCTION: SHIFT RIGHT SINGLE

OPERATION CODE: SRA

EXAMPLE: SRA SHIFTREG,2

The first operand is the register to be shifted and the second operand specifies the number of bit positions to be shifted.

The following example shows a right shift of a negative number:

EXAMPLE

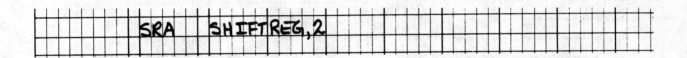

Before Execution:

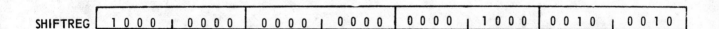

After Execution:

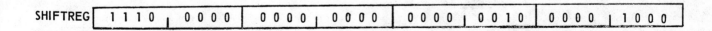

Figure 6 - 68 Example of Shift Right Single Algebraic instruction

Note that when using the shift right single instruction, the sign bit is used as the "filler" bit. Thus, bit positions 0-2 now contain the sign bit ("1"). This is because the negative number illustrated is in two's complement form.

BRANCH TABLE

In the sample program, different types of updating to the master file is done dependent upon the transaction code entered in the update transactions. One method of determining which routine should be entered to process the update is to compare the update code to constants in the program and go to the proper routine based upon an equal condition. Another method is the use of a BRANCH TABLE.

A branch table consists of a series of branch instructions.

```
BRTABLE   EQU   *
          B     ADDREC
          B     DELREC
          B     CHNGQOH
          B     CHNGQOO
          B     CHNGQRSV
          B     CHNGNA
          B     CHNGSRCE
          B     BADTYPE
          B     CHNGUNIT
```

Figure 6-69 Example of a branch table

Each branch instruction in the branch table points to the different routines to process the updates. The branch table is entered by means of an index register in a branch instruction. The following steps illustrate the method to use a branch table:

STEP 1: The input record is read. The transaction code is in the input record.

Figure 6-70 Example of GET Macro

STEP 2: The type of transaction (1-9) is packed to a double word.

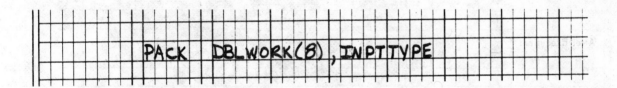

Figure 6-71 Example of Pack instruction

STEP 3: The value of the type (in the example, 4) is converted to a binary value.

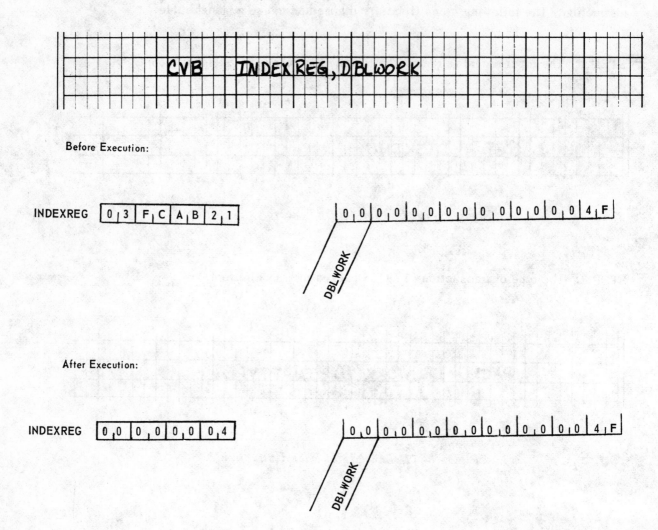

Figure 6-72 Example of Convert to Binary instruction

STEP 4: The value in INDEXREG is multiplied by 4.

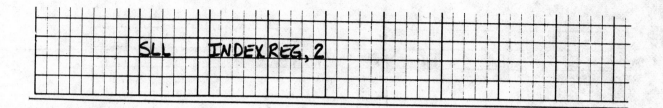

Before Execution:

INDEXREG | 0000 1 0000 | 0000 1 0000 | 0000 1 0000 | 0000 1 0100 |

After Execution:

INDEXREG | 0000 1 0000 | 0000 1 0000 | 0000 1 0000 | 0001 1 0000 |

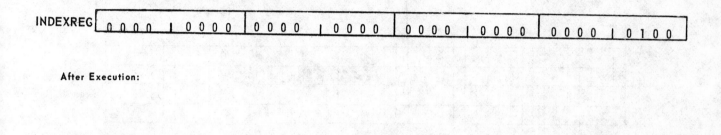

Figure 6-73 Example of SLL instruction to multiply by 2

The SHIFT LEFT LOGICAL instruction is used to multiply the contents of INDEXREG by 4. The value in INDEXREG is now 16.

STEP 5: The address of the branch table less 4 bytes is loaded into BRNCHREG.

Figure 6-74 Example of loading address of branch table into register

STEP 6: Branch to the proper entry in the branch table.

Figure 6-75 Example of branch to address in branch table

A branch is taken into the branch table. The branch address of this instruction is determined by adding the contents of the base register BRNCHREG (BRTABLE−4) plus the value in the index register INDEXREG (16) plus the displacement (0). This address is a net displacement of 12 bytes into the branch table (16-4) and the branch located at that displacement is B CHNGQOO which is the desired branch because a transaction code 4 indicates a change to the quantity on order.

It can be seen that the reason for loading the BRTABLE−4 address in step 5 is that transaction code 0 is invalid. Therefore, transaction code 1 is the first entry in the branch table. In order to get a zero displacement into the branch table for code 1, the branch table address minus 4 was loaded into BRNCHREG. Thus when the index register value of a transaction code 1 (4) is added to the address in BRNCHREG (BRTABLE−4), a zero displacement is the net result and the first branch in the table is taken for transaction code 1 (B ADDREC). If the address of BRTABLE was loaded into BRNCHREG, a dummy branch would have to be inserted in the table to insure correct displacements and this uses 4 bytes of core which do not have to be used.

SAMPLE PROGRAM

The program presented in this chapter randomly updates the inventory master file.

INPUT

The input is the inventory master file and the update transaction records. The format of the update transaction record is illustrated below.

FIELD	FIELD NAME	FORMAT	POSITION	NO. OF DIGITS	LENGTH
Part Number					
Division Number	INPTDIV	N - Z	1 - 2	2	2
Prime Number	INPTPRME	N - Z	3 - 8	6	6
Dash Number	INPTDASH	N - Z	9 - 13	5	5
Description	INPTNAME	AN	14 - 38	25	25
Qty on Hand	INPTQOH	N - Z	39 - 45	7	7
Qty on Order	INPTQOO	N - Z	46 - 52	7	7
Qty Reserved	INPTQRSV	N - Z	53 - 59	7	7
Part Number - NA					
Division - NA	IASYDIV	N - Z	60 - 61	2	2
Prime - NA	IASYPRME	N - Z	62 - 67	6	6
Dash - NA	IASYDASH	N - Z	68 - 72	5	5
Type	INPTTYPE	N - Z	73	1	1
Source	INPTSRCE	N - Z	74	1	1
Unit Price	INPTUNIT	N - Z	75 - 80	6	6

LEGEND: N - Z — Numeric, zoned-decimal   AN — Alpha-numeric

OUTPUT

The output of the sample program is an updated inventory master file and an error exception report. The format of the report is shown below.

```
INVENTORY RECORD                                                    REMARKS                    PAGE XXX
XXXXXXXXXXXXXXXXXXXXXXXXXXXXXXXXXXXXXXXXXXXXXXXXXXXXXXXXXXXXXXXXXXX  XXXXXXXXXXXXXXXXXXXXXXXXXXX XXXXXXXXXXX
END OF UPDATE PROGRAM
```

PROGRAM

The following is a listing of the program to randomly update the inventory master file.

```
000000                         2 MSTUPDAT START 0                                 UPDT0020
                               3        PRINT NOGEN.

                               5 ****
                               6 * THIS PROGRAM UPDATES THE INVENTORY MASTER FILE, WHICH IS AN   UPDT0040
                                 QUENTIAL FILE. IT UPDATES THE FILE IN THREE MAJOR WAYS -        UPDT0050
                                 )ITIONS- IT ADDS PART NUMBERS TO THE FILE.  THE ADDITION.       UPDT0060
                                     UPDATE TRANSACTIONS ARE EDITED IN THE CARD TO DISK          UPDT0070
                                     PROGRAM. THE ONLY ADDITION ERROR REPORTED OUT OF            UPDT0080
                                     THIS UPDATE IS WHEN A DUPLICATE RECORD IS ATTEMPTED         UPDT0090
                              TO BE ADDED. IF A DUPLICATE RECORD IS FOUND, THE DUPLICATE         UPDT0100
                                     IS READ AND IF IT IS A DELETED RECORD, IT IS ADDED.         UPDT0110
                              .ETIONS- ANY PART NUMBER ON THE INVENTORY FILE MAY BE              UPDT0120
                                     DELETED AT ANY TIME. ONE ERROR CAN OCCUR WITH               UPDT0130
                                     DELETIONS - THE PART NUMBER MAY NOT BE PRESENT ON           UPDT0140
                                     THE FILE.                                                   UPDT0150
                              NGES  - CHANGES CAN BE MADE TO ANY RECORD WHICH IS NOT A           UPDT0160
                                     DELETED RECORD. CHANGES CAN BE MADE TO THE                  UPDT0170
                                     FOLLOWING FIELDS - QUANTITY ON HAND, QUANTITY ON            UPDT0180
                                     ORDER, QUANTITY RESERVED, NEXT ASSEMBLY PART                UPDT0190
                                     NUMBER OR SOURCE. WHENEVER A CHANGE IS MADE TO              UPDT0200
                                     QUANTITY ON HAND, A CHANGE IS AUTOMATICALLY MADE            UPDT0210
                                     TO EITHER THE QUANTITY ON ORDER (IT IS DECREASED IF         UPDT0220
                                     THE QUANTITY ON HAND IS INCREASED) OR THE QUANTITY          UPDT0230
                                     RESERVED (IT IS DECREASED IF THE QUANTITY ON HAND           UPDT0240
                                     IS DECREASED).                                              UPDT0250
                                                                                                 UPDT0260
                              ODES IN THE TYPE FIELD TO UPDATE THE FILE ARE -                    UPDT0270
                                                                                                 UPDT0280
                              ADD A RECORD                                                       UPDT0290
                              DELETE A RECORD                                                    UPDT0300
                              CHANGE QUANTITY ON HAND                                            UPDT0310
                              CHANGE QUANTITY ON ORDER                                           UPDT0320
                              CHANGE QUANTITY RESERVED                                           UPDT0330
                              CHANGE NEXT ASSEMBLY NUMBER                                        UPDT0340
                              CHANGE SOURCE                                                      UPDT0350
                              CHANGE UNIT PRICE                                                  UPDT0360
                              ENTRIES IN THE TYPE FIELD ARE INVALID IN THE UPDATE                UPDT0370
                              NS.                                                                UPDT0380
                                                                                                 UPDT0390
                                                                                                 UPDT0400
                                                                                                 UPDT0410
                              SAGE FOR THIS PROGRAM IS AS FOLLOWS                                UPDT0420
                                                                                                 UPDT0430
                                  12                        FIRST BASE REGISTER                  UPDT0440
                                  10                        PRINTER I/O REGISTER                 UPDT0450
                                   9                        DISK INPUT REGISTER                  UPDT0460
                                   8                        DISK OUTPUT REGISTER                 UPDT0470
                                  14                                                             UPDT0480
                                   7                                                             UPDT0490
                                   6                                                             UPDT0500
                                   7                                                             UPDT0510
                                   6                                                             UPDT0520
                                   5                                                             UPDT0530
                                                                                                 UPDT0540
                                                                                                 UPDT0550
                                                                                                 UPDT0560
                                                                                                 UPDT0570

                            R BASEREG1,0              ESTABLISH FIRST BASE REGISTER              UPDT0590
                            NG *,BASEREG1                                                        UPDT0600

                            N PRTFLE,DISKIN,INVMSTR   OPEN FILES                                 UPDT0620
                                  LINKRG14,HEADROU     GO TO PRINT EXCEPTION REPORT HEADER       UPDT0630

                                                                                                 UPDT0650
                            .NE IS ENTERED TO READ THE TRANSACTION FILE AND GO TO THE            UPDT0660
                            )CESSING ROUTINE DEPENDENT UPON THE TYPE CODE ENTERED                UPDT0670
                            .SACTION RECORD.                                                     UPDT0680
                                                                                                 UPDT0690

                            IG INPTDUMY,INPUTREG      USING FOR DISK INPUT AREA                  UPDT0710
                            IG PRTDUMY,PRINTREG       USING FOR PRINTER AREA                     UPDT0720

                               DISKIN                 READ TRANSACTION FILE                      UPDT0740

                            DBLWORD(8),INPTTYPE PACK TYPE TO DOUBLE WORD                         UPDT0760
                            INDEXREG,DBLWORD    CONVERT TYPE TO BINARY                           UPDT0770
                            INDEXREG,2         MULTIPLY BY 4                                     UPDT0780
                            BRNCHREG,BRTABLE-4  LOAD ADDRESS OF BRANCH TABLE                     UPDT0790
                            0(INDEXREG,BRNCHREG) GO TO PROPER ENTRY IN BRANCH TABLE              UPDT0800

                                                                                                 UPDT0820
                            .NG IS THE BRANCH TABLE TO GO TO THE PROPER ROUTINE TO               UPDT0830
```

```
                                     98 * PROCESS THE INPUT RECORD                                  UPDT0840
                                     99 ****                                                        UPDT0850

000040                              101 BRTABLE  EQU   *                                            UPDT0870
000040 47F0 C062           00064    102          B     ADDREC         GO TO ADD A RECORD            UPDT0880
000044 47F0 C25A           0025C    103          B     DELREC         GO TO DELETE A RECORD         UPDT0890
000048 47F0 C26E           00270    104          B     CHNGQOH        GO TO CHANGE QUANTITY ON HAND UPDT0900
00004C 47F0 C2F6           002F8    105          B     CHNGQOO        GO TO CHANGE QUANTITY ON ORDER UPDT0910
000050 47F0 C324           00326    106          B     CHNGQRSV       GO TO CHANGE QUANTITY RESERVED UPDT0920
000054 47F0 C352           00354    107          B     CHNGNA         GO TO CHANGE NEXT ASSEMBLY    UPDT0930
000058 47F0 C362           0C364    108          B     CHNGSRCE       GO TO CHANGE SOURCE           UPDT0940
00005C 47F0 C374           00376    109          B     BADTYPE        IF TYPE = 8,IT IS IN ERROR    UPDT0950
000060 47F0 C37E           00380    110          B     CHNGUNIT       GO TO CHANGE UNIT PRICE       UPDT0960


                                    112 ****                                                        UPDT0980
                                    113 * THE FOLLOWING ROUTINE IS ENTERED TO ADD RECORDS TO THE EXISTING FILE- UPDT0990
                                    114 * RECORDS MAY NOT BE ADDED WHICH ARE ALREADY ACTIVE RECORDS ON THE     UPDT1000
                                    115 * FILE - HOWEVER, IF AN ADD IS ATTEMPTED TO A DELETED RECORD ON THE    UPDT1010
                                    116 * FILE, IT WILL BE ADDED.                                   UPDT1020
                                    117 ****                                                        UPDT1030

000064                              119 ADDREC   EQU   *                                            UPDT1050
000064 4560 C100           00102    120          BAL   LINKREG2,GETBIKEY   GO TO CONVERT KEY TO BINARY  UPDT1060
000068 D206 C488 C4BF 0048A 004C1   121          MVC   MSTRDIV(7),DISKEY   MOVE KEY TO OUTPUT AREA      UPDT1070

00006E D218 C48F 900D 00491 0000D   123          MVC   MSTRNAME(25),INPTNAME MOVE NAME TO OUTPUT   UPDT1090
000074 4570 C0D8           000DA    124          BAL   LINKREG1,GETQOH     GO TO GET QUANTITY ON HAND UPDT1100
000078 D202 C4A8 C45B 004AA 0045D   125          MVC   MSTRQOH(3),BINSTORE+1 MOVE QOH TO OUTPUT    UPDT1110

00007E 4570 C0E2           000E4    127          BAL   LINKREG1,GETQOO     GO TO GET QUANTITY ON ORDER UPDT1130
000082 D202 C4AB C45B 004AD 0045D   128          MVC   MSTRQOO(3),BINSTORE+1 MOVE QTY ON ORDER TO OUTPUT UPDT1140

000088 4570 C0EC           000EE    130          BAL   LINKREG1,GETQRSV    GO TO GET QUANTITY ON RESERVE UPDT1160
00008C D202 C4AE C45B 004B0 0045D   131          MVC   MSTRQRSV(3),BINSTORE+1 MOVE RESERVED QTY TO OUTPUT UPDT1170

000092 4560 C132           00134    133          BAL   LINKREG2,GETNA      GO TO GET NEXT ASSEMBLY NUMBER UPDT1190

000096 4570 C0F6           000F8    135          BAL   LINKREG1,GETUNIT    GO TO GET UNIT PRICE      UPDT1210
00009A D202 C4BA C45B 004BC 0045D   136          MVC   MSTRUNIT(3),BINSTORE+1 MOVE UNIT PRICE TO MASTER UPDT1220

0000A0 92F1 C4B8           004B8    138          MVI   MSTRTYPE,C'1'       SET TYPE CODE TO ACTIVE RECORD UPDT1240
0000A4 D200 C4B9 9049 004BB 00049   139          MVC   MSTRSRCE(1),INPTSRCE MOVE SOURCE TO OUTPUT  UPDT1250
0000AA D201 C4BD C45E 004BF 00460   140          MVC   MSTRXTRA(2),BLANKS   MOVE FILLER BLANKS TO OUTPUT UPDT1260


                                    142 ****                                                        UPDT1280
                                    143 * AT THIS POINT, THE NEW RECORD WILL BE WRITTEN TO THE DISK UPDT1290
                                    144 ****                                                        UPDT1300
0000B0 D236 C518 C488 0051A 0048A   145          MVC   SAVEREC,ISWORK      SAVE REC IN CASE OF DUPLICATE UPDT1310
                                    146          WRITE INVMSTR,NEWKEY      WRITE THE NEW RECORD     UPDT1320

0000CE 91FE C6DC           006DE    152          WAITF INVMSTR             WAIT FOR I/O COMPLETION  UPDT1340
0000D2 4780 C01C           0001E    157          TM    INVMSTRC,X'FE'      ANY ERRORS               UPDT1350
0000D6 47F0 C16E           00170    158          BZ    READINPT            NO, READ NEXT RECORD     UPDT1360
                                    159          B     ADDERROR            YES, GO TO CHECK ERROR   UPDT1370
                                    160 ****                                                        UPDT1380
                                    161 * THESE ROUTINES ARE ENTERED TO PACK THE DESIRED FIELDS TO A UPDT1390
                                    162 * DOUBLEWORD AND GO TO THE CONVERT TO BINARY ROUTINE        UPDT1400
                                    163 ****                                                        UPDT1410

                                    165 *                                                           UPDT1430
                                    166 * QUANTITY ON HAND                                          UPDT1440
                                    167 *                                                           UPDT1450

0000DA                              169 GETQOH   EQU   *                                            UPDT1470
0000DA F276 C44E 9026 00450 00026   170          PACK  DBLWORK(8),INPTQOH(7) PACK QUANTITY ON HAND UPDT1480
0000E0 47F0 C164           00166    171          B     CONVERT             GO TO CONVERT TO BINARY  UPDT1490

                                    173 *                                                           UPDT1510
                                    174 * QUANTITY ON ORDER                                         UPDT1520
                                    175 *                                                           UPDT1530

0000E4                              177 GETQOO   EQU   *                                            UPDT1550
0000E4 F276 C44E 902D 00450 0002D   178          PACK  DBLWORK(8),INPTQOO(7) PACK QUANTITY ON ORDER UPDT1560
0000EA 47F0 C164           00166    179          B     CONVERT             GO TO CONVERT TO BINARY  UPDT1570

                                    181 *                                                           UPDT1590
                                    182 * QUANTITY ON RESERVE                                       UPDT1600
                                    183 *                                                           UPDT1610

0000EE                              185 GETQRSV  EQU   *                                            UPDT1630
0000EE F276 C44E 9034 00450 00034   186          PACK  DBLWORK(8),INPTQRSV(7) PACK QUANTITY RESERVED UPDT1640
0000F4 47F0 C164           00166    187          B     CONVERT             GO TO CONVERT TO BINARY  UPDT1650

                                    189 *                                                           UPDT1670
                                    190 * UNIT PRICE                                                UPDT1680
```

```
                               191 *                                                             UPDT1690
0000F8                         193 GETUNIT  EQU    *                                             UPDT1710
0000F8 F275 C44E 904A 00450 0004A  194          PACK  DBLWORK(8),INPTUNIT(6) PACK UNIT PRICE     UPDT1720
0000FE 47F0 C164         00166  195          B     CONVERT         GO TO CONVERT TO BINARY       UPDT1730


                               197 ****                                                          UPDT1750
                               198 * THE FOLLOWING ROUTINE IS ENTERED TO CONVERT THE KEY TO BINARY. AFTER  UPDT1760
                               199 * IT IS CONVERTED, IT IS STORED IN THE KEYARG FIELD(DISKEY).  UPDT1770
                               200 ****                                                          UPDT1780


000102                         202 GETBIKEY EQU    *                                             UPDT1800
000102 F271 C44E 9000 00450 00000  203          PACK  DBLWORK(8),INPTDIV(2) PACK DIVISION        UPDT1810
000108 4570 C164         00166  204          BAL   LINKREG1,CONVERT  GO TO CONVERT TO BINARY     UPDT1820
00010C D200 C4BF C450 004C1 0045F  205          MVC   DISKKEY(1),BINSTORE+3 MOVE DIVISION TO KEY AREA UPDT1830

000112 F275 C44E 9002 00450 00002  207          PACK  DBLWORK(8),INPTPRME(6) PACK PRIME NUMBER   UPDT1850
000118 4570 C164         00166  208          BAL   LINKREG1,CONVERT  GO TO CONVERT TO BINARY     UPDT1860
00011C D202 C4C0 C45B 004C2 0045B  209          MVC   DISKEY+1(3),BINSTORE+1  MOVE TO KEY AREA   UPDT1870

000122 F274 C44E 9008 00450 00008  211          PACK  DBLWORK(8),INPTDASH(5) PACK DASH NUMBER    UPDT1890
000128 4570 C164         00166  212          BAL   LINKREG1,CONVERT  GO TO CONVERT TO BINARY     UPDT1900
00012C D202 C4C3 C45B 004C5 0045D  213          MVC   DISKEY+4(3),BINSTORE+1 MOVE TO KEY AREA    UPDT1910

000132 07F6                    215          BR    LINKREG2          RETURN TO CALLER             UPDT1930


                               217 ****                                                          UPDT1950
                               218 * THIS ROUTINE IS ENTERED TO CONVERT THE NEXT ASSEMBLY NUMBER UPDT1960
                               219 * TO BINARY                                                   UPDT1970
                               220 ****                                                          UPDT1980


000134                         222 GETNA    EQU    *                                             UPDT2000
000134 F271 C44E 903B 00450 0003B  223          PACK  DBLWORK(8),IASYDIV(2) PACK DIVISION NUMBER UPDT2010
00013A 4570 C164         00166  224          BAL   LINKREG1,CONVERT  GO TO CONVERT TO BINARY     UPDT2020
00013E D200 C4B1 C45D 004B3 0045F  225          MVC   MASYDIV(1),BINSTORE+3 MOVE DIVISION TO OUTPUT UPDT2030

000144 F275 C44E 903D 00450 0003D  227          PACK  DBLWORK(8),IASYPRME(6)  PACK PRIME - NEXT ASSEMBLY UPDT2050
00014A 4570 C164         00166  228          BAL   LINKREG1,CONVERT  GO TO CONVERT TO BINARY     UPDT2060
00014E D202 C4B2 C45B 004B4 0045D  229          MVC   MASYPRME(3),BINSTORE+1 MOVE PRIME TO OUTPUT UPDT2070

000154 F274 C44E 9043 00450 00043  231          PACK  DBLWORK(8),IASYDASH(5) PACK DASH - NEXT ASSEMBLY UPDT2090
00015A 4570 C164         00166  232          BAL   LINKREG1,CONVERT  GO TO CONVERT TO BINARY     UPDT2100
00015E D202 C4B5 C45B 004B7 0045D  233          MVC   MASYDASH(3),BINSTORE+1 MOVE DASH TO OUTPUT UPDT2110

000164 07F6                    235          BR    LINKREG2          RETURN TO CALLER             UPDT2130


                               237 ****                                                          UPDT2150
                               238 * THIS ROUTINE IS ENTERED TO CONVERT PACKED DATA TO BINARY    UPDT2160
                               239 ****                                                          UPDT2170


000166                         241 CONVERT  EQU    *                                             UPDT2190
000166 4F50 C44E         00450  242          CVB   BINREG,DBLWORK    CONVERT DATA TO BINARY      UPDT2200
00016A 5050 C45A         0045C  243          ST    BINREG,BINSTORE   STORE RESULTS IN CORE       UPDT2210
00016E 07F7                    244          BR    LINKREG1          RETURN TO CALLER             UPDT2220


                               246 ****                                                          UPDT2240
                               247 * THIS ROUTINE IS ENTERED WHEN AN ERROR OCCURS IN THE ADD FUNCTION  UPDT2250
                               248 ****                                                          UPDT2260


000170                         250 ADDERROR EQU    *                                             UPDT2280
000170 9180 C6DC        006DE  251          TM    INVMSTRC,X'80'    WAS IT AN INCORRECTABLE ERROR UPDT2290
000174 4710 C192        00194  252          BO    CANERROR          YES, GO TO WRITE MSG AND CANCEL PGM UPDT2300
000178 9140 C6DC        006DE  253          TM    INVMSTRC,X'40'    WAS IT A WRONG LENGTH REC. ERROR UPDT2310
00017C 4710 C1D0        001D2  254          BO    NOTEERROR         YES, GO TO WRITE MSG AND CONTINUE UPDT2320
000180 9104 C6DC        006DE  255          TM    INVMSTRC,X'04'    WAS IT A DUPLICATE KEY ERROR UPDT2330
000184 4710 C1E4        001E6  256          BO    DUPKEY            YES, GO TO SEE IF REC IS DELETED UPDT2340
000188 9102 C6DC        006DE  257          TM    INVMSTRC,X'02'    ARE OVERFLOW AREAS FULL      UPDT2350
00018C 4710 C192        00194  258          BO    CANERROR          YES, GO TO WRITE MSG AND CANCEL PGM UPDT2360
000190 47F0 C192        00194  259          B     CANERROR          ANY OTHER ERROR CAUSES PGM TO CANCEL UPDT2370


                               261 ****                                                          UPDT2390
                               262 * THIS ROUTINE IS ENTERED WHEN AN UNCORRECTABLE ERROR OCCURS. A MESSAGE UPDT2400
                               263 * IS WRITTEN ON THE PRINTER AND THE JOB IS CANCELLED.         UPDT2410
                               264 ****                                                          UPDT2420


000194                         266 CANERROR EQU    *                                             UPDT2440
000194 4570 C394        00396  267          BAL   LINKREG1,TRBYTE   GO TO TRANSLATE ERROR BYTE   UPDT2450
000198 D201 C4CD C4EE 004CF 004F0  268          MVC   CANCBYTE(2),BADBYTE MOVE ERROR BYTE TO MESSAGE UPDT2460
00019E D225 A052 C4C6 00052 004C8  269          MVC   ERRORPT(38),CANCMSG MOVE CANCEL MSG TO I/O AREA UPDT2470
```

```
      LOC  OBJECT CODE    ADDR1 ADDR2  STMT   SOURCE STATEMENT                                   DOS CL3-5 08/26/70
    0001A4 96F0 C1C9         001CB      270         OI    CANCBR+1,X'F0'      SET SWITCH TO CANCEL PROGRAM       UPDT2480


                                        272 ****                                                                 UPDT2500
                                        273 * THE FOLLOWING ROUTINE IS ENTERED TO PRINT THE ERROR MESSAGE ON THE UPDT2510
                                        274 * PRINTER.                                                           UPDT2520
                                        275 ****                                                                 UPDT2530


    0001A8                              277 PRINTIT EQU   *                                                      UPDT2550
    0001A8 D24F A000 9000 00000 00000   278         MVC   RECORDPT(80),INPTDIV  MOVE INPUT RECORD TO REPORT      UPDT2560
                                        279         PUT   PRTFLE                PRINT ERROR MESSAGE              UPDT2570

                                        285         PRTOV PRTFLE,12,HEADROU     IF PAGE OVERFLOW PRINT HEADER    UPDT2590
    0001CA 4700 C408         0040A      292 CANCBR  BC    0,ENDINPUT          IF SWITCH SET, GO TO CANCEL PROGRAM UPDT2610
    0001CE 47F0 C01C         0001E      293         B     READINPT            GO TO READ NEXT INPUT RECORD       UPDT2620


                                        295 ****                                                                 UPDT2640
                                        296 * THIS ROUTINE IS ENTERED IF THE ERROR IS NOT A CANCEL ERROR         UPDT2650
                                        297 ****                                                                 UPDT2660


    0001D2                              299 NOTEEROR EQU  *                                                      UPDT2680
    0001D2 4570 C394         00396      300         BAL   LINKREG1,TRBYTE      GO TO TRANSLATE ERROR BYTE        UPDT2690
    0001D6 D201 C4F7 C4EE 004F9 004F0   301         MVC   NOTEBYTE(2),BADBYTE MOVE ERROR BYTE TO MESSAGE         UPDT2700
    0001DC D225 A052 C4F0 00052 004F7   302 MOVEMSG MVC   ERRORPT(38),NOTEMSG MOVE MSG TO I/O AREA               UPDT2710
    0001E2 47F0 C1A6         001A8      303         B     PRINTIT             GO TO PRINT MESSAGE                UPDT2720


                                        305 ****                                                                 UPDT2740
                                        306 * THIS ROUTINE IS ENTERED IF AN ADD IS ATTEMPTED AND A RECORD WITH A UPDT2750
                                        307 * DUPLICATE KEY IS ALREADY ON THE FILE. IT RETRIEVES THE RECORD ON THE UPDT2760
                                        308 * FILE AND CHECKS IF IT IS A DELETED RECORD. IF SO, IT REPLACES THE  UPDT2770
                                        309 * DELETED RECORD WITH THE NEW RECORD. IF NOT, AN ERROR MESSAGE IS    UPDT2780
                                        310 * PRINTED                                                            UPDT2790
                                        311 ****                                                                 UPDT2800


    0001E6                              313 DUPKEY  EQU   *                                                      UPDT2820
    0001E6 D206 C48F C518 004C1 0051A   314         MVC   DISKEY(7),SAVEREC    MOVE KEY TO KEY AREA              UPDT2830
    0001EC 4570 C20E         00210      315         BAL   LINKREG1,READREC     GO TO READ THE DUPLICATE RECORD   UPDT2840
    0001F0 95F2 C488         004BA      316         CLI   MSTRTYPE,C'2'        IS IT A DELETED RECORD            UPDT2850
    0001F4 4780 C200         00202      317         BE    REWRITE             YES, GO TO PUT NEW RECORD ON FILE  UPDT2860

    0001F8 D201 C4F7 C54F 004F9 00551   319         MVC   NOTEBYTE(2),ZERO4   NO, MOVE DUPLICATE RECORD INDICATOR UPDT2880
    0001FE 47F0 C1DA         001DC      320         B     MOVEMSG             TO MESSAGE - GO TO WRITE MESSAGE   UPDT2890


    000202                              322 REWRITE EQU   *                                                      UPDT2910
    000202 D236 C488 C518 0048A 0051A   323         MVC   ISWORK(55),SAVEREC  MOVE NEW RECORD TO WORK AREA       UPDT2920
    000208 4570 C238         0023A      324         BAL   LINKREG1,WRITEREC   GO TO WRITE THE RECORD             UPDT2930
    00020C 47F0 C01C         0001E      325         B     READINPT            GO TO READ NEXT INPUT RECORD       UPDT2940


                                        327 ****                                                                 UPDT2960
                                        328 * THIS ROUTINE IS ENTERED WHEN A RETRIEVAL FUNCTION IS DESIRED - THAT UPDT2970
                                        329 * IS, A RANDOM READ OF THE MASTER FILE. IT IS ASSUMED THAT THE DESIRED UPDT2980
                                        330 * KEY HAS BEEN MOVED TO THE KEYARG AREA (DISKEY).                    UPDT2990
                                        331 ****                                                                 UPDT3000


    000210                              333 READREC EQU   *                                                      UPDT3020
                                        334         READ  INVMSTR,KEY         READ THE FILE                      UPDT3030

                                        340         WAITF INVMSTR             WAIT FOR SUCCESSFUL COMPLETION     UPDT3050

    000228 91FF C6DC         006DE      346         TM    INVMSTRC,X'FF'      ANY ERRORS                         UPDT3070
    00022C 0787                         347         BCR   8,LINKREG1          NO, RETURN TO CALLER               UPDT3080

    00022E 9110 C6DC         006DE      349         TM    INVMSTRC,X'10'      WAS THE RECORD FOUND               UPDT3100
    000232 4710 C1D0         001D2      350         BO    NOTEEROR            NO, GO TO PRINT MSG AND READ NEXT  UPDT3110
                                        351 *                                 INPUT RECORD                      UPDT3120
    000236 47F0 C192         00194      352         B     CANERROR            ON ANY OTHER ERROR, CANCEL PROGRAM UPDT3130


                                        354 ****                                                                 UPDT3150
                                        355 * THIS ROUTINE IS ENTERED WHEN THE UPDATED RECORD IS TO BE RETURNED  UPDT3160
                                        356 * TO THE FILE. IT IS A WRITE OF THE RECORD RETRIEVED IN THE          UPDT3170
                                        357 * READ REC ROUTINE.                                                 UPDT3180
                                        358 ****                                                                 UPDT3190


    00023A                              360 WRITEREC EQU  *                                                      UPDT3210
                                        361         WRITE INVMSTR,KEY         WRITE RECORD                       UPDT3220

                                        367         WAITF INVMSTR             WAIT FOR I/O COMPLETION            UPDT3240
```

```
000252 91FE C6DC   006DE      373        TM    INVMSTRC,X'FE'      ARE THERE ANY ERRORS         UPDT3260
000256 0787                   374        HCR   8,LINKREG1          NO, RETURN TO CALLER         UPDT3270

000258 47F0 C192        00194 376        B     CANERROR           IF ERROR ON WRITE, CANCEL PGM UPDT3290


                              378 ****                                                         UPDT3310
                              379 * THIS ROUTINE IS ENTERED TO DELETE A RECORD ON THE INVENTORY FILE- UPDT3320
                              380 * THE RECORD IS READ AND A 2 IS MOVED TO THE TYPE CODE, THEN THE    UPDT3330
                              381 * RECORD IS RE-WRITTEN.                                             UPDT3340
                              382 ****                                                         UPDT3350


00025C                        384 DELREC   EQU  *                                             UPDT3370
00025C 4560 C100        00102 385        BAL   LINKREG2,GETBIKEY   GO TO CONVERT KEY TO BINARY  UPDT3380
000260 4570 C20E        00210 386        BAL   LINKREG1,READREC    GO TO READ THE RECORD        UPDT3390
000264 92F2 C4B8   004BA      387        MVI   MSTRTYPE,C'2'       MOVE 2 TO SHOW RECORD IS DELETED UPDT3400
000268 4570 C238        0023A 388        BAL   LINKREG1,WRITEREC   GO TO WRITE THE RECORD       UPDT3410
00026C 47F0 C01C        0001E 389        B     READINPT           GO TO READ THE NEXT RECORD   UPDT3420


                              391 ****                                                         UPDT3440
                              392 * THIS ROUTINE IS ENTERED TO CHANGE THE QUANTITY ON HAND.  IF THE   UPDT3450
                              393 * QUANTITY ON HAND IS INCREASED, THE QUANTITY ON ORDER IS DECREASED  UPDT3460
                              394 * BY THE SMAE AMOUNT BECAUSE THE ORDER FOR THE INCREASE HAS BEEN     UPDT3470
                              395 * FILLED.  IF THE AMOUNT INCREASED IS GREATER THAN THE QTY ORDERED, THE UPDT3480
                              396 * QTY ON ORDER IS MADE ZERO.  IF THE QTY ON HAND IS DECREASED, THE    UPDT3490
                              397 * QTY RESERVED IS DECREASED ALSO BECAUSE RESERVED ORDERS ARE FILLED   UPDT3500
                              398 * FIRST.                                                     UPDT3510
                              399 ****                                                         UPDT3520


000270                        401 CHNGQOH  EQU  *                                             UPDT3540
000270 4560 C100        00102 402        BAL   LINKREG2,GETBIKEY   GO TO CONVERT KEY TO BINARY  UPDT3550
000274 4570 C20E        00210 403        BAL   LINKREG1,READREC    GO TO READ THE RECORD        UPDT3560

000278 D703 C456 C456 00458 0045B 405    XC    FULLWORK,FULLWORK   ZERO FULLWORD WORK AREA      UPDT3580
00027E 4570 C0D8        000DA 406        BAL   LINKREG1,GETQOH     GO TO GET QTY ON HAND TO BINARY UPDT3590
000282 D202 C457 C4A8 00459 004AA 407    MVC   FULLWORK+1(3),MSTRQOH MOVE QTY ON HAND TO WORK AREA UPDT3600
000288 5A50 C456        00458 408        A     BINREG,FULLWORK     ADD QTY ON HAND TO NEW CHANGE UPDT3610
00028C 4740 C2EC        002EE 409        BC    4,BADQOH           IF THE RESULT IS LESS THAN ZERO, UPDT3620
                              410 *                             THE INPUT IS INCORRECT        UPDT3630
000290 5050 C456        00458 411        ST    BINREG,FULLWORK     STORE RESULT INTO FULLWORD   UPDT3640
000294 D202 C4A8 C457 004AA 00459 412    MVC   MSTRQOH(3),FULLWORK+1 MOVE RESULT TO MASTER OUTPUT UPDT3650
00029A D703 C456 C456 00458 0045B 413    XC    FULLWORK,FULLWORK   ZERO WORK AREA               UPDT3660
0002A0 5850 C45A        0045C 414        L     BINREG,BINSTORE     LOAD CHANGE VALUE TO REGISTER UPDT3670
0002A4 1255                   415        LTR   BINREG,BINREG       IS VALUE NEGATIVE            UPDT3680
0002A6 4740 C2C2        002C4 416        BC    4,RSVALTER         YES, GO TO CHANGE RESERVATION UPDT3690

0002AA D202 C457 C4AB 00459 004AD 418    MVC   FULLWORK+1(3),MSTRQOO MOVE QTY ON ORDER TO WORK AREA UPDT3710
0002B0 1155                   419        LNR   BINREG,BINREG       SWITCH SIGN TO NEGATIVE      UPDT3720
0002B2 4570 C2D6        002D8 420        BAL   LINKREG1,ADDQOH     GO TO DO THE ADDITION (SUBTRACTION) UPDT3730
0002B6 D202 C4AB C457 004AD 00459 421    MVC   MSTRQOO(3),FULLWORK+1 MOVE ANSWER TO QTY ON HAND UPDT3740


0002BC                        423 QOHDONE  EQU  *                                             UPDT3760
0002BC 4570 C238        0023A 424        BAL   LINKREG1,WRITEREC   GO TO WRITE RECORD           UPDT3770
0002C0 47F0 C01C        0001E 425        B     READINPT           GO TO READ NEXT UPDATE RECORD UPDT3780


0002C4                        427 RSVALTER EQU  *                                             UPDT3800
0002C4 D202 C457 C4AE 00459 004B0 428    MVC   FULLWORK+1(3),MSTRQRSV MOVE RESERVED QTY TO WORK AREA UPDT3810
0002CA 4570 C2D6        002D8 429        BAL   LINKREG1,ADDQOH     GO TO DO ADDTITION (SUBTRACTION) UPDT3820
0002CE D202 C4AE C457 004B0 00459 430    MVC   MSTRQRSV(3),FULLWORK+1 MOVE ANSWER TO QTY RESERVED UPDT3830
0002D4 47F0 C28A        0028C 431        B     QOHDONE            GO TO WRITE MASTER           UPDT3840


0002D8                        433 ADDQOH   EQU  *                                             UPDT3860
0002D8 5A50 C456        00458 434        A     BINREG,FULLWORK     ADD (SUBTRACT) CHANGED QTY   UPDT3870
0002DC 4740 C2E4        002E6 435        BC    4,*+10             IF RESULT IS LESS THAN 0,GO TO MOVE UPDT3880
0002E0 5050 C456        00458 436        ST    BINREG,FULLWORK     ZERO TO THE FIELD - STORE FIELD UPDT3890
0002E4 07F7                   437        BR    LINKREG1           RETURN TO CALLER             UPDT3900

0002E6 D702 C457 C457 00459 00459 439    XC    FULLWORK+1(3),FULLWORK+1 ZERO WORK AREA         UPDT3920
0002EC 07F7                   440        BR    LINKREG1           RETURN TO CALLER             UPDT3930


0002EE                        442 BADQOH   EQU  *                                             UPDT3950
0002EE D225 A052 C5B3 00052 005B5 443    MVC   ERRORPT(38),BADQMSG MOVE MSG TO I/O AREA        UPDT3960
0002F4 47F0 C1A6        001A8 444        B     PRINTIT            GO TO PRINT ERROR MESSAGE    UPDT3970


                              446 ****                                                         UPDT3990
                              447 * THIS ROUTINE IS ENTERED TO CHANGE THE QUANTITY ON ORDER.  UPDT4000
                              448 ****                                                         UPDT4010


0002F8                        450 CHNGQOO  EQU  *                                             UPDT4030
0002F8 4560 C100        00102 451        BAL   LINKREG2,GETBIKEY   GO TO CONVERT TO BINARY      UPDT4040
0002FC 4570 C20E        00210 452        BAL   LINKREG1,READREC    GO TO READ THE RECORD        UPDT4050
```

```
   LOC  OBJECT CODE    ADDR1 ADDR2  STMT   SOURCE STATEMENT                                   DOS CL3-5 08/26/70

 000300 D703 C456 C456 00458 00458   454        XC    FULLWORK,FULLWORK    ZERO WORK AREA                UPDT4070
 000306 4570 C0E2           000E4    455        BAL   LINKREG1,GETQOO      GET QTY ON ORDER TO BINARY    UPDT4080
 00030A D202 C457 C4AB 00459 004AD   456        MVC   FULLWORK+1(3),MSTRQOO MOVE QTY ON ORD TO WORK AREA UPDT4090
 000310 5A50 C456           00458    457        A     BINREG,FULLWORK      ADD CHANGE TO QTY ON ORDER    UPDT4100
 000314 4740 C2EC           002EE    458        BC    4,BADQOH            IF LESS THAN ZERO, GO TO ERROR ROUT UPDT4110
 000318 5050 C456           00458    459        ST    BINREG,FULLWORK      STORE ANSWER IN FULLWORD      UPDT4120
 00031C D202 C4AB C457 004AD 00459   460        MVC   MSTRQOO(3),FULLWORK+1 MOVE ANSWER TO MASTER        UPDT4130
 000322 47F0 C2BA           002BC    461        B     QOHDONE             GO TO WRITE MASTER            UPDT4140


                                     463  ****                                                          UPDT4160
                                     464  * THIS ROUTINE IS ENTERED TO CHANGE THE QUANTITY RESERVED ON THE UPDT4170
                                     465  * MASTER FILE                                                  UPDT4180
                                     466  ****                                                          UPDT4190


 000326                              468  CHNGQRSV EQU  *                                                UPDT4210
 000326 4560 C100           00102    469        BAL   LINKREG2,GETBIKEY   GO TO CONVERT KEY TO BINARY   UPDT4220
 00032A 4570 C20E           00210    470        BAL   LINKREG1,READREC    GO TO READ THE RECORD         UPDT4230

 00032E D703 C456 C456 00458 00458   472        XC    FULLWORK,FULLWORK    ZERO WORK AREA                UPDT4250
 000334 4570 C0EC           000EE    473        BAL   LINKREG1,GETQRSV    GET QTY RESERVED TO BINARY    UPDT4260
 000338 D202 C457 C4AE 00459 004B0   474        MVC   FULLWORK+1(3),MSTRQRSV MOVE QTY RESERVED TO WORK AREA UPDT4270
 00033E 5A50 C456           00459    475        A     BINREG,FULLWORK      ADD CHANGE TO QTY RESERVED    UPDT4280
 000342 4740 C2EC           002EE    476        BC    4,BADQOH            IF LESS THAN ZERO, GO TO ERROR ROUT UPDT4290
 000346 5050 C456           00458    477        ST    BINREG,FULLWORK      STORE ANSWER                  UPDT4300
 00034A D202 C4AE C457 004B0 00459   478        MVC   MSTRQRSV(3),FULLWORK+1 MOVE ANSWER TO MASTER       UPDT4310
 000350 47F0 C2BA           002BC    479        B     QOHDONE             GO TO WRITE UPDATED MASTER RECORD UPDT4320


                                     481  ****                                                          UPDT4340
                                     482  * THIS ROUTINE IS ENTERED TO CHANGE THE NEXT ASSEMBLY NUMBER  UPDT4350
                                     483  ****                                                          UPDT4360


 000354                              485  CHNGNA   EQU  *                                                UPDT4380
 000354 4560 C100           00102    486        BAL   LINKREG2,GETBIKEY   GO TO CONVERT KEY TO BINARY   UPDT4390
 000358 4570 C20E           00210    487        BAL   LINKREG1,READREC    GO TO READ RECORD             UPDT4400
 00035C 4560 C132           00134    488        BAL   LINKREG2,GETNA      GO TO CONVERT NEXT ASSY NO TO BINARY UPDT4410
                                     489  *                              AND STORE IN MASTER RECORD     UPDT4420
 000360 47F0 C2BA           002BC    490        B     QOHDONE             GO TO WRITE UPDATED MASTER RECORD UPDT4430


                                     492  ****                                                          UPDT4450
                                     493  * THIS ROUTINE IS ENTERED TO CHANGE THE SOURCE OF THE PART    UPDT4460
                                     494  ****                                                          UPDT4470


 000364                              496  CHNGSRCE EQU  *                                                UPDT4490
 000364 4560 C100           00102    497        BAL   LINKREG2,GETBIKEY   CONVERT KEY TO BINARY         UPDT4500
 000368 4570 C20E           00210    498        BAL   LINKREG1,READREC    GO TO READ MASTER RECORD      UPDT4510
 00036C D200 C4B9 9049 004BB 00049   499        MVC   MSTRSRCE(1),INPTSRCE MOVE NEW SOURCE TO MASTER    UPDT4520
 000372 47F0 C2BA           002BC    500        B     QOHDONE             GO TO WRITE UPDATED MASTER RECORD UPDT4530


                                     502  ****                                                          UPDT4550
                                     503  * THIS ROUTINE IS ENTERED IF THE UPDATE TYPE IS INVALID       UPDT4560
                                     504  ****                                                          UPDT4570


 000376                              506  BADTYPE  EQU  *                                                UPDT4590
 000376 D225 A052 C460 00052 00462   507        MVC   ERRORPT(38),BADTYPMS MOVE MSG TO I/O AREA         UPDT4600
 00037C 47F0 C1A6           001A8    508        B     PRINTIT             GO TO PRINT MESSAGE           UPDT4610


                                     510  ****                                                          UPDT4630
                                     511  * THIS ROUTINE IS ENTERED TO CHANGE THE UNIT PRICE           UPDT4640
                                     512  ****                                                          UPDT4650


 000380                              514  CHNGUNIT EQU  *                                                UPDT4670
 000380 4560 C100           00102    515        BAL   LINKREG2,GETBIKEY   CONVERT KEY TO BINARY         UPDT4680
 000384 4570 C20E           00210    516        BAL   LINKREG1,READREC    GO TO READ MASTER RECORD      UPDT4690
 000388 4570 C0F6           000F8    517        BAL   LINKREG1,GETUNIT    CONVERT NEW UNIT PRICE TO BINARY UPDT4700
 00038C D202 C4BA C45B 004BC 0045D   518        MVC   MSTRUNIT(3),BINSTORE+1 MOVE UNIT PRICE TO MASTER  UPDT4710
 000392 47F0 C2BA           002BC    519        B     QOHDONE             GO TO WRITE UPDATED MASTER RECORD UPDT4720


                                     521  ****                                                          UPDT4740
                                     522  * THIS ROUTINE IS ENTERED TO TRANSLATE THE FILENAMEC ERROR BYTE TO UPDT4750
                                     523  * ZONED DECIMAL                                                UPDT4760
                                     524  ****                                                          UPDT4770


 000396 D701 C4EE C4EE 004F0 004F0   526  TRBYTE   XC    BADBYTE,BADBYTE      ZERO BYTES                 UPDT4790
 00039C F110 C4EE C6DC 004F0 006DE   527        MVO   BADBYTE(2),INVMSTRC(1) MOVE FILENAMEC TO ERROR FIELD UPDT4800
 0003A2 F200 C4EF C4EF 004F1 004F1   528        PACK  BADBYTE+1(1),BADBYTE+1(1) PACK SECOND BYTE        UPDT4810
 0003A8 DC01 C4EE C551 004F0 00553   529        TR    BADBYTE(2),TRTBL     TRANSLATE TO ZONED DECIMAL   UPDT4820
```

```
0003AE 07F7                        530          BR    LINKREG1              RETURN TO CALLER           UPDT4830


                                   532 ****                                                            UPDT4850
                                   533 * THIS ROUTINE IS ENTERED TO PRINT THE HEADING ON THE EXCEPTION UPDT4860
                                   534 * REPORT                                                        UPDT4870
                                   535 ****                                                            UPDT4880

0003B0                             537 HEADROU EQU   *                                                 UPDT4900
0003B0 50E0 C59A           0059C   538         ST    LINKRG14,SAVEHD        SAVE RETURN REGISTER        UPDT4910
0003B4 9240 A000     00000         539         MVI   RECORDPT,X'40'         CLEAR PRINTER AREA          UPDT4920
0003B8 D276 A001 A000 00001 00000  540         MVC   RECORDPT+1(119),RECORDPT                          UPDT4930
0003BE FA10 C594 C5FE 00596 00600  541         AP    PAGENO,=P'1'           ADD 1 TO PAGE NUMBER        UPDT4940
0003C4 D203 C590 C596 00592 00598  542         MVC   PAGE(4),PTTRN          MOVE EDIT PATTERN TO HEADER UPDT4950
0003CA DE03 C590 C594 00592 00596  543         ED    PAGE(4),PAGENO         EDIT PAGE NO                UPDT4960
0003D0 D20F A000 C561 00000 00563  544         MVC   RECORDPT(16),INVREC    MOVE HEADERS TO PRINT AREA  UPDT4970
0003D6 D222 A055 C571 00055 00573  545         MVC   ERRORPT+3(35),ACTION   MOVE MSG TO OUTPUT          UPDT4980
                                   546         CNTRL PRTFLE,SK,1            SKIP TO HEAD OF FORMS        UPDT4990

                                   553         PUT   PRTFLE                 PRINT HEADER                UPDT5010

                                   559         CNTRL PRTFLE,SP,2            SPACE TWICE                 UPDT5030

000404 58E0 C59A           0059C   566         L     LINKRG14,SAVEHD        RELOAD RETURN REGISTER      UPDT5050
000408 07FE                        567         BR    LINKRG14               RETURN TO CALLER            UPDT5060


                                   569 ****                                                            UPDT5080
                                   570 * THIS ROUTINE IS ENTERED WHEN END OF FILE IS REACHED ON THE INPUT UPDT5090
                                   571 * FILE OR WHEN A DISK ERROR OCCURS WHICH CAUSES A CANCELLATION OF UPDT5100
                                   572 * THE PROGRAM.                                                  UPDT5110
                                   573 ****                                                            UPDT5120

00040A                             575 ENDINPUT EQU  *                                                 UPDT5140
00040A 9240 A000     00000         576         MVI   RECORDPT,X'40'         CLEAR PRINTER AREA          UPDT5150
00040E D276 A001 A000 00001 00000  577         MVC   RECORDPT+1(119),RECORDPT                          UPDT5160
000414 D214 A000 C59E 00000 005A0  578         MVC   RECORDPT(21),ENDMSG    MOVE END MESSAGE TO PRINT I/O AREA UPDT5170
                                   579         CNTRL PRTFLE,SP,2            SPACE TWICE                 UPDT5180
                                   585         PUT   PRTFLE                 PRINT END MESSAGE           UPDT5190

                                   591         CLOSE PRTFLE,DISKIN,INVMSTR  CLOSE THE FILES             UPDT5210

                                   602         EOJ                         END OF JOB                  UPDT5230
```

```
                                606 ****                                                     UPDT5250
                                607 * CONSTANTS, WORK AREAS, ETC.                             UPDT5260
                                608 ****                                                      UPDT5270

000450                          610 DBLWORD  DS    D                                          UPDT5290
000450                          611 DBLWORK  EQU   DBLWORD                                    UPDT5300
000458                          612 FULLWORK DS    F                                          UPDT5310
00045C                          613 BINSTORE DS    F                                          UPDT5320
000460 4040                     614 BLANKS   DC    CL2' '                                     UPDT5330
000462 C9D5E5C1D3C9C440         615 BADTYPMS DC    CL40'INVALID TYPE-RECORD NOT PROCESSED'    UPDT5340
00048A                          616 ISWORK   DS    0CL55                                      UPDT5350
00048A                          617 MSTRDIV  DS    CL1                                        UPDT5360
00048B                          618 MSTRPRME DS    CL3                                        UPDT5370
00048E                          619 MSTRDASH DS    CL3                                        UPDT5380
000491                          620 MSTRNAME DS    CL25                                       UPDT5390
0004AA                          621 MSTRQOH  DS    CL3                                        UPDT5400
0004AD                          622 MSTRQOO  DS    CL3                                        UPDT5410
0004B0                          623 MSTRQRSV DS    CL3                                        UPDT5420
0004B3                          624 MSTRASSY DS    0CL7                                       UPDT5430
0004B3                          625 MASYDIV  DS    CL1                                        UPDT5440
0004B4                          626 MASYPRME DS    CL3                                        UPDT5450
0004B7                          627 MASYDASH DS    CL3                                        UPDT5460
0004BA                          628 MSTRTYPE DS    CL1                                        UPDT5470
0004BB                          629 MSTRSRCE DS    CL1                                        UPDT5480
0004BC                          630 MSTRUNIT DS    CL3                                        UPDT5490
0004BF                          631 MSTRXTRA DS    CL2                                        UPDT5500
0004C1                          632 DISKKEY  EQU   *                                          UPDT5510
0004C1                          633 DISKEY   DS    CL7                                        UPDT5520
0004C8 E2E3C1E3E4E24040         634 CANCMSG  DC    CL40'STATUS      -***JOB CANCELLED***'     UPDT5530
0004CF                          635 CANCBYTE EQU   CANCMSG+7                                  UPDT5540
0004F0 0000                     636 BADBYTE  DC    X'0000'                                    UPDT5550
0004F2 E2E3C1E3E4E24040         637 NOTEMSG  DC    CL40'STATUS      -RECORD NOT PROCESSED'    UPDT5560
00051A                          638 SAVEREC  DS    CL55                                       UPDT5570
0004F9                          639 NOTEBYTE EQU   NOTEMSG+7                                  UPDT5580
000551 F0F4                     640 ZERO4    DC    C'04'                                      UPDT5590
000553 F0F1F2F3F4F5F6F7         641 TRTBL    DC    X'F0F1F2F3F4F5F6F7F8F9C1C2C3C4C5C6'        UPDT5600
000563 C9D5E5C5D5E3D6D9         642 INVREC   DC    C'INVENTORY RECORD'                        UPDT5610
000573 D9C5D4C1D9D2E240         643 ACTION   DC    C'REMARKS                    PAGE    '     UPDT5620
000596 000C                     644 PAGENO   DC    PL2'0'                                     UPDT5630
000598 40202020                 645 PTTRN    DC    X'40202020'                                UPDT5640
000592                          646 PAGE     EQU   ACTION+31,                                 UPDT5650
00059C                          647 SAVEHD   DS    F                                          UPDT5660
0005A0 C5D5C440D6C640E4         648 ENDMSG   DC    C'END OF UPDATE PROGRAM'                   UPDT5670
0005B5 C4C5C3D9C5C1E2C5         649 BADQMSG  DC    CL40'DECREASE QTY TOO LARGE-NO PROCESS'    UPDT5680
0005E0                          650          LTORG                                            UPDT5690
0005E0 5B5B8C2D6D7C5D540        651          =C'$$BOPEN '
0005E8 5B5B8C2C3D3D6E2C5        652          =C'$$BCLOSE'
0005F0 00000638                 653          =A(DISKIN)
0005F4 000006C0                 654          =A(INVMSTR)
0005F8 00000608                 655          =A(PRTFLE)
0005FC 000003B0                 656          =A(HEADROU)
000600 1C                       657          =P'1'
```

```
                                659 ****                                                              UPDT5710
                                660 * PRINTER FILE                                                    UPDT5720
                                661 ****                                                              UPDT5730


                                663 PRTFLE    DTFPR DEVADDR=SYSLST,IOAREA1=PRT01,BLKSIZE=120,CONTROL=YES,     CUPDT5750
                                          DEVICE=1403,MODNAME=IJDFCPIZ,IOREG=(10),PRINTOV=YES,               CUPDT5760
                                          RECFORM=FIXUNB,IOAREA2=PRT02                                       UPDT5770


                                685 ****                                                              UPDT5790
                                686 * SEQUENTIAL DISK INPUT FILE                                      UPDT5800
                                687 ****                                                              UPDT5810


                                689 DISKIN    DTFSD BLKSIZE=3600,EOFADDR=ENDINPUT,IOAREA1=DISKIN1,          CUPDT5830
                                          IOAREA2=DISKIN2,DEVADDR=SYS006,DEVICE=2311,IOREG=(9),             CUPDT5840
                                          MODNAME=IJGFIZZZ,RECFORM=FIXBLK,RECSIZE=80,                       CUPDT5850
                                          TYPEFLE=INPUT                                                     UPDT5860


                                735 ****                                                              UPDT5880
                                736 * INDEXED SEQUENTIAL INVENTORY MASTER FILE                        UPDT5890
                                737 ****                                                              UPDT5900


                                739 INVMSTR   DTFIS DSKXTNT=3,IOROUT=ADDRTR,KEYLEN=7,NRECDS=65,RECSIZE=55,    CUPDT5920
                                          RECFORM=FIXBLK,CYLOFL=2,DEVICE=2311,                              CUPDT5930
                                          HINDEX=2311,IOAREAL=ISIO,IOAREAR=ISIO,KEYARG=DISKKEY,             CUPDT5940
                                          KEYLOC=1,MODNAME=IJHBARZZ,MSTIND=YES,TYPEFLE=RANDOM,              CUPDT5950
                                          VERIFY=YES,WORKL=ISWORK,WORKR=ISWORK                              UPDT5960
```

6.75

DOS CL3-5 08/26/70

LOC	OBJECT CODE	ADDR1 ADDR2	STMT	SOURCE STATEMENT	

```
                                      862 ****                                                UPDT5980
                                      863 *DISK AND PRINTER I/O AREAS AND WORK AREAS           UPDT5990
                                      864 ****                                                UPDT6000

0008FF 4040404040404040              866 PRT01    DC    CL120' '                              UPDT6020
000977 4040404040404040              867 PRT02    DC    CL120' '                              UPDT6030
0009EF                               868 DISKIN1  DS    CL3600                                UPDT6040
0017FF                               869 DISKIN2  DS    CL3600                                UPDT6050
00260F                               870 ISIO     DS    CL3590                                UPDT6060

000000                               872 INPTDUMY DSECT                                       UPDT6080
000000                               873 INPTDIV  DS    CL2                                   UPDT6090
000002                               874 INPTPRME DS    CL6                                   UPDT6100
000008                               875 INPTDASH DS    CL5                                   UPDT6110
00000D                               876 INPTNAME DS    CL25                                  UPDT6120
000026                               877 INPTQOH  DS    CL7                                   UPDT6130
00002D                               878 INPTQOO  DS    CL7                                   UPDT6140
000034                               879 INPTQRSV DS    CL7                                   UPDT6150
00003B                               880 INPTASSY DS    OCL13                                 UPDT6160
00003B                               881 IASYDIV  DS    CL2                                   UPDT6170
00003D                               882 IASYPRME DS    CL6                                   UPDT6180
000043                               883 IASYDASH DS    CL5                                   UPDT6190
000048                               884 INPTTYPE DS    CL1                                   UPDT6200
000049                               885 INPTSRCE DS    CL1                                   UPDT6210
00004A                               886 INPTUNIT DS    CL6                                   UPDT6220

                                     888 PRTDUMY  DSECT                                       UPDT6240
000000                               889 RECORDPT DS    CL80                                  UPDT6250
000000                               890          DS    CL2                                   UPDT6260
000050                               891 ERRORPI  DS    CL38                                  UPDT6270
000052                               892          END                                        UPDT6280
```

6.76

CHAPTER 6

PROGRAMMING ASSIGNMENT

INSTRUCTIONS

The Sales Master File is to be updated by transactions. Suggested data for these transaction records are contained in the appendices. Using the program from the programming assignment in Chapter 3, create the sequential disk transaction file that is to be used as input to update the Sales Master File.

The Master File should be randomly updated. The following codes indicate the type of update to be performed.

2 – NAME CHANGE
3 – Y-T-D SALES UPDATE
4 – COMMISSION RATE CHANGE
5 – Y-T-D SALES RETURN UPDATE
6 – ADDITION
7 – DELETION

The Y-T-D Sales update is performed by adding Current Sales from the transaction records to the Y-T-D Sales from the master record. A similar procedure is followed in updating the Y-T-D Sales Return Field.

When a Name Change or Commission Rate Change occurs, the fields on the master record should be replaced by the contents of the transaction record.

When a record is to be deleted (code 7), a "2" should be moved to the Type Field in the Master Record indicating that the record is to be considered deleted from the master file. It should be noted that a type "1" is invalid in the transaction record.

CHAPTER 7

SELF-RELOCATING PROGRAMS

INTRODUCTION

The Disk Operating System consists of many programs, modules and macros. As discussed previously, the macros are stored on the system disk pack in the Source Statement Library. Programs utilized by DOS, such as the DOS Sort program, are stored in the CORE IMAGE LIBRARY. In addition, user programs can also be "catalogued" in the core image library (the technique for cataloguing programs is discussed in the appendices).

Programs which are catalogued in the core image library have been processed by the linkage editor before being catalogued and are therefore ready for execution. Each program catalogued in the core image library is called a phase. Thus, the PHASE NAME is the name given to a program catalogued in the core image library. In addition to assigning a phase name to a program, the linkage editor determines the address where the program will be loaded into core storage for execution. In some applications, it is desirable that a program be able to be loaded into different core locations for execution at different times. In order for this to occur, special techniques must be written into the program to make it self-relocating.

SELF-RELOCATING PROGRAMS

A SELF-RELOCATING PROGRAM is a program which can be executed at any location in core storage. As has been previously noted, the use of the base register plus displacement addressing technique allows an address to be generated based on an address loaded into a register and the information supplied in a USING statement. This allows all information under the effect of the USING statement to be addressable no matter where it resides in core storage. When a program is link-edited, however, some addresses are computed as ABSOLUTE addresses, that is, an address which is an exact address in core storage rather than an address computed from a base register plus a displacement. These absolute addresses are computed by the linkage editor by adding the displacement generated by the location counter value of the address in the assembly to the address where the program will be loaded into core.

One type of address which is given an absolute address is the value in an address constant. When the program is assembled, the location counter value for the desired address is placed in the fullword generated by the DC statement.

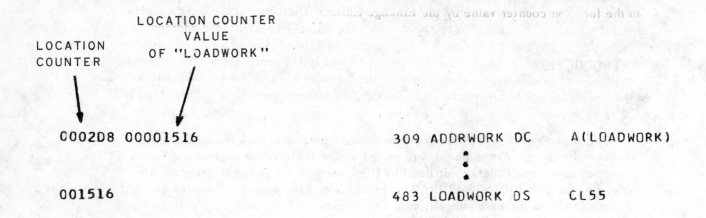

Figure 7-1 Location counter value in address constant

When the program is link-edited, the value in the adcon (001516) will be added to the address where the program will be loaded for execution and that address will replace the location counter value in the adcon field. Thus, the address generated when the program is link-edited is an absolute address and is dependent upon where in core the program is to be loaded. For example, if the program was link-edited to begin at core location 2800, the address which would go into the address field of the DC statement in Figure 7-1 would be 3D16 (= 2800 + 1516). Thus, when the program is executed, it must be loaded at core location 2800 or the address in the address constant will not be correct.

Therefore, in order for a program to be self-relocating, a technique must be established to "resolve" all address constants to the proper value after the program has been loaded into core storage for execution.

The following examples illustrate several techniques which can be used to resolve A-type address constants.

EXAMPLE 1: If a program is catalogued onto the core image library, the load address specified in the phase card can be +0. This indicates that the program can be loaded anywhere in core storage and is commonly done with self-relocating programs. Thus, all the A-type address constants will contain the location counter values when the program is loaded into core storage for execution because a value of 0 has been added to the location counter value by the Linkage Editor. Therefore, if the program adds the address where it is loaded to the value in the address constant, the address constant will contain the proper address. Note that, if the program is loaded into a different core location each time it is executed, the value generated for the address constant will be different. The following steps can be used to resolve the address constant when a phase origin of +0 is used. The address constant to be resolved is shown in Figure 7-1.

STEP 1: Establish base register.

For this example, assume the phase was loaded at core location 2800.

Before Execution:

BASEREG | 0 | 0 | C | 8 | F | 9 | F | F |

After Execution:

BASEREG | 0 | 0 | 0 | 0 | 2 | 8 | 0 | 2 |

Figure 7-2 Establish base register

7.3

After the BALR instruction is executed, the address of the next consecutive core location is loaded into BASEREG. Since the program was loaded at core location 2800, and the BALR instruction is the first instruction executed, the address loaded into BASEREG is 2802 (the BALR instruction uses 2 bytes).

Note that the USING statement is before the BALR instruction instead of behind it as in previous programs. This is because the address in BASEREG is to be modified as shown in Step 2.

STEP 2: Determine the address where the phase was loaded.

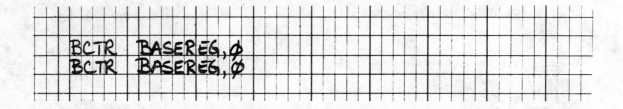

Before Execution:

BASEREG | 0 0 | 0 0 | 2 8 | 0 2 |

After Execution:

BASEREG | 0 0 | 0 0 | 2 8 | 0 0 |

Figure 7-3 Subtract 2 from base register

By using the BCTR instruction twice, the value in BASEREG is reduced by 2 (which is the length of the BALR instruction). Therefore, the value in BASEREG is now equal to the address at which the program was loaded. The value in BASEREG can now be used to resolve the addresses in the A-type address constants in the program.

Note that the USING statement shown in Step 1 will establish proper displacements because the value now in BASEREG is equal to the address of the start of the BALR instruction, and this is the address referenced by the * in the USING statement.

STEP 3: Load the location counter value from the address constant into a register.

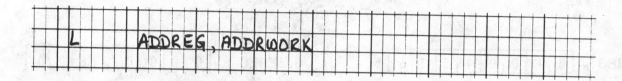

Before Execution:

ADDREG | 0 | 0 | 9 | 8 | F | C | 9 | A |

| 0 | 0 | 0 | 0 | 1 | 5 | 1 | 6 |
ADDRWORK

After Execution:

ADDREG | 0 | 0 | 0 | 0 | 1 | 5 | 1 | 6 |

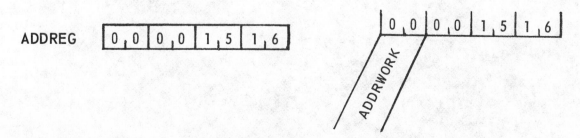

| 0 | 0 | 0 | 0 | 1 | 5 | 1 | 6 |
ADDRWORK

Figure 7-4 Load address constant

Note that the value in the adcon (1516) is loaded into a work register. Since A-type address constants are always established on a fullword boundary, there is no need to move the adcon to a fullword for alignment purposes.

STEP 4: Add the load address to the location counter value.

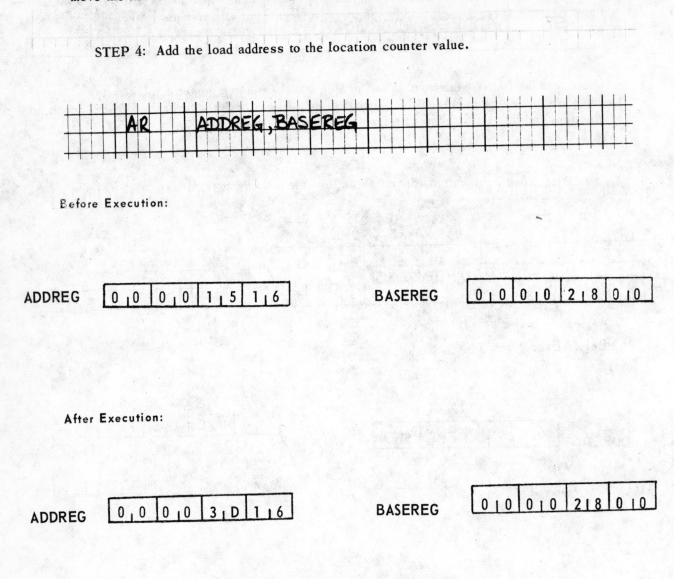

Before Execution:

ADDREG `0 0 0 0 1 5 1 6`   BASEREG `0 0 0 0 2 8 0 0`

After Execution:

ADDREG `0 0 0 0 3 D 1 6`   BASEREG `0 0 0 0 2 8 0 0`

Figure 7-5 Resolve address constant

After the addition, ADDREG contains the exact core address of LOADWORK.

STEP 5: Store the result back in the adcon.

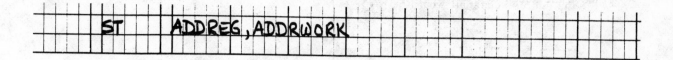

Before Execution:

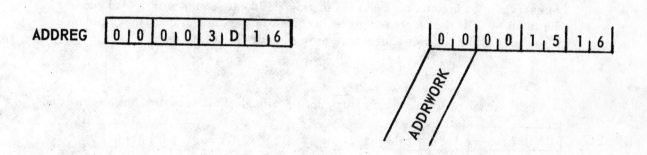

After Execution:

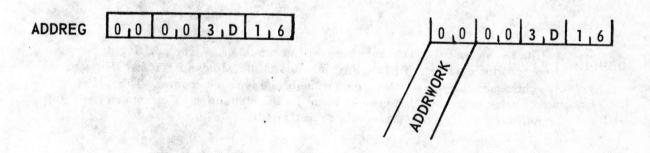

Figure 7-6 Store resolved address constant

After the five steps have been executed, the address constant at ADDRWORK contains the exact core address of LOADWORK.

It can be seen from the example that if the program had been loaded in core location 3600, the address would still have been resolved to point to the exact core location of LOADWORK. Thus, the program could be loaded into core storage at any location and the address constant would be resolved.

EXAMPLE 2: The technique illustrated in Example 1 cannot be used if a program is not catalogued on the core image library with a load address of +0. If the program is catalogued on the core image library with a load address of 2800, the linkage editor resolves all address constants by adding 2800 to the location counter values in the address constants. Therefore, if the technique in Example 1 were used, 2800 would be added twice (once by the linkage editor and once by the program) and the resultant address would be incorrect. Thus, if the program is catalogued with a load address other than +0 or if the program is to be executed from an object deck in a "link and go" mode then the following technique or one similar to it must be used.

STEP 1: When writing the program, define an address constant to get a relocation factor.

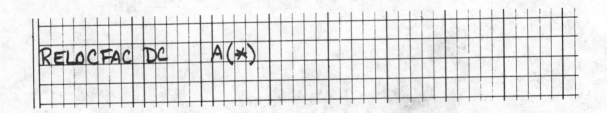

Figure 7-7 Address constant to get relocation factor

The DC statement illustrated above will generate an A-type adcon with the value of the location counter at RELOCFAC inserted in the address constant. The asterisk tells the assembler to use the current value of the location counter. Thus, if the current value of the location counter when the DC instruction is assembled is 0 C 2 C, the following address constant would be generated.

Note that the value generated in the address constant is the same as the value of the location counter.

7.8

STEP 2: When the program is executed, the first step is to load the address of
the relocation factor address constant.

*For this example, assume the phase was catalogued to load at 2800
but was actually loaded at 3600.*

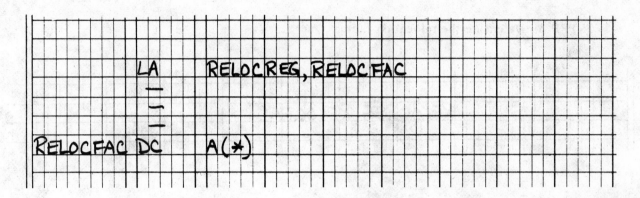

Before Execution:

RELOCREG | 0 | 0 | 0 | C | 0 | F | 2 | 3 |

| 0 | 0 | 0 | 0 | 3 | 4 | 2 | C |
RELOCFAC

Note: RELOCFAC is
located in core storage at
address 422C (= 3600 + C2C)

After Execution:

RELOCREG | 0 | 0 | 0 | 0 | 4 | 2 | 2 | C |

| 0 | 0 | 0 | 0 | 3 | 4 | 2 | C |
RELOCFAC

Figure 7-8 Load address of address constant

Note that by using the Load Address instruction, the absolute address of
RELOCFAC is loaded into RELOCREG. Thus, after this step, both the address
determined by the linkage editor (342C) and the true absolute address (422C) are
known.

STEP 3: Determine the relocation factor.

Before Execution:

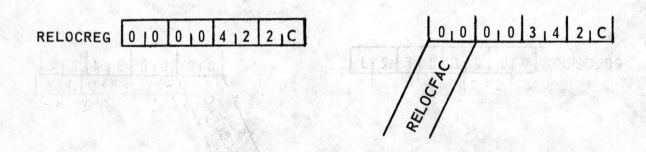

After Execution:

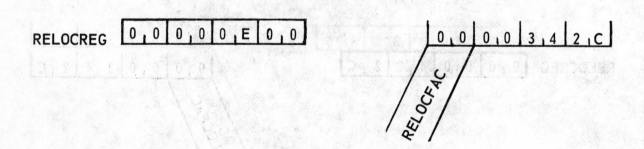

Figure 7 - 9 Determine relocation factor

After the subtraction is executed, RELOCREG contains the "relocation factor". This value is equal to the difference between the absolute core storage address of RELOCFAC and the address determined by the linkage editor when the program was catalogued. This relocation factor will apply to all address constants in the program. Note that the relocation factor is equal to the difference between the address where the program was loaded and the load address used by the linkage editor (3600 - 2800 = 0E00).

STEP 4: Load the constant to be resolved.

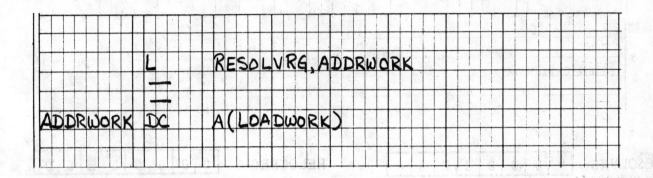

Before Execution:

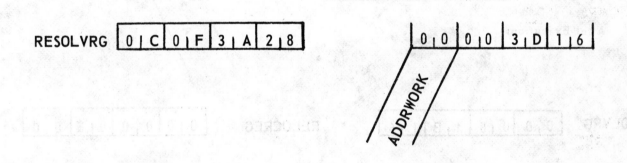

After Execution:

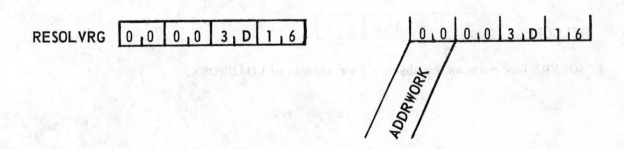

Figure 7-10 Load address constant to be resolved

Note that the value 3D16 was determined by the linkage editor (3D16 = 2800 + 1516).

7.11

STEP 5: Add the relocation factor to the location counter value.

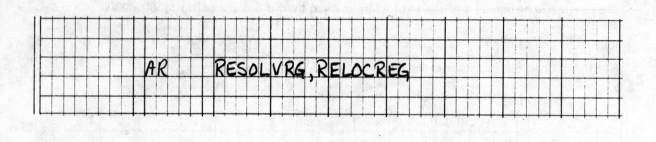

Before Execution:

RESOLVRG | 0 | 0 | 0 | 0 | 3 | D | 1 | 6 |

RELOCREG | 0 | 0 | 0 | 0 | 0 | E | 0 | 0 |

After Execution:

RESOLVRG | 0 | 0 | 0 | 0 | 4 | B | 1 | 6 |

RELOCREG | 0 | 0 | 0 | 0 | 0 | E | 0 | 0 |

Figure 7-11 Add relocation factor to address constant

RESOLVRG now contains the absolute core address of LOADWORK.

STEP 6: Store the absolute address in the adcon.

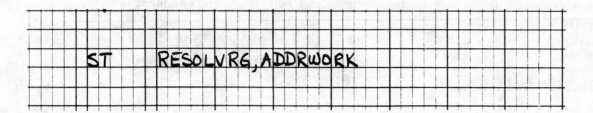

Before Execution:

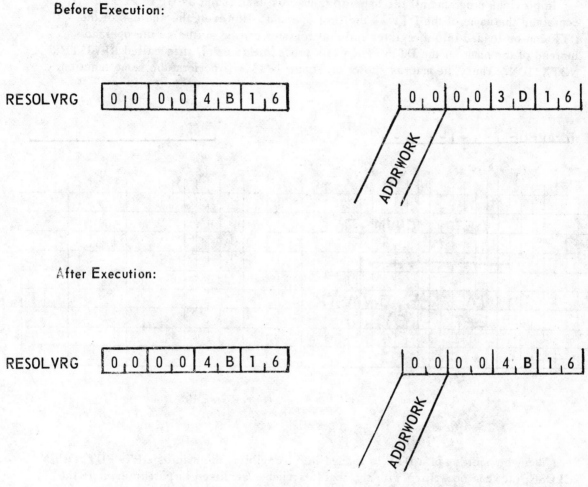

RESOLVRG | 0 0 0 0 4 B 1 6 |

0 0 0 0 3 D 1 6
ADDRWORK

After Execution:

RESOLVRG | 0 0 0 0 4 B 1 6 |

0 0 0 0 4 B 1 6
ADDRWORK

Figure 7-12 Store resolved address in address constant

The absolute address of **LOADWORK** is now in the address constant and ready for use.

The two examples presented above illustrate two methods to use to resolve address constants which are defined in a self-relocating program. There are, however, other considerations before a program can be completely self-relocating and these involve the use of Logical IOCS.

REGISTER NOTATION

In previous programs all the imperative macros used (such as GET, PUT, etc.) contained the name of the DTF as the first operand. However, the address of the DTF can be loaded into a register and that register can be stated as the operand instead of the name of the DTF. When this procedure is used, it is called REGISTER NOTATION. Thus, the macros shown in Figure 7-13 will perform the same function.

EXAMPLE

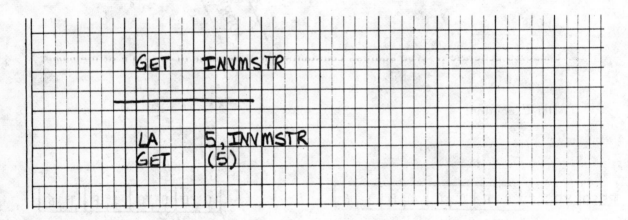

Figure 7-13 GET macro with register notation

When the address of a DTF is loaded into a register, the macros GET, PUT, OPEN, CLOSE, etc. can be written with the register number enclosed in parentheses as the operand instead of the DTF name. If a work area is used with a GET or PUT, its address can also be loaded into a register and register notation can be used.

EXAMPLE

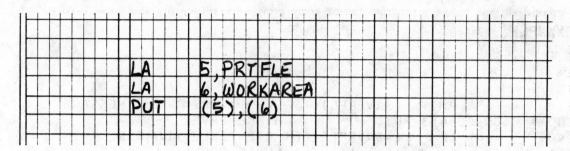

Figure 7-14 PUT macro with register notation

In the example above, the address of the DTF is loaded into register 5 and the address of the work area is loaded into register 6. The register numbers, enclosed in parentheses, are then used as the operands instead of the DTF name and the work area name.

Although register notation is optional in programs which are not self-relocating, it is required when the program is self-relocating. This is because most of the imperative macros generate A-type address constants when the name of the DTF or the name of the work area is used. Figure 7-15 illustrates a partial expansion of the PUT macro.

```
579            PUT    PRTFLE
580+* 360N-CL-453 PUT              CHANGE LEVEL 3-5
581+           L      1,=A(PRTFLE) GET DTF TABLE ADDRESS
```

Figure 7-15 Example of address constant in PUT macro

Note that an A-type address constant is generated for the operand PRTFLE. This adcon is placed in the literal pool and it will be acted upon by the linkage editor in the same manner as other adcons.

However, when register notation is used, no adcons are generated.

EXAMPLE

```
138            PUT    (SAVEREG)           PRINT THE MESSAGE
139+* 360N-CL-453 PUT           CHANGE LEVEL 3-5
140+           LR     1,SAVEREG GET DTF TABLE ADDRESS
141+           L      15,16(1) GET LOGIC MODULE ADDRESS      3-5
142+           BAL    14,12(15) BRANCH TO PUT ROUTINE        3-5
143            BAL    LINKREG1,CLOSEM     GO TO CLOSE THE FILES
```

Figure 7-16 Example of register notation in PUT macro

Note in the example in Figure 7-16 that no address constant is generated. Instead, the address in the register specified in the operand of the macro is loaded into register 1. If desired, the address of the DTF can be loaded into register 1 and register 1 can be stated as the operand (see Figure 7-17).

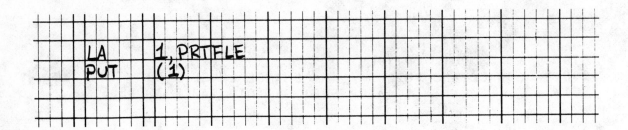

Figure 7-17 PUT macro with special register notation

When "special register notation" is used, that is, the address of the DTF is loaded into register 1 and/or the address of the work area is loaded into register 0, then the macro does not load register 1 and/or register 0.

Thus, in order to avoid the generation of an address constant by an imperative macro, register notation or special register notation should always be used in self-relocating programs.

Address constants are also generated by the DTF macros. These address constants contain such items as the address of the I/O areas and the address of the end-of-file routine.

```
681 ****


683 DISKIN    DTFSD BLKSIZE=3600,EOFADDR=ENDINPUT,IOAREA1=DISKIN1,         C
                    IOAREA2=DISKIN2,DEVADDR=SYS006,DEVICE=2311,IOREG=(9),   C
                    MODNAME=IJGFIZZZ,RECFORM=FIXBLK,RECSIZE=80,             C
                    TYPEFLE=INPUT
684+* 360N-IO-455     DTFSD   CHANGE LEVEL 3-5                              3-5
685+          DC     0D'0'
686+DISKIN    DC     X'000080040000' CCB
687+          DC     AL1(1) LOGICAL UNIT CLASS
688+          DC     AL1(6) LOGICAL UNIT NUMBER
689+          DC     A(IJGC0018) CCB-CCW ADDRESS
690+          DC     4X'00' CCB-ST BYTE,CSW CCW ADDRESS
691+          DC     AL1(0) 3-3
692+          DC     VL3(IJGFIZZZ) LOGIC MODULE ADDRESS
693+          DC     X'20' DTF TYPE
694+          DC     AL1(74) OPEN/CLOSE INDICATORS
695+          DC     CL7'DISKIN' FILENAME
696+          DC     X'00' INDICATE 2311
697+          DC     6X'00' BCCHHR ADDR OF F1 LABEL IN VTOC
698+          DC     2X'00' VOL SEQ NUMBER
699+          DC     X'08' OPEN COMMUNICATIONS BYTE
700+          DC     X'00' XTENT SEQ NO OF CURRENT EXTENT
701+          DC     X'00' XTENT SEQ NO LAST XTENT OPENED
702+          DC     AL3(*) USER'S LABEL ADDRESS
703+          DC     A(DISKIN2) ADDRESS OF SECOND IOAREA
704+          DC     X'80000000' CCHH ADDR OF USER LABEL TRACK
705+          DC     2X'00' LOWER HEAD LIMIT
706+          DC     4X'00' XTENT UPPER LIMIT
707+DISKINS   DC     2X'00' SEEK ADDRESS-BB
708+          DC     X'0000FF00' SEARCH ADDRESS-CCHH
709+          DC     X'00' RECORD NUMBER
710+          DC     AL3(ENDINPUT) EOF ADDRESS
711+          DC     4X'00' CCHH CONTROL FIELD
712+          DC     AL1(1) R    CONTROL FIELD
713+          DC     B'00000100' 3-2
714+          DC     H'3599' SIZE OF BLOCK-1
715+          DC     5X'FF' CCHHR BUCKET                            3-5
716+          DC     3X'00'
717+          L      9,88(1) LOAD USER'S IOREG
718+          DC     A(DISKIN1) DEBLOCKER-INITIAL POINTER
719+          DC     F'80' DEBLOCKER-RECORD SIZE
720+          DC     A(DISKIN1+3600-1) DEBLOCKER-LIMIT
721+          DC     AL1(10) LOGICAL INDICATORS
722+          DC     AL3(0) USER'S ERROR ROUTINE
723+IJGC0018 CCW    7,*-46,64,6 SEEK
724+          CCW    X'31',*-52,64,5 SEARCH ID EQUAL
725+          CCW    8,*-8,0,0 TIC
726+          CCW    6,DISKIN1,0,3600 READ DATA
727+IJJZ0018 EQU    *
```

I/O AREA ADDRESS

END-OF-FILE ROUTINE ADDRESS

Figure 7-18 Address constants in DTFSD macro

In order for these address constants to be resolved in a self-relocating program, the OPENR macro and the CLOSER macro must be used to open and close the file instead of the OPEN macro and the CLOSE macro. The format of the OPENR macro and the CLOSER macro is identical to that of the Open and Close macros.

EXAMPLE

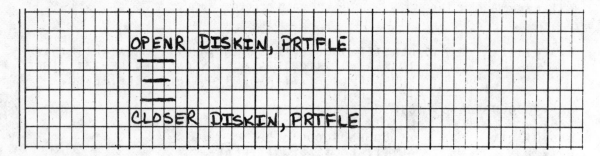

Figure 7-19 OPENR and CLOSER macros

The OPENR and CLOSER macros generate the necessary coding to resolve all the address constants in the DTF's and they must always be used in a self-relocating program.

It should be noted that register notation can also be used with the OPENR and CLOSER macros. When it is used, a requirement of the two macros is that the 8 high-order bits of the registers containing the addresses of the DTFs must be equal to X'00'. Since the Branch and Link instruction, when it is executed, stores the condition code in these 8 high-order bits, any register containing an address calculated by using an address in a register loaded by a Branch and Link instruction will contain the condition code in the 8 high-order bits. The instruction LA BASEREG,0(0,BASEREG) can be used to zero these high-order bits. This is because the Load Address instruction loads an address into the low-order 24 bits of a register and zeros the 8 high-order bits.

MODULAR CONCEPT

The output of an assembly is referred to as an OBJECT MODULE. An object module is made up of one or more CONTROL SECTIONS (defined as a block of code assigned to contiguous main storage locations). One or more object modules are joined by the linkage editor to form a program phase which can then be executed. The MODULAR CONCEPT of programming refers to the concept of joining several or many object modules to form a program phase rather than writing a complete program phase as one object module. Thus, routines which are common to many programs need to be written only once and can then be included in any number of programs which need the function performed by the module.

The Input/Output modules used by Logical IOCS (specified by the MODNAME operand in a DTF) are examples of the use of the modular concept. These routines perform the various functions necessary to process files such as reading or writing records and blocking and deblocking records. Many different programs can use the same I/O modules because the same functions must be performed in each program.

RELOCATABLE LIBRARY

As noted, one of the primary advantages of using modules is that they can be used in more than one program phase. This, in turn, requires that the modules be available to all programs which need to use them. To make these modules available, the Disk Operating System supports a RELOCATABLE LIBRARY. Modules can be catalogued in the Relocatable Library to be retrieved when needed. When an object module is catalogued into the Relocatable Library, it is given a unique name so that it can be identified and retrieved for use by any program. Once the module has been catalogued in the Relocatable Library, the Linkage Editor is used to link the modules together to form a complete program ready for execution. Before discussing how the linkage editor accomplishes this task, it is necessary to understand control sections and linkage between control sections.

CONTROL SECTIONS

As stated previously, a control section is a block of code assigned to contiguous main storage locations. The beginning of a control section is defined by either a START statement or a CSECT statement in the source coding. To define three different control sections in one source module (ie, a single assembly), the coding shown below could be used.

EXAMPLE

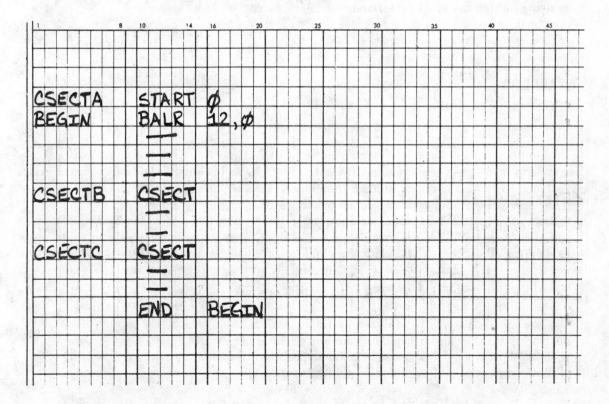

Figure 7-20 Example of multiple control sections in assembly

In the example above, CSECTA is defined through the use of the START instruction and CSECTB and CSECTC are defined through the use of a CSECT instruction. The START instruction can be used to define the first control section only. All others must be defined by a CSECT instruction as shown. The CSECT instruction may contain a label. If it does, it is the name of the new control section. If it does not, the control section is considered unnamed. All unnamed control sections are grouped as a single control section when the object module is produced by the assembler. There are no operands for a CSECT instruction.

When a source module is assembled, each control section is a separate entity. At the start of the control section, the location counter value is reset to the value specified in the START instruction or to zero. Therefore, any USING instruction issued in one control section is not applicable to another control section. Thus, a label defined in CSECTC would not be addressable in CSECTB by using the base register and USING addressing technique from CSECTB. Thus, in order to make labels in one control section addressable by another control section, external labels and entry points are used.

EXTERNAL LABELS AND ENTRY POINTS

External labels and entry points are used to make symbolic labels addressable by many control sections, not just the control section in which they are defined. An ENTRY POINT is a symbolic label defined in one control section that will be used in another control section. An entry point is defined by an ENTRY instruction in the control section in which the label is defined.

EXAMPLE

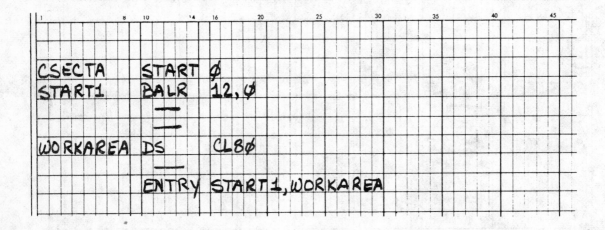

Figure 7-21 Entry points in control section

7.20

In the above example, the symbolic labels START1 and WORKAREA are defined as entry points by the ENTRY instruction. The ENTRY instruction is not an executable instruction. It is used to identify labels within a control section which will be used in another control section. Thus, the labels START1 and WORKAREA in the control section CSECTA will be able to be referenced by other control sections.

A control section which references the labels in CSECTA must define those labels as external labels. An EXTERNAL LABEL is a label which is defined in one control section and is to be used in another control section. An external label can be defined by an EXTRN instruction in the control section which will use the external label.

EXAMPLE

Figure 7-22 External labels in control section

In the above example, START1 and WORKAREA are defined in a control section other than CSECTB but will be referenced in CSECTB.

When an external label is to be referenced, an address constant is used. The address constant is defined in the control section which will use the external label. The following example illustrates the use of external labels.

7.21

EXAMPLE

STEP 1: All entry points and external labels are defined in their respective
control sections.

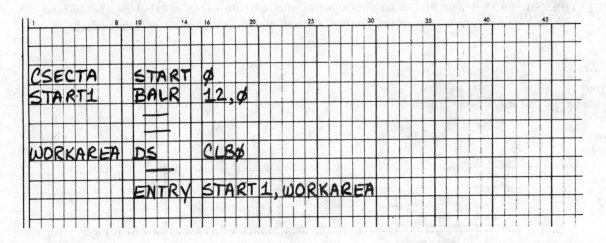

Figure 7-23 *Definition of entry points*

STEP 2: Address constants are defined for all external labels.

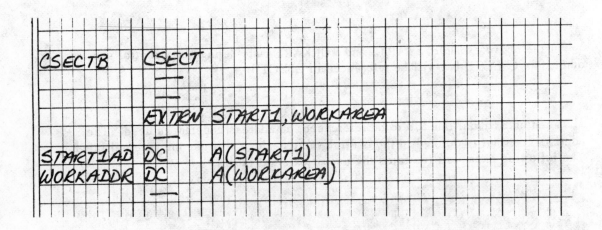

Figure 7-24 *Address constants for external labels*

After the program is link-edited, these address constants can be used in the same manner as address constants defined for symbolic labels in the same control section. Thus, in order to use the routine at START1, the following coding could be used in CSECTB.

STEP 3:

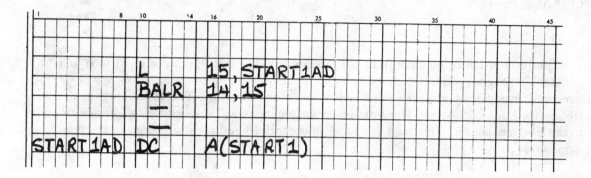

```
        L      15,START1AD
        BALR   14,15
        —
START1AD DC    A(START1)
```

Figure 7-25 Example of the use of an external label

These instructions would load the address of the label START1 in CSECTA into register 15. The BALR instruction would then branch to START1 in CSECTA.

V-TYPE ADDRESS CONSTANTS

As shown previously, the combination of an EXTRN instruction and an A-type address constant can be used to reference an external label. A V-TYPE ADDRESS CONSTANT can be used in place of the EXTRN instruction and A-type address constant to perform the same function. Thus, the two examples shown below are identical.

EXAMPLE

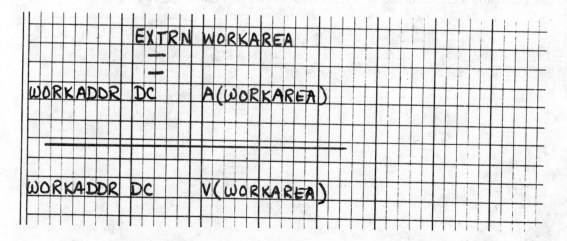

```
            EXTRN WORKAREA
            —
WORKADDR DC       A(WORKAREA)


WORKADDR DC       V(WORKAREA)
```

Figure 7-26 V-type address constant

The V‑type address constant generates the same type of constant as the A‑type address constant and is used in the program in the same manner as an A‑type address constant.

LINKAGE EDITOR

The linkage editor program links all the control sections which are input to it and produces a program phase which is ready for execution. The program phase can be executed immediately after it is link‑edited or it can be catalogued in the core image library for later execution. The linkage editor produces a "link‑edit map" in addition to the program phase. This map shows all the control sections used to make the program phase.

06/11/69	PHASE	XFR-AD	LOCORE	HICORE	DSK-AD	ESD TYPE	LABEL	LOADED	REL-FR
	PHASE***	0028C0	002858	002F47	39 04 2	CSECT	PGMNO13	002858	002858
						CSECT	IJCFZII0	002E18	002E18
						CSECT	IJDFCPIZ	002EA0	002EA0

Figure 7‑27 Linkage editor map

In the link‑edit map shown in Figure 7‑27, the program phase consists of three control sections – PGMNO13, IJCFZII0, and IJDFCPIZ. PGMNO13 is the control section written by the problem programmer and the other two control sections are I/O modules. These I/O modules were included in the program phase because V‑type address constants were included in the DTF as shown in Figure 7‑28.

```
657 PRTFLE    DTFPR DEVADDR=SYSLST,IOAREA1=PRT01,BLKSIZE=120,CONTROL=YES,   C
                    DEVICE=1403,MODNAME=IJDFCPIZ,IOREG=(10),PRINTOV=YES,    C
                    RECFORM=FIXUNB,IOAREA2=PRT02
658+* 360 N-CL-453 DTFPR       CHANGE LEVEL 3-5                             3-5

659+            DC    0D'0'
660+PRTFLE      DC    X'000084000400' RES. COUT,COM. BYTES,STATUS BTS
661+            DC    AL1(0) LOGICAL UNIT CLASS
662+            DC    AL1(3) LOGICAL UNIT
663+            DC    A(*+32) CCW ADDR.
664+            DC    4X'00' CCB-ST BYTE,CSW CCW ADDRESS
665+            DC    AL1(0)
666+            DC    VL3(IJDFCPIZ) ADDRESS OF LOGIC MODULE ←──── ADDRESS OF
667+            DC    X'08' DTF TYPE (PRINTER)                    I/O MODULE
668+            DC    AL1(20) SWITCHES ←──────────────────── ABSOLUTE EXPRESSION
669+            DC    X'09' NORMAL COMM. CODE
670+            DC    X'09' CONTROL COMM. CODE
671+            DC    A(PRT01+0) ADDRESS OF DATA IN IOAREA1
672+            DC    4X'00' BUCKET                              3-5
673+            NOPR  0 PUT LENGTH IN REG12 (ONLY UNDEF.
674+            LA    10,0(14) LOAD USER POINTER REG
675+            DC    2X'00' NOT USED                            3-5
676+            CCW   9,PRT02+0,X'20',120-0
677+IJJZ0017   EQU   *
```

Figure 7-28 V-type address constant and Absolute Expression in DTFPR

It should be noted that, in addition to establishing an address constant and an external label, the V-type address constant indicates to the linkage editor that an AUTOLINK function should be performed. The Autolink function performed by the linkage editor automatically searches the Relocatable Library for control sections containing any external labels which are not included as input to the linkage editor. Thus, external references can be part of a control section or object module contained on the Relocatable Library and be included in the program phase by the linkage editor when autolink is used.

Note that the address constant defined in the DTF in Figure 7-28 is VL3(IJDFCPIZ). This illustrates the use of a length with an address constant. All addresses in the System/360 are calculated using the 24 low-order bits in a register (registers have 32 bits = 4 bytes). The high-order 8 bits are not used for addressing. Thus, in an address constant, the high-order 8 bits are not used for the address of a relocatable expression (that is, a label in a program). Therefore, if desired, the address constant can be defined as three bytes and the correct address will still be contained in the address constant. However, when a length is used, no alignment takes place when the constant is assembled. Thus, when a length is used, it is the programmer's responsibility to ensure that the necessary boundary alignments are correct. Whenever a relocatable expression is used in an address constant, the length may be three or four bytes.

Note also in the DTF illustrated in Figure 7-28 the use of an absolute expression with an address constant. An absolute expression is a constant value which will not change regardless of where the program is loaded into core storage. When an absolute expression is used in an address constant to define a constant value, a length of one to four bytes may be specified. The constant generated in the DTF in Figure 7-28 would be one byte in length and have a hexadecimal value of 14. Thus, the following examples are equivalent to each other.

EXAMPLE

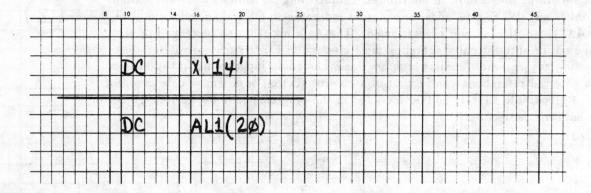

Figure 7-29 Absolute expression for address constant

Note that the value specified in the absolute expression used in the address constant is a decimal value while the value specified in the "X" constant is a hexadecimal value.

SAMPLE PROGRAM

The sample program presented in this chapter performs the same function as the program in Chapter 5, that is, it lists the inventory master file. However, the sample program in this chapter uses external modules and is self-relocating.

The first routine entered in the sample program establishes a base register and resolves the address constants in the program. This routine is illustrated in Figure 7-30.

EXAMPLE

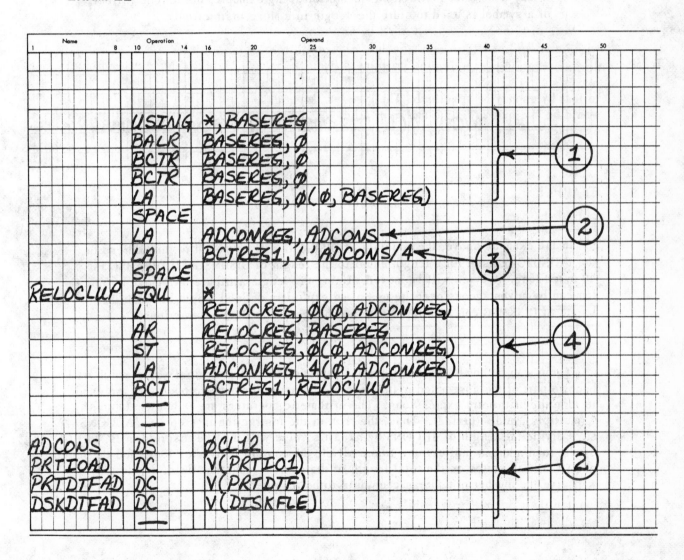

Figure 7-30 Routine to resolve numerous address constants

The routine shown above is capable of resolving any number of address constants in a self-relocating program. Taken step by step, it does the following:

1. A base register is established using the BALR instruction and then the base register value is decremented by 2 so that it contains the address where the program was loaded.

2. The address of the beginning of the address constants to be resolved is loaded into a register.

3. The instruction at step 3 loads the number of address constants to be resolved into BCTREG1. This instruction illustrates one use of the symbolic length attribute and the arithmetic combination of terms. Each symbolic label in an assembly has an implied or explicitly defined length. Whenever the L' symbol is used followed by the name of the label, the length of the symbolic label will be substituted. Thus, in the example, the length of ADCONS (= 12 bytes) is substituted for the expression L' ADCONS. The length attribute can be used in any assembler instruction. In the following example, the length attribute of a symbol is used to state the length in a Move instruction.

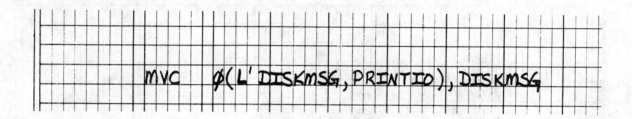

Figure 7-31 Example of length attribute

In the example above, the constant at DISKMSG will be moved to the address in the PRINTIO register for a length equal to the length of DISKMSG. If DISKMSG is 40 bytes long, 40 bytes will be moved. Using the length attribute in a move instruction can be advantageous over the use of an explicitly defined length because the length of DISKMSG can be altered with no change to the Move instruction.

Terms can be combined in arithmetic expressions to form a final value which will become part of the assembled instruction or constant. Arithmetic operators are used to form the arithmetic expressions. The arithmetic operators are + (add), – (minus), * (multiply), and / (divide). Thus, the term in the instruction in step 3 (L'ADCONS/4) says divide the length of ADCONS by 4. This value will then be inserted in BCTREG1 by the load address instruction. Since all the adcons are four bytes long, and the length of ADCONS is stated as the total length of the address constant field, dividing by 4 will give the number of address constants to be resolved.

It should be noted that several arithmetic terms can be combined to give a final value. Thus, the following two instructions could be used to clear a printer I/O area.

EXAMPLE

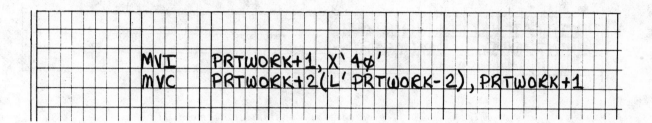

```
MVI     PRTWORK+1, X'40'
MVC     PRTWORK+2(L'PRTWORK-2), PRTWORK+1
```

Figure 7-32 Instruction to clear printer area

In the example above, the number of bytes moved by the MVC instruction will be equal to the length of PRTWORK less 2. Thus, it can be seen that the use of the symbolic length attribute in an instruction can be of help to the programmer because no matter what length changes are made to PRTWORK, the above instructions remain valid to clear the area. If an absolute length had been stated, each time the length of PRTWORK was changed, the MVC instruction would have to be changed.

4. The RELOCLUP routine loads the first address constant into RELOCREG, adds the value in the base register (= address where program was loaded) to the value in the address constant, and then stores the result back in the address constant. It then increments the address to point to the next address constant and continues the process for each address constant defined in the program.

Thus, by performing the above routine, the program is made self-relocating and can be loaded in any location in core for execution.

The program presented in this chapter uses DTF's and I/O areas which are defined as separate control sections and which are catalogued on the relocatable library. This enables more than one program to utilize the same DTF and I/O area. In order to reference the DTF's, V-type address constants are used.

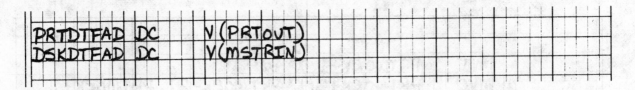

Figure 7-33 V-type address constants for remote DTFs

The V-type address constants specified above provide the addresses of the DTF's PRTOUT and MSTRIN. These DTF's are defined in separate control sections and are named as entry points in the control sections.

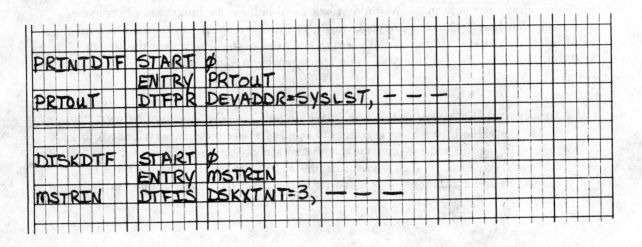

Figure 7-34 Remote DTFs in separate control sections

Thus, as shown, the entry points PRTOUT and MSTRIN are specified as external labels in the sample program through the use of V-type address constants and are therefore addressable in the sample program.

INPUT

The input to the sample program consists of the inventory master file.

FIELD	FIELD NAME	FORMAT	POSITION	NO. OF DIGITS	LENGTH
Part Number					
Division Number	MSTRDIV	N - B	1	2	1
Prime Number	MSTRPRME	N - B	2 - 4	6	3
Dash Number	MSTRDASH	N - B	5 - 7	5	3
Description	MSTRNAME	AN	8 - 32	25	25
Qty on Hand	MSTRQOH	N - B	33 - 35	7	3
Qty on Order	MSTRQOO	N - B	36 - 38	7	3
Qty Reserved	MSTRQRSV	N - B	39 - 41	7	3
Part Number - NA					
Division - NA	MASYDIV	N - B	42	2	1
Prime - NA	MASYPRME	N - B	43 - 45	6	3
Dash - NA	MASYDASH	N - B	46 - 48	5	3
Type	MSTRTYPE	N - Z	49	1	1
Source	MSTRSRCE	N - Z	50	1	1
Unit Price	MSTRUNIT	N - B	51 - 53	6	3
Filler	MSTRXTRA	AN	54 - 55	2	2

LEGEND: N - B — Numeric, Binary   N - Z — Numeric, Zoned Decimal
               AN — Alpha - numeric

OUTPUT

The output of the sample program is the master list report.

	0	1	2	3	4	5	6

```
       0          1          2          3          4          5          6
    1234567890123456789012345678901234567890123456789012345678901234567890
 1
 2     XX/XX/XX                   MASTER LIST                    PAGE XXX
 3
 4     PART NUMBER                                  NEXT ASSEMBLY
 5     DIV PRIME DASH              DESCRIPTION       DIV PRIME DASH   SOURCE
 6
 7  XX XXXXXX XXXXX    XXXXXXXXXXXXXXXXXXXXXXXXXXX XX XXXXXX XXXXX     XXXX
 8
 9
10  END OF MASTER LISTING
11
```

PROGRAM

The program presented in this chapter prints the inventory master file. The program is self-relocating and it uses remote DTFs. The following is the source listing of the program.

```
        SELF-RELOCATING MASTER PRINT                                              PAGE   1

   LOC  OBJECT CODE     ADDR1 ADDR2  STMT   SOURCE STATEMENT              DOS CL3-5 08/26/70

  000000                               2 PRTMASTR START 0                          PRTR0020
                                       3        PRINT NOGEN                        PRTR0030

                                       5 ****                                      PRTR0040
                                       6 * THIS PROGRAM IS USED TO PRINT THE MASTER FILE AFTER IT HAS BEEN   PRTR0050
                                       7 * CREATED. THE PROGRAM IS SELF-RELOCATING AND USES EXTERNAL MODULES PRTR0060
                                       8 * FOR THE DTF'S AND FOR THE I/O AREAS     PRTR0070
                                       9 *                                         PRTR0080
                                      10 * REGISTER USAGE IS AS FOLLOWS            PRTR0090
                                      11 *                                         PRTR0100

  00000C                              13 BASEREG  EQU    12                        PRTR0120
  00000E                              14 LINKRG14 EQU    14                        PRTR0130
  00000B                              15 LINKREG1 EQU    11                        PRTR0140
  00000A                              16 CVDREG   EQU    10                        PRTR0150
  000000                              17 WORKREG  EQU    0                         PRTR0160
  000001                              18 IOREG    EQU    1                         PRTR0170
  000009                              19 INPUTREG EQU    9                         PRTR0180
  000008                              20 OUTPTREG EQU    8                         PRTR0190
  000007                              21 ADCONREG EQU    7                         PRTR0200
  000006                              22 RELOCREG EQU    6                         PRTR0210
  000005                              23 BCTREG1  EQU    5                         PRTR0220

                                      25 ****                                      PRTR0240
                                      26 * THIS ROUTINE ESTABLISHES A BASE REGISTER AND PERFORMS THE   PRTR0250
                                      27 * SELF-RELOCATING FUNCTIONS               PRTR0260
                                      28 ****                                      PRTR0270

  000000                              30        USING *,BASEREG      ESTABLISH BASE REGISTER    PRTR0290
  000000 05C0                         31        BALR  BASEREG,0                    PRTR0300
  000002 06C0                         32        BCTR  BASEREG,0      SUBTRACT 2 TO GET STARTING ADDR  PRTR0310
  000004 06C0                         33        BCTR  BASEREG,0                    PRTR0320
  000006 41CC 0000         00000      34        LA    BASEREG,0(BASEREG)   ZERO HIGH-ORDER BITS  PRTR0330

  00000A 4170 C224         00224      36        LA    ADCONREG,ADCONS   LOAD ADDRESS OF ADDRESS CONSTANTS  PRTR0350
  00000E 4150 0003         00003      37        LA    BCTREG1,L'ADCONS/4  LOAD NUMBER OF ADCONS  PRTR0360

  000012                              39 RELOCLUP EQU   *                          PRTR0380
  000012 5860 7000         00000      40        L     RELOCREG,0(0,ADCONREG) LOAD ADCON INTO REGISTER  PRTR0390
  000016 1A6C                         41        AR    RELOCREG,BASEREG   GET ABSOLUTE ADDRESS  PRTR0400
  000018 5060 7000         00000      42        ST    RELOCREG,0(0,ADCONREG)  STORE ADDRESS  PRTR0410
  00001C 4170 7004         00004      43        LA    ADCONREG,4(0,ADCONREG)  BUMP ADDRESS  PRTR0420
  000020 4650 C012         00012      44        BCT   BCTREG1,RELOCLUP   GO TO NEXT ADCON  PRTR0430

                                      46 ****                                      PRTR0450
                                      47 * THE FOLLOWING ROUTINE OPENS THE FILES AND PRINTS THE HEADINGS  PRTR0460
                                      48 ****                                      PRTR0470

  000024 5850 C228         00228      50        L     5,PRTDTFAD      LOAD ADDRESS OF PRINT DTF  PRTR0490
  000028 5860 C22C         0022C      51        L     6,DSKDTFAD      LOAD ADDRESS OF DISK DTF   PRTR0500

                                      53        OPENR (6),(5)         OPEN FILES                 PRTR0520

                                      67        COMRG                 GET COMM REGION ADDRESS    PRTR0540
  000050 D207 C393 1000 00393 00000   71        MVC   DATEHDR(8),0(1)  MOVE DATE TO HEADER       PRTR0550

  000056 5840 C224         00224      73        L     4,PRTIOAD       LOAD ADDRESS OF PRINT I/O AREA  PRTR0570
  00005A 45E0 C17E         0017E      74        BAL   LINKRG14,HEADROU  PRINT REPORT HEADINGS    PRTR0580

                                      76 ****                                      PRTR0600
                                      77 * THIS ROUTINE IS ENTERED TO SET THE LIMITS FOR THE BEGINNING OF  PRTR0610
                                      78 * SEQUENTIAL PROCESSING AND TO READ THE FIRST RECORD.   PRTR0620
                                      79 ****                                      PRTR0630

  00005E 5810 C22C         0022C      81        L     IOREG,DSKDTFAD  LOAD ADDRESS OF DISK FILE  PRTR0650
                                      82        SETL  (IOREG),BOF     SET LIMITS                 PRTR0660

  00007E                              93 READMSTR EQU   *                          PRTR0680
  00007E 5810 C22C         0022C      94        L     IOREG,DSKDTFAD  LOAD ADDRESS OF DISK DTF   PRTR0690
  000082 4100 C201         002D1      95        LA    WORKREG,MSTRWORK  LOAD ADDRESS OF WORK AREA  PRTR0700
                                      96        GET   (IOREG),(WORKREG)  READ MASTER FILE        PRTR0710
  000092 9120 101E         0001E     102        TM    30(1),X'20'     IS IT END OF FILE          PRTR0720
  000096 4710 C1E0         001E0     103        BO    MSTREND         YES, GO TO EOF ROUTINE     PRTR0730

                                     105 ****                                      PRTR0750
                                     106 * THIS ROUTINE IS ENTERED TO CONVERT THE MASTER RECORD TO PRINTABLE  PRTR0760
                                     107 * FORM                                    PRTR0770
                                     108 ****                                      PRTR0780
```

LOC	OBJECT CODE	ADDR1	ADDR2	STMT	SOURCE STATEMENT		DOS CL3-5 08/26/70
00009A	9240 C309		00309	110	MVI	PRTWORK+1,X'40' CLEAR PRINTER AREA	PRTR0800
00009E	D282 C30A C309	0030A	00309	111	MVC	PRTWORK+2(L'PRTWORK-2),PRTWORK+1	PRTR0810
0000A4	58A0 C240		00240	112	L	CVDREG,FULLZERO ZERO REGISTER	PRTR0820
0000A8	43A0 C2D1		002D1	113	IC	CVDREG,MSTRDIV PUT DIV IN REGISTER	PRTR0830
0000AC	45B0 C178		00178	114	BAL	LINKREG1,CONVERTD+4 CONVERT VALUE TO DECIMAL	PRTR0840
0000B0	F311 C309 C236	00309	00236	115	UNPK	DIVPRT(2),DBLWORD+6(2) UNPACK TO REPORT	PRTR0850
0000B6	96F0 C30A		0030A	116	OI	DIVPRT+1,X'F0' RESET SING	PRTR0860
0000BA	D203 C238 C240	00238	00240	118	MVC	FULLWORD,FULLZERO ZERO FULLWORD	PRTR0880
0000C0	D202 C239 C2D7	00239	002D7	119	MVC	FULLWORD+1(3),MSTRPRME MOVE PRIME TO WORK AREA	PRTR0890
0000C6	45B0 C174		00174	120	BAL	LINKREG1,CONVERTD GO TO CONVERT VALUE TO DECIMAL	PRTR0900
0000CA	F353 C30C C234	0030C	00234	121	UNPK	PRMEPRT(6),DBLWORD+4(4) UPPACK PRIME	PRTR0910
0000D0	96F0 C311		00311	122	OI	PRMEPRT+5,X'F0' RESET SIGN	PRTR0920
0000D4	D202 C239 C2D5	00239	002D5	124	MVC	FULLWORD+1(3),MSTRDASH MOVE DASH TO WORK AREA	PRTR0940
0000DA	45B0 C174		00174	125	BAL	LINKREG1,CONVERTD GO TO CONVERT VALUE TO DECIMAL	PRTR0950
0000DE	F342 C313 C235	00313	00235	126	UNPK	DASHPRT(5),DBLWORD+5(3) UNPACK TO REPORT	PRTR0960
0000E4	96F0 C317		00317	127	OI	DASHPRT+4,X'F0' RESET SIGN	PRTR0970
0000E8	D218 C31A C2D8	0031A	002D8	129	MVC	DESCPRT(25),MSTRNAME MOVE DESCRIPTION TO REPORT	PRTR0990
0000EE	58A0 C240		00240	131	L	CVDREG,FULLZERO ZERO REGISTER	PRTR1010
0000F2	43A0 C2FA		002FA	132	IC	CVDREG,MASYDIV PUT DIVISION IN REGISTER	PRTR1020
0000F6	45B0 C178		00178	133	BAL	LINKREG1,CONVERTD+4 GO TO CONVERT TO DECIMAL	PRTR1030
0000FA	F311 C334 C236	00334	00236	134	UNPK	NADIVPRT(2),DBLWORD+6(2) UNPACK TO REPORT	PRTR1040
000100	96F0 C335		00335	135	OI	NADIVPRT+1,X'F0' RESET SIGN	PRTR1050
000104	D202 C239 C2FB	00239	002FB	137	MVC	FULLWORD+1(3),MASYPRME MOVE PRIME TO WORK AREA	PRTR1070
00010A	45B0 C174		00174	138	BAL	LINKREG1,CONVERTD GO TO CONVERT TO DECIMAL	PRTR1080
00010E	F353 C337 C234	00337	00234	139	UNPK	NAPRMPRT(6),DBLWORD+4(4) UNPACK TO REPORT	PRTR1090
000114	96F0 C33C		0033C	140	OI	NAPRMPRT+5,X'F0' RESET SIGN	PRTR1100
000118	D202 C239 C2FE	00239	002FE	142	MVC	FULLWORD+1(3),MASYDASH MOVE DASH TO WORK AREA	PRTR1120
00011E	45B0 C174		00174	143	BAL	LINKREG1,CONVERTD CONVERT TO DECIMAL	PRTR1130
000122	F342 C33E C235	0033E	00235	144	UNPK	NADASPRT(5),DBLWORD+5(3) UNPACK TO REPORT	PRTR1140
000128	96F0 C342		00342	145	OI	NADASPRT+4,X'F0' RESET SIGN	PRTR1150
00012C	95F1 C302		00302	147	CLI	MSTRSRCE,C'1' IS IT A MANUFACTURED PART	PRTR1170
000130	4770 C13E		0013E	148	BNE	VENDPART NO, GO TO VENDOR ROUTINE	PRTR1180
000134	D203 C346 C538	00346	00538	149	MVC	SRCEPRT(4),=C'MANU' YES, MOVE MANU TO REPORT	PRTR1190
00013A	47F0 C144		00144	150	B	PUTPRT GO TO PRINT RECORD	PRTR1200
00013E				152	VENDPART EQU	*	PRTR1220
00013E	D203 C346 C53C	00346	0053C	153	MVC	SRCEPRT(4),=C'VEND' MOVE VENDOR TO REPORT	PRTR1230
000144				155	PUTPRT EQU	*	PRTR1250
000144	5810 C228		00228	156	L	IOREG,PRTDTFAD LOAD ADDRESS OF PRINT DTF	PRTR1260
000148	D284 4000 C308	00000	00308	157	MVC	0(133,4),PRTWORK MOVE TO PRINTER I/O AREA	PRTR1270
				158	PUT	(IOREG) PRINT RECORD	PRTR1280
000158	9240 C308		00308	163	MVI	SKIP,X'40' MOVE CC CHARACTER TO WORK AREA	PRTR1290
00015C	FA10 C244 C542	00244	00542	164	AP	LNCNT,=P'1' UPDATE LINE COUNT	PRTR1300
000162	F911 C244 C540	00244	00540	165	CP	LNCNT,=P'56' HAVE 56 LINES BEEN PRINTED	PRTR1310
000168	4770 C07E		0007E	166	BNE	READMSTR NO, GOTO READ MASTER	PRTR1320
00016C	45E0 C17E		0017E	167	BAL	LINKRG14,HEADROU GO TO DO HEADER	PRTR1330
000170	47F0 C07E		0007E	168	B	READMSTR GO TO READ MASTER	PRTR1340
				170	****		PRTR1370
				171	* THIS ROUTINE IS ENTERED TO CONVERT BINARY DATA TO PACKED DECIMAL		PRTR1380
				172	* DATA		PRTR1390
				173	****		PRTR1400
000174				175	CONVERTD EQU *		PRTR1420
000174	58A0 C238		00238	176	L	CVDREG,FULLWORD LOAD BINARY DATA TO REGISTER	PRTR1430
000178	4EA0 C230		00230	177	CVD	CVDREG,DBLWORD CONVERT VALUE TO PACKED DECIMAL	PRTR1440
00017C	07FB			178	BR	LINKREG1 RETURN TO CALLER	PRTR1450
				180	****		PRTR1470
				181	* THIS ROUTINE IS ENTERED TO PRINT THE REPORT HEADINGS.		PRTR1480
				182	****		PRTR1490
00017E				184	HEADROU EQU	*	PRTR1510
00017E	50E0 C23C		0023C	185	ST	LINKRG14,SAVE14 SAVE LINK REGISTER	PRTR1520
000182	FB11 C244 C244	00244	00244	186	SP	LNCNT,LNCNT ZERO LINE COUNTER	PRTR1530
000188	FA10 C246 C542	00246	00542	187	AP	PGCNT,=P'1' ADD 1 TO PAGE NUMBER	PRTR1540
00018E	D203 C3CC C248	003CC	00248	188	MVC	PGNOHDR-1(4),PGEDIT MOVE EDIT PATTERN TO HEADER	PRTR1550
000194	DE03 C3CC C246	003CC	00246	189	ED	PGNOHDR-1(4),PGCNT EDIT PAGE COUNT	PRTR1560
00019A	5810 C228		00228	190	L	IOREG,PRTDTFAD LOAD ADDRESS OF PRINT DTF	PRTR1570
00019E	D284 4000 C38D	00000	0038D	191	MVC	0(133,4),HEAD1 MOVE HEADER1 TO PRINT I/O AREA	PRTR1580
				192	PUT	(IOREG) PRINT RECORD	PRTR1590
0001AE	D284 4000 C413	00000	00413	198	MVC	0(133,4),HEAD2 MOVE HEADER2 TO PRINT I/O AREA	PRTR1610
0001B4	5810 C228		00228	199	L	IOREG,PRTDTFAD LOAD ADDRESS OF DTF	PRTR1620
				200	PUT	(IOREG) PRINT RECORD	PRTR1630
0001C2	5810 C228		00228	206	L	IOREG,PRTDTFAD LOAD ADDRESS OF DTF	PRTR1650
0001C6	D284 4000 C498	00000	00498	207	MVC	0(133,4),HEAD3 MOVE HEADER3 TO I/O AREA	PRTR1660
				208	PUT	(IOREG) PRINT REOCRD	PRTR1670

DOS CL3-5 08/26/70

LOC	OBJECT CODE	ADDR1	ADDR2	STMT	SOURCE STATEMENT			
0001D6	92F0 C308	00308		214	*	MVI	SKIP,C'0'	MOVE CONTROL CHARACTER FOR FIRST	PRTR1690
				215	*			LINE OF REPORT AFTER HEADING	PRTR1700
0001DA	58E0 C23C		0023C	216		L	LINKRG14,SAVE14	RELOAD RETURN REGISTER	PRTR1710
0001DE	07FE			217		BR	LINKRG14	RETURN TO CALLER	PRTR1720

```
                                219 ****                                                           PRTR1740
                                220 * THIS ROUTINE IS ENTERED WHEN END-OF-FILE IS REACHED ON THE   PRTR1750
                                221 * MASTER FILE                                                  PRTR1760
                                222 ****                                                           PRTR1770

0001E0                          224 MSTREND  EQU    *                                              PRTR1790
0001E0 5810 C228         00228  225          L      IOREG,PRTDTFAD    LOAD ADDRESS OF DTF          PRTR1800
0001E4 D283 4000 C24C 00000 0024C 226        MVC    0(132,4),ENDMSG     MOVE END MSG TO PRINTER    PRTR1810
                                227          PUT    (IOREG)             PRINT RECORD               PRTR1820
0001F4 5850 C228         00228  232          L      5,PRTDTFAD        LOAD ADDRESS OF PRINT FILE   PRTR1830
0001F8 5860 C22C         0022C  233          L      6,DSKDTFAD        LOAD ADDRESS OF DISK FILE    PRTR1840
                                234          ESETL (6)                 END SEQ RETRIEVAL           PRTR1850
                                239          CLOSER (5),(6)          CLOSE FILES                   PRTR1860
                                251          EOJ                     END OF JOB                    PRTR1870
```

```
  LOC  OBJECT CODE    ADDR1 ADDR2 STMT   SOURCE STATEMENT                              DOS CL3-5 08/26/70

                                  255 ****                                            PRTR1890
                                  256 * CONSTANTS, WORK AREAS, ETC.                    PRTR1900
                                  257 ****                                            PRTR1910

  000224                          259 ADCONS   DS    OCL12                            PRTR1930
  000224 00000000                 260 PRTIOAD  DC    V(PRTIO1)                        PRTR1940
  000228 00000000                 261 PRTDTFAD DC    V(PRTDTF)                        PRTR1950
  00022C 00000000                 262 DSKDTFAD DC    V(DISKFLE)                       PRTR1960

  000230                          264 DBLWORD  DS    D                                PRTR1980
  000238                          265 FULLWORD DS    F                                PRTR1990
  00023C                          266 SAVE14   DS    F                                PRTR2000
  000240 00000000                 267 FULLZERO DC    F'0'                             PRTR2010
  000244 000C                     268 LNCNT    DC    X'000C'                          PRTR2020
  000246 000C                     269 PGCNT    DC    X'000C'                          PRTR2030
  000248 40202020                 270 PGEDIT   DC    X'40202020'                      PRTR2040
  00024C                          271 ENDMSG   DS    OCL133                           PRTR2050
  00024C 60                       272          DC    C'-'                             PRTR2060
  00024D C5D5C440D6C640D4         273          DC    CL132'END OF MASTER LISTING'     PRTR2070

  0002D1                          275 MSTRWORK DS    OCL55                            PRTR2090
  0002D1                          276 MSTRDIV  DS    CL1                              PRTR2100
  0002D2                          277 MSTRPRME DS    CL3                              PRTR2110
  0002D5                          278 MSTRDASH DS    CL3                              PRTR2120
  0002D8                          279 MSTRNAME DS    CL25                             PRTR2130
  0002F1                          280          DS    CL9                              PRTR2140
  0002FA                          281 MSTRASSY DS    OCL7                             PRTR2150
  0002FA                          282 MASYDIV  DS    CL1                              PRTR2160
  0002FB                          283 MASYPRME DS    CL3                              PRTR2170
  0002FE                          284 MASYDASH DS    CL3                              PRTR2180
  000301                          285          DS    CL1                              PRTR2190
  000302                          286 MSTRSRCE DS    CL1                              PRTR2200
  000303                          287          DS    CL5                              PRTR2210

  000308                          289 PRTWORK  DS    OCL133                           PRTR2230
  000308                          290 SKIP     DS    CL1                              PRTR2240
  000309                          291 DIVPRT   DS    CL2                              PRTR2250
  00030B                          292          DS    CL1                              PRTR2260
  00030C                          293 PRMEPRT  DS    CL6                              PRTR2270
  000312                          294          DS    CL1                              PRTR2280
  000313                          295 DASHPRT  DS    CL5                              PRTR2290
  000318                          296          DS    CL2                              PRTR2300
  00031A                          297 DESCPRT  DS    CL25                             PRTR2310
  000333                          298          DS    CL1                              PRTR2320
  000334                          299 NADIVPRT DS    CL2                              PRTR2330
  000336                          300          DS    CL1                              PRTR2340
  000337                          301 NAPRMPRT DS    CL6                              PRTR2350
  00033D                          302          DS    CL1                              PRTR2360
  00033E                          303 NADASPRT DS    CL5                              PRTR2370
  000343                          304          DS    CL3                              PRTR2380
  000346                          305 SRCEPRT  DS    CL4                              PRTR2390
  00034A                          306          DS    CL55                             PRTR2400
  000381                          307          DS    CL12                             PRTR2410

  00038D                          309 HEAD1    DS    OCL133                           PRTR2430
  00038D F140                     310          DC    C'1 '                            PRTR2440
  00038F 40404040                 311          DC    CL4' '                           PRTR2450
  000393                          312 DATEHDR  DS    CL8                              PRTR2460
  00039B 4040404040404040         313          DC    C'          MASTER LIST                 PAGE '   PRTR2470
  0003CD                          314 PGNOHDR  DS    CL3                              PRTR2480
  0003D0 4040404040404040         315          DC    CL67' '                          PRTR2490

  000413                          317 HEAD2    DS    OCL133                           PRTR2510
  000413 F040                     318          DC    C'0 '                            PRTR2520
  000415 D7C1D9E340D5E4D4         319          DC    C'PART NUMBER'                   PRTR2530
  000420 4040404040404040         320          DC    CL31' '                          PRTR2540
  00043F D5C5E7E340C1E2E2         321          DC    C'NEXT ASSEMBLY'                 PRTR2550
  00044C 4040404040404040         322          DC    CL76' '                          PRTR2560

  000498                          324 HEAD3    DS    OCL133                           PRTR2580
  000498 40                       325          DC    C' '                             PRTR2590
                                  326          DC    C'DIV PRIME DASH       DESCRIPTION       DIV PRIME DC   PRTR2600
  000499 C4C9E54007D9C9D4                            ASH    SOURCE'                   PRTR2610
  0004DB 4040404040404040         327          DC    CL66' '                          PRTR2620
                                  328          END                                   PRTR2630
  000520 5B5BC2D6D7C5D5D9         329          =C'$$BOPENR'
  000528 5B5BC2E2C5E3D340         330          =C'$$BSETL '
  000530 5B5BC2C3D3D6E2C5         331          =C'$$BCLOSE'
  000538 D4C1D5E4                 332          =C'MANU'
  00053C E5C5D5C4                 333          =C'VEND'
  000540 056C                     334          =P'56'
  000542 1C                       335          =P'1'
```

```
LOC  OBJECT CODE    ADDR1 ADDR2 STMT   SOURCE STATEMENT                                    DOS CL3-5 08/26/70

000000                           1 PRINT1   START  0                                              PRTO0010
                                 2          ENTRY  PRTDTF,PRTIO1                                   PRTO0020
                                 3 PRTDTF   DTFPR  DEVADDR=SYSLST,IOAREA1=PRTIO1,BLKSIZE=133,CTLCHR=ASA,   CPRTO0030
                                                   DEVICE=1403,MODNAME=IJDFAZZZ,RECFORM=FIXUNB           PRTO0040
                                 4+** 360 N-CL-453 DTFPR    CHANGE LEVEL 3-5                        3-5
000000                           5+         DC     0D'0'
000000 000080000000              6+PRTDTF   DC     X'000080000000' RES. COUNT,COM. BYTES,STATUS BTS
000006 00                        7+         DC     AL1(0) LOGICAL UNIT CLASS
000007 03                        8+         DC     AL1(3) LOGICAL UNIT
000008 00000028                  9+         DC     A(*+32) CCW  ADDR.
00000C 00000000                 10+         DC     4X'00' CCB-ST BYTE,CSW CCW ADDRESS
000010 00                       11+         DC     AL1(0)
000011 000000                   12+         DC     VL3(IJDFAZZZ) ADDRESS OF LOGIC MODULE
000014 08                       13+         DC     X'08' DTF TYPE  (PRINTER)
000015 30                       14+         DC     AL1(48) SWITCHES
000016 09                       15+         DC     X'09' NORMAL  COMM. CODE
000017 09                       16+         DC     X'09' CONTROL COMM. CODE
000018 00000031                 17+         DC     A(PRTIO1+1) ADDRESS OF DATA IN IOAREA1
00001C 00000000                 18+         DC     4X'00' BUCKET                            3-5
000020 0700                     19+         NOPR   0 PUT LENGTH IN REG12 (ONLY UNDEF.)
000022 4700 0000          00000 20+         NOP    0 LOAD USER POINTER REG
000026 0000                     21+         DC     2X'00' NOT USED                          3-5
000028 0900003120000084         22+         CCW    9,PRTIO1+1,X'20',133-1
000030                          23+IJJZ0001 EQU    *


000030 4040404040404040         25 PRTIO1   DC     CL133' '                          666      PRTO0060
                                26          END                                               PRTO0070
```

```
LOC  OBJECT CODE    ADDR1 ADDR2 STMT   SOURCE STATEMENT                                    DOS CL3-5 08/26/70

                                 1 DISK1      START 0                                            DISK0010
000000                           2            ENTRY DISKFLE,DISKKEY,DISKIO1,DISKIOW             DISK0020
                                 3 DISKFLE DTFIS DSKXTNT=3,IOROUT=RETRVE,KEYLEN=7,NRECDS=65,    CDISK0030
                                        RECFORM=FIXBLK,RECSIZE=55,CYLOFL=2,DEVICE=2311,         CDISK0040
                                        HINDEX=2311,IOAREAS=DISKIO1,KEYARG=DISKKEY,KEYLOC=1,    CDISK0050
                                        MODNAME=IJHZRSZZ,MSTIND=YES,TYPEFLE=SEQNTL,WORKS=YES     DISK0060
                                 4+* 360N-IO-457 DTFIS   CHANGE LEVEL 3-4                              3-4
                                 5+* 360N-IO-457 DTFIS1  CHANGE LEVEL 3-4                              3-4
                                 6+         DC    0D'0' 3-4
000000                           7+DISKFLE DC    X'000008' 3-4
000000 000008                    8+         DC    XL5'0' 3-4
000003 0000000000                9+         DC    A(DISKFLEB) CCW ADDR
000008 00000008                 10+         DC    XL4'0'
00000C 00000000                 11+         DC    V(IJHZRSZZ) ADDR LOGIC MODULE
000010 00000000                 12+         DC    AL1(38) TYPE FILE INDICATOR
000014 26                       13+         DC    B'00001000' OPTION C03-4
000015 08                       14+         DC    CL7'DISKFLE' FILE NAME
000016 C4C9E2D2C603C5           15+         DC    AL1(0) PRIME DATA DEVICE TYPE INDICATOR
00001D 00                       16+DISKFLEC DC    XL1'0' STATUS INDICATORS
00001E 00                       17+         DC    AL1(0) INDEX DEVICE TYPE INDICATOR
00001F 00                       18+         DC    AL1((DISKFLEE-DISKFLE)/4) REL POS XTNT-CEL  TABLE
000020 46                       19+         DC    XL3'000000' HHR FIRST DATA RECORD IN CYL.
000021 000000                   20+         DC    H'0' HH LAST PRIME DATA TRK IN CYL
000024 0000                     21+         DC    XL1'00' HI RECORD # ON MAST.NDX/CYL.NDX
000026 00                       22+         DC    XL1'00' HI RECORD # ON PRIME DATA TRACK
000027 00                       23+         DC    XL1'00' HI RECORD # ON OVFLO TRACK
000028 00                       24+         DC    XL1'00' HI RECORD # ON SHARED TRACK
000029 00                       25+         DC    XL1'00' HI RECORD # ON TI TRACK
00002A 00                       26+         DC    B'01000000' RETRIEVAL SWITCH
00002B 40                       27+         DC    XL7'00' PRIME DATA START
00002C 00000000000000           28+         DC    XL7'00' MBBCCH CYL INDEX START
000033 00000000000000           29+         DC    XL7'00' MBBCCH MST INDEX START
00003A 00C00000000000           30+         DC    X'00' INDEX LEVEL NUMBER
000041 00                       31+         DC    XL8'00' MBBCCHHR LAST PR.DATA RCD ADDR.
000042 0000000000000000         32+         DC    H'0' RECORD LENGTH
00004A 0000                     33+         DC    H'0' KEY LENGTH
00004C 0000                     34+         DC    H'0' BLOCKSIZE
00004E 0000                     35+         DC    H'0' RL+10
000050 0000                     36+         DC    H'0' BLOCKING FACTOR
000052 0000                     37+         DC    H'0' INDEX ENTRY LENGTH KL+10
000054 0000                     38+         DC    H'0' PR.DATA REC. KEY+DATA
000056 0000                     39+         DC    H'0' OVFLO KEY AND DATA KL+RL
000058 0000                     40+         DC    H'0' KL+NRCDS*RL+8
00005A 0000                     41+         DC    H'0' KL+RL+18
00005C 0000                     42+         DC    H'0' KEY LOCATION
00005E 0000                     43+         DC    H'5' 5
000060 0005                     44+         DC    H'10'
000062 000A                     45+         DC    Y(DISKFLE2-DISKFLE) BASE FOR TABLE2
000064 007C                     46+         DC    Y(DISKFLEB-DISKFLE) BASE FOR TABLE3
000066 00D8                     47+DISKFLES DC    5H'0' COMMON SEEK/SEARCH BUC.
000068 00000000000000           48+DISKFLEW DC    5H'0' CWORKAREA USED IN MACRO
000072 0000000000000000         49+DISKFLEM EQU   *
00007C                          50+******************* SECOND PART OF TABLE ********************
                                51+DISKFLE2 EQU   *
00007C                          52+         DC    A(DISKFLES+3) ADDR OF COMMON SEEK/SEARCH BUC.
00007C 0000006B                 53+         DC    A(DISKFLEW) ADDR OF RANDOM SEQ BUCKET
000080 00000072                 54+         DC    A(DISKIO1) ADDR OF IOAREAS
000084 0000012F                 55+         DC    F'0' ADDR IOAREA2                       3-4
000088 00000000                 56+         DC    A(DISKKEY) ADDR OF KEYARG
00008C 00000128                 57+         DC    F'0' ADDR OF WORKR
000090 00000000                 58+         DC    F'0' SEQ CURRENT IOAREA
000094 00000000                 59+         NOP   0
000098 4700 0000        00000   60+         DC    X'00' NO VERIFY
00009C 00                       61+         DC    X'00' BLOCKED
00009D 00                       62+         DC    3H'0' CCHHR            LIMITS FOR SEQ.
00009E 000000000000             63+         DC    H'0' BLOCKED.
0000A4 0000                     64+         DC    X'C7'
0000A6 C7                       65+         DC    X'0000000000'
0000A7 0000000000               66+DISKFLEH DC    4H'0' MBBCCHHR        CURRENT DISKADDR FOR SEQ
0000AC 0000000000000000         67+         DC    4H'0' MBBCCHHR        CURRENT OVFL. ENTRY FOR SEQ.
0000B4 0000000000000000         68+         DC    H'0' SEQ RECORD COUNTER
0000BC 0000                     69+         DC    H'0' HR CURRENT TRCNDX ENTRY FOR SEQ.
0000BE 0000                     70+DISKFLET DC    H'0' NUMBER OF RECORDS TAGGED
0000C0 0000                     71+         DS    2D RESERVED.
0000C8                          72+****************** THIRD PART OF TABLE ********************
0000D8 0700006940000006         73+DISKFLEB CCW   X'07',DISKFLES+1,X'40',6 SEEK
0000E0 0000000000000000         74+         DC    7D'0'
000118 0000000000000000         75+DISKFLEE DC    3F'0' MODULE CELL TABLE
000124 FFFFFFFF                 76+         DC    X'FFFFFFFF'

000128 00000000000000.          78 DISKKEY DC    XL7'00'                                    DISK0080
00012F                          79 DISKIO1 DS    CL3575                                     DISK0090
000F26                          80 DISKIOW DS    CL55                                       DISK0100
                                81         END                                             DISK0110
```

7.38

CHAPTER 7

PROGRAMMING ASSIGNMENT

INSTRUCTIONS

The program presented in the programming assignment in Chapter 5 should be rewritten to make it self-relocating using remote DTF's and I/O areas.

CHAPTER 8

OVERLAYS

INTRODUCTION

Although the inventory master file established in Chapter 4 and stored on the disk as an indexed sequential file contains the most up-to-date information, it is relatively useless unless this information can be presented in a usable form. Normally this information is presented as a printed report. Printed reports from the master file can be in many forms and present different information, dependent upon the needs of the users. In the sample programs developed in this chapter two reports are to be prepared: an Inventory Master Report which will contain all the data in each data record, and a Spares/Shortages Report which lists those records which have spares or shortages. The report layout for these two reports is shown in Figure 8-1.

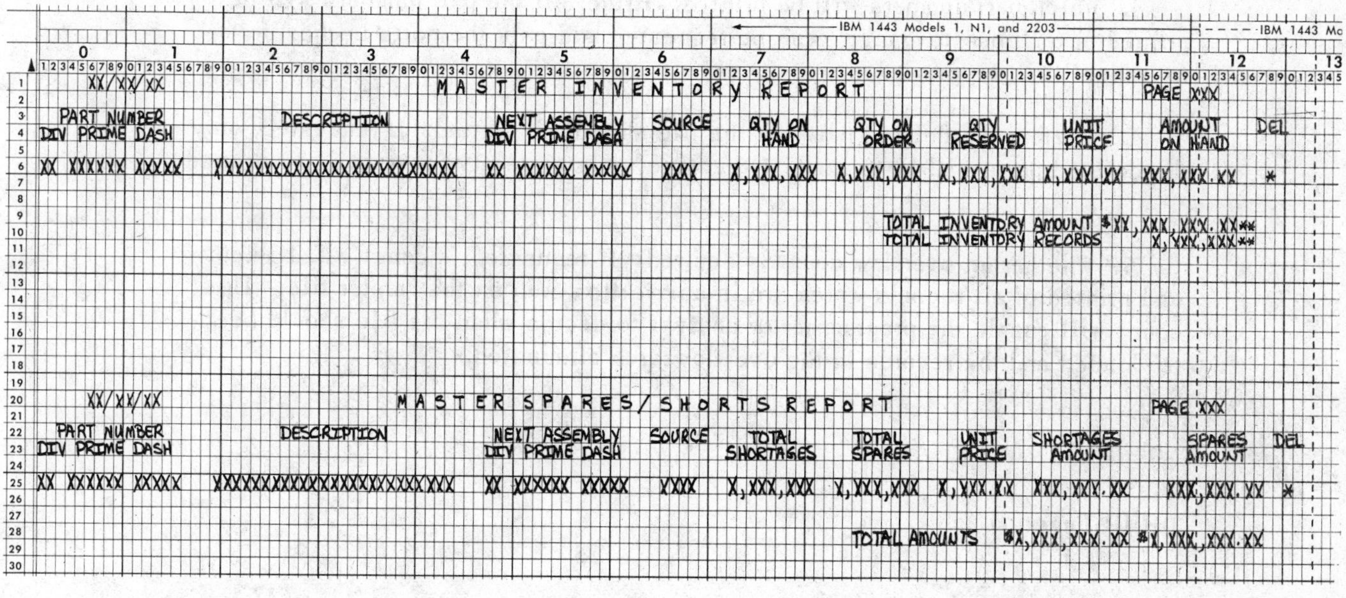

Figure 8-1 Report Layouts

In addition to these reports, a back-up file is necessary for the master file. This back-up file is to be produced on magnetic tape and will be used to restore the inventory master file in case it becomes unusable.

It was decided that both the print function (to prepare the two reports) and the "dump" function (to create the back-up file) could be performed within the same program. To perform both functions within a single program, the program will read a control card and determine which function should be performed. In addition, certain control features will be introduced to the program through the use of the control card. The functions to be controlled by the control card include the following:

PRINT Function

1. Which report will be produced. Either the Inventory Master Report or the Spares/Shortages Report will be printed.

2. Which division will be printed. Either the complete inventory file or a single division can be printed.

3. Which part numbers will be printed. Either all the part numbers will be printed or a "from-to-range" can be requested and only the parts in the "from-to-range" will be printed.

4. Whether the deleted parts on the file should be printed. If requested, only the deleted parts will be printed. Otherwise, only the active parts will be printed.

5. Whether an overflow count is desired. If requested, a count will be kept and printed of all records which are in an overflow area on the master file. This count will enable the programmer or analyst to decide when the file should be re-loaded and the records in the overflow area eliminated.

DUMP Function

1. Whether the deleted records on the master file should be dumped on the back-up tape. If requested, the deleted records and the active records on the master file will be put on the back-up tape. Otherwise, only the active records will be dumped onto the back-up tape.

In addition to the above requirements, the program must be able to fit in 10,000 bytes of core storage (10K) and must be able to be loaded into any core location and be executed. In order for the core requirements to be met, the concept of OVERLAYS must be understood.

OVERLAYS

In some applications, such as the sample program presented in this chapter, there are core requirements placed on a program, that is, the program can be no larger than a given number of bytes. In some instances this presents no problem because the entire program can fit into the required number of bytes. In other instances, however, the entire program may be too large to fit into the core storage area alloted for the program. When this occurs, it is necessary to break the program up into a number of independent segments which can then be executed as a single program to produce the required results. All of these independent segments cannot be in core storage at one time because together they are too large for the core requirements. Therefore, these segments must OVERLAY one another. Overlaying is the technique of replacing one segment of a program in core storage with another segment of the same program. The segment which is brought into core storage can then be executed until it has completed its task at which time it can be overlayed by another segment. Thus, a number of different segments of a program can each be executed in the same area of core storage. These separate segments are referred to as OVERLAYS.

In the sample program, the core requirement states that the program must be less than 10K in length. It is not possible, however, for the entire program to be included in 10K or less; therefore, overlays are used.

The sample program has three distinct functions: Interpret the control card, dump the inventory master file onto tape, and print the desired reports from the master file. Thus, the program could logically be broken into three overlay segments. By making one overlay to interpret the card, one to dump the inventory master and one to print the reports, the program could satisfy the core requirements. Therefore, the program is designed to use three overlay phases.

In order to use overlays in a program, each overlay phase must be catalogued in the core image library with a phase name. The program can then bring the desired overlay phase into core. In the sample program developed in this chapter the three overlay phase names are MSTRUTIL, DUMPINV and PRINTINV.

One of two macros can be used to bring an overlay phase into core storage from the core image library: the LOAD macro or the FETCH macro.

8.3

The LOAD macro can be used to load an overlay phase into core storage. It locates the phase in the core image library and places the phase into core storage at the address specified. Two different methods of using the Load macro can be used and these are illustrated in the following diagrams.

The following example illustrates the use of the Load macro to bring the overlay phase DUMPINV from the core image library to core storage. This phase (DUMPINV) creates the back-up of the master file.

METHOD 1: Load Macro Without Register Notation

STEP 1: Issue Load Macro.

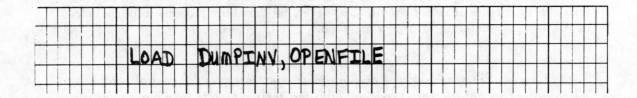

Figure 8-2 Example of Load macro

The Load macro has one or two operands. The first operand is the name of the phase which will be retrieved from the core image library and placed in core storage. The first operand is required. It must be the same name that was used in the Phase control card when the phase was catalogued. The technique for cataloguing a phase in the core image library is explained in the appendices.

If the second operand is used, it specifies the beginning address in core storage where the phase will be loaded. Thus, the Load macro will load the phase at the address specified in the second operand. This address must be defined in the calling program and begin on a doubleword boundary. In the example above the phase DUMPINV will be loaded at OPENFILE.

If the second operand is not used, the overlay phase is loaded into core storage at the address determined by the linkage editor at the time the phase was catalogued. This address is determined by entries in the phase card.

The second operand is used when the beginning address for a phase as determined by the linkage editor is not the same as the address where it should be loaded for use in the program. This may occur when different programs use the same overlay phase or when the overlay phase is self-relocating.

After the overlay phase has been loaded into core storage, the Load macro returns the address of the ENTRY POINT in register 1. The entry point is the address in the overlay phase where execution is to begin. Therefore, the next step is to Branch to the address in register 1 by use of the Branch Register Instruction.

STEP 2: Branch to the loaded overlay phase.

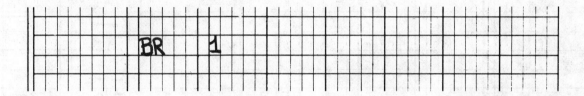

Figure 8-3 Branch Register instruction

The entry point is established when the program is link-edited. This entry point will be either the first byte of the program if no operand is used in the END statement of the program being loaded or the address of the operand in the END statement.

The following illustration shows an example of the entry point in a called overlay phase being determined by the operand in the END statement.

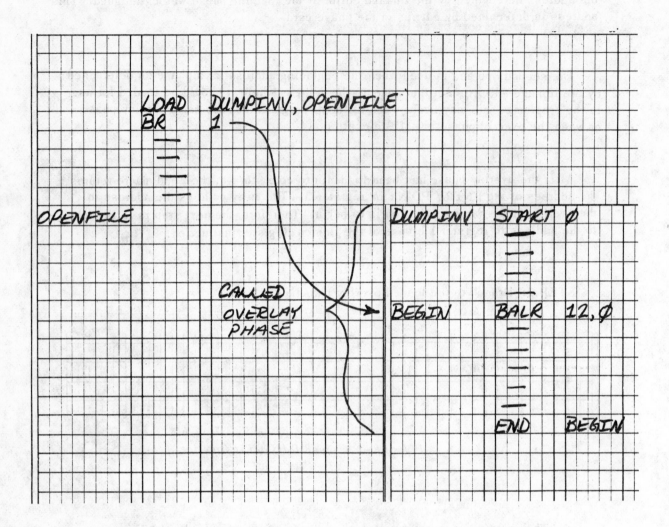

Figure 8-4 Illustration of entry point determined by END statement

Note that the operand BEGIN was used in the END statement in the called overlay phase DUMPINV. Therefore, the linkage editor determined the address of BEGIN to be the entry point of DUMPINV. This address is returned in register 1 after the overlay phase is loaded into core storage and the BR 1 instruction branches to the address of BEGIN.

As can be seen, it is the responsibility of the calling program (that is, the program which issues the Load macro) to branch to the called program (that is, the overlay phase which was loaded). Therefore, it is necessary that the called program not be loaded in a core storage address which will cause the load routine in the calling program to be overlayed.

...ustrates another method of loading the overlay phase ...e library to core storage.

...e name as a constant.

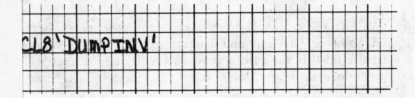

8-5 DC instruction to define phase name

...be loaded must be set up as an 8 byte character constant. ...PINV" is only seven characters, 8 bytes are used for the ...s are padded with trailing blanks by the linkage editor to

...f the constant into a register.

Load Address instruction to load address of phase name

"LOADREG" could be equated to any general register. However, if general register 1 is used, core and time are both saved. Thus in the example above, if LOADREG is equated to register 1, after the Load Address Instruction is executed the ADDRESS of the constant 'DUMPINV ' is loaded into register 1.

STEP 3: Load into a register the address specifying where the overlay phase will be loaded.

Figure 8-7 Use of Load Address instruction to load address of load point

"ENTRYREG" could be equated to any general register. If general register 0 is used, however, both core and time are saved. In this example OPENFILE is the symbolic label in the calling program specifying the address where the overlay phase is to be loaded.

STEP 4: Issue the Load macro.

Figure 8-8 Example of Load macro

LOADREG contains the address of the constant specifying the name of the phase to be loaded and ENTRYREG contains the address where the phase will be loaded. Whenever register notation is used with the Load macro, the register numbers or their equated names are placed in parentheses as shown. The parentheses must be used because they are the means by which the macro can determine if the name specified is a label, as in method 1, or is a register. The Load macro above loads the phase name referenced in the first operand (DUMPINV as specified in the DC statement) at the beginning address specified in the second operand. Note that ENTRYREG was loaded with the address of OPENFILE.

STEP 5: Branch to the loaded phase.

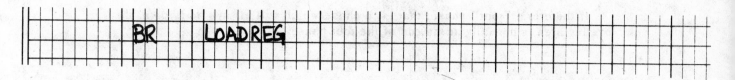

Figure 8-9 Use of Branch Register instruction to go to called phase

The branch is taken to the loaded phase by branching to the address returned in register 1 (LOADREG EQU 1). Thus the branch to the called phase is the same whether method 1 or method 2 are used.

There are valid reasons for using both method 1 and method 2 of the Load macro. Obviously, from the two examples just presented, method 1 is easier to code. It also provides better program documentation because the phase name being loaded and the load address are used as operands in the macro.

There are, however, significant reasons for using the second method. First, only one Load macro need be coded for any number of phases to be loaded. The addresses can be loaded anywhere in the calling program and then the single Load macro can be executed. Second, register notation should be used whenever the calling program is a self-relocating program.

There are a number of ways for allocating core storage when overlays are used. The following examples illustrate two commonly used methods.

EXAMPLE 1 - ROOT PHASE

If there is a "root" phase, that is, a phase which will always be in core, then the overlay area is normally at the end of the root phase.

The following diagram illustrates the allocation of core storage when both a root phase and overlay phase are used.

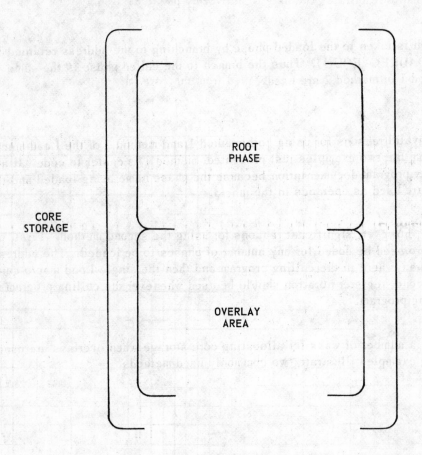

Figure 8-10 Root phase and overlay phase in core storage

As shown in the figure above, the root phase would remain in core at all times and the overlay phases would be loaded into the overlay area. Normally, after the overlay phase has completed its task, it returns control to the root phase which can then call the next desired overlay phase.

The root phase can communicate with the overlay phase through the use of registers. For example, after the Load macro is executed, the address of the entry point of the called phase is returned in register 1. Instead of executing an unconditional branch to the called phase, a BALR instruction could be used. The BALR instruction stores the next sequential address of the next instruction in the register specified in the first operand and branches to the address specified in the second operand. Thus, when the called overlay is complete, it can return to the root phase with a BR instruction. The called overlay phase thus is used in the same manner as a subroutine written in the root phase itself.

The following example illustrates the use of an overlay phase as a subroutine in a root phase.

OVPHASE is the name of the phase to be loaded from the core image library.

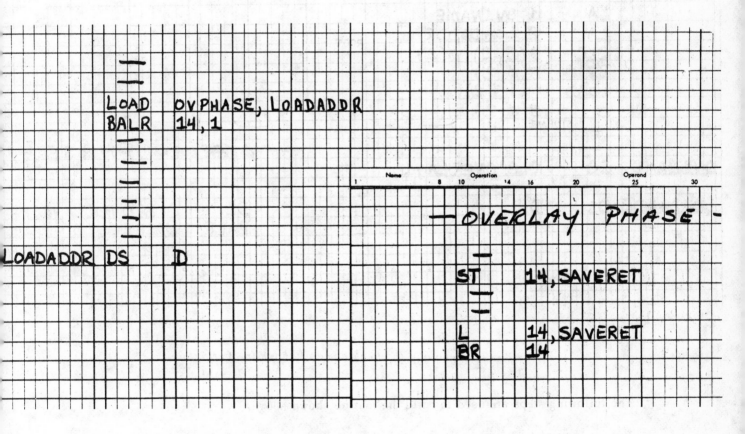

Figure 8-11 Overlay phase used as a subroutine

Note that the overlay phase will return contol to the root phase at the address following the BALR instruction.

The technique of using a root phase is normally done when the root phase is a control phase of some kind. The root phase will normally call many different phases to accomplish different tasks much in the same way a subroutine is used.

If a root phase is calling numerous overlay phases, it may happen that the desired overlay phase is already in core storage. If the root phase can determine this, a great deal of time can be saved because the overlay phase will not have to be loaded into core storage. One technique to check if the phase is in core is shown in the following example.

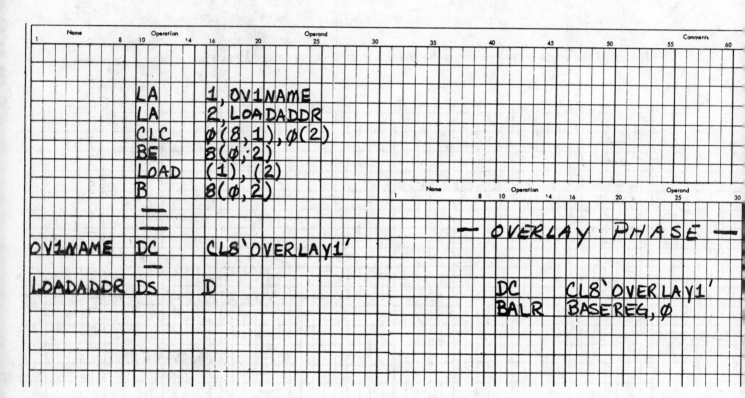

Figure 8-12 Technique to check name of phase in overlay area

The following steps are used to build the routine shown above.

EXAMPLE

STEP 1: The name of the overlay phase is put in the first 8 bytes of the phase.

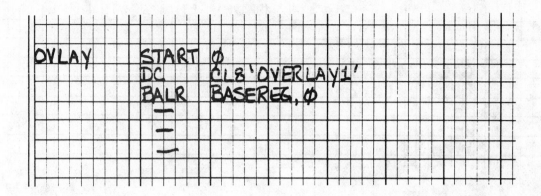

Figure 8 - 13 Definition of phase name

Note that the name of the phase (OVERLAY1) is in the first 8 bytes of the overlay phase. Then, after the phase name, the normal coding for the program begins.

STEP 2: The root phase loads the address of the desired phase into a register and the address of the load point into another.

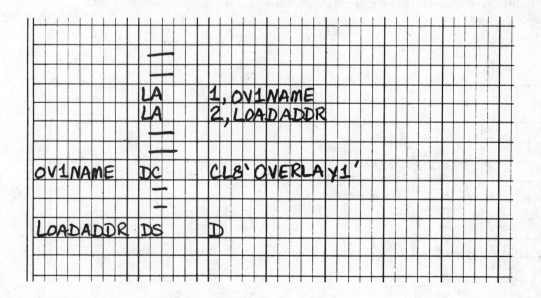

Figure 8 - 14 Loading of addresses of phase name and load point

The address of the load point is LOADADDR, which is a doubleword. The address should always be on a doubleword boundary.

STEP 3: The root phase checks to determine if the desired phase is in core and, if so, branches to it.

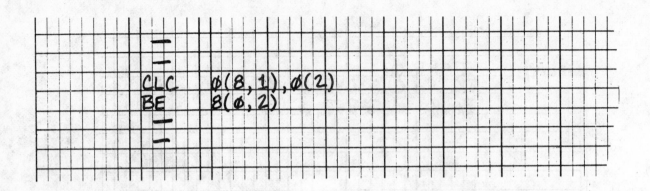

Figure 8-15 Checking name of phase in overlay area

The address contained in register 1 is the address of the phase name. The address in register 2 is the address of the load point. Thus, the compare instruction compares the desired phase name with the name of the phase in core. If they are equal, the root phase will branch to the overlay phase. Note that the branch is to the load point plus 8 because the phase name occupies the first 8 bytes of the overlay phase.

STEP 4: If the names are not equal, the desired phase must be loaded and then entered.

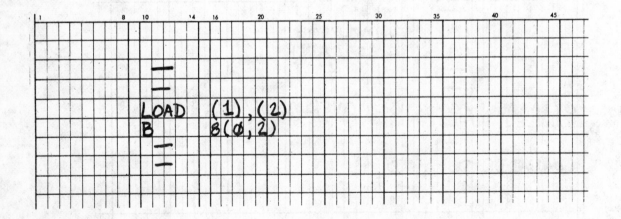

Figure 8-16 Loading overlay phase

The root phase loads the overlay phase and branches to the first instruction in the overlay phase.

8.14

As mentioned previously, it may be desirable to have a return point in the root phase. Thus, the routine shown in the above example could be written as illustrated in Figure 8-17.

EXAMPLE

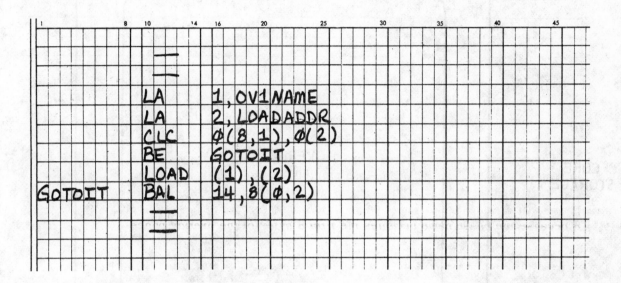

Figure 8-17 Use of Branch and Link instruction to go to overlay phase

In the example above, the return address to the root phase would be stored in register 14 before the overlay phase is entered.

EXAMPLE 2 - NO ROOT PHASE

If a root phase is not needed in an application, then the calling program can be completely overlayed by the overlay phase.

In the sample program presented in this chapter, it is not necessary to have a root phase because each function to be performed can be done separately. The control card must be interpreted and then the back-up tape or the report is to be produced. Once the control card is interpreted, therefore, the phase which performs that function is no longer needed.

The following diagram illustrates the allocation of core storage when the calling program is overlayed by the called program, such as occurs in the sample program.

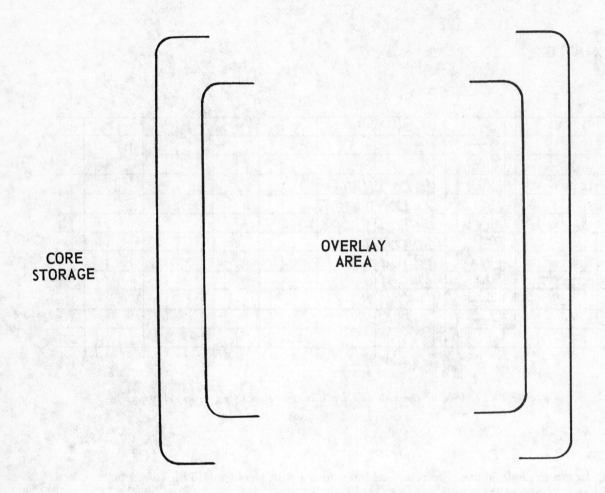

CORE
STORAGE

OVERLAY
AREA

Figure 8 - 18 Core storage with no root phase

Thus, as shown in Figure 8-18, almost all the core storage can be used for overlay purposes. The only part which cannot be overlayed is the Load macro and the branch instruction to the overlay phase. Therefore, when using no root phase, the Load macro and branch instruction should be at the front of the program as shown in Figure 8-19.

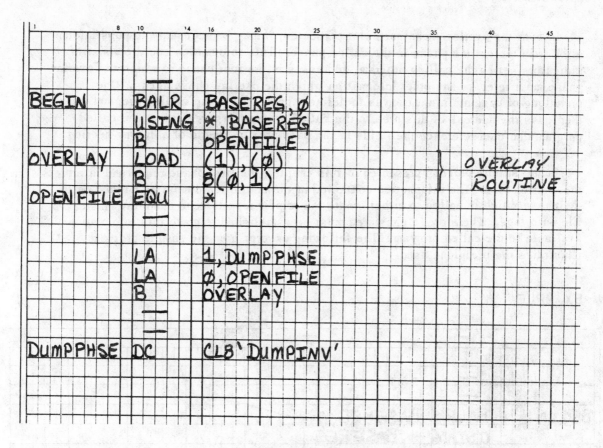

```
BEGIN      BALR    BASEREG,0
           USING   *,BASEREG
           B       OPENFILE
OVERLAY    LOAD    (1),(0)              }  OVERLAY
           B       8(0,1)               }  ROUTINE
OPENFILE   EQU     *
           —
           LA      1,DUMPPHSE
           LA      0,OPENFILE
           B       OVERLAY
           —

DUMPPHSE   DC      CL8'DUMPINV'
```

Figure 8-19 Load macro and Branch instruction at front of program

In this routine, after the base register is assigned, the load routine is bypassed by use of the branch instruction. The B OPENFILE causes execution of the first instruction in the calling program. When it is determined which overlay phase should be loaded, the address of a constant containing a phase name, and the address of the load point are loaded into registers 1 and 0 respectively. The main processing routine then branches to the overlay routine which loads the desired overlay phase and branches to it.

If the address of OPENFILE is loaded into register 0, the overlay phase will be loaded immediately following the branch instruction (B 8(0,1)).

It should be noted that no check was made to see if the desired overlay phase was already in core storage. This is because a different phase must always be loaded when no root phase is used and the desired phase could never be in core storage. Also, there will never be a situation where a return is desired because there is no root phase to return to.

PASS AREAS

In both the overlay techniques just presented, it may be necessary to pass information from the calling phase to the called phase. This information could consist of indicators set by the calling program, addresses in the root phase to which the overlay phase must refer, or any other information which the overlay phase needs. One technique of passing information is to define a pass area in the calling program and then pass the address of this area to the called program in a register. The called program can then reference the fields in the pass area by means of a dummy section.

In the sample program presented in this chapter, the first phase reads and interprets the control card. The information contained in the control card must be passed on to the phase which is called to either create the printer reports or to dump the master file onto tape. Therefore, a pass area must be established to make this information available to the called program. The following excerpt from the sample program illustrates the technique used.

EXAMPLE

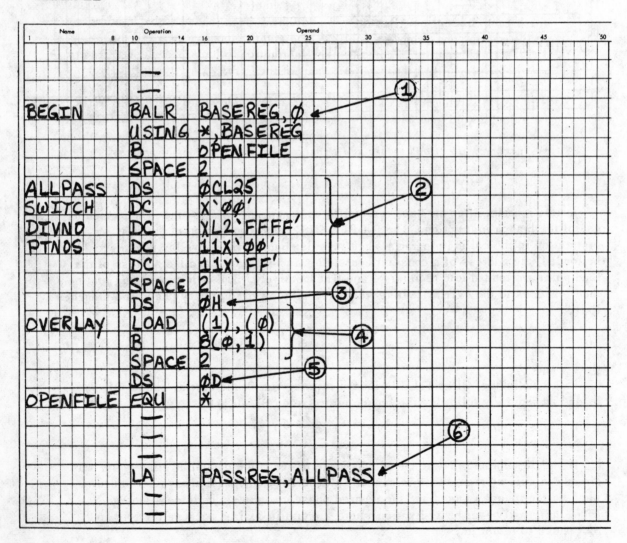

Figure 8-20 Using a pass area with overlays

8.18

The following points should be noted:

1. A base register is established before the pass area and Load macro. This is done to provide addressability of the pass area and the load routine in the calling program.

2. The pass area (ALLPASS), which contains the information to be passed to the called overlay phase, is located before the load point. If it was located after the load point, it would be overlayed and would not be available to the called program.

3. The DS 0H statement is used to insure that the Load macro coding will begin on a halfword boundary. All instructions must begin on a halfword boundary and the length of the pass area may be such that the instruction following it would not be on a halfword boundary if the DS statement were not used.

4. The load routine is located prior to the load point of the overlay program. As shown previously, this is necessary so that the overlay phase will not overlay the branch instruction. Registers 1 and 0 have been loaded with the address of the overlay phase name and of the load point respectively before the "OVERLAY" routine is entered. The instructions which load these registers can be overlayed and thus are not a part of the "OVERLAY" routine.

5. The DS 0D statement is used to insure that the address at "OPENFILE" is on a doubleword boundary. This is done because the load address for the overlay area must be on a doubleword boundary and "OPENFILE" is to be used as the load point.

6. Before the "OVERLAY" routine is entered, the address of the pass area (ALLPASS) is loaded into a register which will not be used before the overlay phase is loaded. Thus, after the overlay phase is in core, the pass area is addressable in the overlay phase by using the loaded register.

The example below illustrates how the register could be used.

EXAMPLE

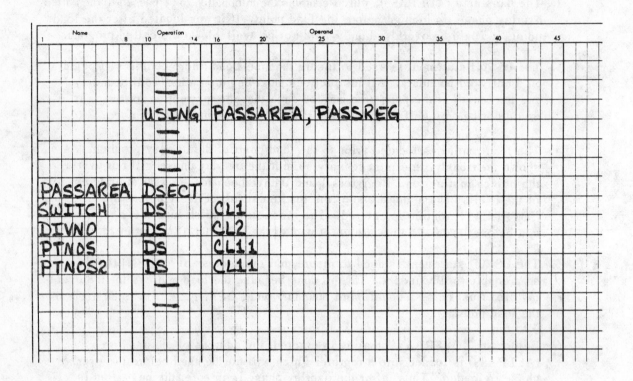

Figure 8-21 Dummy section to reference pass area

Note that the dummy section is defined the same as the pass area so that the pass area can be referenced by the dummy section.

REGISTER STORAGE

When overlay phases are loaded, it is normally desirable that they be able to use all of the general purpose registers. In some applications, however, the registers may contain information from the root phase, such as the return address, which cannot be destroyed. Therefore, a common practice in each overlay phase is to store all the registers when the phase is entered and to reload them just before returning to the root phase. This could be accomplished, of course, by using sixteen store instructions and sixteen load instructions. A better technique, however, is to use the store multiple and load multiple instructions.

STORE MULTIPLE Instruction

INSTRUCTION: STORE MULTIPLE

OPERATION CODE: STM

EXAMPLE: STM   4,7,SAVEREGS

The STORE MULTIPLE instruction is used to store more than one register in core storage. Beginning with the register specified in the first operand, each consecutive register up to and including the register specified in the second operand is stored in core storage beginning at the address specified in the third operand. The third operand must begin on a fullword boundary and be large enough to contain the range of registers specified in the first and second operands. The following example illustrates the use of the Store Multiple instruction to store four registers.

EXAMPLE

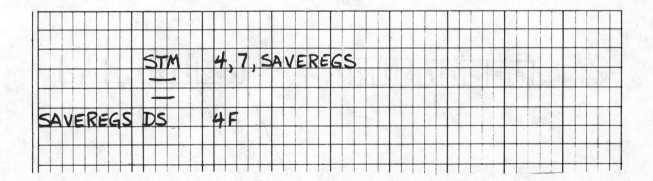

```
         STM    4,7,SAVEREGS

SAVEREGS DS    4F
```

Before Execution:

Register 4 | 0 | 0 | 0 | 0 | C | 1 | 2 | 4 |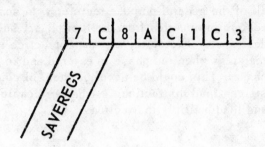

Register 5 | 0 | 0 | 0 | 0 | 0 | C | 2 | C |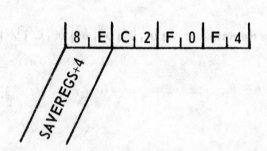

Register 6 | 0 | 0 | 0 | 0 | 0 | A | 0 | 0 |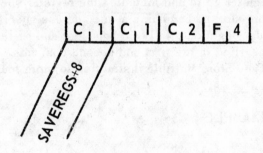

Register 7 | F | F | F | F | F | 0 | 0 | 2 |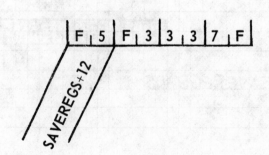

After Execution:

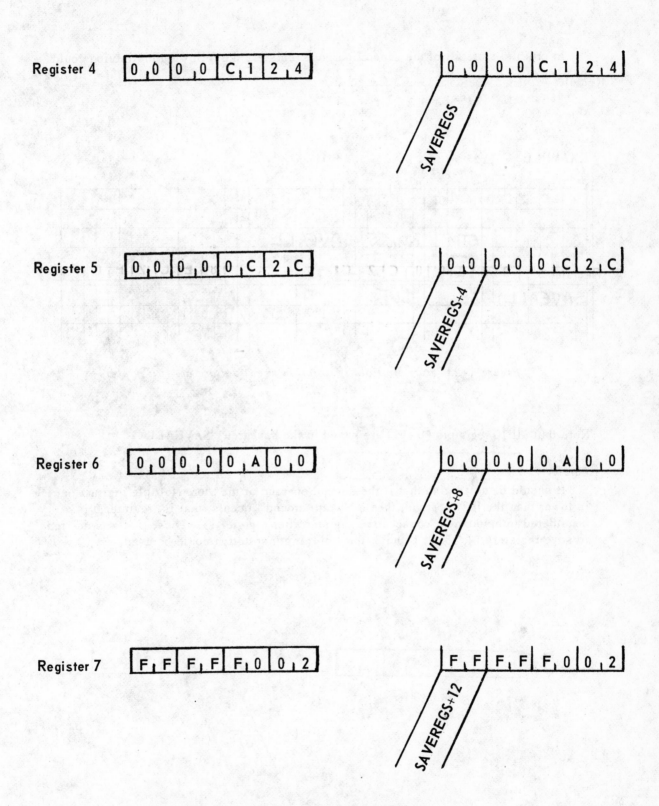

Figure 8-22 Example of Store Multiple instruction

Note that the storage area is defined in the example as SAVEREGS DS 4F. Thus, four fullwords, beginning on a fullword boundary, are used for storage of the registers.

In order to store all of the general purpose registers the following instruction could be used.

EXAMPLE

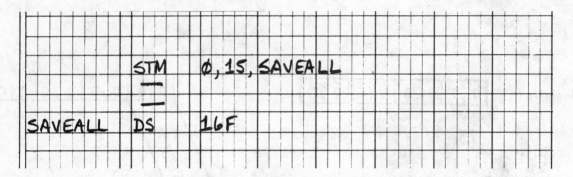

Figure 8-23 Store Multiple instruction used to store all 16 registers

Note that all 16 registers (0-15) are saved in the savearea "SAVEALL".

It should be noted also that if the second operand of the Store Multiple instruction is lower than the first operand, then a "wrap-around" occurs, that is, register 0 is considered to be the next consecutive register after register 15. Thus, if it was desired to save registers 14, 15, 0, 1 and 2, the following instruction could be used.

EXAMPLE

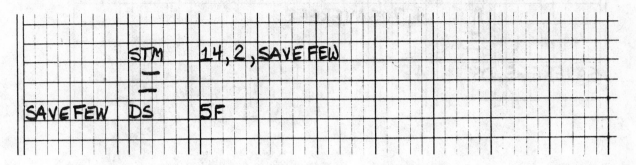

```
            STM    14,2,SAVEFEW
             —
             —
SAVEFEW DS   5F
```

Figure 8-24 "Wrap-around" feature of Store Multiple instruction

In the example above, register 14 would be stored at the fullword SAVEFEW, register 15 would be stored at SAVEFEW+4, register 0 would be stored at SAVEFEW+8, register 1 would be stored at SAVEFEW+12 and register 2 would be stored at SAVEFEW+16.

LOAD MULTIPLE Instruction

The LOAD MULTIPLE instruction can be used to load consecutive registers from core storage.

INSTRUCTION: LOAD MULTIPLE

OPERATION CODE: LM

EXAMPLE: LM   4,7,SAVEREGS

When the Load Multiple instruction is executed, the contents of core storage beginning at the address specified in the third operand are loaded into consecutive registers beginning with the register specified in the first operand and continuing until the register specified in the second operand has been loaded. The example below illustrates the use of the Load Multiple instruction when loading four registers.

EXAMPLE

```
          LM     4,7,SAVEREGS
          =
          =
SAVEREGS DS     4F
```

Before Execution:

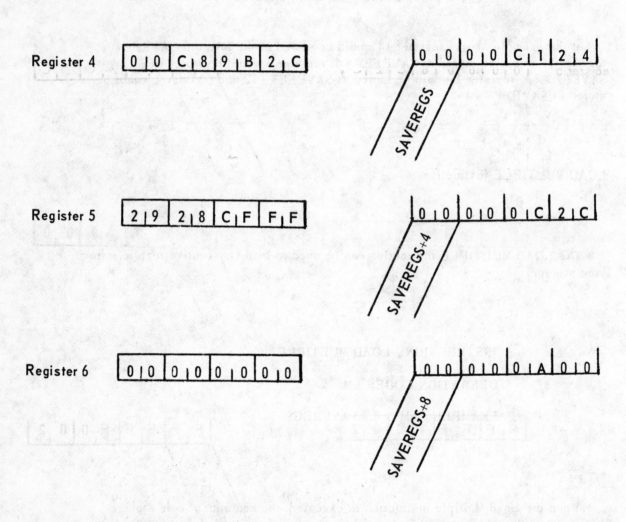

Register 4   `0 0 C 8 9 B 2 C`   `0 0 0 0 C 1 2 4`
                                         SAVEREGS

Register 5   `2 9 2 8 C F F F`   `0 0 0 0 0 C 2 C`
                                         SAVEREGS+4

Register 6   `0 0 0 0 0 0 0 0`   `0 0 0 0 0 A 0 0`
                                         SAVEREGS+8

Register 7   `F F F F 9 3 2 C`   `F F F F F 0 0 2`
                                         SAVEREGS+12

8.26

After Execution:

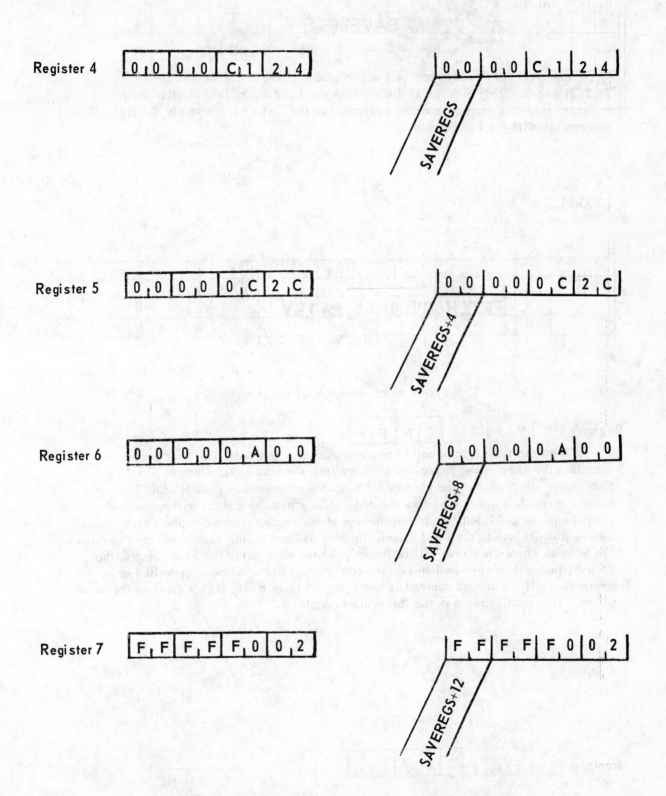

Figure 8-25 Example of Load Multiple instruction

As with the Store Multiple instruction, if the second operand is lower than the first operand, a "wrap-around" occurs.

FETCH MACRO

The second macro which can be used to load a phase into core storage is the FETCH macro. The Fetch macro differs from the Load macro in that after the phase is loaded into core storage, control is returned to the CALLED phase not the CALLING program, as with the Load macro.

EXAMPLE

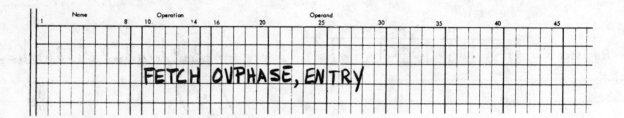

Figure 8 - 26 Example of Fetch macro

As with the Load macro, one or two operands can be used. The first operand specifies the name of the phase to be loaded from the core image library. It is the phase name which was in the phase card when the program was catalogued. The second operand, if used, specifies the address to which the control will be passed after the phase is loaded. Note that the use of the second operand in the Fetch macro differs from the use in the Load macro. In the Load macro, the second operand specifies the address where the phase will be loaded. Thus, when using the Fetch macro, the called phase will always be loaded into core storage at the address specified in the phase card. If the second operand is used, as in Figure 8 - 26, it is a label in the called phase. This is illustrated in the following example.

EXAMPLE

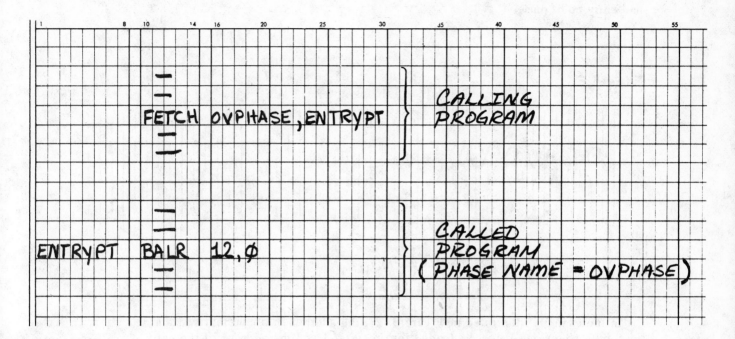

Figure 8-27 Fetch macro and overlay phase entry point

In the example above, the phase OVPHASE is to be loaded into core storage at the address specified in the phase card under which the phase was catalogued in the core image library. The second operand in the Fetch macro specifies a symbolic name (that is, a label) in the called phase. In the example, this name is ENTRYPT. Thus, after the phase OVPHASE is loaded into core storage, the Fetch macro will return control to the BALR instruction in the called phase.

As with the Load macro, register notation can be used in place of the phase name and entry point name.

EXAMPLE

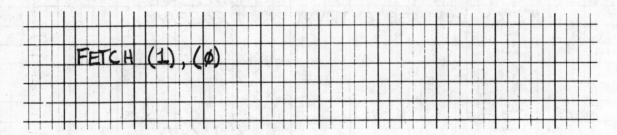

Figure 8-28 Fetch macro using register notation

In the example illustrated in Figure 8-28, the address of a constant containing the 8 byte phase name must be loaded into register 1 and the address of the entry point in the called phase must be loaded into register 0 before the Fetch macro is issued. The phase will be loaded and control will be returned at the address loaded into register 0.

The Fetch macro can be used, in many instances, in the same manner as the Load macro. It can be especially advantageous when the called phase will overlay the calling phase. Since control is passed to the called phase, it is not necessary to have instructions following the Fetch macro, as with the Load macro. Thus, with the exception of any common pass areas, a calling phase may be completely overlayed by a called phase.

The major disadvantage of the Fetch macro, however, is that it cannot be used in calling self-relocating programs.

SAMPLE PROGRAM CONTROL CARD

In the program presented in this chapter, the control card must be interpreted and the information in it passed along to the "dump" phase or print phase. The control card format uses positional operands, that is, the first operand can begin in any column in the card and the following operands must follow in a specific order. The formats for the dump and print cards are illustrated below.

PRINT Control Card

First entry: 'PRINT' — This operand is required. It specifies that the print function is to be performed.

Second entry: 'MASTER' or 'SPARES' — One of these two words is required. They specify whether the master report or spares/shortages report is to be printed.

Third entry: XX or omitted — If desired, a two digit division number is specified. If this entry is used, only the division stated will be printed. This entry is optional.

Fourth entry: XXXXXXXXXXX or omitted — If desired, an 11 digit number (prime and dash of part number) is specified for the first part number to be printed. When this entry is used, only part numbers with a prime/dash number equal to or greater than the specified number will be printed. This entry is optional.

Fifth entry: XXXXXXXXXXX or omitted — If desired, an 11 digit number (prime and dash of part number) is specified for the last part number to be printed. When this entry is used, only part numbers with a prime/dash less than or equal to the specified number will be printed. This entry is optional.

Sixth entry: 'Y' or omitted — If desired, this entry can be a 'Y' which specifies a listing of only the deleted parts on the file. If it is used, only the deleted parts on the master file will be printed. If not, only the active parts are printed.

Seventh entry: 'Y' or omitted — This operand is coded 'Y' if a count of records in the overflow area is desired. If it is used, a count of records in the overflow area will be printed at the end of the report. If not, no count is printed.

DUMP Control Card

First entry: 'DUMP' — This operand is required. It specifies that the dump function is to be performed.

Second entry: 'Y' or omitted — This operand, if coded 'Y', specifies that the deleted records, as well as the active records, are to be copied onto the back-up tape. If this entry is coded 'Y', delete cards are punched for each deleted record so that if the file is reloaded from the tape, the delete cards can be processed against the file. It should be noted that the type code in all the records placed on the tape is changed to 8 (that is, the load code) so that the programs presented in Chapters 3 and 4 can be used to reload the file.

As noted previously, the entries in the control card are positional. Thus, the first entry must always be first, the second entry second, etc. Since there are optional operands, which may be omitted, their absence must be indicated through the use of a delimeter. The delimeter chosen for the control card is a comma. Thus, each operand in the control card must be separated by a comma and if an operand is omitted, a comma must be present to indicate its absence. The example illustrated below is a typical entry in the control card for the print function.

PRINT,MASTER,10,,,Y

Figure 8 - 29 Example of control card

The control card above specifies the print function is to be performed and that the master file report is to be printed. It also states that only division 10 is to be printed. The next two operands stating beginning and ending part numbers are omitted. This omission is indicated by two consecutive commas. The last operand in the example specifies that only the deleted parts are to be printed.

Note that, although one more operand could be specified (ie. take overflow count) it is omitted and there is no comma indicating its omission. This is because no more operands are to be specified and the blank indicates the end of the entries in the control card.

The entry in the control card to just print the spares/shortages report is shown below.

PRINT,SPARES

Figure 8 - 30 Example of control card

Note that even though more operands could be specified, none are specified after the SPARES entry so the remainder of the card is blank.

The following entry in the control card is in error:

PRINT,SPARES,,,Y

Figure 8-31 Example of invalid control card

The 'Y' is stated as the fifth operand and this is an invalid value. The value must be an 11 digit part number.

The following entry in the control card is also invalid:

PRINT,MASTER,,,,Y,

Figure 8-32 Example of invalid control card

The operands specified are valid but the comma following the 'Y' indicates another operand is to follow, and there is no operand.

TRANSLATE AND TEST Instruction

In order to interpret the control card, some method of scanning the card must be developed to recognize where the entries begin and end and what their values are. The Translate and Test instruction is commonly used to scan data with variable entries.

INSTRUCTION: TRANSLATE AND TEST

OPERATION CODE: TRT

EXAMPLE: TRT   0(80,CARDREG),TRTABLE

The Translate and Test instruction uses successive bytes in the field defined in the first operand to enter and search a table defined in the second operand. It uses the same technique as the Translate instruction, that is, it adds the hexadecimal value of the byte in the field in the first operand to the address specified in the second operand and the byte at the resultant address in the table is examined. If the byte in the table is equal to X'00', the next successive byte in the field in the first operand is used to search the table. This procedure continues until the number of bytes specified in the first operand have been processed or until a value other than X'00' is found in the table.

If all the bytes examined in the table were X'00', the condition code is set to a mask of 8. If a byte with a value other than X'00' is found in the table, the address of the byte in the first operand is inserted into register 1 and the byte from the table is inserted in the low-order 8 bits of register 2. The condition code is set to a mask of 4 if the byte in the first operand is not the last byte of the field. If it is the last byte of the field, the condition code is set to a mask of 2.

Thus, the Translate and Test instruction can be used to search for specific values in a byte within a field. For example, if it was necessary to find all the blanks in a field and accumulate a count, the routine shown on page 8.42 could be used. Taken step-by-step, the routine does the following.

RSC ZRTN EQU *
ERR
does parcel id
match HOLD ID ?

if no then print
error msg

DATEST
for
LSTD
& EXPR

MTG TESTS

TAXTEST

entries except for the entry at X'40' (blank).

Table for use with Translate and Test instruction

Note in the translate table that the only entry which has a value other than X'00' is the entry for the EBCDIC representation of a blank. Thus, when the Translate and Test instruction is executed, a blank is the only character which will stop the instruction.

STEP 2: Since the Translate and Test instruction is normally executed through the use of an Execute instruction, the next step is to write the TRT instruction outside of the normal sequence of instructions.

```
TRTINST   TRT   Ø(Ø,FIELDREG),TRTABLE



FIELDREG  EQU   8
```

Figure 8-34 Definition of Translate and Test instruction

Note that the address of the field to be checked will be in FIELDREG but that no length is stated for the instruction (the format for the TRT instruction is TRT D1(L,B1),D2(B2)). This length will be determined by the execute instruction.

STEP 3: Load the address of the field to be tested into FIELDREG.

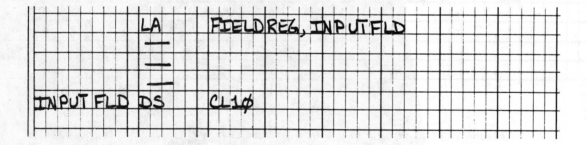

```
          LA    FIELDREG,INPUTFLD



INPUTFLD  DS    CL1Ø
```

STEP 4: Load the length of the input field less 1 into a register to be used with the execute instruction.

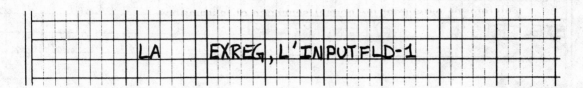

Figure 8 - 36 Load length of input field less one byte

Note the use of the length attribute to determine the length of the input field.

STEP 5: Zero register 2.

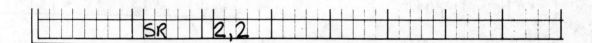

Figure 8 - 37 Zero register 2

Register 2 is the register in which the byte from the table is inserted. It is normally set to zero so that comparisons can be made to it after the TRT instruction to determine what character stopped the instruction.

STEP 6: Execute the translate instruction.

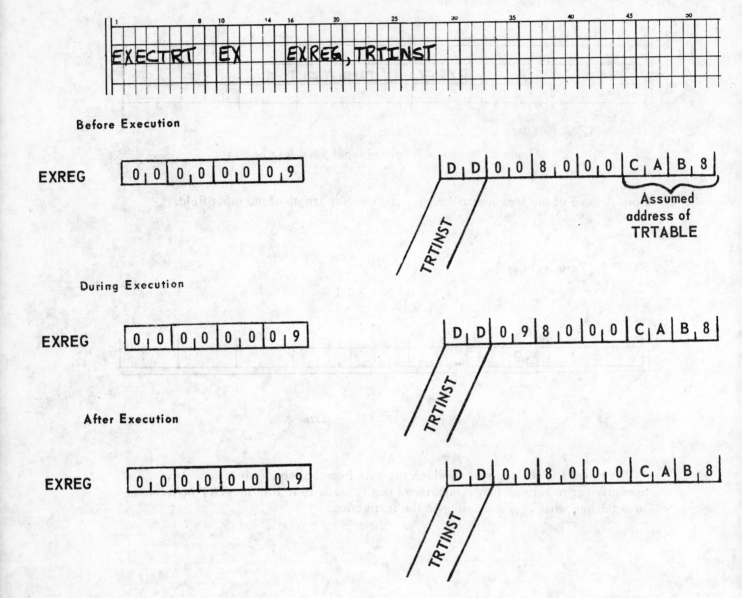

Figure 8-38 Execute the Translate and Test instruction

Note that 10 bytes will be examined.

STEP 7: Test if the end of the field has been reached.

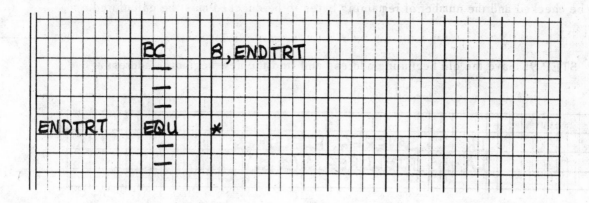

Figure 8-39 Branch if end of input field

If the condition code is equal to a mask of 8 after the TRT instruction, it indicates that the field has been completed. Thus, no more testing needs to be done.

STEP 8: Test if the last character was a blank.

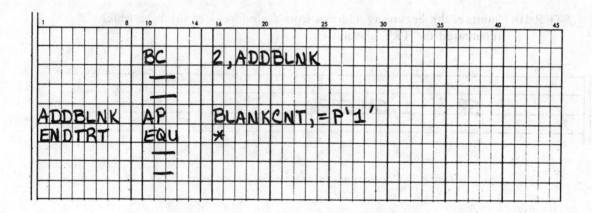

Figure 8-40 Branch if last character was a blank

If the condition code is equal to a mask of 2 after the TRT instruction, it indicates that a blank was found as the last character in the field. Thus, a branch is taken to add 1 to the counter and then continue processing.

If a blank was found, but it was not the last character in the field, it indicates that more of the field must be checked. Thus, both the new beginning address of the field to be checked and the number of remaining bytes to be checked must be calculated.

STEP 9: Save the old beginning address and find the new beginning address.

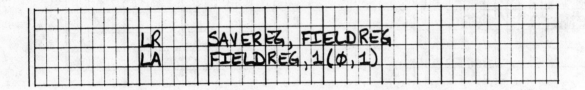

Figure 8-41 Save beginning address and load new address

The address in FIELDREG, which is the beginning address for the TRT instruction, is loaded into another register (SAVEREG) to be used for calculations. The new beginning address is then loaded into FIELDREG. As noted, after the TRT instruction is completed, the address of the byte in the first operand which terminated the instruction is returned in register 1. Thus, by adding 1 to that address, the address of the next byte in the field is determined.

STEP 10: Subtract the beginning address from the address of the byte which terminated the TRT instruction.

Figure 8-42 Determine number of bytes processed

The result of this subtraction gives the number of bytes less 1 which were actually processed by the TRT instruction. Thus, if the beginning address of the field was 2000, and the third byte stopped the instruction, the address returned in register 1 would be 2002 and the result of this subtraction would be 2, one less than the number of bytes processed.

STEP 11: Subtract the number of bytes processed from the original number of bytes.

Figure 8-43 Determine number of bytes left to process

The result in this subtraction is the number of bytes left to process. However, since the length code for all machine language instructions must be one less than the number of bytes to be processed, 1 must be subtracted from this value.

STEP 12: Subtract 1 to get correct length.

Figure 8-44 Determine length attribute for TRT instruction

STEP 13: Add 1 to the count for blanks.

Figure 8-45 Add 1 to blank count

Note that the Execute instruction with a zero first operand is used to add 1 to the blank count.

STEP 14: Return to check the rest of the field.

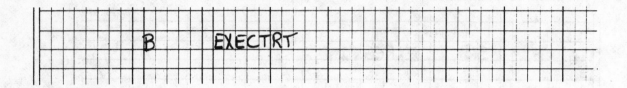

Figure 8 - 46 Return to check the rest of the input field

The entire routine appears as follows:

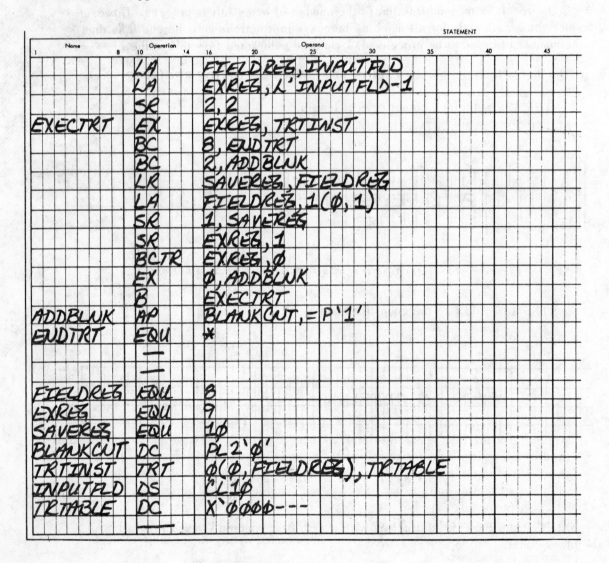

Figure 8 - 47 Scan routine

8.42

As has been noted, the Translate and Test instruction can be used to flag any characters in the EBCDIC coding structure. Thus, in the sample program, the Translate and Test instruction is used to flag the commas and blanks in the control card.

It should be noted that, since the Translate and Test instruction utilizes registers 1 and 2, care must be taken not to have permanent information in those two registers when the TRT instruction is executed.

FIXED-LENGTH MULTIPLICATION AND DIVISION

As shown previously, fixed-length add and subtract instructions can be used to perform arithmetic operations on numbers in the binary format. In addition, multiplication and division can be performed on binary numbers. The multiply instructions are MULTIPLY FULLWORD, MULTIPLY HALFWORD and MULTIPLY REGISTER. The divide instructions are DIVIDE FULLWORD and DIVIDE REGISTER.

MULTIPLY FULLWORD Instruction

The Multiply Fullword instruction is used to multiply a value in a register by a value stored in a fullword in core storage.

INSTRUCTION: MULTIPLY FULLWORD

OPERATION CODE: M

EXAMPLE: M   2,FULLWORD

The second operand in the Multiply Fullword instruction is a fullword in core storage and the data in the fullword is the multiplier. The first operand is the even numbered register of an even/odd pair of registers. Thus, in the above example, register 2 in the first operand references both register 2 and register 3. The multiplicand in the multiply operation is stored in the ODD numbered register of the even/odd pair. Thus, in the example above, the multiplicand would be stored in register 3. Both the multiplier and the multiplicand are considered to be signed binary numbers. The product is stored in both the even and odd registers with the low-order 32 bits in the odd register and the high-order 31 bits plus sign in the even register. The contents of the even-numbered register are ignored during the execution of the multiply instruction.

The following example illustrates the use of the multiply instruction.

EXAMPLE

Before Execution:

Register 2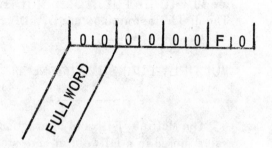

Register 3 | 0 | 0 | 0 | 0 | 0 | 0 | 6 | 4 |

After Execution:

Register 2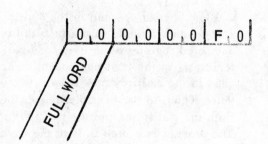

Register 3 | 0 | 0 | 0 | 0 | 0 | 9 | 6 | 0 |

Figure 8-48 Example of Multiply Fullword instruction

In the example above, the value in the odd register (register 3) is multiplied by the value in core storage in the fullword FULLWORD and the answer is placed in the even/odd numbered registers (registers 2 and 3). The contents of register 2 are ignored when the multiply operation takes place.

Note again that the even numbered register of the even/odd pair of registers is specified in the first operand of the instruction but that the multiplicand must be contained in the odd numbered register.

MULTIPLY REGISTER Instruction

The Multiply Register instruction can be used to multiply two binary values contained in registers.

INSTRUCTION: MULTIPLY REGISTER

OPERATION CODE: MR

EXAMPLE: MR   4,7

The second operand specifies a register which contains the multiplier. The first operand specifies the even numbered register of the even/odd numbered registers which are used in the same manner as with the Multiply Fullword instruction. The multiplicand must be loaded into the odd numbered register in the even/odd pair of registers. The product is stored in both the even and odd registers in the same manner as the Multiply Fullword instruction.

MULTIPLY HALFWORD Instruction

The Multiply Halfword is used to multiply a value in a register by a value in a half-word in core storage.

INSTRUCTION: MULTIPLY HALFWORD

OPERATION CODE: MH

EXAMPLE: MH   7,HALFWORD

The first operand specifies a single register which contains the multiplicand. It does not specify an even/odd pair of registers and thus can be any general purpose register. The second operand specifies a halfword in core storage which contains the multiplier. The product is stored in the register specified in the first operand.

It should be noted that the possibility exists that the product will be a number larger than what can be stored in a single register. Since there is no indication given by the computer that the product is too large, care must be taken with the Multiply Halfword instruction to ensure that the multiplier and multiplicand will not produce a product too large to be stored in a register.

The example below illustrates the use of the Multiply Halfword instruction.

EXAMPLE

Before Execution:

Register 7 | 0 0 | 0 0 | 0 C | 8

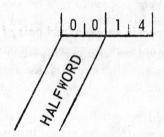

After Execution:

Register 7 | 0 0 | 0 0 | 0 F | A 0

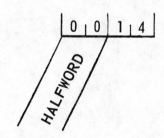

Figure 8-49 Example of Multiply Halfword instruction

In the example above, the value in register 7 is multiplied by the value in HALFWORD and the product is stored in register 7.

It should be noted that in all fixed-length multiply instructions, the multiplier and multiplicand are considered signed numbers. Thus, numbers which are negative will be stored in two's complement form.

8.47

DIVIDE FULLWORD Instruction

The Divide Fullword instruction is used to divide a single signed binary value contained in an even/odd pair of registers by a value in a fullword in core storage.

INSTRUCTION: DIVIDE FULLWORD

OPERATION CODE: D

EXAMPLE: D 4,FULL

The second operand is a fullword in core storage which contains the divisor. The first operand is the even numbered register of an even/odd pair of registers which contain the dividend. Thus, in the example above, register 4 and register 5 together contain the dividend with the low-order positions in register 5 and the high-order positions in register 4. After the division is performed, the quotient is placed in the odd numbered register and the remainder is placed in the even numbered register, both as signed binary numbers.

The example below illustrates the use of the Divide Fullword instruction.

EXAMPLE

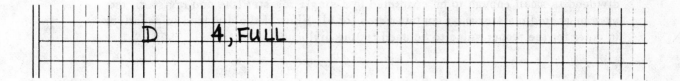

Before Execution:

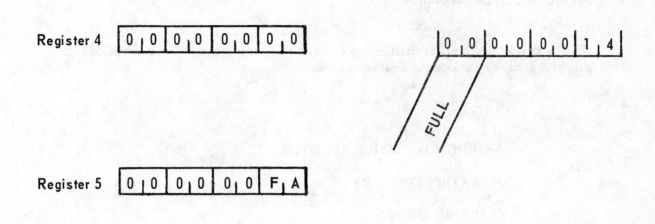

Register 4

| 0 | 0 | 0 | 0 | 0 | 0 | 0 | 0 |

| 0 | 0 | 0 | 0 | 0 | 0 | 1 | 4 |

FULL

Register 5

| 0 | 0 | 0 | 0 | 0 | 0 | F | A |

After Execution:

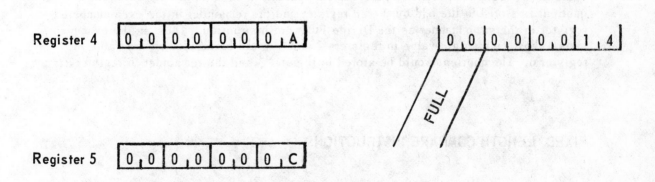

Register 4

| 0 | 0 | 0 | 0 | 0 | 0 | 0 | A |

| 0 | 0 | 0 | 0 | 0 | 0 | 1 | 4 |

FULL

Register 5

| 0 | 0 | 0 | 0 | 0 | 0 | 0 | C |

Figure 8-50 Example of Divide Fullword instruction

In the example above, the decimal value 250 (X'FA') is divided by the decimal value 20 (X'14'). The quotient (decimal 12 = X'0C') is stored in the odd numbered register (register 5) of the even/odd pair and the remainder (decimal 10 = X'0A') is stored in the even numbered register (register 4).

It should be noted that the contents of both registers in the even/odd pair of registers is considered a single number to be used as the dividend. Thus, if the dividend is small enough to be contained in a single register (the odd register), the even numbered register must contain zeros (or all 1 bits if the dividend is negative) in order for the proper value to be used for the dividend.

It should also be noted that a divisor of zero is invalid. Thus, a check should be made before the divide instruction to insure the divisor is not equal to zero.

DIVIDE REGISTER Instruction

The Divide Register instruction can be used to divide the value in an even/odd pair of registers by a value in another register.

INSTRUCTION: DIVIDE REGISTER

OPERATION CODE: DR

EXAMPLE: DR   2,6

The first operand specifies the even numbered register of an even/odd pair of registers which contains the signed binary value to be used as the dividend. The value in the register specified in the second operand is used as the divisor. The quotient is stored in the odd numbered register and the remainder in the even numbered register in the same manner as the Divide Fullword instruction. Thus, in the example shown above, the single value in registers 2 and 3 would be divided by the value in register 6. The quotient would be stored in register 3 and the remainder in register 2.

FIXED-LENGTH COMPARE INSTRUCTIONS

Fixed-length compare instructions are used to compare data of fixed length, that is, data contained in a register and in a fullword or halfword in core storage. A series of five fixed-length compare instructions are available: COMPARE REGISTER, COMPARE FULLWORD, COMPARE HALFWORD, COMPARE LOGICAL REGISTER and COMPARE LOGICAL FULLWORD.

COMPARE REGISTER Instruction

The Compare Register instruction is used to perform an algebraic compare between two registers.

> INSTRUCTIONS: COMPARE REGISTER
>
> OPERATION CODE: CR
>
> EXAMPLE: CR 8,11

In the example shown, the contents of register 8 are compared with the contents of register 11. The values in the registers are considered to be signed binary values. Thus, in the comparison, a negative value (that is, one in two's complement form) is considered lower than a positive value. The condition code set is dependent on whether the first operand is high, low, or equal.

COMPARE FULLWORD Instruction

> INSTRUCTION: COMPARE FULLWORD
>
> OPERATION CODE: C
>
> EXAMPLE: C FUNCREG,FULLONE

The Compare Fullword instruction is used to compare the contents of the register specified in the first operand to the contents of the fullword specified in the second operand. The compare is an algebraic compare, that is, the high-order bit in the register and the high-order bit in the fullword are considered to be "signs" and negative values are considered lower than positive values.

COMPARE HALFWORD Instruction

INSTRUCTION: COMPARE HALFWORD

OPERATION CODE: CH

EXAMPLE: CH   2,HALF

The halfword specified in the second operand is expanded to a fullword by propagating the sign bit. The contents of the register specified in the first operand are then algebraically compared with the expanded halfword. The condition code is set dependent upon whether the contents of the register are high, low, or equal.

COMPARE LOGICAL REGISTER Instruction

INSTRUCTION: COMPARE LOGICAL REGISTER

OPERATION CODE: CLR

EXAMPLE: CLR   8,6

The Compare Logical Register instruction is used to perform a logical comparison between the contents of the register specified in the first operand and the register specified in the second operand. A logical compare is a bit-by-bit comparison with no sign considered. Thus, in a logical comparison, a negative binary number will be considered higher than a positive binary number because the high-order bit of a negative number is equal to 1.

COMPARE LOGICAL FULLWORD Instruction

INSTRUCTION: COMPARE LOGICAL FULLWORD

OPERATION CODE: CL

EXAMPLE: CL   5,FULL

The contents of the register specified in the first operand are logically compared to the contents of the fullword specified in the second operand. Neither value is considered to be a signed number.

ORG Instruction

The ORG instruction is an instruction to the assembler telling it what value to place in the location counter. In a normal assembly, the location counter value is incremented by the length of an instruction, storage area, or constant defined in the program. Thus, in Figure 8-51, the location counter is incremented by the length of the instructions.

```
00018C 9104 4000      00000        209      TM    SWITCH,X'04'
000190 4780 C192             001A0  210      BZ    NODELETE
000194 95F2 3030      00030        211      CLI   MSTRTYPE,C'2'
000198 4770 C2FC             0030A  212      BNE   GETNEXT
00019C 47F0 C19A             001A8  213      B     CONTINUE
```

Figure 8-51 Example of location counter in assembly

Note that as each 4 byte instruction is processed, the location counter value is incremented by 4.

The ORG instruction is used to alter the normal sequence of the location counter.

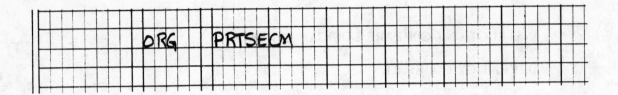

Figure 8-52 Example of ORG instruction

The only operand of the ORG instruction is a previously defined label in the assembly. When the ORG instruction is encountered, the location counter value is set to the value it had at the label specified in the operand. Thus, if the location counter value of PRTSECM was 0008DD, when the ORG instruction above was encountered, the value in the location counter would be set to 0008DD.

The ORG instruction can be used to "redefine" a section of core storage, that is, more than one set of labels can be applied to the same location in core storage. In the sample program presented in this chapter, the first 69 bytes of the master report and the spares/shorts reports are identical. The next 64 bytes, however, vary dependent upon which report is being created. The ORG instruction can be used to redefine these 64 bytes so that the different labels from the different reports can all reference the same 64 bytes of core storage.

8.54

The following example illustrates the use of the ORG instruction to redefine a printer area.

000898		663	PRTFIRST DS	OCL69
000898		664	SKIP DS	CL1
000899		665	DIVR DS	CL2
00089B	40	666	DC	C' '
00089C		667	PRIMER DS	CL6
0008A2	40	668	DC	C' '
0008A3		669	DASHR DS	CL5
0008A8	404040	670	DC	CL3' '
0008AB		671	DESCR DS	CL25
0008C4	404040	672	DC	CL3' '
0008C7		673	NADIVR DS	CL2
0008C9	40	674	DC	C' '
0008CA		675	NAPRIMER DS	CL6
0008D0	40	676	DC	C' '
0008D1		677	NADASHR DS	CL5
0008D6	404040	678	DC	CL3' '
0008D9		679	SOURCER DS	CL4
0008DD		680	PRTSECM DS	OCL64
0008DD		681	DS	CL3
0008E0		682	QOHRM DS	CL9
0008E9		683	DS	CL2
0008EB		684	QOORM DS	CL9
0008F4		685	DS	CL2
0008F6		686	QRSVRM DS	CL9
0008FF		687	DS	CL2
000901		688	UNITRM DS	CL8
000909		689	DS	CL2
00090B		690	AMOUNTRM DS	CL10
000915		691	DS	CL3
000918		692	DELRM DS	CL1
000919		693	DS	CL4
0008DD		694	ORG	PRTSECM
0008DD		695	DS	CL3
0008E0		696	SHORTRS DS	CL9
0008E9		697	DS	CL2
0008EB		698	SPARERS DS	CL9
0008F4		699	DS	CL2
0008F6		700	UNITRS DS	CL8
0008FE		701	DS	CL2
000900		702	SHTAMTRS DS	CL10
00090A		703	DS	CL4
00090E		704	SPAMTRS DS	CL10
000918		705	DS	CL2
00091A		706	DELRS DS	CL1
00091B		707	DS	CL2

Figure 8-53 Example of the use of the ORG instruction

Note in the excerpt from the sample program illustrated above that the first 69 bytes (labelled PRTFIRST) begin with the location counter equal to a value of 000898. The next 64 bytes (labelled PRTSECM) begin with the location counter value equal to 0008DD. The ORG instruction at statement number 694 resets the location counter to the value it had at the label PRTSECM (that is, the value is reset to 0008DD). Thus, the labels following the ORG statement will reference the same core storage locations as the labels following the DS instruction labelled PRTSECM. It should be noted that once the location counter has been set by the ORG instruction it is incremented by the assembler in the normal manner.

SAMPLE PROGRAM

The sample program, as has been noted, produces one of two printed reports or a back-up tape, dependent upon the entries in a control card. The sample program utilizes overlays and is self-relocating.

INPUT

The input to the sample program is the inventory master file and the control card as described previously.

OUTPUT

The output is either a back-up tape or one of two printed reports. The formats of the reports are illustrated below.

```
         0         1         2         3         4         5         6         7         8         9         10        11        12
   1234567890123456789012345678901234567890123456789012345678901234567890123456789012345678901234567890123456789012345678901234567890123
 1    XX/XX/XX                        M A S T E R   I N V E N T O R Y   R E P O R T                              PAGE XXX
 2
 3    PART NUMBER              DESCRIPTION              NEXT ASSEMBLY    SOURCE    QTY ON       QTY ON       QTY         UNIT      AMOUNT      DEL
 4    DIV PRIME DASH                                    DIV PRIME DASH             HAND         ORDER        RESERVED    PRICE     ON HAND
 5
 6    XX XXXXXX XXXXX    XXXXXXXXXXXXXXXXXXXXXXXXXX      XX XXXXXX XXXXX    XXXX    X,XXX,XXX   X,XXX,XXX   X,XXX,XXX   X,XXX.XX   XXX,XXX.XX   *
 7
 8
 9                                                                        TOTAL INVENTORY AMOUNT $XX,XXX,XXX.XX**
10                                                                        TOTAL INVENTORY RECORDS    X,XXX,XXX**
11
12
13
14
15
16
17
18
19
20    XX/XX/XX                      M A S T E R   S P A R E S / S H O R T S   R E P O R T                        PAGE XXX
21
22    PART NUMBER              DESCRIPTION              NEXT ASSEMBLY    SOURCE    TOTAL        TOTAL        UNIT        SHORTAGES   SPARES     DEL
23    DIV PRIME DASH                                    DIV PRIME DASH             SHORTAGES    SPARES       PRICE       AMOUNT      AMOUNT
24
25    XX XXXXXX XXXXX    XXXXXXXXXXXXXXXXXXXXXXXXXX      XX XXXXXX XXXXX    XXXX    X,XXX,XXX   X,XXX,XXX   X,XXX.XX   XXX,XXX.XX   XXX,XXX.XX   *
26
27
28                                                                        TOTAL AMOUNTS  $X,XXX,XXX.XX  $X,XXX,XXX.XX
29
30
```

8.57

PROGRAM

```
  LOC  OBJECT CODE    ADDR1 ADDR2 STMT  SOURCE STATEMENT                                     DOS CL3-5 08/26/70

 000000                            2 MSTRUTIL START 0                                                 UTIL0020
                                   3         PRINT NOGEN


                                   5 ****                                                             UTIL0040
                                   6 * THIS PROGRAM IS USED AS AN UTILITY PROGRAM FOR THE INVENTORY MASTER  UTIL0050
                                   7 * FILE. IT IS THE ROOT PHASE FOR A PROGRAM WHICH PRINTS THE INVENTORY  UTIL0060
                                   8 * MASTER IN ONE OF TWO REPORTS - A COMPLETE MASTER FILE REPORT OR A    UTIL0070
                                   9 * SHORTS AND SPARES REPORT, OR FOR A PROGRAM WHICH DUMPS THE MASTER    UTIL0080
                                  10 * FILE ONTO MAGNETIC TAPE AS BACK-UP AND AS A SOURCE TO RE-LOAD       UTIL0090
                                  11 * THE FILE                                                           UTIL0100
                                  12 *                                                                    UTIL0110
                                  13 * THIS PROGRAM LOADS A CONTROL CARD, INTERPRETS THE INFORMATION AND   UTIL0120
                                  14 * PASSES THE INFORMATION TO THE DUMP OR PRINT PHASE                  UTIL0130
                                  15 *                                                                    UTIL0140
                                  16 *                                                                    UTIL0150
                                  17 * THE CONTROL CARD WHICH IS READ BY THIS PROGRAM HAS THE FOLLOWING   UTIL0160
                                  18 * FORMAT (NOTE THAT THE FORMAT IS 'FREEFORM' - THIS MEANS THAT THE   UTIL0170
                                  19 * OPERANDS CAN START IN ANY COLUMN - AND THAT IT IS POSITIONAL, WHICH UTIL0180
                                  20 * MEANS IF ONE OPERAND IS OMITTED AND ONE FOLLOWS, THE OMITTED OPERAND UTIL0190
                                  21 * MUST BE INDICATED BY A COMMA                                        UTIL0200
                                  22 *                                                                    UTIL0210
                                  23 *   PRINT CARD - THE FIRST ENTRY IN THE PRINT CARD IS THE WORD 'PRINT'. UTIL0220
                                  24 *               THE NEXT ENTRY IS THE WORD 'MASTER' IF A LISTING OF  UTIL0230
                                  25 *                 THE COMPLETE MASTER IS DESIRED OR THE WORD 'SPARES' UTIL0240
                                  26 *                 IF THE SPARES AND SHORTS LISTING IS DESIRED.       UTIL0250
                                  27 *               THE NEXT ENTRY, IF DESIRED, IS A PARTICULAR DIVISION UTIL0260
                                  28 *                 NUMBER TO BE PRINTED. IF OMITTED, ALL DIVISIONS    UTIL0270
                                  29 *                 ARE PRINTED                                       UTIL0280
                                  30 *               THE NEXT 2 ENTRIES, IF DESIRED, ARE A FROM-TO RANGE OF UTIL0290
                                  31 *                 PART NUMBERS TO BE PRINTED. IF OMITTED, ALL PART   UTIL0300
                                  32 *                 NUMBERS ARE PRINTED.                              UTIL0310
                                  33 *               THE NEXT ENTRY IS A 'Y' IF A DELETED PARTS LISTING IS UTIL0320
                                  34 *                 DESIRED. THE DEFAULT IS TO PRINT ONLY THE VALID    UTIL0330
                                  35 *                 PARTS.                                            UTIL0340
                                  36 *               THE NEXT ENTRY IS A 'Y' IF A COUNT IS DESIRED ON THE UTIL0350
                                  37 *                 NUMBER OF RECORDS IN THE OVERFLOW AREA.           UTIL0360
                                  38 *   A SAMPLE CARD MIGHT APPEAR AS:                                  UTIL0370
                                  39 *                                                                  UTIL0380
                                  40 *       PRINT,MASTER,21,,,,Y                                        UTIL0390
                                  41 *                                                                  UTIL0400
                                  42 *                                                                  UTIL0410
                                  43 *   DUMP CARD  - THE FIRST ENTRY IS THE WORD 'DUMP'                UTIL0420
                                  44 *               THE SECOND ENTRY IS = 'Y' IF THE DELETES ARE TO BE UTIL0430
                                  45 *                 DUMPED AS WELL AS THE ACTIVE RECORDS.            UTIL0440
                                  46 *                                                                  UTIL0450
                                  47 *                                                                  UTIL0460
                                  48 * REGISTER USAGE IS AS FOLLOWS:                                    UTIL0470

 00000C                           50 BASEREG  EQU  12                                                   UTIL0490
 000005                           51 PRINTREG EQU  5                                                    UTIL0500
 000006                           52 CUMPREG  EQU  6                                                    UTIL0510
 000001                           53 READREG  EQU  1          REGISTER TO CONTAIN DTF ADDRESSES         UTIL0520
 00000B                           54 CARDREG  EQU  11         CONTAINS ADDRESS OF CARD I/O AREA         UTIL0530
 00000A                           55 TRREG    EQU  10         CONTAINS LENGTH FOR TRT INSTRUCTION       UTIL0540
 000002                           56 FUNCREG  EQU  2          CONTAINS FUNCTION BYTE FROM TRT           UTIL0550
 000001                           57 ADDRREG  EQU  1          CONTAINS ADDRESS OF DELIMETER FOR TR      UTIL0560
 000009                           58 SAVEREG  EQU  9          USED AS SAVE REGISTER FOR ADDRREG         UTIL0570
 000008                           59 LINKREG1 EQU  8          USED AS LINKAGE REGISTER                  UTIL0580
 000001                           60 LOADREG  EQU  1          CONTAINS ADDRESS OF PHASE NAME -LOAD      UTIL0590
 000000                           61 ENTRYREG EQU  0          CONTAINS ADDR OF LOAD POINT FOR LOAD      UTIL0600
 000007                           62 BCTREG1  EQU  7          USED FOR BCT COUNT                        UTIL0610
 000005                           63 SAVEREG1 EQU  5          USED AS A SAVE REGISTER                   UTIL0620
 000004                           64 PASSREG  EQU  4          USED TO PASS ADDRESS TO OVERLAYS          UTIL0630
 000003                           65 REGBASE  EQU  3                                                    UTIL0640
 000002                           66 ADCONREG EQU  2                                                    UTIL0650
 000005                           67 RELOCREG EQU  5                                                    UTIL0660
                                  68 ****                                                               UTIL0670


                                  70 ****                                                               UTIL0690
                                  71 * THE FOLLOWING ESTABLISHES A BASE REGISTER AND OPENS THE FILES     UTIL0700
                                  72 ****                                                               UTIL0710


 000000 05C0                      74 BEGIN    BALR BASEREG,0       ESTABLISH BASE REGISTER              UTIL0730
 000002                           75         USING *,BASEREG                                            UTIL0740
 000002 47F0 C026          00028  76         B    OPENFILE                                              UTIL0750


                                  78 ****                                                               UTIL0770
                                  79 *PASSING AREA                                                      UTIL0780
                                  80 ****                                                               UTIL0790


 000006                           82 ALLPASS  DS   0CL25                                                UTIL0810
 000006 00                        83 SWITCH   DC   X'00'                                                UTIL0820
 000007 FFFF                      84 DIVNO    DC   XL2'FFFF'                                             UTIL0830
 000009 0000000000000000          85 PTNOS    DC   11X'00'                                              UTIL0840
 000014 FFFFFFFFFFFFFFFF          86         DC   11X'FF'                                               UTIL0850
```

```
LOC   OBJECT CODE   ADDR1 ADDR2 STMT   SOURCE STATEMENT                                      DOS CL3-5 08/26/70

                                88 OVERLAY  LOAD  (1),(0)              LOAD DESIRED PHASE              UTIL0870
000022 47F0 1008         00008  92         B     8(0,1)              GO TO LOADED PHASE             UTIL0880


000028                          94         DS    0D                                                 UTIL0900
000028 4120 C32A         0032C  95 OPENFILE LA    ADCONREG,ADCONS     LOAD ADDRESS OF BEGINNING OF ADCONS UTIL0910
00002C 41CC 0000         00000  96         LA    BASEREG,0(BASEREG)  ZERO HIGH-ORDER BITS           UTIL0920
000030 183C                     97         LR    REGBASE,BASEREG     LOAD BASE REGISTER             UTIL0930
000032 0630                     98         BCTR  REGBASE,0           SUBTRACT 2 FROM ADDRESS        UTIL0940
000034 0630                     99         BCTR  REGBASE,0             IN BASE REGISTER             UTIL0950
000036 4170 0004         00004 100         LA    BCTREG1,L'ADCONS/4  LOAD NUMBER OF ADCONS          UTIL0960
00003A                         101 RELOCLUP EQU  *                                                  UTIL0970
00003A 5850 2000         00000 102         L     RELOCREG,0(0,ADCONREG) LOAD ADCON INTO REGISTER    UTIL0980
00003E 1453                    103         AR    RELOCREG,REGBASE    GET ABSOLUTE ADDRESS           UTIL0990
000040 5050 2000         00000 104         ST    RELOCREG,0(0,ADCONREG) STORE ANSWER BACK IN ADCON  UTIL1000
000044 4122 0004         00004 105         LA    ADCONREG,4(ADCONREG) BUMP TO LOOK AT NEXT ADCON    UTIL1010
000048 4670 C038         0003A 106         BCT   BCTREG1,RELOCLUP    GO TO GET NEXT ADCON           UTIL1020
00004C 5850 C32A         0032C 107         L     5,CARDFLE           LOAD ADDRESS OF CARD FILE DTF  UTIL1030
000050 5860 C32E         00330 108         L     6,PRTFLE            LOAD ADDRESS OF PRINT FILE DTF UTIL1040
                               109         OPENR (5),(6)             OPEN FILES                     UTIL1050


                               123 ****                                                             UTIL1070
                               124 * THE FOLLOWING READS A CARD AND SCANS IT FOR LEADING BLANKS-WHEN THE UTIL1080
                               125 * FIRST ENTRY IS FOUND, IT GOES TO CHECK IT                     UTIL1090
                               126 ****                                                            UTIL1100

000072 41A0 C0CC         000CE 128         LA    10,CDERROR          IF NO CARD, THERE IS AN ERROR  UTIL1120
                               129 *                                 REGISTER 10 MUST CONTAIN THE ADDRESS UTIL1124
                               130 *                                 OF THE CARD EOF ROUTINE        UTIL1125
000076 5810 C32A         0032C 131         L     READREG,CARDFLE     LOAD ADDRESS OF CARDFLE DTF    UTIL1130
                               132         GET   (READREG)           READ A CARD                    UTIL1140

000084 1B22                    138         SR    FUNCREG,FUNCREG     ZERO REGISTER                  UTIL1160
000086 58B0 C332         00334 139         L     CARDREG,CARDIO2A    LOAD ADDRESS OF CARDIO AREA    UTIL1170
00008A 41A0 004F         0004F 140         LA    TRREG,79            LOAD NUMBER OF BYTES - 1 TO CHECK UTIL1180
00008E                         141 EXECTRT  EQU  *                                                  UTIL1190
00008E 44A0 C31E         00320 142         EX    TRREG,TRTINST       EXECUTE THE TRANSLATE AND TEST UTIL1200
000092 4780 C0CC         000CE 143         BC    8,CDERROR            IF END, GO TO ERROR           UTIL1210
000096 4720 C0CC         000CE 144         BC    2,CDERROR            IF END, GO TO ERROR           UTIL1220
00009A 1891                    145         LR    SAVEREG,ADDRREG     SAVE ADDRESS OF STOP BYTE      UTIL1230
00009C 1B1B                    146         SR    ADDRREG,CARDREG     GET LENGTH OF FIELD            UTIL1240
00009E 4770 C0B2         000B4 147         BC    7,NOTZERO1          IF ANSWER NOT 0, GO TO CHECK FIELD UTIL1250
0000A2 5920 C402         00404 148         C     FUNCREG,FULLONE     WAS IT STOPPED BY A BLANK      UTIL1254
0000A6 4770 C0CC         000CE 149         BNE   CDERROR             NO, CARD IS IN ERROR           UTIL1255
0000AA 41B0 B001         00001 150         LA    CARDREG,1(0,CARDREG) BUMP TEST AREA BY 1           UTIL1260
0000AE 06A0                    151         BCTR  TRREG,0             SUBTRACT 1 FROM LENGTH         UTIL1270
0000B0 47F0 C08C         0008E 152         B     EXECTRT             GO TO EXECUTE NEXT TRT         UTIL1280


                               154 ****                                                             UTIL1300
                               155 * THIS ROUTINE IS ENTERED WHEN SOMETHING OTHER THAN A BLANK IS FOUND- UTIL1310
                               156 * IT CHECKS IF THE WORK IS DUMP OR PRINT                         UTIL1320
                               157 ****                                                            UTIL1330

0000B4                         159 NOTZERO1 EQU  *                                                  UTIL1350
0000B4 0610                    160         BCTR  ADDRREG,0           SUBTRACT 1 FROM COMPARE REGISTER UTIL1360
0000B6 4160 C40A         0040C 161         LA    COMPREG,COMPTBL     LOAD ADDRESS OF CONSTANT TABLE UTIL1370
0000BA 4410 C324         00326 162         EX    ADDRREG,CLCINST     IS WORD = PRINT                UTIL1380
0000BE 4780 C16A         0016C 163         BE    PRINTROU            YES, GO TO PRINT ROUTINE       UTIL1390
0000C2 4160 6005         00005 164         LA    COMPREG,5(0,COMPREG) BUMP ADDRESS                  UTIL1400
0000C6 4410 C324         00326 165         EX    ADDRREG,CLCINST     IS WORK = DUMP                 UTIL1410
0000CA 4780 C112         00114 166         BE    DUMPROU                                            UTIL1420


                               168 ****                                                             UTIL1440
                               169 * IF AN ERROR IS FOUND IN THE CONTROL CARD, THIS ROUTINE IS ENTERED. UTIL1450
                               170 * IT PRINTS A MESSAGE ON THE PRINTER AND CANCELS THE JOB         UTIL1460
                               171 ****                                                            UTIL1470

0000CE                         173 CDERROR  EQU  *                                                  UTIL1490
0000CE 5890 C32E         00330 174         L     SAVEREG,PRTFLE      LOAD ADDRESS OF PRINT FILE     UTIL1500
0000D2 5850 C336         00338 175         L     PRINTREG,PRTIO1A    LOAD ADDRESS OF I/O AREA       UTIL1510
0000D6 D283 5000 C530 00000 00532 176     MVC   0(132,PRINTREG),BADCARD MOVE MSG TO I/O AREA       UTIL1520
                               177         PUT   (SAVEREG)           PRINT THE MESSAGE              UTIL1530
0000E6 4580 C0EE         000F0 182         BAL   LINKREG1,CLOSEM     GO TO CLOSE THE FILES          UTIL1540
                               183         CANCEL ALL                                               UTIL1550


                               188 ****                                                             UTIL1570
                               189 * THIS ROUTINE IS ENTERED TO CLOSE THE FILES                     UTIL1580
                               190 ****                                                            UTIL1590

0000F0                         192 CLOSEM   EQU  *                                                  UTIL1610
0000F0 5850 C32A         0032C 193         L     5,CARDFLE           LOAD ADDRESS OF CARD FILE      UTIL1620
0000F4 5860 C32E         00330 194         L     6,PRTFLE            LOAD ADDRESS OF PRINT FILE     UTIL1630
                               195         CLOSER (5),(6)            LOAD FILES                     UTIL1640
```

```
  LOC   OBJECT CODE    ADOR1 ADDR2   STMT   SOURCE STATEMENT                              DOS CL3-5 08/26/70

000112 07F8                           207         BR   LINKREG1            RETURN TO CALLER             UTIL1650


                                      209 ****                                                         UTIL1670
                                      210 * THIS ROUTINE IS ENTERED WHEN THE DUMP ROUTINE IS REQUESTED UTIL1680
                                      211 ****                                                         UTIL1690

000114                                213 DUMPROU EQU  *                                              UTIL1710
000114 5920 C402             00404    214         C    FUNCREG,FULLONE     IS IT BLANK                 UTIL1720
000118 4780 C156             0015B    215         BE   LOADDUMP            YES, GO TO LOAD DUMP PHASE  UTIL1730
00011C 41B0 9001             00001    216         LA   CARDREG,1(0,SAVEREG) BUMP TRT ADDR BY 1         UTIL1740
000120 41A0 0002             00002    217         LA   TRREG,2             LOAD LENGTH FOR TRT INST    UTIL1750
000124 4166 0010             0001C    218         LA   COMPREG,16(COMPREG) BUMP COMPARE TABLE ADDRESS  UTIL1760
000128 44A0 C31E             00320    219         EX   TRREG,TRTINST       EXECUTE TRANSLATE AND TEST  UTIL1770
00012C 4780 COCC             000CE    220         BC   8,CDERROR           IF NO DELIMETER, CARD ERROR UTIL1780
000130 1891                           221         LR   SAVEREG,ADDRREG     SAVE START REGISTER         UTIL1790
000132 1B1B                           222         SR   ADDRREG,CARDREG     GET LENGTH OF FILD          UTIL1800
000134 4770 C140             00142    223         BC   7,NOTZERO2          IF LENGTH NOT ZERO, GO TO CHECK UTIL1810
000138 47F0 COCC             000CE    224         B    CDERROR                IF ZERO, GO TO CARD ERROR UTIL1820

00013C D201 C005 B000 00007 00000    226 MOVEDIV MVC  DIVNO(2),0(CARDREG) MOVE DIV NO TO PASS AREA    UTIL1850
000142                                227 NOTZERO2 EQU *                                              UTIL1860
000142 5920 C402             00404    228         C    FUNCREG,FULLONE     IS DELIMETER A BLANK        UTIL1870
000146 4770 COCC             000CE    229         BNE  CDERROR             NO, GO TO CARD ERROR        UTIL1880
00014A 0610                           230         BCTR ADDRREG,0           SUBTRACT 1 FOR COMPARE      UTIL1890
00014C 4410 C324             00326    231         EX   ADDRREG,CLCINST     EXECUTE COMPARE INSTRUCTION UTIL1900
000150 4770 COCC             000CE    232         BNE  CDERROR             IF NOT = 'Y', CARD IS IN ERROR UTIL1910
000154 9601 C004             00006    233         OI   SWITCH,X'01'        INDICATE DUMP DELETES AND GOOD RECS UTIL1920


                                      235 ****                                                         UTIL1940
                                      236 * THIS ROUTINE IS ENTERED TO LOAD THE DUMP PHASE OF THIS PROGRAM UTIL1950
                                      237 ****                                                         UTIL1960

000158                                239 LOADDUMP EQU *                                              UTIL1980
000158 4580 COEE             000F0    240         BAL  LINKREG1,CLOSEM        GO TO CLOSE FILES        UTIL1990
00015C 4110 C528             0052A    241         LA   LOADREG,DUMPPHSE       LOAD ADDRESS OF NAME OF PHASE UTIL2000
000160 4100 C026             00028    242 GOTOLOAD LA  ENTRYREG,OPENFILE   LOAD ADDRESS OF ENTRY AREA FOR PHASE UTIL2010
000164 4140 C004             00006    243         LA   PASSREG,ALLPASS     LOAD ADDRESS OF PASS AREA   UTIL2020
000168 47F0 C01E             00020    244         B    OVERLAY             GO TO LOAD PHASE INTO CORE  UTIL2030


                                      246 ****                                                         UTIL2050
                                      247 * THE FOLLOWING ROUTINE IS ENTERED WHEN A PRINT CONTROL CARD IS READ UTIL2060
                                      248 ****                                                         UTIL2070

00016C                                250 PRINTROU EQU *                                              UTIL2090
00016C 5920 C402             00404    251         C    FUNCREG,FULLONE     WAS DELIMETER A BLANK       UTIL2100
000170 4780 COCC             000CE    252         BE   CDERROR             YES, CARD IS IN ERROR       UTIL2110
000174 41B9 0001             00001    253         LA   CARDREG,1(SAVEREG)  BUMP TO LOOK AT NEXT FIELD  UTIL2120
000178 41A0 0006             00006    254         LA   TRREG,6             LOAD LENGTH OF FIELD TO EXAMINE UTIL2130
00017C 4166 0009             00009    255         LA   COMPREG,9(COMPREG)  BUMP COMPARE TABLE BY NINE POSITIONS UTIL2140
000180 44A0 C31E             00320    256         EX   TRREG,TRTINST       EXECUTE TRANSLATE AND TEST INST UTIL2150
000184 4780 COCC             000CE    257         BC   8,CDERROR           IF NO DELIMETER FOUND, CARD IN ERROR UTIL2160
000188 1891                           258         LR   SAVEREG,ADDRREG     SAVE START ADDRESS          UTIL2170
00018A 1B1B                           259         SR   ADDRREG,CARDREG     GET LENGTH                  UTIL2180
00018C 4770 C192             00194    260         BC   7,NOTZERO4          IF NOT ZERO, GO CHECK CONTENTS UTIL2190
000190 47F0 COCC             000CE    261         B    CDERROR             IF ZERO, PARAMETER IS OMITTED AND UTIL2200
                                      262 *                                CARD IS IN ERROR           UTIL2210

000194                                264 NOTZERO4 EQU *                                              UTIL2230
000194 0610                           265         BCTR ADDRREG,0           SUBTRACT 1 FROM LENGTH      UTIL2240
000196 4410 C324             00326    266         EX   ADDRREG,CLCINST     COMPARE IF MASTER PRINT     UTIL2250
00019A 4770 C148             001AA    267         BNE  CHKSPARE            IF NOT MASTER, CHECK IF SPARES UTIL2260
00019E 9602 C004             00006    268         OI   SWITCH,X'02'        SET SWITCH INDICATING MASTER REPORT UTIL2270
0001A2 4166 0006             00006    269         LA   COMPREG,6(COMPREG)  BUMP COMPARE ADDRESS        UTIL2280
0001A6 47F0 C1B8             001BA    270         B    PRINT2              GO TO CHECK NEXT PARAMETER  UTIL2290

0001AA                                272 CHKSPARE EQU *                                              UTIL2310
0001AA 4166 0006             00006    273         LA   COMPREG,6(COMPREG)  UPDATE COMPARE ADDRESS      UTIL2320
0001AE 4410 C324             00326    274         EX   ADDRREG,CLCINST     IS IT A SPARES REPORT DESIRED UTIL2330
0001B2 4770 COCC             000CE    275         BNE  CDERROR             IF NOT SPARES, CARD IS IN ERROR UTIL2340
0001B6 9640 C004             00006    276         OI   SWITCH,X'40'        SET SWITCH INDICATING SPARES RPT UTIL2350

0001BA                                278 PRINT2  EQU  *                                              UTIL2370
0001BA 5920 C402             00404    279         C    FUNCREG,FULLONE     WAS IT A BLANK WHICH STOPPED TRT UTIL2380
0001BE 4780 C312             00314    280         BE   LOADPRT             YES, GO TO LOAD PRINT PHASE UTIL2390
0001C2 4166 0006             00006    281         LA   COMPREG,6(COMPREG)  UPDATE COMPARE ADDRESS      UTIL2400
0001C6 41B9 0001             00001    282         LA   CARDREG,1(SAVEREG)  UPDATE ARGUMENT ADDRESS     UTIL2410
0001CA 41A0 0002             00002    283         LA   TRREG,2             LOAD LENGTH FOR TRT INSTRUCTION UTIL2420
0001CE 44A0 C31E             00320    284         EX   TRREG,TRTINST       EXECUTE TRANSLATE AND TEST INST.-DIV UTIL2430
0001D2 4780 COCC             000CE    285         BC   8,CDERROR           IF NO DELIMETER, GO TO ERROR UTIL2440
0001D6 1891                           286         LR   SAVEREG,ADDRREG     SAVE ADDRESS                UTIL2450
0001D8 1B1B                           287         SR   ADDRREG,CARDREG     GET LENGTH                  UTIL2460
0001DA 4770 C1EB             001EA    288         BC   7,NOTZERO5          IF NOT ZERO, GO CHECK CONTENTS UTIL2470
0001DE 5920 C402             00404    289         C    FUNCREG,FULLONE     WAS DELIMETER A BLANK       UTIL2480
```

8.60

```
LOC   OBJECT CODE      ADDR1 ADDR2  STMT   SOURCE STATEMENT                                  DOS CL3-5 08/26/70

0001E2 4780 C0CC             000CE   290          BE    CDERROR          YES, CARD IS IN ERROR               UTIL2490
0001E6 47F0 C204             00206   291          B     PRINT3           GO TO CHECK NEXT FIELD              UTIL2500


0001EA                               293 NOTZERO5 EQU   *                                                    UTIL2520
0001EA 95F0 B000       00000         294          CLI   0(CARDREG),C'0'  IS FIRST DIV NO LESS THAN ZERO      UTIL2530
0001EE C0CC                  000CE   295          BL    CDERROR          YES, GO TO ERROR                    UTIL2540
0001F2 95F0 B001       00001         296          CLI   1(CARDREG),C'0'  IS SEC DIV NO LESS THAN ZERO        UTIL2550
0001F6 4740 C0CC             000CE   297          BL    CDERROR          YES, GO TO ERROR                    UTIL2560
0001FA 4400 C13A             0013C   298          EX    0,MOVEDIV        MOVE DIVISION NUMBER TO PASS AREA   UTIL2570
0001FE 5920 C402             00404   299          C     FUNCREG,FULLONE  WAS DELIMETER A BLANK               UTIL2580
000202 4780 C312             00314   300          BE    LOADPRT          YES, GO TO LOAD PRINT PHASE         UTIL2590


000206                               302 PRINT3   EQU   *                                                    UTIL2610
000206 41B9 0001             00001   303          LA    CARDREG,1(SAVEREG) LOAD ADDRESS FOR TRT              UTIL2620
00020A 41A0 000B             0000B   304          LA    TRREG,11         LOAD SIZE LESS 1 TO CHECK           UTIL2630
00020E 44A0 C31E             00320   305          EX    TRREG,TRTINST    EXECUTE TRT INSTRUCTION             UTIL2640
000212 4780 C0CC             000CE   306          BC    8,CDERROR        IF DELIMETER NOT FOUND, CARD ERROR  UTIL2650
000216 1891                          307          LR    SAVEREG,ADDRREG  SAVE ENDING ADDRESS                 UTIL2660
000218 1B1B                          308          SR    ADDRREG,CARDREG  GET LENGTH                          UTIL2670
00021A 4770 C228             0022A   309          BC    7,NOTZERO6       IF NOT ZERO, GO TO CHECK CONTENTS   UTIL2680
00021E 5920 C402             00404   310          C     FUNCREG,FULLONE  WAS DELIMETER BLANK                 UTIL2690
000222 4780 C0CC             000CE   311          BE    CDERROR          YES, GO TO ERROR ROUTINE            UTIL2700
000226 47F0 C250             00252   312          B     PRINT4           GO TO CHECK NEXT FIELD              UTIL2710


00022A                               314 NOTZERO6 EQU   *                                                    UTIL2730
00022A 1871                          315          LR    BCTREG1,ADDRREG  SAVE LENGTH FOR MOVE                UTIL2740
00022C 185B                          316          LR    SAVEREG1,CARDREG SAVE STARTING ADDRESS               UTIL2750
00022E                               317 COMPLUP1 EQU   *                                                    UTIL2760
00022E 95F0 B000       00000         318          CLI   0(CARDREG),C'0'  IS PART NO LESS THAN 0              UTIL2770
000232 4740 C0CC             000CE   319          BL    CDERROR          YES, CARD IS IN ERROR               UTIL2780
000236 95F9 B000       00000         320          CLI   0(CARDREG),C'9'  IS PART NO GREATER THAN 9           UTIL2790
00023A C0CC                  000CE   321          BH    CDERROR          YES, CARD ERROR                     UTIL2800
00023E 41BB 0001             00001   322          LA    CARDREG,1(CARDREG) BUMP ADDRESS BY 1                 UTIL2810
000242 4670 C22C             0022E   323          BCT   BCTREG1,COMPLUP1 GO TO CHECK REST OF FIELD           UTIL2820


000246 0610                          325          BCTR  ADDRREG,0        SUBTRACT 1 FROM REGISTER            UTIL2840
000248 4210 C24B             0024D   326          STC   ADDRREG,MVC1+1   STORE LENGTH IN INSTRUCTION         UTIL2850
00024C D200 C007 5000  00009 00000   327 MVC1     MVC   PTNOS(1),0(SAVEREG1) MOVE FIRST DIGITS OF PART NUMBER UTIL2860


000252                               329 PRINT4   EQU   *                                                    UTIL2880
000252 5920 C402             00404   330          C     FUNCREG,FULLONE  WAS DELIMETER A BLANK               UTIL2890
000256 4780 C312             00314   331          BE    LOADPRT          YES, GO TO LOAD PRINT PROGRAM       UTIL2900
00025A 41B9 0001             00001   332          LA    CARDREG,1(SAVEREG) LOAD STARTING ADDRESS TO REG      UTIL2910
00025E 41A0 000B             0000B   333          LA    TRREG,11         LOAD LENGTH LESS 1 TO CHECK         UTIL2920
000262 44A0 C31E             00320   334          EX    TRREG,TRTINST    EXECUTE TRANSLATE AND TEST INST     UTIL2930
000266 4780 C0CC             000CE   335          BC    8,CDERROR        IF NO DELIMETER, CARD IN ERROR      UTIL2940
00026A 1891                          336          LR    SAVEREG,ADDRREG  SAVE ENDING ADDRESS                 UTIL2950
00026C 1B1B                          337          SR    ADDRREG,CARDREG  GET LENGTH                          UTIL2960
00026E 4770 C27C             0027E   338          BC    7,NOTZERO7       IF NOT ZERO, GO TO CHECK CONTENTS   UTIL2970
000272 5920 C402             00404   339          C     FUNCREG,FULLONE  WAS DELIMETER A BLANK               UTIL2980
000276 4780 C0CC             000CE   340          BE    CDERROR          YES, CARD IS IN ERROR               UTIL2990
00027A 47F0 C2A4             002A6   341          B     PRINT5               GO TO CHECK NEXT FIEKD           UTIL3000


00027E                               343 NOTZERO7 EQU   *                                                    UTIL3020
00027E 1871                          344          LR    BCTREG1,ADDRREG  SAVE LENGTH FOR MOVE                UTIL3030
000280 185B                          345          LR    SAVEREG1,CARDREG SAVE STARTING ADDRESS               UTIL3040
000282                               346 COMPLUP2 EQU   *                                                    UTIL3050
000282 95F0 B000       00000         347          CLI   0(CARDREG),X'F0' IS PART NO LESS THAN ZERO           UTIL3060
000286 4740 C0CC             000CE   348          BL    CDERROR          YES, CARD IS IN ERROR               UTIL3070
00028A 95F9 B000       00000         349          CLI   0(CARDREG),X'F9' IS PART NO GREATER THAN NINE        UTIL3080
00028E C0CC                  000CE   350          BH    CDERROR          YES, CARD IS IN ERROR               UTIL3090
000292 41BB 0001             00001   351          LA    CARDREG,1(CARDREG) BUMP COMPARE ADDRESS BY 1         UTIL3100
000296 4670 C280             00282   352          BCT   BCTREG1,COMPLUP2 GO TO CHECK REST OF FIELD           UTIL3110


00029A 0610                          354          BCTR  ADDRREG,0        SUBTRACT 1 TO GET LENGTH            UTIL3130
00029C 4210 C29F             002A1   355          STC   ADDRREG,MVC2+1   STORE LENGTH IN MOVE INSTRUCTION    UTIL3140
0002A0 D200 C012 5000  00014 00000   356 MVC2     MVC   PTNOS+11(1),0(SAVEREG1) MOVE PART NUMBER             UTIL3150


0002A6                               358 PRINT5   EQU   *                                                    UTIL3170
0002A6 5920 C402             00404   359          C     FUNCREG,FULLONE  WAS LAST DELIMETER A BLANK          UTIL3180
0002AA 4780 C312             00314   360          BE    LOADPRT          YES, GO TO LOAD PRINT PHASE         UTIL3190
0002AE 41B9 0001             00001   361          LA    CARDREG,1(SAVEREG) LOAD START ADDR FOR TRT           UTIL3200
0002B2 41A0 0001             00001   362          LA    TRREG,1          LOAD LENGTH LESS 1                  UTIL3210
0002B6 44A0 C31E             00320   363          EX    TRREG,TRTINST    EXECUTE TRT INSTRUCTION             UTIL3220
0002BA 4780 C0CC             000CE   364          BC    8,CDERROR        IF NO DELIMETER, CARD IN ERROR      UTIL3230
0002BE 1891                          365          LR    SAVEREG,ADDRREG      SAVE ADDRESS                    UTIL3240
0002C0 1B1B                          366          SR    ADDRREG,CARDREG  GET LENGTH                          UTIL3250
0002C2 4770 C2D0             002D2   367          BC    7,NOTZERO8       IF NOT ZERO, GO TO CHECK FIELD      UTIL3260
0002C6 5920 C402             00404   368          C     FUNCREG,FULLONE  IF BLANK, CARD IN ERROR             UTIL3270
0002CA 4780 C0CC             000CE   369          BE    CDERROR          GO TO ERROR ROUTINE                 UTIL3280
0002CE 47F0 C2E6             002E8   370          B     PRINT6           IF NOT BLANK, GO TO CHECK NEXT FIELD UTIL3290


0002D2                               372 NOTZERO8 EQU   *                                                    UTIL3310
0002D2 0610                          373          BCTR  ADDRREG,0        SUBTRACT 1 FOR COMPARE              UTIL3320
0002D4 4410 C324             00326   374          EX    ADDRREG,CLCINST  COMPARE FIELD TO 'Y'                UTIL3330
0002D8 4770 C0CC             000CE   375          BNE   CDERROR          IF NOT =, CARD ERROR                UTIL3340
0002DC 9604 C004       00006         376          OI    SWITCH,X'04'     INDICATE WANT DELETED PARTS LIST    UTIL3350
```

LOC   OBJECT CODE   ADDR1 ADDR2 STMT   SOURCE STATEMENT   DOS CL3-5 08/26/70

```
0002E0 5920 C402           00404  377        C    FUNCREG,FULLONE    WAS LAST DELIMETER A BLANK         UTIL3360
0002E4 4780 C312           00314  378        BE   LOADPRT            YES, GO TO LOAD PRINT PROGRAM      UTIL3370


0002E8                            380 PRINT6 EQU  *                                                    UTIL3390
0002E8 4189 0001           00001  381        LA   CARDREG,1(SAVEREG) LOAD START ADDR FOR TRT           UTIL3400
0002EC 41A0 0001           00001  382        LA   TRREG,1            LOAD TRT LENGTH                   UTIL3410
0002F0 44A0 C31E           00320  383        EX   TRREG,TRTINST      EXECUTE THE TRANSLATE AND TEST INST UTIL3420
0002F4 4780 C0CC           000CE  384        BC   8,CDERROR          IF NO DELIMETER, CARD IS IN ERROR UTIL3430
0002F8 1B1B                       385        SR   ADDRREG,CARDREG    SUBTRACT TO GET LENGTH            UTIL3440
0002FA 4780 C0CC           000CE  386        BC   8,CDERROR          IF LENGTH ZERO, CARD IS IN ERROR  UTIL3450
0002FE 5920 C402           00404  387        C    FUNCREG,FULLONE    IF DELIMETER NOT BLANK, CARD ERROR UTIL3460
000302 4770 C0CC           000CE  388        BNE  CDERROR            GO TO ERROR ROUTINE               UTIL3470
000306 0610                       389        BCTR ADDRREG,0          SUBTRACT 1 FROM LENGTH            UTIL3480
000308 4410 C324           00326  390        EX   ADDRREG,CLCINST    IS CARD =Y                        UTIL3490
00030C 4770 C0CC           000CE  391        BNE  CDERROR            NO, CARD IS BAD                   UTIL3500
000310 9608 C004     00006        392        OI   SWITCH,X'08'       SET SWITCH TO GET OVERFLOW COUNT  UTIL3510


000314                            394 LOADPRT EQU *                                                    UTIL3530
000314 4580 C0EE           000F0  395        BAL  LINKREG1,CLOSEM    GO TO CLOSE FILES                 UTIL3540
000318 4110 C520           00522  396        LA   1,PRTPHASE         LOAD ADDRESS OF PRINT PHASE       UTIL3550
00031C 47F0 C15E           00160  397        B    GOTOLOAD           GO TO LOAD PHASE                  UTIL3560
```

      LOC   OBJECT CODE   ADDR1 ADDR2 STMT   SOURCE STATEMENT   DOS CL3-5 08/26/70
                                          399 ****   UTIL3580
                                          400 * EXECUTED INSTRUCTIONS   UTIL3590
                                          401 ****   UTIL3600

   000320 DD00 B000 C420 00000 00422   403 TRTINST TRT   0(0,CARDREG),TRTABLE   UTIL3620
   000326 D500 B000 6000 00000 00000   404 CLCINST CLC   0(0,CARDREG),0(COMPREG)   UTIL3630

```
                                   406 ****                                                    UTIL3650
                                   407 * CONSTANTS, I/O AREAS, ETC.                             UTIL3660
                                   408 ****                                                    UTIL3670

00032C                             410          DS    OF                                       UTIL3690
00032C                             411 ADCONS   DS    OCL16                                    UTIL3700
00032C 00000000                    412 CARDFLE  DC    V(CARDDTF)                               UTIL3710
000330 00000000                    413 PRTFLE   DC    V(PRTDTF)                                UTIL3720
000334 00000000                    414 CARDIO2A DC    V(CARDIO2)                               UTIL3730
000338 00000000                    415 PRTIO1A  DC    V(PRTIO1)                                UTIL3740
00033C                             416 CARDIO   DS    CL80                                     UTIL3750
00038C                             417 PRINTIO  DS    CL120                                    UTIL3760
000404 00000001                    418 FULLONE  DC    F'1'                                     UTIL3770
000408 00000000                    419 FULLZERO DC    F'0'                                     UTIL3780
00040C                             420 COMPTBL  DS    OCL48                                    UTIL3790
00040C D7D9C9D5E3                  421          DC    C'PRINT'                                 UTIL3800
000411 C4E4D4D7                    422          DC    C'DUMP'                                  UTIL3810
000415 D4C1E2E3C5D9                423          DC    C'MASTER'                                UTIL3820
00041B E2D7C1D9C5E2                424          DC    C'SPARES'                                UTIL3830
000421 E8                          425          DC    C'Y'                                     UTIL3840
000422 0000000000000000            426 TRTABLE  DC    XL64'00'                                 UTIL3850
000462 01                          427          DC    X'01'                                    UTIL3860
000463 0000000000000000            428          DC    XL42'00'                                 UTIL3870
00048D 02                          429          DC    X'02'                                    UTIL3880
00048E 0000000000000000            430          DC    XL148'00'                                UTIL3890
000522 D7D9C9D5E3C9D5E5            431 PRTPHASE DC    CL8'PRINTINV'                            UTIL3900
00052A C4E4D4D7C9D5E540            432 DUMPPHSE DC    CL8'DUMPINV'                             UTIL3910
000532 F1C9D5E5C1D3C9C4            433 BADCARD  DC    CL133'IINVALID CONTROL CARD-CORRECT AND RESUBMIT***' UTIL3920
000000                             434          END   BEGIN                                    UTIL3930
0005B8 5B5BC2D6D7C5D5D9            435                =C'$$BOPENR'
0005C0 5B5BC2C3D3D6E2C5            436                =C'$$BCLOSE'
```

```
  LCC  OBJECT CODE    ADDR1 ADDR2  STMT   SOURCE STATEMENT                              DOS CL3-5 08/26/70

000000                                2 DUMPINV  START 0                                         DUMP0020
000000 C4E4D4D7C9D5E540                3          DC    CL8'DUMPINV'                             DUMP0030


                                      5          PRINT NOGEN
                                      6 ****                                                     DUMP0050
                                      7 * THE FOLLOWING PROGRAM PHASE IS USED TO DUMP THE INVENTORY MASTER   DUMP0060
                                      8 * FILE ONTO A MAGNETIC TAPE FOR BACK-UP. DEPENDENT UPON PARAMETERS   DUMP0070
                                      9 * SET IN THE ROOT PHASE, EITHER THE COMPLETE FILE (INCLUDING THE     DUMP0080
                                     10 * DELETED RECORDS) IS DUMPED OR JUST THE GOOD RECORDS. ALL RECORDS   DUMP0090
                                     11 * DUMPED HAVE THEIR TYPE CODE CHANGED TO 8 BEFORE THEY ARE DUMPED SO DUMP0100
                                     12 * THAT THEY CAN BE LOADED USING THE COMMON LOAD ROUTINE. IF THE      DUMP0110
                                     13 * DELETED RECORDS ARE DUMPED, A DELETE CARD IS PUNCHED FOR EACH DELETED DUMP0120
                                     14 * RECORD SO THAT THE FILE CAN BE RESTORED EXACTLY.                   DUMP0130
                                     15 *                                                                    DUMP0140
                                     16 * IF A DIVISION IS ENTERED IN THE CONTROL CARD, JUST THE DIVISION IS DUMP0150
                                     17 * DUMPED.                                                            DUMP0160
                                     18 *                                                                    DUMP0170
                                     19 * THE FOLLOWING ARE REGISTER USES                                    DUMP0180
                                     20 *                                                                    DUMP0190
                                     21 *                                                                    DUMP0200

00000C                               23 BASEREG  EQU   12                    BASE REGISTER                   DUMP0220
000004                               24 PASSREG  EQU   4                     CONTAINS PASS AREA ADDRESS      DUMP0230
00000B                               25 RELOCREG EQU   11                    USED FOR SELF-RELOCATION ADCONS DUMP0240
000007                               26 TAPEREG  EQU   7                                                     DUMP0250
000006                               27 DISKREG  EQU   6                                                     DUMP0260
00000B                               28 LINKREG1 EQU   11                    LINK REGISTER                   DUMP0270
00000A                               29 CVDREG   EQU   10                    USED AS CONVERT TO DECIMAL REGISTER DUMP0280
000009                               30 ADCONREG EQU   9                                                     DUMP0290
000008                               31 REGBASE  EQU   8                                                     DUMP0300
000007                               32 BCTREG   EQU   7                                                     DUMP0310
000005                               33 MOVEREG  EQU   5                                                     DUMP0320
000003                               34 DSKIOREG EQU   3                                                     DUMP0330
000008                               35 TAPEIORG EQU   8                                                     DUMP0340
000008                               36 PRINTIO  EQU   8                                                     DUMP0350
000009                               37 CARDIORG EQU   9                                                     DUMP0360
000002                               38 CARDREG  EQU   2                                                     DUMP0370
00000B                               39 SAVIORG  EQU   11                                                    DUMP0380


                                     41 ****                                                                 DUMP0400
                                     42 * THE FOLLOWING ROUTINE ESTABLISHES A BASE REGISTER AND RELOCATES THE DUMP0410
                                     43 * ADCONS                                                             DUMP0420
                                     44 ****                                                                 DUMP0430

000000                               46          USING *-8,1            USING FROM MSTRUTIL                  DUMP0450
000000 900F 1288          00288      47          STM   0,15,SAVEREGG     SAVE ENTRY REGISTERS                DUMP0460
00000C 05C0                          48          BALR  BASEREG,0         ESTABLISH BASE REGISTER             DUMP0470
00000E                               49          USING *,BASEREG                                             DUMP0480
                                     50          DROP  1                                                     DUMP0490
000000                               51          USING DISKDSEC,3        USING FOR DISK I/O AREA             DUMP0500
000000                               52          USING TAPEDSEC,8        USING FOR TAPE I/O AREA             DUMP0510
000000                               53          USING PASSAREA,PASSREG  USING FOR PASS AREA FROM ROOT       DUMP0520
00000E 4190 C2BA          002C8      54          LA    ADCONREG,ADCONS   LOAD ADDRESS OF BEGINNING OF ADCONS DUMP0530
000012 41CC 0000          00000      55          LA    BASEREG,0(BASEREG) ZERO HIGH-ORDER BITS               DUMP0540
000016 18CC                          56          LR    REGBASE,BASEREG   LOAD BASE ADDRESS                   DUMP0550
000018 4B80 C352          00360      57          SH    REGBASE,=H'14'    SUBTRACT 14 TO GET PROPER DISPLACE  DUMP0560
00001C 4170 0009          00009      58          LA    BCTREG,L'ADCONS/4  LOAD NUMBER OF ADCONS             DUMP0570
000020                               59 RELOCLUP EQU   *                                                     DUMP0580
000020 58B0 9000          00000      60          L     RELOCREG,0(0,ADCONREG) LOAD ADCON INTO REGISTER       DUMP0590
000024 1AB8                          61          AR    RELOCREG,REGBASE  GET ABSOLUTE ADDRESS                DUMP0600
000026 50B0 9000          00000      62          ST    RELOCREG,0(0,ADCONREG) STORE ANSWER BACK IN ADCON     DUMP0610
00002A 4199 0004          00004      63          LA    ADCONREG,4(ADCONREG)  BUMP TO LOOK AT NEXT ADCON      DUMP0620
00002E 4670 C012          00020      64          BCT   BCTREG,RELOCLUP   GO TO GET NEXT ADCON               DUMP0630


                                     66 ****                                                                 DUMP0650
                                     67 * THE FOLLOWING ROUTINE OPENS THE FILES, POSITIONS THE INDEXED       DUMP0660
                                     68 * SEQUENTIAL FILE AT THE CORRECT RECORD AND READS THE RECORD.        DUMP0670
                                     69 ****                                                                 DUMP0680
000032 5880 C2CA          002D8      70          L     8,PRINTADR        LOAD ADDRESS OF PRINT DTF          DUMP0690
000036 5860 C2BE          002CC      71          L     6,DISKADDR        LOAD ADDRESS OF DISK FILE          DUMP0700
00003A 5850 C2C2          002D0      72          L     5,TAPEADDR        LOAD ADDRESS OF TAPE FILE          DUMP0710
00003E 5870 C2C6          002D4      73          L     7,CARDADDR        LOAD ADDRESS OF CARD FILE          DUMP0720
                                     74          OPENR (5),(6),(7),(8)                                      DUMP0730
000072 5830 C2CE          002DC      91          L     DSKIOREG,DSKIOADR LOAD ADDRESS OF DISK I/O AREA      DUMP0740
                                     92          SETL  (6),BOF           START AT THE BEGINNING OF THE FILE DUMP0750
000092 45B0 C1C6          001D4     102          BAL   LINKREG1,GETDISK  GO TO READ DISK                    DUMP0760
000096 47F0 C0AC          000BA     103          B     DUMPREC           GO TO DUMP RECORDS                 DUMP0770
00009A 5810 C2CA          002D8     104 PUTMSG   L     1,PRINTADR        LOAD ADDRESS OF DTF                DUMP0780
                                    105          PUT   (1)               PRINT MSG                          DUMP0790
                                    110          ESETL (6)               END SEQUENTIAL RETRIEVAL            DUMP0800
0000BD 45B0 C208          00216    115          BAL   LINKREG1,CLOSEM   GO TO CLOSE FILES                  DUMP0810
                                    116          CANCEL ALL              CANCEL PROGRAM                     DUMP0820


                                    121 ****                                                                DUMP0840
                                    122 * THIS ROUTINE IS ENTERED WHEN THE PROPER MASTER RECORD HAS BEEN    DUMP0850
                                    123 * RETRIEVED- IT DUMPS THE RECORD ONTO TAPE. IF DELETED RECORDS ARE  DUMP0860
                                    124 * TO BE DUMPED, A DELETE CARD IS ALSO PUNCHED                       DUMP0870
                                    125 ****                                                                DUMP0880
```

```
  LOC   OBJECT CODE    ADDR1 ADDR2   STMT   SOURCE STATEMENT                                  DOS CL3-5 08/26/70

0000BA                                 127 DUMPREC  EQU   *                                                     DUMP0900
0000BA 5890 C2DA          002E8         128          L     CARDIORG,CARDIOAD   LOAD ADDRESS OF CARD I/O AREA     DUMP0910
0000BE 5820 C2C6          002D4         129          L     CARDREG,CARDADDR    LOAD ADDRESS OF CARD FILE         DUMP0920
0000C2 5870 C2C2          002D0         130          L     TAPEREG,TAPEADDR    LOAD ADDRESS OF TAPE FILE         DUMP0930


0000C6 95F2 3030          00030         132 DODUMP   CLI   MSTRTYPE,C'2'       IS IT A DELETED RECORD            DUMP0950
0000CA 4770 C0CC          000DA         133          BNE   *+16                BYPASS CHECK                      DUMP0960
0000CE 9101 4000          00000         134          TM    SWITCH,X'01'        SHOULD WE DUMP DELETES            DUMP0970
0000D2 4780 C198          001A6         135          BZ    GETREC              NO, GO TO READ NEXT RECORD        DUMP0980
0000D6 96F0 C195          001A3         136          OI    CARDBR+1,X'F0'      SET TO UNCONDITIONAL BRANCH       DUMP0990
0000DA D703 C30E C30E 0031C 0031C       137          XC    BINSTORE(4),BINSTORE ZERO FULLWORD WORK AREA          DUMP1000
0000E0 D200 C311 3000 0031F 00000       138          MVC   BINSTORE+3(1),MSTRDIV MOVE DIVISION TO HOLD AREA      DUMP1010
0000E6 45B0 C1EC          001FA         139          BAL   LINKREG1,CONVERT    GO TO CONVERT TO DECIMAL          DUMP1020
0000EA F311 8000 C278 00000 00286       140          UNPK  TAPEDIV(2),DBLWORK+6(2) UNPACK DIVISION               DUMP1030

0000F0 D202 C30F 3001 0031D 00001       142          MVC   BINSTORE+1(3),MSTRPRME MOVE PRIME TO HOLD             DUMP1050
0000F6 45B0 C1EC          001FA         143          BAL   LINKREG1,CONVERT    GO TO CONVERT TO DECIMAL          DUMP1060
0000FA F353 8002 C276 00002 00284       144          UNPK  TAPEPRME(6),DBLWORK+4(4) UNPACK PRIME NUMBER          DUMP1070

000100 D202 C30F 3004 0031D 00004       146          MVC   BINSTORE+1(3),MSTRDASH MOVE DASH TO HOLD              DUMP1090
000106 45B0 C1EC          001FA         147          BAL   LINKREG1,CONVERT    GO TO CONVERT TO DECIMAL          DUMP1100
00010A F342 8008 C277 00008 00285       148          UNPK  TAPEDASH(5),DBLWORK+5(3) UNPACK DASH NUMBER           DUMP1110

000110 D218 8000 3007 00000 0000D       150          MVC   TAPENAME(25),MSTRNAME MOVE NAME TO TAPE AREA          DUMP1130

000116 D202 C30F 3020 0031D 00020       152          MVC   BINSTORE+1(3),MSTRQOH MOVE QTY ON HAND TO HOLD        DUMP1150
00011C 45B0 C1EC          001FA         153          BAL   LINKREG1,CONVERT    GO TO CONVERT TO DECIMAL          DUMP1160
000120 F363 8026 C276 00026 00284       154          UNPK  TAPEQOH(7),DBLWORK+4(4) UNPACK QUANTITY ON HAND       DUMP1170

000126 D202 C30F 3023 0031D 00023       156          MVC   BINSTORE+1(3),MSTRQOO MOVE QTY ON ORDER TO HOLD       DUMP1190
00012C 45B0 C1EC          001FA         157          BAL   LINKREG1,CONVERT    GO TO CONVERT TO DECIMAL          DUMP1200
000130 F363 802D C276 0002D 00284       158          UNPK  TAPEQOO(7),DBLWORK+4(4)  UNPACK QUANTITY ON ORDER     DUMP1210

000136 D202 C30F 3026 0031D 00026       160          MVC   BINSTORE+1(3),MSTRQRSV  MOVE QTY RSV TO HOLD          DUMP1230
00013C 45B0 C1EC          001FA         161          BAL   LINKREG1,CONVERT        GO TO CONVERT TO DECIMAL      DUMP1240
000140 F363 8034 C276 00034 00284       162          UNPK  TAPEQRSV(7),DBLWORK+4(4) UNPACK QTY ON ORDER          DUMP1250

000146 D703 C30E C30E 0031C 0031C       164          XC    BINSTORE(4),BINSTORE ZERO HOLD AREA                   DUMP1270
00014C D200 C311 3029 0031F 00029       165          MVC   BINSTORE+3(1),MASYDIV MOVE NEXT ASSY DIV NO TO HOLD   DUMP1280
000152 45B0 C1EC          001FA         166          BAL   LINKREG1,CONVERT        GO TO CONVERT TO DECIMAL      DUMP1290
000156 F311 803B C278 0003B 00286       167          UNPK  TASYDIV(2),DBLWORK+6(2) UNPACK N.A. DIVISION NO       DUMP1300

00015C D202 C30F 302A 0031D 0002A       169          MVC   BINSTORE+1(3),MASYPRME  MOVE N.A. PRIME TO HOLD       DUMP1320
000162 45B0 C1EC          001FA         170          BAL   LINKREG1,CONVERT        GO TO CONVERT TO DECIMAL      DUMP1330
000166 F353 803D C276 0003D 00284       171          UNPK  TASYPRME(6),DBLWORK+4(4) UNPACK N.A. PRIME            DUMP1340

00016C D202 C30F 302D 0031D 0002D       173          MVC   BINSTORE+1(3),MASYDASH  MOVE N.A. DASH TO HOLD        DUMP1360
000172 45B0 C1EC          001FA         174          BAL   LINKREG1,CONVERT        GO TO CONVERT TO DECIMAL      DUMP1370
000176 F342 8043 C277 00043 00285       175          UNPK  TASYDASH(5),DBLWORK+5(3) UNPACK N.A. DASH             DUMP1380

00017C 92F8 8048          00048         177          MVI   TAPETYPE,C'8'           SET TYPE TO BE ABLE TO LOAD   DUMP1400
000180 D200 8049 3031 00049 00031       178          MVC   TAPESRCE(1),MSTRSRCE MOVE SOURCE TO TAPE              DUMP1410

000186 D202 C30F 3032 0031D 00032       180          MVC   BINSTORE+1(3),MSTRUNIT  MOVE UNIT PRICE TO HOLD       DUMP1430
00018C 45B0 C1EC          001FA         181          BAL   LINKREG1,CONVERT        GO TO CONVERT TO DECIMAL      DUMP1440
000190 F353 804A C276 0004A 00284       182          UNPK  TAPEUNIT(6),DBLWORK+4(4) UNPACK UNIT PRICE            DUMP1450


000196 18B8                             184          LR    SAVIORG,TAPEIORG    SAVE I/O AREA ADDRESS             DUMP1470
                                        185          PUT   (TAPEREG)           WRITE TAPE RECORD                 DUMP1480
0001A2 4700 C1AA          001B8         190 CARDBR   BC    0,DELREC            IF SET ON, GO TO PUNCH CARD       DUMP1490

0001A6                                  192 GETREC   EQU   *                                                     DUMP1510
0001A6 45B0 C1C6          001D4         193          BAL   LINKREG1,GETDISK    GO TO READ NEXT DISK RECORD       DUMP1520
0001AA D501 3000 4001 00000 00001       194          CLC   MSTRDIV(2),DIVNO    HAVE WE REACHED END OF PRINT      DUMP1530
0001B0 4720 C266          00274         195          BH    ENDJOB              YES, GO TO END OF JOB ROUTINE     DUMP1540
0001B4 47F0 C0B8          000C6         196          B     DODUMP              GO TO DUMP RECORD                 DUMP1550


                                        198 ****                                                                DUMP1570
                                        199 * THIS ROUTINE IS ENTERED WHEN A DELETE CARD MUST BE PUNCHED. IT IS DUMP1580
                                        200 * PUNCHED FROM THE SAME DATA THAT IS ON THE TAPE                    DUMP1590
                                        201 ****                                                                DUMP1600


0001B8                                  203 DELREC   EQU   *                                                     DUMP1620
0001B8 940F C195          001A3         204          NI    CARDBR+1,X'0F'      TURN OFF UNCONDITIONAL BRANCH     DUMP1630
0001BC D24F 9000 B000 00000 00000       205          MVC   0(80,CARDIORG),0(SAVIORG) MOVE TAPE REC TO CARD I/O AREA DUMP1640
0001C2 92F2 9048          00048         206          MVI   72(CARDIORG),C'2'   MAKE IT A DELETE CARD             DUMP1650
                                        207          PUT   (CARDREG)           PUNCH CARD                        DUMP1660
0001D0 47F0 C198          001A6         212          B     GETREC              GO TO READ NEXT RECORD            DUMP1670


                                        214 ****                                                                DUMP1690
                                        215 * THIS ROUTINE IS ENTERED TO READ THE DISK FILE                     DUMP1700
                                        216 ****                                                                DUMP1710


0001D4                                  218 GETDISK  EQU   *                                                     DUMP1730
                                        219          GET   (6),(DSKIOREG)      READ DISK                         DUMP1740
0001E0 9180 101E          0001E         225          TM    30(1),X'80'         WAS IT UNCORRECTABLE DASD ERROR   DUMP1750
```

```
0001E4 4710 C1FA          00208   226         BO    BADERROR              YES, GO TO PUT MSG AND STOP JOB   DUMP1760
0001E8 9140 101E    0001E         227         TM    30(1),X'40'           WAS IT WRONG LENGTH              DUMP1770
0001EC 4710 C1FA          00208   228         BO    BADERROR              YES, GO TO STOP JOB             DUMP1780
0001F0 9120 101E    0001E         229         TM    30(1),X'20'           WAS IT END OF FILE             DUMP1790
0001F4 4710 C266          00274   230         BO    ENDJOB                YES, GO TO END OF JOB          DUMP1800
0001F8 07FB                       231         BR    LINKREG1              NO, RETURN TO CALLER           DUMP1810


                                  233   ****                                                           DUMP1830
                                  234   * THIS ROUTINE IS ENTERED TO CONVERT THE BINARY DATA TO PACKED DUMP1840
                                  235   * DECIMAL DATA                                                 DUMP1850
                                  236   ****                                                           DUMP1860

0001FA                            238   CONVERT EQU   *                                                DUMP1880
0001FA 58A0 C30E          0031C   239         L     CVDREG,BINSTORE       LOAD VALUE TO BE CONVERTED    DUMP1890
0001FE 4EA0 C272          002B0   240         CVD   CVDREG,DBLWORK        CONVERT TO DECIMAL            DUMP1900
000202 960F C279          00287   241         OI    DBLWORK+7,X'OF'       RESET SIGN                   DUMP1910
000206 07FB                       242         BR    LINKREG1              RETURN TO CALLER             DUMP1920


                                  244   ****                                                           DUMP1940
                                  245   * THIS ROUTINE IS ENTERED WHENEVER AN UNCORRECTABLE ERROR OCCURS DUMP1950
                                  246   * ON A DISK READ                                               DUMP1960
                                  247   ****                                                           DUMP1970

000208                            249   BADERROR EQU  *                                                DUMP1990
000208 5880 C2D2          002E0   250         L     PRINTIO,PRTIOADR      LOAD ADDRESS OF PRINT I/O AREA DUMP2000
00020C D225 8000 C312 00000 00320 251         MVC   0(L'DISKMSG,PRINTIO),DISKMSG  MOVE ERROR MSG TO PRINT DUMP2010
000212 47F0 C08C          0009A   252         B     PUTMSG                GO TO WRITE MSG AND CANCEL PGM DUMP2020


                                  254   ****                                                           DUMP2040
                                  255   * THIS ROUTINE IS ENTERED TO CLOSE ALL THE FILES              DUMP2050
                                  256   ****                                                           DUMP2060

000216                            258   CLOSEM EQU   *,PRINTADR,          DUMP2080
000216 5880 C2CA          002D8   259         L     8,PRINTADR            LOAD ADDRESS OF PRINT DTF    DUMP2090
00021A 5860 C2BE          002CC   260         L     6,DISKADDR            LOAD ADDRESS OF DISK DTF     DUMP2100
00021E 5850 C2C2          002D0   261         L     5,TAPEADDR            LOAD ADDRESS OF TAPE DTF     DUMP2110
000222 5870 C2C6          002D4   262         L     7,CARDADDR            LOAD ADDRESS OF CARD DTF     DUMP2120
000226 5890 C2DA          002E8   263         L     CARDIORG,CARDIOAD     LOAD ADDRESS OF CARD I/O AREA DUMP2130
00022A 9240 9000    00000        264         MVI   0(CARDIORG),X'40'     MOVE BLANKS TO CARD I/O AREA DUMP2140
00022E D24E 9001 9000 00001 00000 265         MVC   1(79,CARDIORG),0(CARDIORG) DUMP2150
                                  266         PUT   (7)                   PUNCH BLANK CARD             DUMP2160

                                  272         ESETL (6)                   END SEQUENTIAL RETRIEVAL     DUMP2180
                                  277         CLOSER (5),(6),(7),(8)      CLOSE FILES                  DUMP2190
000272 07FB                       293         BR    LINKREG1              RETURN TO CALLER             DUMP2200


                                  295   ****                                                           DUMP2220
                                  296   * THIS ROUTINE IS ENTERED WHEN THE JOB IS TO BE TERMINATED     DUMP2230
                                  297   * IN A NORAM MANNER                                            DUMP2240
                                  298   ****                                                           DUMP2250

000274                            300   ENDJOB EQU   *                                                DUMP2270
000274 45B0 C208          00216   301         BAL   LINKREG1,CLOSEM       GO TO CLOSE FILES            DUMP2280
                                  302         EOJ                         END OF JOB                   DUMP2290
```

```
  LOC  OBJECT CODE    ADDR1 ADDR2  STMT   SOURCE STATEMENT                              DOS CL3-5 08/26/70

                                   306 ****                                             DUMP2310
                                   307 * CONSTANTS                                      DUMP2320
                                   308 ****                                             DUMP2330

000280                             310 DBLWORK  DS    D
000288                             311 SAVEREGG DS    16F                               DUMP2350
0002C8                             312 ADCONS   DS    0CL36                             DUMP2360
0002C8 00000000                    313 KEYARG   DC    V(DISKKEY)                        DUMP2370
0002CC 00000000                    314 DISKADDR DC    V(DISKFLE)                        DUMP2380
0002D0 00000000                    315 TAPEADDR DC    V(TAPEFLE)                        DUMP2390
0002D4 00000000                    316 CARDADDR DC    V(CARDFLE)                        DUMP2400
0002D8 00000000                    317 PRINTADR DC    V(PRTDTF)                         DUMP2410
0002DC 00000000                    318 DSKIOADR DC    V(DISKIOW)                        DUMP2420
0002E0 00000000                    319 PRTIOADR DC    V(PRTIO1)                         DUMP2430
0002E4 00000000                    320 TAPEIOAD DC    V(TAPEIO1)                        DUMP2440
0002E8 00000000                    321 CARDIOAD DC    V(CARDIO1)                        DUMP2450
0002EC FFFF                        322 HIGHVALU DC    X'FFFF'                           DUMP2460
0002EE C4C9E5C9E2C9D6D5            323 DIVMSG   DC    C'DIVISION REQUESTED NOT ON FILE-JOB CANCELLED'  DUMP2470
00031A 0000                                                                            DUMP2480
00031C 00000000                    324 BINSTORE DC    F'0'
000320 E4D5C3D6D9D9C5C3            325 DISKMSG  DC    C'UNCORRECTABLE DISK ERROR-JOB CANCELLED'  DUMP2490
000000                             326 PASSAREA DSECT                                   DUMP2500
000000                             327 SWITCH   DS    CL1                               DUMP2510
000001                             328 DIVNO    DS    CL2                               DUMP2520
000003                             329 PTNOS    DS    CL22                              DUMP2530
                                                                                       DUMP2540
```

```
                                        331 ****                                                             DUMP2560
                                        332 * DUMMY SECTIONS FOR DISK AND TAPE I/O AREAS                     DUMP2570
                                        333 ****                                                             DUMP2580

000000                                  335 DISKDSEC DSECT                                                   DUMP2600
000000                                  336 MSTRDIV  DS    CL1                                               DUMP2610
000001                                  337 MSTRPRME DS    CL3                                               DUMP2620
000004                                  338 MSTRDASH DS    CL3                                               DUMP2630
000007                                  339 MSTRNAME DS    CL25                                              DUMP2640
000020                                  340 MSTRQOH  DS    CL3                                               DUMP2650
000023                                  341 MSTRQOO  DS    CL3                                               DUMP2660
000026                                  342 MSTRQRSV DS    CL3                                               DUMP2670
000029                                  343 MSTRASSY DS    0CL7                                              DUMP2680
000029                                  344 MASYDIV  DS    CL1                                               DUMP2690
00002A                                  345 MASYPRME DS    CL3                                               DUMP2700
00002D                                  346 MASYDASH DS    CL3                                               DUMP2710
000030                                  347 MSTRTYPE DS    CL1                                               DUMP2720
000031                                  348 MSTRSRCE DS    CL1                                               DUMP2730
000032                                  349 MSTRUNIT DS    CL3                                               DUMP2740
000035                                  350 MSTRXTRA DS    CL2                                               DUMP2750


000000                                  352 TAPEDSEC DSECT                                                   DUMP2770
000000                                  353 TAPEDIV  DS    CL2                                               DUMP2780
000002                                  354 TAPEPRME DS    CL6                                               DUMP2790
000008                                  355 TAPEDASH DS    CL5                                               DUMP2800
00000D                                  356 TAPENAME DS    CL25                                              DUMP2810
000026                                  357 TAPEQOH  DS    CL7                                               DUMP2820
00002D                                  358 TAPEQOO  DS    CL7                                               DUMP2830
000034                                  359 TAPEQRSV DS    CL7                                               DUMP2840
00003B                                  360 TAPEASSY DS    0CL13                                             DUMP2850
00003B                                  361 TASYDIV  DS    CL2                                               DUMP2860
00003D                                  362 TASYPRME DS    CL6                                               DUMP2870
000043                                  363 TASYDASH DS    CL5                                               DUMP2880
000048                                  364 TAPETYPE DS    CL1                                               DUMP2890
000049                                  365 TAPESRCE DS    CL1                                               DUMP2900
00004A                                  366 TAPEUNIT DS    CL6                                               DUMP2910
                                        367          END                                                    DUMP2920
000348 5B5BC2D6D7C5D5D9                 368               =C'$$BOPENR'
000350 5B5BC2E2C5E3D340                 369               =C'$$BSCTL '
000358 5B5BC2C3D3D6E2C5                 370               =C'$$BCLOSE'
000360 000E                            371               =H'14'
```

8.69

```
000000                                2 PRINTINV  START 0                                              PRTI0020
000000 D7D9C9D5E3C9D5E5               3           DC    CL8'PRINTINV'                                  PRTI0030
                                      4           PRINT NOGEN


                                      6 ****                                                           PRTI0050
                                      7 * THIS PROGRAM PHASE IS USED TO PRINT THE MASTER FILE. IT GENERATES ONE PRTI0060
                                      8 * OF TWO REPORTS - A COMPLETE LISTING OF THE MASTER FILE SHOWING ALL     PRTI0070
                                      9 *RECORDS ON THE MASTER FILE OR A LISTING OF SHORTS (PARTS WHICH HAVE     PRTI0080
                                     10 * MORE PARTS  ON RESERVATION THAN ON ORDER AND ON HAND) AND SPARES       PRTI0090
                                     11 * (PARTS HAVING MORE PARTS ON HAND AND ON ORDER THAN RESERVED). THIS     PRTI0100
                                     12 * PROGRAM IS ENTERED FROM THE ROOT PHASE WHICH HAS INTERPRETED THE       PRTI0110
                                     13 * CONTROL CARD AND SET THE APPROPRIATE SWITCHES, ETC.                    PRTI0120
                                     14 * IF A SPECIFIC DIVISION IS ENTERED ON THE CONTROL CARD, ONLY THAT       PRTI0140
                                     15 * DIVISION IS PRINTED.  IF A PART NUMBER RANGE (PRIME AND DASH) IS       PRTI0150
                                     16 * ENTERED ON THE CONTROL CARD, ONLY PART NUMBERS FALLING IN  THE         PRTI0160
                                     17 * RANGE ARE PRINTED.  IF A DELETED PARTS LIST IS REQUESTED, ONLY THOSE   PRTI0170
                                     18 * PART NUMBERS WHICH ARE DELETED ARE PRINTED. OTHERWISE, ONLY THE        PRTI0180
                                     19 * ACTIVE PART NUMBERS ARE PRINTED.  IF DESIRED A TOTAL OF ALL RECORDS    PRTI0190
                                     20 * PROCESSED FROM AN OVERFLOW AREA WILL BE GIVEN. THIS OPTION WILL ALLOW  PRTI0200
                                     21 * THE PROGRAMMER TO DECIDE WHEN THE FILE SHOULD BE ORGANIZED TO          PRTI0210
                                     22 * ELIMINATE RECORDS IN THE OVERFLOW AREAS.                               PRTI0220
                                     23 *                                                                        PRTI0230
                                     24 * REGISTER USAGE IS AS FOLLOWS                                           PRTI0240
                                     25 *                                                                        PRTI0250
                                     26 *                                                                        PRTI0260

00000C                               28 BASEREG  EQU   12                                              PRTI0280
000004                               29 PASSREG  EQU   4                                               PRTI0290
00000B                               30 CVDREG   EQU   11                                              PRTI0300
00000B                               31 ADCONREG EQU   11                                              PRTI0310
00000A                               32 REGBASE  EQU   10                                              PRTI0320
000009                               33 BCTREG   EQU   9                                               PRTI0330
000008                               34 RELOCREG EQU   8                                               PRTI0340
00000A                               35 DISKREG  EQU   10                                              PRTI0350
000008                               36 PRINTREG EQU   8                                               PRTI0360
000007                               37 DISKIORG EQU   7                                               PRTI0370
000006                               38 PRTIORG  EQU   6                                               PRTI0380
000005                               39 LINKREG1 EQU   5                                               PRTI0390
000003                               40 MOVEREG  EQU   3                                               PRTI0400
00000E                               41 LINKRG14 EQU   14                                              PRTI0410
000000                               42 MULTREG1 EQU   0                                               PRTI0420
000001                               43 MULTREG2 EQU   1                                               PRTI0430
                                     44 ****                                                           PRTI0440


000000                               46           USING *-8,1           USING FROM MSTRUTIL            PRTI0460
000000 900F 15EC             005EC   47           STM   0,15,SAVEREGS    SAVE ALL REGISTERS            PRTI0470
00000C 05C0                          48           BALR  BASEREG,0        ESTABLISH BASE REGISTER       PRTI0480
00000E                               49           USING *,BASEREG                                      PRTI0490
                                     50           DROP  1                                              PRTI0500

000000                               52           USING PASSAREA,PASSREG  USING FOR PASS AREA FROM ROOT PRTI0520
000000                               53           USING DISKDSEC,DISKIORG USING FOR DISK I/O AREA      PRTI0530
00000E 41CC 0000           00000     54           LA    BASEREG,0(BASEREG)  ZERO HIGH-ORDER BITS       PRTI0540
000012 41B0 C61E           0062C     55           LA    ADCONREG,ADCONS  LOAD ADDRESS OF BEGINNING OF ADCONS PRTI0550
000016 18AC                          56           LR    REGBASE,BASEREG  LOAD BASE ADDRESS             PRTI0560
000018 4BA0 C5CA           005D8     57           SH    REGBASE,=H'14'        SUBTRACT TO GET START ADDRESS PRTI0570
00001C 4190 0005           00005     58           LA    BCTREG,L'ADCONS/4  LOAD NUMBER OF ADCONS       PRTI0580
000020                               59 RELOCLUP EQU   *                                               PRTI0590
000020 5880 B000           00000     60           L     RELOCREG,0(0,ADCONREG) LOAD ADCON INTO REGISTER PRTI0600
000024 1A8A                          61           AR    RELOCREG,REGBASE  GET ABSOLUTE ADDRESS          PRTI0610
000026 5080 B000           00000     62           ST    RELOCREG,0(0,ADCONREG)  STORE BACK IN ADCON     PRTI0620
00002A 41B0 B004           00004     63           LA    ADCONREG,4(0,ADCONREG) BUMP TO LOOK AT NEXT ADCON PRTI0630
00002E 4690 C012           00020     64           BCT   BCTREG,RELOCLUP  GO TO GET NEXT ADCON          PRTI0640


                                     66 ****                                                           PRTI0660
                                     67 * THE FOLLOWING ROUTINE OPENS THE FILES, LOADS ADDRESSES, AND            PRTI0670
                                     68 * POSITIONS THE INDEXED SEQUENTIAL FILE AT THE CORRECT RECORD            PRTI0680
                                     69 ****                                                           PRTI0690
000032 5870 C626           00634     70           L     DISKIORG,DISKIOAD  LOAD DISK I/O ADDRESS        PRTI0700
000036 5860 C62A           00638     71           L     PRTIORG,PRTIOAD  LOAD PRINTER ADDRESS          PRTI0710


00003A 58A0 C61E           0062C     73           L     DISKREG,DISKADDR  LOAD ADDRESS OF DISK DTF      PRTI0730
00003E 5880 C622           00630     74           L     PRINTREG,PRTADDR  LOAD ADDRESS OF PRINT DTF    PRTI0740

                                     76           OPENR (DISKREG),(PRINTREG) OPEN FILES                PRTI0760


000062 5830 C62E           0063C     90           L     MOVEREG,KEYARG   LOAD ADDRESS OF KEYARG FIELD  PRTI0780
000066 D501 4001 C632 00001 00640    91           CLC   DIVNO(2),HIGHVALU IS THERE A DIVISION DUMP REQUESTED PRTI0790
00006C 4770 C084           00092     92           BNE   DIVPRINT         YES, GO TO DETERMINE WHERE TO START PRTI0800

                                     94           SETL  (DISKREG),BOF    START AT BEGINNING OF FILE    PRTI0820

00008A 4550 C3B8           003C6     105          BAL   LINKREG1,GETDISK  GO TO READ THE DISK           PRTI0840
00008E 47F0 C0DC           000EA     106          B     PRINTREC         GO TO PRINT THE RECORD        PRTI0850


                                     108 ****                                                          PRTI0870
                                     109 * THIS ROUTINE IS ENTERED WHEN A DIVISION PRINT IS REQUESTED.          PRTI0880
```

8.70

```
 LOC  OBJECT CODE   ADDR1 ADDR2  STMT   SOURCE STATEMENT                      DOS CL3-5 08/26/70

                                  110 ****                                              PRTI0890

000092                            112 DIVPRINT EQU  *                                   PRTI0910
000092 F271 C5D2 4001 005E0 00001 113          PACK DBLWORK(8),DIVNO(2) PACK DIVISION   PRTI0920
000098 4550 C3A4            003B2 114          BAL  LINKREG1,CONVERTB   CONVERT DIVISION NUMBER TO BINARY  PRTI0930
00009C 42B0 3000            00000 115          STC  CVDREG,0(0,MOVEREG) STORE DIVISION IN KEY  PRTI0940

                                  117          SETL (DISKREG),GKEY     FIND BLOCK CONTAINING CORRECT DIV  PRTI0960

0000BA                            128 GETDIV   EQU  *                                   PRTI0980
0000BA 4550 C3B8            003C6 129          BAL  LINKREG1,GETDISK    GO TO READ DISK RECORD  PRTI0990

0000BE D500 7000 3000 00000 00000 131          CLC  MSTRDIV(1),0(MOVEREG) IS DIVISION EQUAL  PRTI1010
0000C4 4780 C0DC            000EA 132          BE   PRINTREC           YES, GO TO PRINT   PRTI1020
0000C8 4740 C0AC            000BA 133          BL   GETDIV             IF LOW, HAVE NOT REACHED DIVISION  PRTI1030

0000CC D22B 6001 C638 00001 00646 135          MVC  1(L'BADMSG,PRTIORG),BADMSG    MOVE MESSAGE TO PRINTER   PRTI1050
0000D2 92F1 6000      00000       136          MVI  0(PRTIORG),C'1'    MOVE CONTROL CHARACTER TO I/O AREA  PRTI1060
0000D6                            137 PUTERROR EQU  *                                   PRTI1070
                                  138          PUT  (PRINTREG)         PRINT ERROR MESSAGE   PRTI1080
0000E0 4550 C58E            0059C 143          BAL  LINKREG1,CLOSEM    GO TO CLOSE FILES   PRTI1090
                                  144          CANCEL ALL                                PRTI1100


                                  149 ****                                              PRTI1120
                                  150 * THIS ROUTINE IS ENTERED WHEN THE FIRST RECORD HAS BEEN RETRIEVED. IT  PRTI1130
                                  151 * DETERMINES IF THE RECORD SHOULD BE PRINTED, PUTS THE RECORD IN THE    PRTI1140
                                  152 * PROPER REPORT FORMAT AND PRINTS THE RECORD.     PRTI1150
                                  153 ****                                              PRTI1160


0000EA                            155 PRINTREC EQU  *                                   PRTI1180
0000EA D501 4001 C632 00001 00640 156          CLC  DIVNO(2),HIGHVALU   HAS DIVISION DUMP BEEN REQUESTED   PRTI1190
0000F0 4770 C0EC            000FA 157          BNE  CHKPRME            YES, GO TO CHECK PRIME NO   PRTI1200
0000F4 D200 3000 4001 00000 00001 158          MVC  0(1,MOVEREG),DIVNO MOVE X'FF' TO DIVISION NO   PRTI1210
0000FA D502 4003 C635 00003 00643 159 CHKPRME  CLC  PTNOS(3),LOWVALU   IS LOW PART NO = ZEROS    PRTI1220
000100 4780 C106            00114 160          BE   CHKDASH            NYES, CHECK LOW DASH NUMBER   PRTI1230

000104 F275 C5D2 4003 005E0 00003 162          PACK DBLWORK(8),PTNOS(6) PACK PRIME      PRTI1250
00010A 4550 C3A4            003B2 163          BAL  LINKREG1,CONVERTB   GO TO CONVERT KEY TO BINARY   PRTI1260
00010E D202 3001 C5DB 00001 005E9 164          MVC  1(3,MOVEREG),BINSTORE+1 MOVE VALUE TO KEY COMPARE AREA   PRTI1270

000114                            166 CHKDASH  EQU  *                                   PRTI1290
000114 D502 4009 C635 00009 00643 167          CLC  PTNOS+6(3),LOWVALU  IS LOW DASH = ZEROS    PRTI1300
00011A 4780 C120            0012E 168          BE   CHKHIGH            YES. CHECK HIGH PRIME NUMBER   PRTI1310

00011E F274 C5D2 4009 005E0 00009 170          PACK DBLWORK(8),PTNOS+6(5) PACK DASH NUMBER    PRTI1330
000124 4550 C3A4            003B2 171          BAL  LINKREG1,CONVERTB   GO TO CONVERT TO BINARY    PRTI1340
000128 D202 3004 C5DB 00004 005E9 172          MVC  4(3,MOVEREG),BINSTORE+1 MOVE DASH NO TO COMPARE AREA   PRTI1350

00012E                            174 CHKHIGH  EQU  *                                   PRTI1370
00012E D502 400E C632 0000E 00640 175          CLC  PTNOS2(3),HIGHVALU  IS PRIME = X'FF'     PRTI1380
000134 4780 C13A            00148 176          BE   CHKDASHH           YES, CHECK HIGH DASH NUMBER   PRTI1390

000138 F275 C5D2 400E 005E0 0000E 178          PACK DBLWORK(8),PTNOS2(6) PACK PRIME       PRTI1410
00013E 4550 C3A4            003B2 179          BAL  LINKREG1,CONVERTB   GO TO CONVERT TO BINARY    PRTI1420
000142 D202 C664 C5DB 00672 005E9 180          MVC  HIGHKEY(3),BINSTORE+1  MOVE PRIME TO COMPARE AREA    PRTI1430

000148                            182 CHKDASHH EQU  *                                   PRTI1450
000148 D502 4014 C632 00014 00640 183          CLC  PTNOS2+6(3),HIGHVALU IS DASH = X'FF'     PRTI1460
00014E 4780 C154            00162 184          BE   PROCREC            YES, GO TO PROCESS    PRTI1470

000152 F274 C5D2 4014 005E0 00014 186          PACK DBLWORK(8),PTNOS2+6(5) PACK DASH NUMBER    PRTI1490
000158 4550 C3A4            003B2 187          BAL  LINKREG1,CONVERTB                          PRTI1500
00015C D202 C667 C5DB 00675 005E9 188          MVC  HIGHKEY+3(3),BINSTORE+1  MOVE DASH TO COMPARE AREA   PRTI1510

000162                            190 PROCREC  EQU  *                                   PRTI1530
000162 45E0 C402            00410 191          BAL  LINKRG14,HEADROU    GO T3 WRITE HEADER RECORD   PRTI1540

000166                            193 WRITEREC EQU  *                                   PRTI1560
000166 D500 7000 3000 00000 00000 194          CLC  MSTRDIV(1),0(MOVEREG) IS DIV IN DESIRED RANGE   PRTI1570
00016C 4720 C4BC            004CA 195          BH   ENDOFRPT            NO, GO TO END OF REPORT   PRTI1580
000170 D505 7001 3001 00001 00001 196          CLC  MSTRPRME(6),1(MOVEREG) IS PRIME LOW   PRTI1590
000176 4740 C2FA            00308 197          BL   GETNEXT            YES, GO TO READ NEXT RECORD   PRTI1600
00017A D505 7001 C664 00001 00672 198          CLC  MSTRPRME(6),HIGHKEY IS PART NO HIGH   PRTI1610
000180 4720 C2FA            00308 199          BH   GETNEXT            YES, GO TO READ NEXT REC   PRTI1620

                                  201 *                                                 PRTI1640
                                  202 * AT THIS POINT, THE DIVISION AND PART (UMBERS ARE OK TO PRINT   PRTI1650
                                  203 *                                                 PRTI1660

000184 9104 4000      00000       205          TM   SWITCH,X'04'       IS DELETED PARTS LIST DESIRED   PRTI1680
000188 4780 C18A            00198 206          BZ   NODELETE           NO, CHECK REMAINDER   PRTI1690
00018C 95F2 7030      00030       207          CLI  MSTRTYPE,C'2'      YES, IS PART A DELETED PART   PRTI1700
000190 4770 C2FA            00308 208          BNE  GETNEXT            NO, GO TO READ NEXT RECORD   PRTI1710
000194 47F0 C192            001A0 209          B    CONTINUE           GO TO PROCESS NEXT RECORD   PRTI1720

000198                            211 NODELETE EQU  *                                   PRTI1740
000198 95F2 7030      00030       212          CLI  MSTRTYPE,C'2'      IS IT A DELETED REOCRD    PRTI1750
00019C 4780 C2FA            00308 213          BE   GETNEXT            YES, BYPASS AND READ NEXT RECORD   PRTI1760

0001A0                            215 CONTINUE EQU  *                                   PRTI1780
```

8.71

```
LOC   OBJECT CODE   ADDR1 ADDR2  STMT   SOURCE STATEMENT

0001A0 9240 C922       00930     216          MVI   PRTFIRST+1,X'40'      BLANK PRINT LINE-LEAVE CARRIAGE   PRTI1790
0001A4 D282 C923 C922 00931 00930 217 BLANKIT MVC   PRTFIRST+2(131),PRTFIRST+1  CONTROL ALONE              PRTI1800

0001AA 1BBB                     219          SR    CVDREG,CVDREG          ZERO REGISTER                     PRTI1820
0001AC 4380 7000       00000    220          IC    CVDREG,MSTRDIV         INSERT DIVISION NUMBER            PRTI1830
0001B0 4550 C3B2       003C0    221          BAL   LINKREG1,CONVERTD+4    GO TO CONVERT TO DECIMAL          PRTI1840
0001B4 F311 C922 C5D8 00930 005E6 222        UNPK  DIVR(2),DBLWORK+6(2)   UNPACK DIVISION NUMBER TO REPORT  PRTI1850
0001BA 96F0 C923       00931    223          OI    DIVR+1,X'F0'           RESET SIGN                        PRTI1860

0001BE D703 C5DA C5DA 005E8 005E8 225 ZEROWORK XC  BINSTORE,BINSTORE      ZERO WORK AREA                    PRTI1880
0001C4 D202 C5DB 7001 005E9 00001 226        MVC   BINSTORE+1(3),MSTRPRME MOVE PRIME TO WRK AREA            PRTI1890
0001CA 4550 C3AE       003BC    227          BAL   LINKREG1,CONVERTD      GO TO CONVERT TO DECIMAL          PRTI1900
0001CE F353 C925 C5D6 00933 005E4 228        UNPK  PRIMER(6),DBLWORK+4(4) UNPACK PRIME NUMBER               PRTI1910
0001D4 96F0 C92A       00938    229          OI    PRIMER+5,X'F0'         RESET SIGN                        PRTI1920

0001D8 D202 C5DB 7004 005E9 00004 231        MVC   BINSTORE+1(3),MSTRDASH MOVE DASH TO WORK AREA            PRTI1940
0001DE 4550 C3AE       003BC    232          BAL   LINKREG1,CONVERTD      GO TO CONVERT TO DECIMAL          PRTI1950
0001E2 F342 C92C C5D7 0093A 005E5 233        UNPK  DASHR(5),DBLWORK+5(3)  UNPACK DASH NUMBER                PRTI1960
0001E8 96F0 C930       0093E    234          OI    DASHR+4,X'F0'          RESET SIGN                        PRTI1970
0001EC D218 C934 7007 00942 00007 236        MVC   DESCR(25),MSTRNAME     MOVE DESCRIPTION TO PRINT         PRTI1990

0001F2 1BBB                     238          SR    CVDREG,CVDREG          ZERO THE REGISTER                 PRTI2010
0001F4 4380 7029       00029    239          IC    CVDREG,MASYDIV         INSERT DIVISION-NEXT ASSEMBLY     PRTI2020
0001F8 4550 C3AE       003BC    240          BAL   LINKREG1,CONVERTD      GO TO CONVERT TO DECIMAL          PRTI2030
0001FC F311 C950 C5D8 0095E 005E6 241        UNPK  NADIVR(2),DBLWORK+6(2) UNPACK DIVISION NUMBER-N/A        PRTI2040
000202 96F0 C951       0095F    242          OI    NADIVR+1,X'F0'         RESET SIGN                        PRTI2050

000206 D202 C5DB 702A 005E9 0002A 244        MVC   BINSTORE+1(3),MASYPRME MOVE PRIME TO WRK AREA            PRTI2070
00020C 4550 C3AE       003BC    245          BAL   LINKREG1,CONVERTD      CONVERT TO DECIMAL                PRTI2080
000210 F353 C953 C5D6 00961 005E4 246        UNPK  NAPRIMER(6),DBLWORK+4(4) UNPACK PRIME-NEXT ASSY          PRTI2090
000216 96F0 C958       00966    247          OI    NAPRIMER+5,X'F0'       RESET SIGN                        PRTI2100

00021A D202 C5DB 702D 005E9 0002D 249        MVC   BINSTORE+1(3),MASYDASH MOVE DASH TO WORK AREA            PRTI2120
000220 4550 C3AE       003BC    250          BAL   LINKREG1,CONVERTD      CONVERT TO DECIMAL                PRTI2130
000224 F342 C95A C5D7 00968 005E5 251        UNPK  NADASHR(5),DBLWORK+5(3) UNPACK DASH - NEXT ASSEMBLY      PRTI2140
00022A 96F0 C95E       0096C    252          OI    NADASHR+4,X'F0'        RESET SIGN                        PRTI2150

00022E 95F1 7031       00031    254          CLI   MSTRSRCE,C'1'          IS IT A MANUFACTURED PART         PRTI2170
000232 4780 C232       00240    255          BE    MANU                   YES, GO TO MOVE MANU TO REPORT    PRTI2180
000236 D203 C962 C5C2 00970 005D0 256        MVC   SOURCER,=C'VEND'       NO, MOVE VENDOR TO REPORT         PRTI2190
00023C 47F0 C238       00246    257          B     *+10                   BYPASS NEXT MOVE                  PRTI2200
000240 D203 C962 C5C6 00970 005D4 258 MANU   MVC   SOURCER,=C'MANU'       MOVE MANUFACTURED TO RPT          PRTI2210

                                260 ****                                                                    PRTI2230
                                261 * THE COMMON PORTION OF THE REPORT LINE HAS NOW BEEN COMPLETED. IT IS   PRTI2240
                                262 * NECESSARY TO SEE WHICH REPORT IS DESIRED AND COMPLETE THE PRINT LINE. PRTI2250
                                263 ****                                                                    PRTI2260

000246 95F2 7030       00030    265          CLI   MSTRTYPE,C'2'          IS IT A DELETED RECORD            PRTI2280
00024A 4770 C244       00252    266          BNE   *+8                    NO, BYPASS NEXT MOVE              PRTI2290
00024E 925C C9A1       009AF    267          MVI   DELRM,C'*'             YES, MOVE ASTERICK TO INDICATE DEL PRTI2300
000252 9140 4000       00000    268          TM    SWITCH,X'40'           IS IT A SPARES/SHORTS REPORT      PRTI2310
000256 4710 C302       00310    269          BO    SPSHORT                YES, GO TO PROCESS                PRTI2320
00025A D202 C5DB 7020 005E9 00020 270 MVCQOH MVC   BINSTORE+1(3),MSTRQOH       MOVE QTY ON HAND TO WORK ARE PRTI2330
000260 5810 C5DA       005E8    271          L     MULTREG2,BINSTORE      LOAD QTY ON HAND TO REGISTER      PRTI2340
000264 4550 C3AE       003BC    272          BAL   LINKREG1,CONVERTD      GO TO CONVERT QTY ON HAND TO DEC  PRTI2350
000268 D209 C968 C9EE 00976 009FC 273        MVC   QOHRM-1(10),QTYEDIT    MOVE EDIT PATTERN TO PRINT LINE   PRTI2360
00026E DE09 C968 C5D6 00976 005E4 274        ED    QOHRM-1(10),DBLWORK+4  EDIT QTY ON HAND                  PRTI2370
000274 D202 C5DB 7032 005E9 00032 275 MVCUNIT MVC  BINSTORE+1(3),MSTRUNIT MOVE UNIT PRICE TO WORK AREA      PRTI2380
00027A 5C00 C5DA       005E8    276          M     MULTREG1,BINSTORE      MULTIPLY TO GET ANSWER-AMOUNT     PRTI2390
000280 1BB1                     277          LR    CVDREG,MULTREG2        LOAD ANSWER TO CVD REGISTER       PRTI2400
000280 4550 C382       003C0    278          BAL   LINKREG1,CONVERTD+4    CONVERT TO DECIMAL                PRTI2410
000284 D20B C992 C9E2 009A0 009F0 279        MVC   AMOUNTRM-2(12),AMTEDIT MOVE EDIT PATTERN TO PRINT        PRTI2420
00028A DE0B C992 C5D5 009A0 005E3 280        ED    AMOUNTRM-2(12),DBLWORK+3 EDIT AMT                        PRTI2430
000290 FA54 CA06 C5D5 00A14 005E3 281        AP    AMTCNTR1,DBLWORK+3(5)  ADD TOTAL TO COUNTER              PRTI2440

000296 4400 C1B0       001BE    283          EX    0,ZEROWORK             ZERO WORK AREA                    PRTI2460
00029A 4400 C266       00274    284          EX    0,MVCUNIT              MOVE UNIT TO WRK AREA             PRTI2470
00029E 4550 C3AE       003BC    285          BAL   LINKREG1,CONVERTD      GO TO CONVERT TO DECIMAL          PRTI2480
0002A2 D209 C988 C9F8 00996 00A06 286        MVC   UNITRM-2(10),UNITEDIT  MOVE EDIT WORD TO PRINT           PRTI2490
0002A8 DE09 C988 C5D6 00996 005E4 287        ED    UNITRM-2(10),DBLWORK+4 EDIT UNIT PRICE                   PRTI2500

0002AE D202 C5DB 7026 005E9 00026 289 MVCQRSV MVC  BINSTORE+1(3),MSTRQRSV MOVE QUANTITY RESERVED TO WORK    PRTI2520
0002B4 4550 C3AE       003BC    290          BAL   LINKREG1,CONVERTD      GO TO CONVERT TO DECIMAL          PRTI2530
0002B8 D209 C97E C9EE 0098C 009FC 291        MVC   QRSVRM-1(10),QTYEDIT   MOVE EDIT PATTERN                 PRTI2540
0002BE DE09 C97E C5D6 0098C 005E4 292        ED    QRSVRM-1(10),DBLWORK+4 EDIT QUANTITY RESERVED            PRTI2550

0002C4 D202 C5DB 7023 005E9 00023 294 MVCQOO MVC   BINSTORE+1(3),MSTRQOO       MOVE QTY ON ORDER TO WORK    PRTI2570
0002CA 4550 C3AE       003BC    295          BAL   LINKREG1,CONVERTD      GO TO CONVERT TO DECIMAL          PRTI2580
0002CE D209 C973 C9EE 00981 009FC 296        MVC   QOORM-1(10),QTYEDIT    MOVE EDIT PATTERN TO PRINT        PRTI2590
0002D4 DE09 C973 C5D6 00981 005E4 297        ED    QOORM-1(10),DBLWORK+4  EDIT QTY ON ORDER                 PRTI2600

                                299 *                                                                       PRTI2620
                                300 * AT THIS POINT THE REPORT LINE HAS BEEN COMPLETED AND IS READY         PRTI2630
                                301 * TO BE PRINTED.                                                        PRTI2640
                                302 *                                                                       PRTI2650

0002DA D284 6000 C921 00000 0092F 304 PRINTLNE MVC 0(133,PRTIORG),PRTFIRST MOVE PRINT LINE TO I/O AREA      PRTI2670

                                306          PUT   (PRINTREG)            PRINT LINE                         PRTI2690
```

```
0002EA FA30 CA02 C5CE 00A10 005DC   312           AP    RECCNT,=P'1'  ADD 1 TO RECORD COUNT         PRTI2710
0002F0 9240 C921      0092F          313           MVI   SKIP,X'40'    MOVE BLANK FOR 1 LINE SKIP    PRTI2720
0002F4 FA10 CA12 C5CE 00A20 005DC   314           AP    LNECOUNT,=P'1'   ADD ONE TO LINE COUNT      PRTI2730
0002FA F911 CA12 C5CC 00A20 005DA   315           CP    LNECOUNT,=P'56'  HAVE WE PRINTED 56 LINES   PRTI2740
000300 4770 C2FA      00308          316           BNE   *+8           NO, BYPASS HEADER ROUTINE     PRTI2750
000304 45E0 C402      00410          317           BAL   LINKRG14,HEADROU  YES, GO TO PRINT HEADER   PRTI2760

000308 4550 C3B8      003C6          319  GETNEXT  BAL   LINKREG1,GETDISK  GO TO READ DISK RECORD    PRTI2780
00030C 47F0 C158      00166          320           B     WRITEREC      GO TO WRITE NEXT RECORD       PRTI2790


                                    322  ****                                                        PRTI2810
                                    323  * THIS ROUTINE IS ENTERED TO PRINT THE SPARES/SHORTS REPORT. IT MOVES  PRTI2820
                                    324  * ALL THE DATA FROM THE MASTER TO THE REPORT AND PERFORMS THE          PRTI2830
                                    325  * NECESSARY CALCULATIONS FOR THE REPORT.                               PRTI2840
                                    326  ****                                                        PRTI2850

000310                              328  SPSHORT  EQU   *                                            PRTI2870
000310 4400 C1B0      001BE         329           EX    0,ZEROWORK    ZERO WRK AREA                  PRTI2880
000314 4400 C24C      0025A         330           EX    0,MVCQOH      MOVE QTY ON HAND TO WORKAREA   PRTI2890
000318 58B0 C5DA      005E8         331           L     CVDREG,HINSTORE  LOAD QTY ON HAND TO REG     PRTI2900
00031C 4400 C286      002C4         332           EX    0,MVCQOO      MOVE QTY ON ORDER TO WORK      PRTI2910
000320 5AB0 C5DA      005E8         333           A     CVDREG,BINSTORE  ADD TO QTY ON HAND         PRTI2920
000324 4400 C2A0      002AE         334           EX    0,MVCQRSV     MOVE QTY RESERVED TO WORK AREA PRTI2930
000328 5BB0 C5DA      005E8         335           S     CVDREG,BINSTORE  SUBTRACT QTY RESERED FROM OTHER 2  PRTI2940
00032C 4780 C2FA      00308         336           BC    8,GETNEXT     IF RESULT = 0, NO SPARES OR SHORTS  PRTI2950
000330 4740 C35C      0036A         337           BC    4,SHORTS      IF LESS THAN ZERO, QTY RSV IS  PRTI2960
                                    338  *                           GREATER - THUS HAVE SHORTS     PRTI2970


                                    340  *                                                           PRTI2990
                                    341  * ENTERED WHEN HAVE SPARES - THAT IS, QTY ON HAND + QTY ON ORDER IS    PRTI3000
                                    342  * GREATER THAN QTY RESERVED                                           PRTI3010
                                    343  *                                                           PRTI3020

000334 4550 C3B2      003C0         345           BAL   LINKREG1,CONVERTD+4 GO TO CONVERT SPARES TO DECIMAL  PRTI3040
000338 D209 C973 C9EE 00981 009FC   346           MVC   SPARERS-1(10),QTYEDIT  MOVE EDIT PATTERN TO PRINT  PRTI3050
00033E DE09 C973 C5D6 00981 005E4   347           ED    SPARERS-1(10),DBLWORK+4  EDIT SPARES QTY    PRTI3060
000344 181B                         348           LR    MULTREG2,CVDREG   LOAD SPARES  QTY TO MULTIPLY REG  PRTI3070
000346 4400 C266      00274         349           EX    0,MVCUNIT     MOVE UNIT PRICE TO WORK AREA   PRTI3080
00034A 5C00 C5DA      005E8         350           M     MULTREG1,BINSTORE  MULTIPLY TO GET AMOUNT    PRTI3090
00034E 18B1                         351           LR    CVDREG,MULTREG2   LOAD ANSWER TO CVD REGISTER  PRTI3100
000350 4550 C382      003C0         352           BAL   LINKREG1,CONVERTD  GO TO CONVERT TO DECIMAL   PRTI3110
000354 D20B C995 C9E2 009A3 009F0   353           MVC   SPAMTRS-2(12),AMTEDIT  MOVE EDIT PATTERN TO REPORT LINE  PRTI3120
00035A DE0B C995 C5D5 009A3 005E3   354           ED    SPAMTRS-2(12),DBLWORK+3  EDIT SPARES  AMOUNT  PRTI3130
000360 FA54 CA0C C5D5 00A1A 005E3   355           AP    AMTCNTR2,DBLWORK+3(5)  ADD SPARES AMT TO COUNTER  PRTI3140
000366 47F0 C390      0039E         356           B     UNITSPSH      GO TO MOVE UNIT PRICE TO REPORT  PRTI3150


                                    358  *                                                           PRTI3170
                                    359  * THIS ROUTINE IS ENTERED WHEN THERE ARE SHORTAGES OF A PART-THAT IS,  PRTI3190
                                    360  * THE QTY RESERVED IS GREATER THAN QTY ON HAND + QTY ON ORDER          PRTI3200
                                    361  *                                                           PRTI3210

00036A                              363  SHORTS   EQU   *                                            PRTI3230
00036A 10BB                         364           LPR   CVDREG,CVDREG     MAKE SHORTS A POSITIVE VALUE  PRTI3240
00036C 4550 C382      003C0         365           BAL   LINKREG1,CONVERTD+4  GO TO CONVERT SHORTS TO DEC  PRTI3250
000370 D209 C968 C9EE 00976 009FC   366           MVC   SHORTRS-1(10),QTYEDIT  MOVE EDIT PATTERN TO RPT LINE  PRTI3260
000376 DE09 C968 C5D6 00976 005E4   367           ED    SHORTRS-1(10),DBLWORK+4  EDIT SHORT QUANTITY  PRTI3270
00037C 181B                         368           LR    MULTREG2,CVDREG  LOAD SHORTS TO MULTIPLY REG  PRTI3280
00037E 4400 C266      00274         369           EX    0,MVCUNIT     MOVE UNIT PRICE TO WORK AREA   PRTI3290
000382 5C00 C5DA      005E8         370           M     MULTREG1,BINSTORE  MULTIPLY TO GET AMOUNT    PRTI3300
000386 18B1                         371           LR    CVDREG,MULTREG2   LOAD ANSWER TO CVD REG      PRTI3310
000388 4550 C382      003C0         372           BAL   LINKREG1,CONVERTD+4  GO TO CONVERT AMT TO DECIMAL  PRTI3320
00038C D20B C987 C9E2 00995 009F0   373           MVC   SHTAMTRS-2(12),AMTEDIT  MOVE EDIT PATTERN TO RPT LINE  PRTI3330
000392 DE0B C987 C5D5 00995 005E3   374           ED    SHTAMTRS-2(12),DBLWORK+3  EDIT SHORTS  AMT   PRTI3340
000398 FA54 CA06 C5D5 00A14 005E3   375           AP    AMTCNTR1,DBLWORK+3(5)  ADD SHORTS AMT TO COUNTER  PRTI3350

00039E                              377  UNITSPSH EQU   *                                            PRTI3370
00039E 4550 C3AE      003BC         378           BAL   LINKREG1,CONVERTD  GO TO CONVERT UNIT PRICE TO DECIMAL  PRTI3380
0003A2 D209 C97D C9F8 0098B 00A06   379           MVC   UNITRS-2(10),UNITEDIT  MOVE EDIT PATTERN TO PRINT AREA  PRTI3390
0003A8 DE09 C97D C5D6 0098B 005E4   380           ED    UNITRS-2(10),DBLWORK+4  EDIT UNIT PRICE       PRTI3400
0003AE 47F0 C2CC      002DA         381           B     PRINTLNE      GO TO PRINT THE LINE           PRTI3410


                                    383  ****                                                        PRTI3430
                                    384  * THIS ROUTINE IS ENTERED TO CONVERT PACKED DECIMAL DATA TO BINARY     PRTI3440
                                    385  ****                                                        PRTI3450

0003B2                              387  CONVERTB EQU   *                                            PRTI3470
0003B2 4FB0 C5D2      005E0         388           CVB   CVDREG,DBLWORK    CONVERT VALUE TO BINARY    PRTI3480
0003B6 50B0 C5DA      005E8         389           ST    CVDREG,BINSTORE   STORE VALUE IN FULLWORK    PRTI3490
0003BA 07F5                         390           BR    LINKREG1          RETURN TO CALLER           PRTI3500


                                    392  ****                                                        PRTI3520
                                    393  * THIS ROUTINE IS ENTERED TO CONVERT BINARY DATA TO PACKED DECIMAL     PRTI3530
                                    394  ****                                                        PRTI3540
```

LOC   OBJECT CODE   ADDR1 ADDR2   STMT   SOURCE STATEMENT   DOS CL3-5 08/26/70

```
0003BC                             396 CONVERTD  EQU   *                                                        PRTI3560
0003BC 58B0 C50A         005E8     397          L     CVDREG,BINSTORE     LOAD BINARY VALUE TO REGISTER          PRTI3570
0003C0 4EB0 C5D2         005E0     398          CVD   CVDREG,DBLWORK      CONVERT VALUE TO DECIMAL               PRTI3580
0003C4 07F5                        399          BR    LINKREG1            GO TO CALLER                           PRTI3590


                                   401 ****                                                                      PRTI3610
                                   402 * THIS ROUTINE IS ENTERED TO READ THE DISK FILE                           PRTI3620
                                   403 ****                                                                      PRTI3630


0003C6                             405 GETDISK   EQU   *                                                         PRTI3650
                                   406          GET   (DISKREG),(DISKIORG)  READ RECORD                          PRTI3660

0003D2 9180 A01E   0001E           413          TM    30(DISKREG),X'80'   WAS THERE AN UNCORRECTABLE ERROR       PRTI3680
0003D6 4710 C3EA         003F9     414          BO    BADDISK             YES, GO TO PROCESS                     PRTI3690
0003DA 9140 A01E   0001E           415          TM    30(DISKREG),X'40'   WAS IT WRONG LENGTH ERROR              PRTI3700
0003DE 4710 C3F8         00406     416          BO    WRNGLENG            YES, GO TO PROCESS                     PRTI3710
0003E2 9120 A01E   0001E           417          TM    30(DISKREG),X'20'   WAS IT END OF FILE                     PRTI3720
0003E6 4710 C4BC         004CA     418          BO    ENDOFRPT            YES, GO TO COMPLETE REPORT             PRTI3730
0003EA 9101 A01E   0001E           419          TM    30(DISKREG),X'01'   WAS RECORD FROM OVERFLOW AREA          PRTI3740
0003EE 0785                        420          BCR   8,LINKREG1          NO, RETURN TO CALLER                   PRTI3750
0003F0 FA10 CA45 C5CE 00A53 005DC  421          AP    OVCOUNT,=P'1'       YES, ADD 1 TO COUNT                    PRTI3760
0003F6 07F5                        422          BR    LINKREG1            RETURN TO CALLER                       PRTI3770


                                   424 ****                                                                      PRTI3790
                                   425 * THIS ROUTINE IS ENTERED WHEN AN UNCORRECTABLE DISK ERROR OCCURS.  IT    PRTI3800
                                   426 * MOVES AN ERROR MSG TO THE PRINT I/O AREA, THEN GOES TO CANCEL THE       PRTI3810
                                   427 * PROGRAM                                                                 PRTI3820
                                   428 ****                                                                      PRTI3830


0003F8                             430 BADDISK   EQU   *                                                         PRTI3850
0003F8 D225 6001 C8DA 00001 008E8  431          MVC   1(L'DISKERR,PRTIORG),DISKERR MOVE ERROR MSG               PRTI3860
0003FE 92F1 6000   00000           432 GOPUT    MVI   0(PRTIORG),C'1'     MOVE HEAD OF FORMS TO I/O AREA         PRTI3870
000402 47F0 C0C8         000D6     433          B     PUTERROR            GO TO PRINT ERROR AND CANCEL PGM       PRTI3880


                                   435 ****                                                                      PRTI3900
                                   436 * ENTERED FOR WRONG LENGTH ERROR. MOVES ERROR MSG TO PRINT AND CANCELS    PRTI3910
                                   437 * THE PROGRAM                                                             PRTI3920
                                   438 ****                                                                      PRTI3930


000406                             440 WRNGLENG  EQU   *                                                         PRTI3950
000406 D220 6001 C900 00001 0090E  441          MVC   1(L'LENGMSG,PRTIORG),LENGMSG  MOVE ERROR MESSAGE          PRTI3960
00040C 47F0 C3F0         003FE     442          B     GOPUT               GO TO PRINT MSG                        PRTI3970


                                   444 ****                                                                      PRTI3990
                                   445 * THIS ROUTINE IS ENTERED TO PRINT THE HEADINGS FOR THE REPORTS           PRTI4000
                                   446 ****                                                                      PRTI4010


000410                             448 HEADROU   EQU   *                                                         PRTI4030
000410 50E0 C5DA         005E8     449          ST    LINKRG14,BINSTORE   SAVE LINK REGISTER                     PRTI4040
000414 4700 C41A         00428     450          BC    0,AFTERFRS          BYPASS NEXT STUFF IF SECOND TIME       PRTI4050
000418 96F0 C407   00415           451          OI    *-3,X'F0'           SET BRANCH                             PRTI4060
                                   452          COMRG                     GET COMM, REGION DATE                  PRTI4070
000422 D207 C670 1000 0067E 00000  456          MVC   MOHEAD(8),0(1)      MOVE DATE TO REPORT                   PRTI4080
000428                             457 AFTERFRS  EQU   *                                                         PRTI4090
000428 FA10 C8D4 C5CE 008E2 005DC  458          AP    PGCNT,=P'1'         ADD 1 TO PAGE COUNT                    PRTI4100
00042E D203 C6E2 C8D6 006F0 008E4  459          MVC   PGNOHEAD-1(4),PGEDIT  MOVE EDIT PATTERN TO PAGE NO        PRTI4110
000434 DE03 C6E2 C8D4 006F0 008E2  460          ED    PGNOHEAD-1(4),PGCNT  EDIT PAGE NUMBER                     PRTI4120
00043A FB11 CA12 CA12 00A20 00A20  461          SP    LNECOUNT,LNECOUNT   ZERO LINE COUNT                        PRTI4130
000440 9260 C921       0092F       462          MVI   SKIP,C'-'           MOVE TRIPLE SPACE CONTROL CHAR TO      PRTI4140
                                   463 *                                  PRINT LINE                             PRTI4150
000444 9140 4000   00000           464          TM    SWITCH,X'40'        IS IT A SPARES/SHORTS REPORT           PRTI4160
000448 4710 C486         00494     465          BO    SPSHEAD             YES, GO TO PREPARE SP/SH HEADING       PRTI4170

00044C D22C C690 C6EF 0069E 006FD  467          MVC   MAINHEAD(L'INVHEAD),INVHEAD  MOVE TITLE TO HEADER         PRTI4190
000452 D284 6000 C66A 00000 00678  468 MVCHEAD  MVC   0(133,PRTIORG),HEADER1  MOVE HEADER TO I/O AREA           PRTI4200
                                   469          PUT   (PRINTREG)          PRINT FIRST LINE                       PRTI4210

000462 D245 6000 C74F 00000 0075D  475 EXLN2    MVC   0(L'FRSTLN2,PRTIORG),FRSTLN2  MOVE FIRST PART OF SEC LNE   PRTI4230
000468 D23E 6046 C795 00046 007A3  476          MVC   L'FRSTLN2(L'SECLN2M,PRTIORG),SECLN2M  MOVE SECOND PART     PRTI4240
                                   477          PUT   (PRINTREG)          PRINT SECOND LINE                      PRTI4250

000478 D246 6000 C813 00000 00821  483 EXLN3    MVC   0(L'FRSTLN3,PRTIORG),FRSTLN3  MOVE FIRST PART OF LINE 3    PRTI4270
00047E D23C 6047 C85A 00047 00868  484          MVC   L'FRSTLN3(L'SECLN3M,PRTIORG),SECLN3M  MOVE SECOND PART     PRTI4280
                                   485 HEADRETN PUT   (PRINTREG)          PRINT THIRD LINE                       PRTI4290

00048E 58E0 C5DA         005E8     491          L     LINKRG14,BINSTORE   RELOAD RETURN REGISTER                 PRTI4310
000492 07FE                        492          BR    LINKRG14            RETURN TO CALLER                       PRTI4320


                                   494 *                                                                         PRTI4340
                                   495 * ENTERED FOR SPARES/SHORTS HEADINGS                                      PRTI4350
                                   496 *                                                                         PRTI4360

000494                             498 SPSHEAD   EQU   *                                                         PRTI4380
```

LOC	OBJECT CODE	ADDR1	ADDR2	STMT	SOURCE STATEMENT	

```
000494 D232 C690 C71C 0069E 0072A   499        MVC   MAINHEAD(L'SPARHEAD),SPARHEAD MOVE TITLE TO HEADER   PRTI4390
00049A 4400 C444           00452     500        EX    0,MVCHEAD                MOVE HEADING TO PRINT LINE   PRTI4400
                                     501        PUT   (PRINTREG)               PRINT THE LINE              PRTI4410

0004A8 4400 C454           00462     507        EX    0,EXLN2                  MOVE FIRST PART OF SECOND LINE   PRTI4430
0004AC D23E 6046 C7D4 00046 007E2   508        MVC   L'FRSTLN2(L'SECLN2S,PRTIORG),SECLN2S MOVE SECOND PART   PRTI4440
                                     509        PUT   (PRINTREG)               PRINT THE LINE              PRTI4450

0004BC 4400 C46A           00478     515        EX    0,EXLN3                  MOVE FIRST PART OF LINE 3   PRTI4470
0004C0 D23C 6047 C897 00047 008A5   516        MVC   L'FRSTLN3(L'SECLN3S,PRTIORG),SECLN3S MOVE SECOND PART   PRTI4480
0004C6 47F0 C476           004B4     517        B     HEADRETN                 GO TO PRINT AND RETURN     PRTI4490


                                     519 ****                                                              PRTI4510
                                     520 * THIS ROUTINE IS ENTERED WHEN END OF FILE IS REACHED ON THE DISK INPUT PRTI4520
                                     521 * OR WHEN THE DESIRED DIVISION BEING PRINTED IS DONE              PRTI4530
                                     522 ****                                                              PRTI4540


0004CA                               524 ENDOFRPT EQU  *                                                   PRTI4560
0004CA 9240 C922           00930     525        MVI   PRTFIRST+1,X'40'         MOVE SPACES TO PRINT AREA   PRTI4570
0004CE 4400 C196           001A4     526        EX    0,BLANKIT                                            PRTI4580
0004D2 9260 C921           0092F     527        MVI   SKIP,C'-'                MOVE TRIPLE SPACE TO CTLCHR   PRTI4590
0004D6 9140 4000           00000     528        TM    SWITCH,X'40'             IS IT A SPARES/SHORTS REPORT   PRTI4600
0004DA 4710 C562           00570     529        BO    SPSHEND                  YES, GO TO PRINT CORRECT TOTALS   PRTI4610

0004DE D215 C979 C9A6 00987 009B4   531        MVC   CONSILN1(L'TOTICONA),TOTICONA MOVE CONSTANT TO END LINE PRTI4630
0004E4 D20E C98F CA14 0099D 00A22   532        MVC   AMTILN1-1(15),TOTAEDIT   MOVE EDIT WORD TO PRINT LINE   PRTI4640
0004EA DE0E C98F CA06 00990 00A14   533        ED    AMTILN1-1(15),AMTCNTR1   EDIT AMOUNT                 PRTI4650
0004F0 925B C990           0099E     534        MVI   AMTILN1,C'$'             MOVE DOLLAR SIGN TO LINE   PRTI4660
0004F4 4400 C2CC           002DA     535 EXPRTLN EX   0,PRINTLNE               MOVE LINE TO PRINT I/O AREA   PRTI4670
0004F8 D201 C99E C9E0 009AC 009EE   536        MVC   TOASTIL1,ASTS            MOVE ASTERICKS TO REPORT   PRTI4680
                                     537        PUT   (PRINTREG)               PRINT LINE                 PRTI4690


000508 9240 C966           00974     543        MVI   PRTSECM,X'40'            MOVE BLANKS TO PRINT LINE   PRTI4710
00050C D23E C967 C966 00975 00974   544        MVC   PRTSECM+1(63),PRTSECM                                PRTI4720
000512 D216 C979 C9BC 00987 009CA   545        MVC   CONSILN2(L'TOTICONR),TOTICONR MOVE CONSTANT         PRTI4730
000518 D209 C994 C9EE 009A2 009FC   546        MVC   RECSILN2-1(10),QTYEDIT   MOVE EDIT PATTERN TO PRINT   PRTI4740
00051E DE09 C994 CA02 009A2 00A10   547        ED    RECSILN2-1(10),RECCNT    EDIT RECORD COUNT          PRTI4750
000524 D201 C99E C9E0 009AC 009EE   548        MVC   TOASTIL2,ASTS            MOVE ASTERICKS TO REPORT   PRTI4760
00052A 9240 C921           0092F     549        MVI   SKIP,X'40'               MOVE SINGLE LINE SKIP TO CTLCHR   PRTI4770
00052E 4400 C2CC           002DA     550 ENDPUT  EX   0,PRINTLNE               MOVE LINE TO PRINT I/O AREA   PRTI4780
                                     551        PUT   (PRINTREG)               PRINT LINE                 PRTI4790


00053C 9108 4000           00000     557        TM    SWITCH,X'08'             DESIRE OVERFLOW COUNT?     PRTI4810
000540 4780 C55C           0056A     558        BZ    NOOV                     NO, GO TO END JOB          PRTI4820

000544 DE03 CA30 CA45 00A3E 00A53   560        ED    TOTALOVF(4),OVCOUNT EDIT OVERFLOW COUNT             PRTI4840
00054A 9240 C922           00930     561        MVI   PRTFIRST+1,X'40'         CLEAR PRINTER AREA         PRTI4850
00054E 4400 C196           001A4     562        EX    0,BLANKIT                                           PRTI4860
000552 92F1 C921           0092F     563        MVI   SKIP,C'1'                MOVE HEAD OF FORMS TO CTLCHR   PRTI4870
000556 D214 C922 CA30 00930 00A3E   564        MVC   PRTFIRST+1(21),TOTALOVF  MOVE TOTAL TO PRINT        PRTI4880
00055C 4400 C2CC           002DA     565        EX    0,PRINTLNE               MOVE TO PRINTER I/O AREA   PRTI4890
                                     566        PUT   (PRINTREG)               PRINT TOTAL OVERFLOW RECORDS   PRTI4900


00056A                               572 NOOV    EQU  *                                                   PRTI4920
00056A 4550 C58E           0059C     573        BAL   LINKREG1,CLOSEM          GO TO CLOSE FILES          PRTI4930
                                     574        EOJ                            END OF JOB                 PRTI4940


                                     578 *                                                                PRTI4960
                                     579 * THIS ROUTINE IS ENTERED TO PRINT THE TOTAL LINE FOR THE SPARES/SHORTS PRTI4970
                                     580 * REPORT                                                          PRTI4980
                                     581 *                                                                PRTI4990


000570                               583 SPSHEND EQU  *                                                   PRTI5010
000570 D20C C994 CA23 009A2 00A31   584        MVC   AMT2SLN1(13),TOTEDITS    MOVE EDIT PATTERN          PRTI5020
000576 DE0C C994 CA0D 009A2 00A1B   585        ED    AMT2SLN1(13),AMTCNTR2+1  EDIT TOTAL AMOUNT OF SPARES   PRTI5030
00057C 925B C994           009A2     586        MVI   AMT2SLN1,C'$'            MOVE $ TO AMOUNTS          PRTI5040
000580 D20C C986 CA23 00994 00A31   587        MVC   AMT1SLN1(13),TOTEDITS    MOVE EDIT PATTERN          PRTI5050
000586 DE0C C986 CA07 00994 00A15   588        ED    AMT1SLN1(13),AMTCNTR1+1  EDIT TOTAL AMOUNT OF SHORTS   PRTI5060
00058C 925B C986           00994     589        MVI   AMT1SLN1,C'$'            MOVE $ TO AMOUNTS          PRTI5070
000590 D20C C976 C9D3 00984 009E1   590        MVC   CONSSLN1(L'TOTSCONA),TOTSCONA MOVE CONSTANT TO PRINT   PRTI5080
000596 47F0 C520           0052E     591        B     ENDPUT                   GO TO PRINT LINE AND END JOB   PRTI5090


                                     593 ****                                                             PRTI5110
                                     594 * THIS ROUTINE IS ENTERED TO CLOSE THE FILES                     PRTI5120
                                     595 ****                                                             PRTI5130


                                     597 CLOSEM  CLOSER (DISKREG),(PRINTREG)  CLOSE FILES                PRTI5150
0005B6 07F5                          609        BR    LINKREG1                 RETURN TO CALLER           PRTI5160


0005B8                               611        LTORG                                                     PRTI5180
0005B8 5B5BC2D6D7C5D5D9              612              =C'$$BOPENR'
0005C0 5B5BC2E2C5E3D340              613              =C'$$BSETL '
0005C8 5B5BC2C3D3D6E2C5              614              =C'$$BCLOSE'

0005D0 E5C5D5C4                      615              =C'VEND'
0005D4 D4C1D5E4                      616              =C'MANU'
0005D8 000E                          617              =H'14'
0005DA 056C                          618              =P'56'
0005DC 1C                            619              =P'1'
```

```
LOC   OBJECT CODE    ADDR1 ADDR2 STMT   SOURCE STATEMENT                                          DOS CL3-5 08/26/70

                                 621 ****                                                          PRTI5200
                                 622 * CONSTANTS, I/O AREAS, ETC.                                   PRTI5210
                                 623 ****                                                          PRTI5220

0005E0                           625 DBLWORK  DS    D                                              PRTI5240
0005E8                           626 BINSTORE DS    F                                              PRTI5250
0005EC                           627 SAVEREGS DS    16F                                            PRTI5260
00062C                           628 ADCONS   DS    0CL20                                          PRTI5270
00062C 00000000                  629 DISKADDR DC    V(DISKFLE)                                     PRTI5280
000630 00000000                  630 PRTADDR  DC    V(PRTDTF)                                      PRTI5290
000634 00000000                  631 DISKLOAD DC    V(DISKIOW)                                     PRTI5300
000638 00000000                  632 PRTLOAD  DC    V(PRTIO1)                                      PRTI5310
00063C 00000000                  633 KEYARG   DC    V(DISKKEY)                                     PRTI5320
000640 FFFFFF                    634 HIGHVALU DC    X'FFFFFF'                                      PRTI5330
000643 000000                    635 LOWVALU  DC    X'000000'                                      PRTI5340
000646 D9C5D8E4C5E2E3C5          636 RADMSG   DC    C'REQUESTED DIVISION NOT ON FILE-JOB CANCELLED' PRTI5350
000672 FFFFFFFFFFFF              637 HIGHKEY  DC    X'FFFFFFFFFFFF'                                PRTI5360
000678                           638 HEADER1  DS    0CL133                                         PRTI5370
000678 F1                        639          DC    C'1'                          CARRIAGE CONTROL CHARACTER PRTI5380
000679 4040404040               640          DC    CL5' '                                         PRTI5390
00067E 4040                      641 MOHEAD   DC    CL2' '                                         PRTI5400
000680 60                        642          DC    C'-'                                           PRTI5410
000681 4040                      643 DAHEAD   DC    CL2' '                                         PRTI5420
000683 60                        644          DC    C'-'                                           PRTI5430
000684 4040                      645 YRHEAD   DC    CL2' '                                         PRTI5440
000686 40404040404040           646          DC    CL24' '                                        PRTI5450
00069E 40404040404040           647 MAINHEAD DC    CL51' '                                        PRTI5460
0006D1 404040404040             648          DC    CL27' '                                        PRTI5470
0006EC D7C1C7C540               649          DC    CL5'PAGE'                                       PRTI5480
0006F1 404040                   650 PGNOHEAD DC    CL3' '                                         PRTI5490
0006F4 4040404040404040         651          DC    CL9' '                                         PRTI5500
0006FD D440C140E240E340         652 INVHEAD  DC    C'M A S T E R   I N V E N T O R Y   R E P O R T' PRTI5510
00072A D440C140E240E340         653 SPARHEAD DC    C'M A S T E R   S P A R E S / S H O R T S   R E P O R T' PRTI5520
00075D F04040D7C1D9E340         654 FRSTLN2  DC    C'0  PART NUMBER          DESCRIPTION          NEXT ACPRTI5530
                                                    SSEMBLY    SOURCE'                             PRTI5540
0007A3 40404040D8E3E840         655 SECLN2M  DC    C'  QTY ON      QTY ON      QTY     UNIT     AMOUNT CPRTI5550
                                                    DEL    '                                       PRTI5560
0007E2 40404040C3D6E3C1         656 SECLN2S  DC    C'  TOTAL       TOTAL      UNIT    SHORTAGES    SPARCPRTI5570
                                                    ES  DEL '                                      PRTI5580
000821 40C4C9E540D7D9C9         657 FRSTLN3  DC    C'  DIV PRIME DASH                          DIV PRICPRTI5590
                                                    ME DASH         '                              PRTI5600
000868 40404040C8C1D5C4         658 SECLN3M  DC    C'    HAND       ORDER     RESERVED    PRICE   ON HAND CPRTI5610
                                                                                                  PRTI5620
0008A5 40E2C8D6D9E3C1C7         659 SECLN3S  DC    C'  SHORTAGES    SPARES      PRICE     AMOUNT    AMOUNCPRTI5630
                                                    T   '                                          PRTI5640
0008E2 000C                     660 PGCNT    DC    PL2'0'                                          PRTI5650
0008E4 40202020                 661 PGEDIT   DC    X'40202020'                                    PRTI5660
0008E8 E405C3D6D9D9C5C3         662 DISKERR  DC    C'UNCORRECTABLE DISK ERROR-JOB CANCELLED'      PRTI5670
00090E E6D9D6D5C760D3C5         663 LENGMSG  DC    C'WRONG-LENGTH RECORD-JOB CANCELLED'           PRTI5680
00092F                          664 PRTFIRST DS    0CL69                                          PRTI5690
00092F                          665 SKIP     DS    CL1                                            PRTI5700
000930                          666 DIVR     DS    CL2                                            PRTI5710
000932 40                       667          DC    C' '                                           PRTI5720
000933                          668 PRIMER   DS    CL6                                            PRTI5730
000939 40                       669          DC    C' '                                           PRTI5740
00093A                          670 DASHR    DS    CL5                                            PRTI5750
00093F 404040                   671          DC    CL3' '                                         PRTI5760
000942                          672 DESCR    DS    CL25                                           PRTI5770
00095B 404040                   673          DC    CL3' '                                         PRTI5780
00095E                          674 NADIVR   DS    CL2                                            PRTI5790
000960 40                       675          DC    C' '                                           PRTI5800
000961                          676 NAPRIMER DS    CL6                                            PRTI5810
000967 40                       677          DC    C' '                                           PRTI5820
000968                          678 NADASHR  DS    CL5                                            PRTI5830
00096D 404040                   679          DC    CL3' '                                         PRTI5840
000970                          680 SOURCER  DS    CL4                                            PRTI5850
000974                          681 PRTSECM  DS    0CL64                                          PRTI5860
000974                          682          DS    CL3                                            PRTI5870
000977                          683 QOHRM    DS    CL9                                            PRTI5880
000980                          684          DS    CL3                                            PRTI5890
000982                          685 QOORM    DS    CL9                                            PRTI5900
00098B                          686          DS    CL2                                            PRTI5910
00098D                          687 QRSVRM   DS    CL9                                            PRTI5920
000996                          688          DS    CL2                                            PRTI5930
000998                          689 UNITRM   DS    CL8                                            PRTI5940
0009A0                          690          DS    CL2                                            PRTI5950
0009A2                          691 AMOUNTRM DS    CL10                                           PRTI5960
0009AC                          692          DS    CL3                                            PRTI5970
0009AF                          693 DELRM    DS    CL1                                            PRTI5980
0009B0                          694          DS    CL4                                            PRTI5990
000974                          695          ORG   PRTSECM                                        PRTI6000
000974                          696          DS    CL3                                            PRTI6010
000977                          697 SHORTRS  DS    CL9                                            PRTI6020
000980                          698          DS    CL2                                            PRTI6030
000982                          699 SPARERS  DS    CL9                                            PRTI6040
00098B                          700          DS    CL2                                            PRTI6050
00098D                          701 UNITRS   DS    CL8                                            PRTI6060
000995                          702          DS    CL2                                            PRTI6070
000997                          703 SHTAMTRS DS    CL10                                           PRTI6080
0009A1                          704          DS    CL4                                            PRTI6090
0009A5                          705 SPAMTRS  DS    CL10                                           PRTI6100
0009AF                          706          DS    CL2                                            PRTI6110
0009B1                          707 DELRS    DS    CL1                                            PRTI6120
```

```
    LOC   OBJECT CODE     ADDR1 ADDR2 STMT   SOURCE STATEMENT                            DOS CL3-5 08/26/70

    0009B2                            708          DS      CL2                                PRTI6130
    000974                            709          ORG     PRTSECM                            PRTI6140
    000974                            710          DS      CL19                               PRTI6150
    000987                            711  CONSILN1 DS      CL22                               PRTI6160
    00099D                            712          DS      CL1                                PRTI6170
    00099E                            713  AMTILN1  DS      CL14                               PRTI6180
    0009AC                            714  TOASTIL1 DS      CL2                                PRTI6190
    0009AE                            715          DS      CL6                                PRTI6200
    000974                            716          ORG     PRTSECM                            PRTI6210
    000974                            717          DS      CL19                               PRTI6220
    000987                            718  CONSILN2 DS      CL23                               PRTI6230
    00099E                            719          DS      CL5                                PRTI6240
    0009A3                            720  RECSILN2 DS      CL9                                PRTI6250
    0009AC                            721  TOASTIL2 DS      CL2                                PRTI6260
    0009AE                            722          DS      CL6                                PRTI6270
    000974                            723          ORG     PRTSECM                            PRTI6280
    000974                            724          DS      CL16                               PRTI6290
    000984                            725  CONSSLN1 DS      CL13                               PRTI6300
    000991                            726          DS      CL3                                PRTI6310
    000994                            727  AMTISLN1 DS      CL13                               PRTI6320
    0009A1                            728          DS      CL1                                PRTI6330
    0009A2                            729  AMT2SLN1 DS      CL13                               PRTI6340
    0009AF                            730          DS      CL5                                PRTI6350
    0009B4 E3D6E3C1D340C9D5           731  TOTICONA DC      C'TOTAL INVENTORY AMOUNT'          PRTI6360
    0009CA E3D6E3C1D340C9D5           732  TOTICONR DC      C'TOTAL INVENTORY RECORDS'         PRTI6370
    0009E1 E3D6E3C1D340C1D4           733  TOTSCONA DC      C'TOTAL AMOUNTS'                   PRTI6380
    0009EE 5C5C                       734  ASTS     DC      C'**'                              PRTI6390
    0009F0 4020202020 6B2020         735  AMTEDIT  DC      X'40202020206B2020214B2020'        PRTI6400
    0009FC 40206B2020206B20          736  QTYEDIT  DC      X'40206B2020206B202020'            PRTI6410
    000A06 40202 06B2020214B         737  UNITEDIT DC      X'40202 06B2020214B2020'           PRTI6420
    000A10 0000000C                  738  RECCNT   DC      X'0000000C'                        PRTI6430
    000A14 00000000000C              739  AMTCNTR1 DC      X'00000000000C'                    PRTI6440
    000A1A 00000000000C              740  AMTCNTR2 DC      X'00000000000C'                    PRTI6450
    000A20 000C                      741  LNECOUNT DC      PL2'0'                             PRTI6460
    000A22 4020202 06B202020         742  TOTAEDIT DC      X'40202020206B2020206B2020214B2020' PRTI6470
    000A31 40206B2020206B20          743  TOTEDITS DC      X'40206B2020206B202020214B2020'    PRTI6480
    000A3E 40202021                  744  TOTALOVF DC      X'40202021'                        PRTI6490
    000A42 40D6E5C5D9C6D3D6          745           DC      C' OVERFLOW RECORDS'               PRTI6500
    000A53 000C                      746  OVCOUNT  DC      X'000C'                            PRTI6510
```

8.77

```
  LOC  OBJECT CODE    ADDR1 ADDR2 STMT   SOURCE STATEMENT                        DOS CL3-5 08/26/70

                                  748 ****                                       PRTI6530
                                  749 * PASS AREA DUMMY SECTION                  PRTI6540
                                  750 ****                                       PRTI6550

 000000                          752 PASSAREA DSECT                              PRTI6570
 000000                          753 SWITCH   DS    CL1                          PRTI6580
 000001                          754 DIVNO    DS    CL2                          PRTI6590
 000003                          755 PTNOS    DS    CL11                         PRTI6600
 00000E                          756 PTNOS2   DS    CL11                         PRTI6610


                                  758 ****                                       PRTI6630
                                  759 * MASTER RECORD DUMMY SECTION              PRTI6640
                                  760 ****                                       PRTI6650

 000000                          762 DISKDSEC DSECT                              PRTI6670
 000000                          763 MSTRDIV  DS    CL1                          PRTI6680
 000001                          764 MSTRPRME DS    CL3                          PRTI6690
 000004                          765 MSTRDASH DS    CL3                          PRTI6700
 000007                          766 MSTRNAME DS    CL25                         PRTI6710
 000020                          767 MSTRQOH  DS    CL3                          PRTI6720
 000023                          768 MSTRQOO  DS    CL3                          PRTI6730
 000026                          769 MSTRQRSV DS    CL3                          PRTI6740
 000029                          770 MSTRASSU DS    0CL7                         PRTI6750
 000029                          771 MASYDIV  DS    CL1                          PRTI6760
 00002A                          772 MASYPRME DS    CL3                          PRTI6770
 00002D                          773 MASYDASH DS    CL3                          PRTI6780
 000030                          774 MSTRTYPE DS    CL1                          PRTI6790
 000031                          775 MSTRSRCE DS    CL1                          PRTI6800
 000032                          776 MSTRUNIT DS    CL3                          PRTI6810
 000035                          777 MSTRXTRA DS    CL2                          PRTI6820
                                  778          END                              PRTI6830
```

```
LOC   OBJECT CODE     ADDR1 ADDR2 STMT   SOURCE STATEMENT                              DOS CL3-5 08/26/70

000000                            1 DISK1     START 0                                             DISK0010
                                  2           ENTRY DISKFLE,DISKKEY,DISKIO1,DISKIOW             DISK0020
                                  3 DISKFLE   DTFIS DSKXTNT=3,IOROUT=RETRVE,KEYLEN=7,NRECDS=65,  CDISK0030
                                              RECFORM=FIXBLK,RECSIZE=55,CYLOFL=2,DEVICE=2311,    CDISK0040
                                              HINDEX=2311,IOAREAS=DISKIO1,KEYARG=DISKKEY,KEYLOC=1, CDISK0050
                                              MODNAME=IJHZRSZZ,MSTIND=YES,TYPEFLE=SEQNTL,WORKS=YES DISK0060
                                  4+** 360N-IO-457 DTFIS   CHANGE LEVEL 3-4                       3-4
                                  5+** 360N-IO-457 DTFIS1  CHANGE LEVEL 3-4                       3-4
000000                            6+        DC      0D'0' 3-4
000000 000008                     7+DISKFLE DC      X'000008' 3-4
000003 0000000000                 8+        DC      XL5'0' 3-4
000008 00000008                   9+        DC      A(DISKFLEH) CCW ADDR
00000C 00000000                  10+        DC      XL4'0'
000010 00000000                  11+        DC      V(IJHZRSZZ) ADDR LOGIC MODULE
000014 26                        12+        DC      AL1(38) TYPE FILE INDICATOR
000015 08                        13+        DC      B'00001000' OPTION CO3-4
000016 C4C9E2D2C6D3C5            14+        DC      CL7'DISKFLE' FILE NAME
00001D 00                        15+        DC      AL1(0) PRIME DATA DEVICE TYPE INDICATOR
00001E 00                        16+DISKFLEC DC     XL1'0' STATUS INDICATORS
00001F 00                        17+        DC      AL1(0) INDEX DEVICE TYPE INDICATOR
000020 46                        18+        DC      AL1((DISKFLEE-DISKFLE)/4) REL POS XTNT-CELL TABLE
000021 000000                    19+        DC      XL3'000000' HHR FIRST DATA RECORD IN CYL.
000024 0000                      20+        DC      H'0' HH LAST PRIME DATA TRK IN CYL
000026 00                        21+        DC      XL1'00' HI RECORD # ON MAST.NDX/CYL.NDX
000027 00                        22+        DC      XL1'00' HI RECORD # ON PRIME DATA TRACK
000028 00                        23+        DC      XL1'00' HI RECORD # ON OVFLO TRACK
000029 00                        24+        DC      XL1'00' HI RECORD # ON SHARED TRACK
00002A 00                        25+        DC      XL1'00' HI RECORD # ON TI TRACK
00002B 40                        26+        DC      B'01000000' RETRIEVAL SWITCH
00002C 0000000000000000          27+        DC      XL7'00' PRIME DATA START
000033 0000000000000000          28+        DC      XL7'00' MBBCCH CYL INDEX START
00003A 00C00000000000000         29+        DC      XL7'00' MBBCCH MST INDEX START
000041 00                        30+        DC      X'00' INDEX LEVEL NUMBER
000042 0000000000000000          31+        DC      XL8'00' MBBCCHHR LAST PR.DATA RCD ADDR.
00004A 0000                      32+        DC      H'0' RECORD LENGTH
00004C 0000                      33+        DC      H'0' KEY LENGTH
00004E 0000                      34+        DC      H'0' BLOCKSIZE
000050 0000                      35+        DC      H'0' RL+10
000052 0000                      36+        DC      H'0' BLOCKING FACTOR
000054 0000                      37+        DC      H'0' INDEX ENTRY LENGTH KL+10
000056 0000                      38+        DC      H'0' PR.DATA REC. KEY+DATA
000058 0000                      39+        DC      H'0' OVFLO KEY AND DATA KL+NRCDS$RL
00005A 0000                      40+        DC      H'0' KL*NRCDS*RL+8
00005C 0000                      41+        DC      H'0' KL+RL+18
00005E 0000                      42+        DC      H'0' KEY LOCATION
000060 0005                      43+        DC      H'5' 5
000062 000A                      44+        DC      H'10'
000064 007C                      45+        DC      Y(DISKFLE2-DISKFLE) BASE FOR TABLE2
000066 00D8                      46+        DC      Y(DISKFLEB-DISKFLE) BASE FOR TABLE3
000068 0000000000000000          47+DISKFLES DC     5H'0' COMMON SEEK/SEARCH BUC.
000072 0000000000000000          48+DISKFLEW DC     5H'0' CWORKAREA USED IN MACRO
00007C                           49+DISKFLEM EQU    *
                                 50+********************* SECOND PART OF TABLE *******************
00007C                           51+DISKFLE2 EQU    *
00007C 0000006B                  52+        DC      A(DISKFLES+3) ADDR OF COMMON SEEK/SEARCH BUC.
000080 00000072                  53+        DC      A(DISKFLEW) ADDR OF RANDOM SEQ BUCKET
000084 0000012F                  54+        DC      A(DISKIO1) ADDR OF IOAREAS
000088 00000000                  55+        DC      F'0' ADDR IOAREA2                    3-4
00008C 00000128                  56+        DC      A(DISKKEY) ADDR OF KEYARG
000090 00000000                  57+        DC      F'0' ADDR OF WORKR
000094 00000000                  58+        DC      F'0' SEQ CURRENT IOAREA
000098 4700 0000        00000    59+        NOP     0
00009C 00                        60+        DC      X'00' NO VERIFY
00009D 00                        61+        DC      X'00' BLOCKED
00009E 000000000000              62+        DC      3H'0' CCHHR          LIMITS FOR SEQ.
0000A4 0000                      63+        DC      H'0' BLOCKED.
0000A6 C7                        64+        DC      X'C7'
0000A7 0000000000                65+        DC      X'0000000000'
0000AC 0000000000000000          66+DISKFLEH DC     4H'0' MBBCCHHR      CURRENT DISKADDR FOR SEQ
0000B4 0000000000000000          67+        DC      4H'0' MBBCCHHR      CURRENT OVFL. ENTRY FOR SEQ.
0000BC 0000                      68+        DC      H'0' SEQ RECORD COUNTER
0000BE 0000                      69+        DC      H'0' HR CURRENT TRCNDX ENTRY FOR SEQ.
0000C0 0000                      70+DISKFLET DC     H'0' NUMBER OF RECORDS TAGGED
0000C8                           71+        DS      2D RESERVED.
                                 72+********************* THIRD PART OF TABLE *********************
0000D8 0700006940000006          73+DISKFLEB CCW    X'07',DISKFLES+1,X'40',6 SEEK
0000E0 0000000000000000          74+        DC      7D'0'
000118 0000000000000000          75+DISKFLEE DC     3F'0' MODULE CELL TABLE
000124 FFFFFFFF                  76+        DC      X'FFFFFFFF'

000128 00000000000000            78 DISKKEY  DC      XL7'00'                                      DISK0080
00012F                           79 DISKIO1  DS      CL3575                                       DISK0090
000F26                           80 DISKIOW  DS      CL55                                         DISK0100
                                 81          END                                                  DISK0110
```

8.79

```
    LOC   OBJECT CODE    ADDR1 ADDR2  STMT   SOURCE STATEMENT                                              DOS CL3-5 08/26/70

  000000                                 1 TAPE1    START 0                                                          TAPE0010
                                         2          ENTRY TAPEFLE,TAPEIO1                                            TAPE0020
                                         3 TAPEFLE  DTFMT BLKSIZE=3600,DEVADDR=SYS009,FILABL=STD,IOAREA1=TAPEIO1,    CTAPE0030
                                                          MODNAME=IJFFZZZZ,READ=FORWARD,RECFORM=FIXBLK,             CTAPE0040
                                                          RECSIZE=80,REWIND=UNLOAD,TYPEFLE=OUTPUT,IOREG=(8)          TAPE0050
                                         4+* 360N-IO-456 DTFMT    CHANGE LEVEL 3-7                          3-7
  000000                                 5+        DC    0D'0'
  000000 000080000000                    6+TAPEFLE  DC    X'000080000000' CCB
  000006 01                              7+        DC    AL1(1) LOGICAL UNIT CLASS
  000007 09                              8+        DC    AL1(9) LOGICAL UNIT
  000008 00000038                        9+        DC    AL4(IJF10001) CCW ADDRESS
  00000C 00000000                       10+        DC    4X'00' CCB-ST BYTE,CSW CCW ADDRESS
  000010 00                             11+        DC    AL1(0) 3-7
  000011 000000                         12+        DC    VL3(IJFFZZZZ) ADDRESS OF LOGIC MODULE
  000014 12                             13+        DC    X'12' DTF TYPE
  000015 40                             14+        DC    AL1(64) LOGICAL IOCS SWITCHES
  000016 E3C1D7C5C6D3C540               15+        DC    CL8'TAPEFLE'
  00001E 01                             16+        DC    X'01'
  00001F 64                             17+        DC    AL1(100) SWITCHES FOR OPEN                         3-3
  000020 A0                             18+        DC    AL1(160) SWITCH ONE FOR OPEN AND CLOSE
  000021 000000                         19+        DC    AL3(0) USER LABEL ROUTINE
  000024 00                             20+        DC    AL1(0) SWITCH FOR OPEN AND CLOSE
  000025 000025                         21+        DC    AL3(*)
  000028 00000000                       22+        DC    F'0' BLOCKCOUNT
  00002C 868C F018           00018      23+        BXH   11,12,24(15) DEBLOCKING FORWARD
  000030 41EE 0001           00001      24+        LA    14,1(14) INCREASE BLOCKCOUNT BY ONE
  000034 5881 0044           00044      25+        L     8,IJF20001-TAPEFLE(1) LOAD USER IOREG
  000038 0100006820000E10               26+IJF10001 CCW  X'01',TAPEIO1,X'20',3600
  000040 00000068                       27+        DC    A(TAPEIO1) ONE IOAREA
  000044 00000068                       28+IJF20001 DC   A(TAPEIO1) DEBLOCKER 1
  000048 00000050                       29+        DC    F'80' DEBLOCKER 2
  00004C 00000E77                       30+        DC    A(TAPEIO1+3600-1) DEBLOCKER 3
  000050 0E10                           31+        DC    Y(3600) BLOCKSIZE
  000052 0E0F                           32+        DC    Y(3600-1) BLOCKSIZE-1
  000054 004F                           33+        DC    Y(80-1) RECSIZE-1
  000056 0000                           34+        DC    2X'00' RESERVED
  000058 0000                           35+        DC    2X'00' RESERVED FOR OPEN
  00005A 000000000000                   36+        DC    6X'00' FILE SERIAL NO.
  000060 00000000                       37+        DC    4X'00' VOLUME SEQUENCE NO.
  000064 00000000                       38+        DC    4X'00' FILE SEQUENCE NO.

  000068                                40 TAPEIO1  DS    CL3600                                             TAPE0070
                                        41           END                                                     TAPE0080
```

```
  LOC  OBJECT CODE    ADDR1 ADDR2  STMT   SOURCE STATEMENT                                       DOS CL3-5 08/26/70

 000000                             1 CARD1    START 0                                                          CDOT0010
                                    2          ENTRY CARDFLE,CARDIO1                                            CDOT0020
                                    3 CARDFLE  DTFCD DEVADDR=SYSPCH,IOAREA1=CARDIO1,BLKSIZE=80,DEVICE=1442,     CCDOT0030
                                                     MODNAME=IJCFZOZ1,TYPEFLE=OUTPUT                            CDOT0040
 000000                             4+** 360N-CL-453.DTFCD     CHANGE LEVEL 3-7                        3-7
 000000 000080000000               5+         DC    0D'0'
 000006 00                         6+CARDFLE  DC    X'000080000000' RES. COUNT,COM. BYTES,STATUS BTS
 000007 02                         7+         DC    AL1(0) LOGICAL UNIT CLASS
 000008 00000028                   8+         DC    AL1(2) LOGICAL UNIT
 00000C 00000000                   9+         DC    A(IJCX0001) CCW ADDRESS
 000010 00                        10+         DC    4X'00' CCB-ST BYTE,CSW CCW ADDR.
 000011 000000                    11+         DC    AL1(0)
 000014 04                        12+         DC    VL3(IJCFZOZ1) ADDRESS OF LOGIC MODULE
 000015 10                        13+         DC    X'04' DTF TYPE = PUNCH
 000016 81                        14+         DC    AL1(16) SWITCHES
 000017 81                        15+         DC    AL1(129) NORMAL  COMM. CODE
 000018 00000030                  16+         DC    AL1(129) CONTROL COMM. CODE
 00001C 40404040                  17+         DC    A(CARDIO1+0) ADDR.OF DATA IN IOAREA1
 000020 0700                      18+         DC    CL4' ' BUCKET
 000022 4700 0000          00000  19+         NOPR  0 PUT LENGTH IN REG12(ONLY UNDEF)
 000026 02                        20+         NOP   0 LOAD USER POINTER REG
 000027 40                        21+         DC    X'02' SWITCH2
 000028 8100003020000050          22+         DC    C' ' BLANK FOR EJECT LAST PRG. CARD
 000030                           23+IJCX0001 CCW   129,CARDIO1+0,X'20',80-0
                                  24+IJJZ0001 EQU   *

 000030                           26 CARDIO1  DS    CL80                                                        CDOT0060
                                  27          END                                                              CDOT0070
```

8.81

```
  LOC  OBJECT CODE    ADDR1 ADDR2  STMT   SOURCE STATEMENT                                      DOS CL3-5 08/26/70

 000000                             1 CARD2     START 0                                          CDIN0010
                                    2           ENTRY CARDDTF,CARDIO2,ENDCARD2                   CDIN0020
                                    3 CARDDTF   DTFCD DEVADDR=SYSIPT,IOAREA1=CARDIO2,BLKSIZE=80,DEVICE=2501,  CCDIN0030
                                                      EOFADDR=ENDCARD2,MODNAME=IJCFZIZ3,RECFORM=FIXUNB,       CDIN0040
                                                      TYPEFLE=INPUT                              CDIN0050
                                    4+* 360N-CL-453 DTFCD    CHANGE LEVEL 3-7                            3-7
 000000                             5+        DC    0D'0'
 000000 000080000000                6+CARDDTF  DC    X'000080000000' RES. COUNT,COM. BYTES,STATUS BTS
 000006 00                          7+        DC    AL1(0) LOGICAL UNIT CLASS
 000007 01                          8+        DC    AL1(1) LOGICAL UNIT
 000008 00000020                    9+        DC    A(IJCX0001) CCW ADDRESS
 00000C 00000000                   10+        DC    4X'00' CCB-ST BYTE,CSW CCW ADDR.
 000010 00                         11+        DC    AL1(0)
 000011 000000                     12+        DC    VL3(IJCFZIZ3) ADDRESS OF LOGIC MODULE
 000014 02                         13+        DC    X'02' DTF TYPE (READER)
 000015 00                         14+        DC    AL1(0) SWITCHES
 000016 02                         15+        DC    AL1(2) NORMAL COMM.CODE
 000017 02                         16+        DC    AL1(2) CNTROL COMM.CODE
 000018 00000032                   17+        DC    A(CARDIO2) ADDR. OF IOAREA1
 00001C 00000082                   18+        DC    A(ENDCARD2) EOF ADDRESS
 000020 0200003220000050           19+IJCX0001 CCW  2,CARDIO2,X'20',80
 000028 4700 0000         00000    20+        NOP   0 LOAD USER POINTER REG.
 00002C 4700 0000         00000    21+        NOP   0 MOVE IOAREA TO WORKA
 000030 0000                       22+        DC    X'0000'
 000032                            23+IJJZ0001 EQU  *

 000032                            25 CARDIO2  DS    CL80                                         CDIN0070

 000082 07FA                       27 ENDCARD2 BR    10                                           CDIN0090
                                   28           END                                              CDIN0100
```

8.82

```
     LOC   OBJECT CODE      ADDR1 ADDR2 STMT   SOURCE STATEMENT                                          DOS CL3-5 08/26/70

   000000                                 1 PRINT1    START  0                                              PRTO0010
                                          2           ENTRY  PRTDTF,PRTIO1                                   PRTO0020
                                          3 PRTDTF    DTFPR  DEVADDR=SYSLST,IOAREA1=PRTIO1,BLKSIZE=133,CTLCHR=ASA,   CPRTO0030
                                                             DEVICE=1403,MODNAME=IJDFAZZZ,RECFORM=FIXUNB             PRTO0040
                                          4+** 360 N-CL-453 DTFPR        CHANGE LEVEL 3-5                       3-5
   000000                                 5+          DC     0D'0'
   000000 000080000000                    6+*PRTDTF   DC     X'000080000000' RES. COUNT,COM. BYTES,STATUS BTS
   000006 00                              7+          DC     AL1(0) LOGICAL UNIT CLASS
   000007 03                              8+          DC     AL1(3) LOGICAL UNIT
   000008 00000028                        9+          DC     A(*+32) CCW  ADDR.
   00000C 00000000                       10+          DC     4X'00' CCB-ST BYTE,CSW CCW ADDRESS
   000010 00                             11+          DC     AL1(0)
   000011 000000                         12+          DC     VL3(IJDFAZZZ) ADDRESS OF LOGIC MODULE
   000014 08                             13+          DC     X'08' DTF TYPE  (PRINTER)
   000015 30                             14+          DC     AL1(48) SWITCHES
   000016 09                             15+          DC     X'09' NORMAL  COMM. CODE
   000017 09                             16+          DC     X'09' CONTROL COMM. CODE
   000018 00000031                       17+          DC     A(PRTIO1+1) ADDRESS OF DATA IN IOAREA1
   00001C 00000000                       18+          DC     4X'00' BUCKET                                   3-5
   000020 0700                           19+          NOPR   0 PUT LENGTH IN REG12 (ONLY UNDEF.
   000022 4700 0000           00000      20+          NOP    0 LOAD USER POINTER REG
   000026 0000                           21+          DC     2X'00' NOT USED                                3-5
   000028 0900003120000084               22+          CCW    9,PRTIO1+1,X'20',133-1
   000030                                23+IJJZ0001  EQU    *

   000030 4040404040404040               25 PRTIO1    DC     CL133' '                                666     PRTO0060
                                         26           END                                                   PRTO0070
```

CHAPTER 8

PROGRAMMING ASSIGNMENT

INSTRUCTIONS

From the Sales Master File created in Chapter 4, two reports are to be prepared, a Net Sales Report and a Commission Report. In addition, a back-up tape for the Sales Master File is to be created.

The Net Sales Report is to contain the Department Number, Salesman Number, Salesman Name, Y-T-D Sales, Y-T-D Sales Returns and the Net Sales (Y-T-D Sales — Sales Returns).

The Commission Report is to contain the Department Number, the Salesman Number, Salesman Name, Net Sales, Commission Rate, and Commision (Commission Rate x Net Sales).

The back-up tape should include all fields on the master record.

A control card is to be used to determine whether the reports or the tape back-up are to be produced.

Other functions to be determined by the control card include the following:

Print Function

1. Which report will be produced. Either the Net Sales Report or the Commission Report.

2. Which Department will be printed. Either the complete Sales Master File or a single department.

3. Which Salesman Numbers will be printed. Either all salesman numbers will be printed or a "From-TO" range will be printed.

The entries in the control card will be the following:

1. "DUMP" — This entry indicates that a backup file is to be created.

2. "PRINT" — This indicates that one of the two printed reports is to be produced.

   A. "NET" — This indicates that the Net Sales Report is to be produced.

                                    or

   B. "COMMISSION" — This indicates that the Commission Report is to be produced.

   C. "XX" or omitted — If present, this entry specifies a department to be printed. If omitted, all departments are printed.

   D. "XXX" or omitted — If present, this entry specifies a beginning salesman number for the report.

   E. "XXX" or omitted — If present, this entry specifies an ending salesman number for the report.

The control card should be free-form with each positional entry separated by a comma.

In addition, the program should be segmented into three overlay sections — one to read and interpret the control cards, one to create the back-up file and one to create the printed reports.

CHAPTER 9

PHYSICAL IOCS

INTRODUCTION

All of the programs presented thus far have utilized logical IOCS to process data files. Logical IOCS performs such functions as making data records available from data files, opening and closing files, blocking and deblocking records and servicing end-of-file and end-of-volume conditions. It is utilized through the use of macros such as GET, PUT, READ, WRITE, CNTRL, DTF--, etc.

As shown previously, Logical IOCS uses common Input/Output modules to accomplish its tasks. In order to effect a transfer of data, for example, read a card, the logical IOCS I/O modules use a series of routines referred to as Physical IOCS. The PHYSICAL IOCS routines are contained in the DOS supervisor and these routines issue the actual I/O commands to the channel and device to begin the transfer of data between main storage and the device.

Although the instructions issued in the supervisor which begin the transfer of data from a peripheral device to main storage or vice versa are PRIVILEGED INSTRUCTIONS (that is, they can only be issued by the supervisor), the instructions issued in the I/O modules which call the Physical IOCS routines can be used in any problem program. When they are used in a problem program, the program is said to use Physical IOCS rather than Logical IOCS.

USE OF PHYSICAL IOCS

If a problem program uses Physical IOCS rather than Logical IOCS, it must perform many of the same functions provided by Logical IOCS in order to process the data files in a similar manner. Therefore, such things as end-of-volume processing, end-of-file processing, and blocking and deblocking must be handled by the problem program rather than relying on the Logical IOCS I/O modules. Since the programming involved in performing these functions has already been done in Logical IOCS, many installations prefer to use logical IOCS because additional programming time is necessary to develop the file management routines if Logical IOCS is not used.

Physical IOCS does, however, offer several significant advantages for certain applications. Programs written using Physical IOCS normally consume less core storage than programs using Logical IOCS and usually have a faster execution time. This is because the Logical IOCS routines are generalized routines and the routines written in conjunction with Physical IOCS are specialized routines for the problem being solved. Also, when using Physical IOCS for card and printer files, no blocking or involved end-of-file, end-of-volume processing needs to be done. Thus, in some instances, Physical IOCS can be used in a problem program with no increased effort on the programmer's part but with the advantages mentioned above.

In order to perform I/O using Physical IOCS, the program must make use of the CCW instruction.

CCW Instruction

When an input/output operation is to be accomplished on the System 360, a "channel program" must be presented to the channel. The channel then acts as a separate computer and executes the channel program to read or write data from an I/O device. Therefore, before any data can be transferred, a channel program must be written by the problem program. The channel program is written by using the CCW (Channel Command Word) instruction.

The CCW instruction is used to build a channel program by supplying a command code, a data address, a data length and some control flags. The CCW used to construct the channel program to read a card on a 2540 card reader is shown in Figure 9-1.

EXAMPLE

Figure 9-1 Example of CCW instruction

The name CARDCCWI is used to identify the CCW and must be present on the first CCW of any channel program. The first operand of the CCW instruction is the command code for the device. It specifies what operation will be performed. In the example, the X'02' is the command code to read a card and place it in pocket 1 of the card reader. The second operand is the address of the I/O area into which the data will be read. Thus, the card will be read into the area beginning at the address specified by the label CARDINIO. The I/O area is normally defined by a DS instruction in the same manner used for I/O areas when using logical IOCS. The third operand is an indicator which controls the action of the channel program. The fourth operand of the CCW instruction specifies the number of bytes of data which are to be read. This count, specified as a decimal value, is normally the length of the record being read or written by the channel program.

The CCW instruction reserves 8 bytes of storage on a doubleword boundary which contain the values specified in the instruction. The 8 bytes contain the following:

Byte 0: Command Code

Byte 1-3: Data Address

Byte 4: Flags

Byte 5: Not used, set to zero.

Byte 6-7: Count

Figure 9-2 Contents of CCW instruction

Thus, the 8 bytes are available to the problem program by referencing the name given to the CCW as byte 0.

COMMAND CHAINING

A channel program consists of one or more CCW's. Each CCW in a channel program specifies an operation to be executed by the channel and device. In order to execute more than one command in a channel program, COMMAND CHAINING must occur. Command chaining is specified by a X'40' value in the third operand of the CCW. This indicates to the channel that when the first command of the channel program has been completed then the command of the next sequential CCW should be executed immediately without terminating the channel program.

The technique of command chaining is illustrated in the following series of examples. A record is to be printed on the 1403 printer. Normally, the record is printed and then the printer is spaced to be ready for the next print line. The CCW to accomplish this is shown in Figure 9-3.

EXAMPLE

PRTCCW   CCW   X'09', PRTIO, X'00', 80

Figure 9-3 CCW to print single line on printer

The command code X'09' causes the channel program to write a single line and then skip one line after the print operation. The I/O area is PRTIO and 80 bytes will be printed.

If the above CCW were executed all the time, the printing would run from one page to another with no skip to head of forms when printing reached the bottom of the page. In order to skip to head of forms at the appropriate time, a second CCW can be included in the channel program.

EXAMPLE

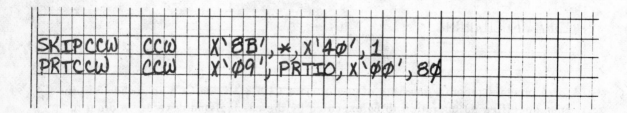

SKIPCCW   CCW   X'8B', *, X'40', 1
PRTCCW   CCW   X'09', PRTIO, X'00', 80

Figure 9-4 CCWs to skip to head of page and print a line

In the example above, the first CCW (SKIPCCW) is chained to the second CCW (PRTCCW). This means that immediately after the first command is executed the second command will be executed. The command for the CCW SKIPCCW is X'8B'. This is the command to skip to channel 1 in the carriage control tape. Thus, when the CCW is executed, the paper will be restored to head of forms. If the SKIPCCW is chained to a print CCW, as shown in Figure 9-4, a line will be printed immediately after the skip to head of forms. Thus, if the CCW's are written as shown, the first line of the report will be printed after a skip to head of forms. However, it is not desirable to skip to head of forms before each line on the report. Therefore, after the first line is printed a NO-OP command must be moved to the SKIPCCW CCW. A NO-OP command will cause no operation to take place. Thus, the instruction MVI SKIPCCW,X'03' could be used to move the NO-OP command to the CCW. After the instruction, the CCWs would appear as shown below.

```
SKIPCCW    CCW    X'03',*,X'40',1
PRTCCW     CCW    X'09',PRTIO,X'00',80
```

Figure 9-5 Chained CCWs with NO-OP Command

When the NO-OP command is in the SKIPCCW CCW, only the contents of PRTIO will be printed and no skip to head of forms will take place. However, after 55 lines have been printed, it is again desired to print on a new page. Thus the following routine could be used to check when a skip to head of forms should take place.

```
Name        Operation    Operand
            CP           LNCOUNT,=P'55'
            BNE          DOPRINT
            MVI          SKIPCCW,X'8B'
            SP           LNCOUNT,LNCOUNT
DOPRINT     EQU          *
```

Figure 9-6 Routine to check for page overflow

In the routine shown above, a line counter is checked to determine if 55 lines have been printed. If so, the command code in SKIPCCW is changed from a NOP to a skip to Channel 1 command code. This is done by moving the command code X'8B' to the CCW.

9.5

Thus, by altering the channel commands in the CCW, the desirable channel program can be produced.

DATA CHAINING AND SUPPRESS TRANSFER OF DATA INDICATORS

When a channel program is written as shown in the previous examples, the data in the record read is transferred to the storage location beginning with the address specified in the second operand and the number of bytes read or written is normally equal to the count supplied in the fourth operand.

The DATA CHAINING indicator can be used in the CCW to use different I/O areas in the same channel program. This indicator is X'80' in the CCW indicator byte. When DATA CHAINING is used, data is read into (or written from) data areas defined in consecutive CCW's.

EXAMPLE

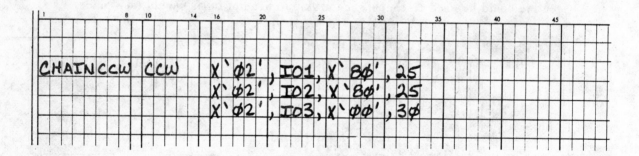

Figure 9-7 Example of data chaining

In the example above, data chaining is used because the indicator bytes in the first two CCW's of the channel program are X'80'. Thus, when the channel program is executed, the first 25 bytes of the card will be read into IO1, the second 25 bytes will be read into IO2 and the last 30 bytes will be read into IO3. As can be seen from the above channel program, data chaining can be used to move data to desired areas in core storage instead of reading the data into one large I/O area and then moving the data to the desired areas by using a move instruction. Execution time in a program can some times be saved using this technique because the move instructions do not have to be executed after the channel program is complete. It should be noted that when data chaining is used, the command issued in the first CCW is the command used for the complete channel program.

9.6

Field selection can be accomplished in an input record through the use of the SUPPRESS TRANSFER OF DATA INDICATOR (or SKIP indicator). This indicator (X'10') indicates to the channel program to read the data on the input record but to not transfer the data to main storage. Using the skip indicator with the data chaining indicator will allow specific fields in an input record to be moved to a specific I/O area. (See Figure 9-8).

EXAMPLE

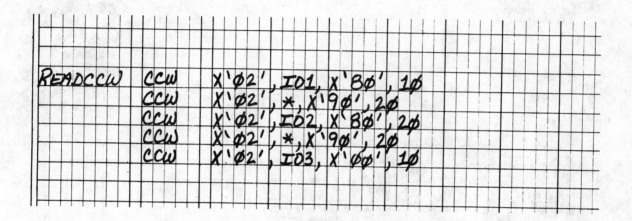

```
READCCW   CCW      X'Ø2',IO1,X'8Ø',1Ø
          CCW      X'Ø2',*,X'9Ø',2Ø
          CCW      X'Ø2',IO2,X'8Ø',2Ø
          CCW      X'Ø2',*,X'9Ø',2Ø
          CCW      X'Ø2',IO3,X'ØØ',1Ø
```

Figure 9-8 Example of field selecting an input record

In the example above, data chaining (X'80') is used with the Skip flag (X'10') to selectively read portions of an input record into core storage. The first 10 bytes of the input record will be read into the core storage location IO1. The next 20 bytes of the record will be read by the channel but will not be transferred to main storage because the skip indicator is on (X'90' = X'80' + X'10'). The next 20 bytes of the input record will be read into the core storage location IO2. The next 20 bytes will then be skipped and the last 10 bytes will be read into IO3. Thus, by using the data chaining and skip indicators, selected fields in an input record can be read and transferred to the desired I/O areas.

It should be noted that when command chaining is used, each command in the channel program is considered to apply to a new physical record. Thus, if three read commands were chained together, three physical records would be read. When data chaining is indicated, each CCW in the channel program is considered to apply to one physical record. Thus, when data chaining is used, the complete channel program applies to one record which is placed in the core storage locations defined in the chained CCWs.

TRANSFER IN CHANNEL COMMAND

When a channel program is begun and chaining is used, the normal sequence of execution is from one CCW (located on a doubleword boundary) to the next sequentially consecutive CCW. The TRANSFER IN CHANNEL command (TIC) can be used to alter the sequence of execution of a channel program. Thus, a TIC command can be used in a channel program to effectively branch from one CCW to another. The example below illustrates the use of the TIC command to execute a CCW command which does not follow sequentially.

EXAMPLE

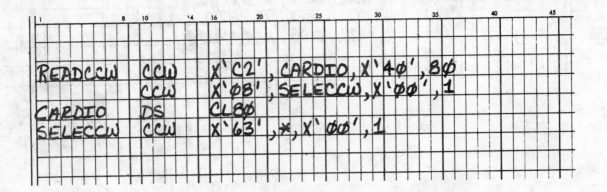

Figure 9-9 Example of Transfer in Channel Command

In the example above, the first CCW reads a card but does not stacker select the card (that is, the data is read into main storage but the card is not processed through the card reader and into a pocket). The TIC command is then used to transfer control to the SELECCW command which stacker selects the card into pocket 2. Note that command chaining is used in the first CCW so that the TIC command will be executed. The two restrictions on the TIC command are that it cannot be the first CCW specified in a channel program and that two TIC commands cannot be issued consecutively, that is, one TIC command cannot point to another TIC command.

As can be seen from the previous examples, there are many commands which can be issued for the various peripheral devices on the System/360. A complete list of these commands is given in the appendices.

COMMAND CONTROL BLOCK

Before a channel program begins execution, it must have certain information, such as the I/O unit on which the I/O is to be performed. The COMMAND CONTROL BLOCK is used to present the necessary information to the channel. In addition, when the channel program is complete, the channel posts information, such as any errors incurred during the I/O operation, in the Command Control Block. This information is then available for the problem program to test.

The Command Control Block can be defined through the use of the CCB macro. The CCB for a 2540 card reader is illustrated in Figure 9-10.

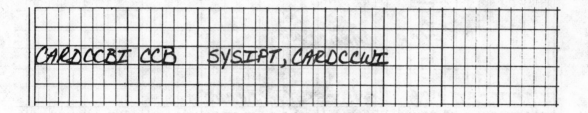

CARDCCBI CCB   SYSIPT, CARDCCWI

Figure 9-10 Example of CCB macro

The label (in the example, CARDCCBI) is required on all CCB macros. The first operand of the CCB is the SYS number which will be assigned to the device on which the I/O will take place. In the example, the device assigned to SYSIPT is to be used. The second operand is the label name of the first CCW to be executed in the channel program. The CCB macro expands into a sixteen byte table which communicates the necessary information to the Physical IOCS routine in the supervisor so that it can perform the I/O operation. The table is also used to post information after the channel program is complete. A CCB must be defined for each I/O device that is to be used by Physical IOCS macro instructions.

EXECUTE CHANNEL PROGRAM Macro

As has been mentioned, a CCW and a CCB must be defined for the channel program which is to be executed. In order to execute the channel program, the EXCP macro (EXecute Channel Program) is used. The EXCP macro to read a card on a 2540 card reader (assigned to SYSIPT) is illustrated in Figure 9-11.

EXAMPLE

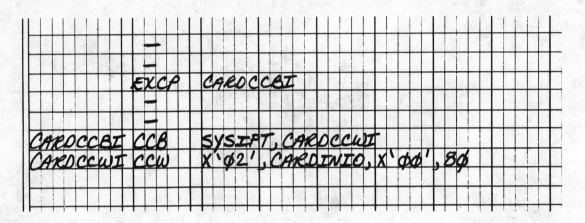

Figure 9-11 Example of EXCP macro

In the example above, the channel program is defined by the CCW at CARDCCWI. The command control block is defined by the CCB macro at CARDCCBI. The EXCP macro is used to begin the channel program. The only operand, which is required, is the name of the command control block as defined by the CCB. When the EXCP macro is executed, the supervisor Physical IOCS routine is entered to begin the channel program.

WAIT Macro

When a channel program begins, the data transfer begins between the device and main storage. Control is then returned to the problem program (the program which issued the EXCP macro). The problem program can then execute instructions while the data transfer is taking place, that is, the problem program and the channel program execute concurrently. However, when the problem program is going to reference data being read by the channel program, it must wait until the channel program is complete before it attempts to manipulate the data. Thus, when the problem program has completed all the processing it can perform without referencing the incoming or outgoing data, it must issue the WAIT macro.

EXAMPLE

Figure 9-12 Example of WAIT macro

The WAIT macro may or may not have a label name. The only operand is the name of the command control block and it is required. The WAIT macro halts the problem program execution until the channel program is complete. When the channel program is completed, the Physical IOCS routines post a "traffic bit" which indicates the channel program is complete and then return control to the problem program which can then reference the data which is in core.

SAMPLE PROGRAM

The sample program presented in this chapter is used to resequence COBOL and Assembler Language source decks. COBOL, a source language commonly used in business applications, uses a source coding sheet as shown in Figure 9-13.

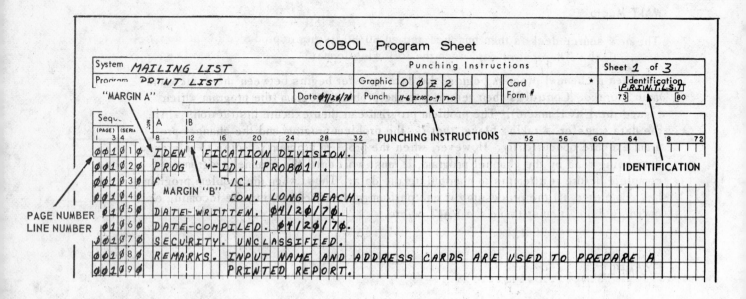

Figure 9-13 Example of COBOL coding sheet

Note that the first six columns in a COBOL source deck contain a page and line number (the first 3 numbers are the page number and the next 3 numbers are the line number). Normally, each 20-25 lines are given a new page number because the coding sheet has 25 lines on it. In addition, there is an identification name which can go into columns 73-80 to identify the program. When a COBOL program is originally coded, the page/line numbers and the identification are normally keypunched in the source cards. However, when the program is tested and changed, some times page and line numbers become out of sequence or the identification is left off when an additional card is inserted in the program. Thus, after the program is debugged and completed, the source deck may not be completely documented as it should be. The same situation may occur with the identification field in columns 73-80 in an assembler language program.

The purpose of the sample program, therefore, is to repunch either a COBOL or an Assembler Language source deck with the proper information punched in the source deck.

In order to accomplish this, a control card is read followed by the source deck. The new source deck is then punched and an 80/80 listing is produced of the new source deck. The control card uses the following format:

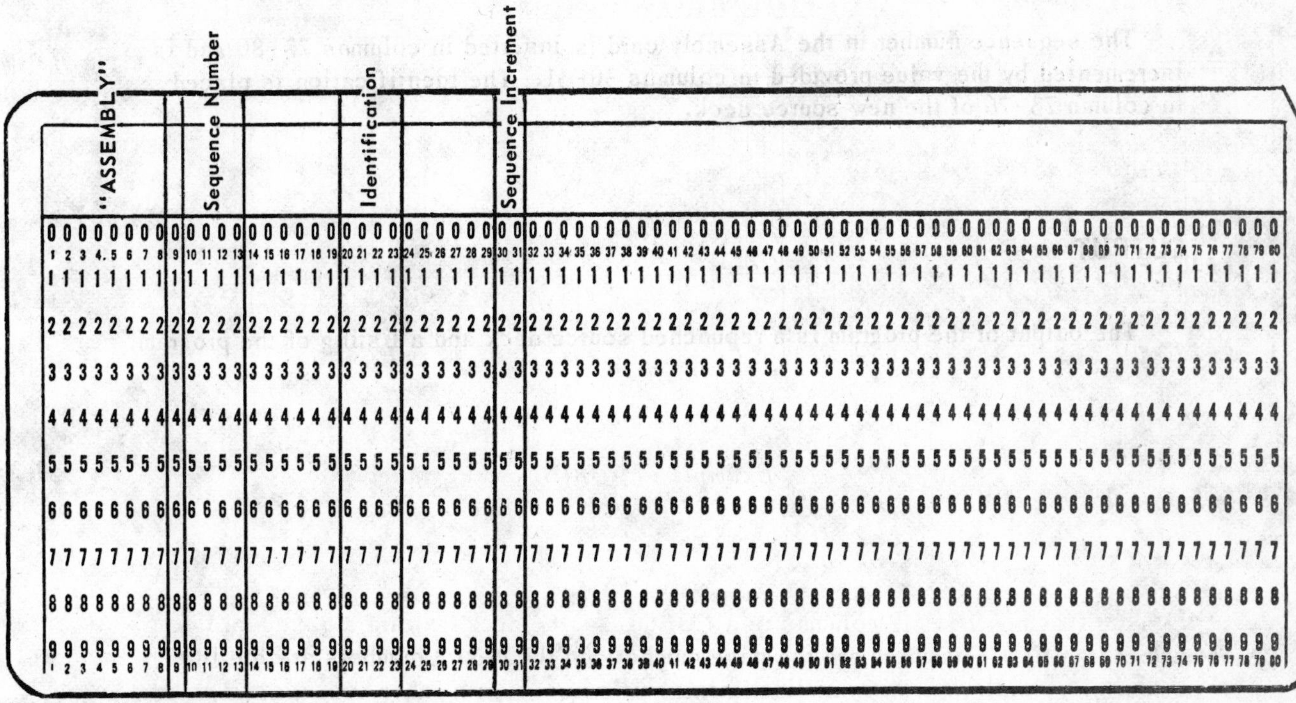

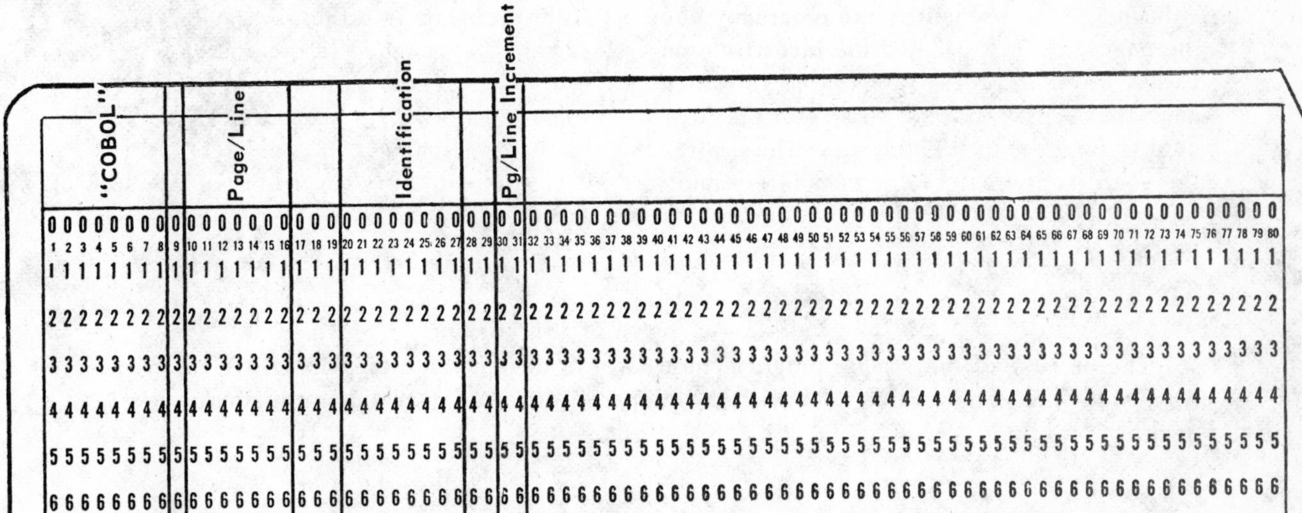

Figure 9-14 Control card formats

The page/line number in the COBOL card provides the beginning page and line number and it is incremented by the increment value in columns 30-31. The identification in columns 20-27 is inserted in columns 73-80 of the source card.

The sequence number in the Assembly card is inserted in columns 77-80 and is incremented by the value provided in columns 30-31. The identification is placed in column 73-76 of the new source deck.

OUTPUT

The output of the program is a repunched source deck and a listing of the program.

PROGRAM

```
            SOURCE DECK SEQUENCING                                                                    PAGE    1

    LOC   OBJECT CODE      ADDR1 ADDR2  STMT    SOURCE STATEMENT                              DOS CL3-5 08/26/70
   000000                               2 DECKSEQ  START 0                                           DSEQ0020

                                        4            PRINT NOGEN
                                        5 ****                                                       DSEQ0040
                                        6 * THIS PROGRAM IS USED TO RESEQUENCE ASSEMBLER AND COBOL SOURCE DECKS   DSEQ0050
                                        7 * FOR COBOL PROGRAMS, IT PUNCHES AN INCREMENTING PAGE AND LINE NUMBER   DSEQ0060
                                        8 * STARTING WITH THE PAGE AND LINE NO SPECIFIED IN THE CONTROL CARD.     DSEQ0070
                                        9 * IT ALSO PUNCHES AN IDENTIFICATION IN COLS 73-80 IF ONE IS SPECIFIED   DSEQ0080
                                       10 * IN THE CONTROL CARD.                                     DSEQ0090
                                       11 *                                                          DSEQ0100
                                       12 * FOR ASSEMBLER PROGRAMS IT PUNCHES AN IDENTIFICATION NUMBER AND AN     DSEQ0110
                                       13 * IDENTIFICATION NAME IN COLS 73-80                         DSEQ0120
                                       14 *                                                          DSEQ0130
                                       15 * A LISTING OF THE NEW DECK IS ALSO PRODUCED.               DSEQ0140
                                       16 *                                                          DSEQ0150
                                       17 * BASE REGISTER USAGE IS AS FOLLOWS                         DSEQ0160
                                       18 *                                                          DSEQ0170
   00000C                             20 BASEREG  EQU   12                                           DSEQ0190
   00000B                             21 LINKREG1 EQU   11                                           DSEQ0200

   000000 05C0                        23          BALR  BASEREG,0            ESTABLISH BASE REGISTER    DSEQ0220
   000002                             24          USING *,BASEREG                                    DSEQ0230

                                       26          EXCP  CARDCCBI            READ A CARD               DSEQ0250
                                       30          WAIT  CARDCCBI            WAIT FOR I/O              DSEQ0260
   000016 D504 C20E C354 00210 00356  37          CLC   NAMEI(5),=C'COBOL'  IS IT COBOL CARD         DSEQ0280
   00001C 4780 C042           00044    38          BE    CBL                YES, GO TO PROCESS       DSEQ0290
   000020 D507 C20E C336 00210 00338  39          CLC   NAMEI(8),=C'ASSEMBLY' IS IT AN ASSEMBLY CARD  DSEQ0300
   000026 4780 C11A           0011C   40          BE    ASSEM              YES, GO TO PROCESS       DSEQ0310

                                       42          EXCP  CONCCB             WRITE ERROR MSG ON CONSOLE DSEQ0330
                                       46          WAIT  CONCCB             WAIT FOR I/O             DSEQ0340
                                       52          CANCEL ALL               CANCEL PGM              DSEQ0350

                                       57 ****                                                       DSEQ0370
                                       58 * THIS ROUTINE IS ENTERED WHEN COBOL CARDS ARE TO BE PUNCHED            DSEQ0380
                                       59 ****                                                       DSEQ0390

   000044                             61 CBL      EQU   *                                            DSE00410
   000044 F235 C2FE C217 00300 00219  62          PACK  NUMBPACK(4),NUMBERI(6)  PACK PG/LN          DSEQ0420
   00004A F211 C302 C22B 00304 0022D  63          PACK  INCRPACK(2),INCRI(2)    PACK INCREMENT      DSEQ0430
   000050 D207 C304 C221 00306 00223  64          MVC   HOLDID(8),IDI       MOVE I.D. TO HOLD AREA   DSEQ0440
   000056 D201 C30C C300 0030E 00302  65          MVC   HOLDNUMB(2),NUMBPACK+2  SAVE STARTING PAGE NUMBER DSEQ0450
   00005C                             66 ALLCOB   EQU   *                                            DSEQ0460
   00005C 45B0 C0C4           000C6   67          BAL   LINKREG1,READCARD   GO TO READ NEXT CARD    DSEQ0470

   000060 F353 C20E C2FE 00210 00300  69          UNPK  PGLN(6),NUMBPACK(4) UNPACK PG/LN            DSEQ0490
   000066 96F0 C213           00215   70          OI    PGLN+5,X'F0'        RESET SIGN              DSEQ0500
   00006A D207 C256 C304 00258 00306  71          MVC   COBID(8),HOLDID     MOVE ID TO OUTPUT       DSEQ0510
   000070 D24F C25E C20E 00260 00210  72          MVC   CARDOUT,CARDINIO    MOVE CARD TO OUTPUT     DSEQ0520

                                       74          EXCP  CARDCCBO            PUNCH CARD              DSEQ0540
   00007C D24F C2AE C20E 002B0 00210  78          MVC   PRTIO,CARDINIO      MOVE CARD TO PRINT OUT   DSEQ0550
   000082 45B0 C0F8           000FA   79          BAL   LINKREG1,PRTCARD    GO TO PRINT CARD        DSEQ0560
   000086 FA31 C2FE C302 00300 00304  80          AP    NUMBPACK(4),INCRPACK(2) ADD TO PG/LN COUNT  DSEQ0570
   00008C F911 C300 C34E 00302 00350  81          CP    NUMBPACK+2(2),=P'250'  IS IT GREATER THAN 250 DSEQ0580
   000092 47D0 C0A0           000A2   82          BNH   NOTOVERC           NO, CONTINUE TO NEXT CARD DSEQ0590
   000096 D201 C300 C30C 00302 0030E  83          MVC   NUMBPACK+2(2),HOLDNUMB  RESET NUMBER FOR NEW PAGE DSEQ0600
   00009C FA32 C2FE C359 00300 0035B  84          AP    NUMBPACK(4),=P'1000'   SET NEW PAGE NUMBER  DSEQ0610

   0000A2                             86 NOTOVERC EQU   *                                            DSEQ0630
                                       87          WAIT  PRTCCB             WAIT FOR PRINTER        DSEQ0640
   0000B0 9203 C1E6           001E8   93          MVI   SKIPCCW,X'03'       RESET SKIP TO NOP       DSEQ0650
                                       94          WAIT  CARDCCBO           WAIT FOR CARD PUNCH I/O  DSEQ0660
   0000C2 47F0 C05A           0005C   100         B     ALLCOB             GO TO READ NEXT CARD     DSEQ0670

                                       102 ****                                                      DSEQ0690
                                       103 * THIS ROUTINE IS ENTERED TO READ CARDS                   DSEQ0700
                                       104 ****                                                      DSEQ0710

   0000C6                             106 READCARD EQU   *                                            DSEQ0730
                                       107         EXCP  CARDCCBI           READ A CARD             DSEQ0740
                                       111         WAIT  CARDCCBI           WAIT FOR I/O            DSEQ0750
   0000DA D501 C20E C350 00210 00352  118         CLC   CARDINIO(2),=C'/*'  IS IT END OF FILE       DSEQ0770
   0000E0 4780 C180           00182   119         BE    EOF                YES, GO TO END OF FILE  DSEQ0780
   0000E4 D504 C20E C354 00210 00356  120         CLC   CARDINIO(5),=C'COBOL'  IS IT NEW COBOL DECK DSEQ0790
   0000EA 4780 C042           00044   121         BE    CBL                YES, GO TO PROCESS NEW DECK DSEQ0800
   0000EE D507 C20E C336 00210 00338  122         CLC   CARDINIO(8),=C'ASSEMBLY' IS IT NEW ASSEMBLY DSEQ0810
   0000F4 4780 C11A           0011C   123         BE    ASSEM              YES, GO TO PROCESS NEW DECK DSEQ0820
   0000F8 07FB                        124         BR    LINKREG1           NO, RETURN TO CALLER    DSEQ0830
```

```
                                126 ****  THIS ROUTINE IS ENTERED TO PRINT THE RECORD. IT FIRST CHECKS IF    DSEQ0850
                                127 * THIS ROUTINE IS ENTERED TO PRINT THE RECORD. IT FIRST CHECKS IF        DSEQ0860
                                128 * 55 LINES HAVE BEEN PRINTED AND IF SO, CHAINS TO A CCW TO GO TO         DSEQ0870
                                129 * HEAD OF FORMS AFTER THE LINE IS PRINTED.                                DSEQ0880
                                130 ****                                                                      DSEQ0890

0000FA                          132 PRTCARD EQU   *                                                           DSEQ0910
0000FA F911 C30E C352 00310 00354  133         CP    LNCOUNT,=P'55'      HAVE WE PRINTED 55 LINES           DSEQ0920
000100 4770 C10C           0010E 134         BNE   DOPRINT             NO, BYPASS NEXT INST               DSEQ0930
000104 928B C1E6           001E8 135         MVI   SKIPCCW,X'8B'       YES, SET UP CHAIN TO GO TO HEAD OF  DSEQ0940
                                136 *                                   FORMS AFTER LINE IS PRINTED         DSEQ0950
000108 FB11 C30E C30E 00310 00310  137         SP    LNCOUNT,LNCOUNT     ZERO COUNTER                       DSEQ0960
                                138 DOPRINT EXCP  PRTCCB              WRITE LINE                         DSEQ0970
000114 FA10 C30E C35C 00310 0035E  142         AP    LNCOUNT,=P'1'       ADD 1 TO LINE COUNTER              DSEQ0980
00011A 07F6                       143         BR    LINKREG1            RETURN TO CALLER                   DSEQ0990


                                145 ****                                                                      DSEQ1010
                                146 * THIS ROUTINE IS ENTERED WHEN AN ASSEMBLY DECK IS TO BE REPUNCHED       DSEQ1020
                                147 ****                                                                      DSEQ1030

00011C                          149 ASSEM   EQU   *                                                           DSEQ1050
00011C F223 C2FE C217 00300 00219  150         PACK  NUMBPACK(3),NUMBERI(4)  PACK I.D. NUMBER               DSEQ1060
000122 F211 C302 C22B 00304 0022D  151         PACK  INCRPACK(2),INCRI(2)    PACK INCREMENT                 DSEQ1070
000128 D203 C304 C221 00306 00223  152         MVC   HOLDID(4),IDI           MOVE AND HOLD I.D.             DSEQ1080

00012E                          154 ALLASSEM EQU  *                                                           DSEQ1100
00012E 45B0 C0C4           000C6 155         BAL   LINKREG1,READCARD   GO TO READ NEXT CARD               DSEQ1110
000132 F332 C25A C2FE 0025C 00300  156         UNPK  ASSEMID+4(4),NUMBPACK(3) UNPACK NUMBER               DSEQ1120
000138 96F0 C25D           0025F 157         OI    ASSEMID+7,X'F0'     RESET SIGN                         DSEQ1130
00013C D203 C256 C304 00258 00306  158         MVC   ASSEMID(4),HOLDID   MOVE I.D. TO CARD                  DSEQ1140
000142 D24F C25E C20E 00260 00210  159         MVC   CARDOUT,CARDINIO    MOVE CARD TO OUTPUT AREA           DSEQ1150

                                161         EXCP  CARDCCBO            PUNCH CARD                         DSEQ1170

00014C D24F C2AE C20E 002B0 00210  166         MVC   PRTIO,CARDINIO      MOVE CARD TO PRINTER I/O AREA      DSEQ1190
000154 45B0 C0F8           000FA 167         BAL   LINKREG1,PRTCARD    GO TO PRINT CARD                   DSEQ1200
000158 FA21 C2FE C302 00300 00304  168         AP    NUMBPACK(3),INCRPACK(2)  INCREMENT I.D. NUMBER        DSEQ1210

                                170         WAIT  PRTCCB              WAIT FOR PRINTER I/O               DSEQ1230
00016C 9203 C1E6           001E8 176         MVI   SKIPCCW,X'03'       RESET NOP FOR HEAD OF FORMS        DSEQ1240
                                177         WAIT  CARDCCBO            WAIT FOR CARD PUNCH                DSEQ1250
00017E 47F0 C12C           0012E 183         B     ALLASSEM            GO TO READ NEXT CARD               DSEQ1260


                                185 ****                                                                      DSEQ1280
                                186 * THIS ROUTINE IS ENTERED WHEN END-OF-FILE IS REACHED                    DSEQ1290
                                187 ****                                                                      DSEQ1300

000182                          189 EOF     EQU   *                                                           DSEQ1320
000182 9240 C25E           00260 190         MVI   CARDOUT,X'40'       MOVE BLANKS TO CARD OUTPUT         DSEQ1330
000186 D24E C25F C25E 00261 00260  191         MVC   CARDOUT+1(L'CARDOUT-1),CARDOUT                        DSEQ1340
                                192         EXCP  CARDCCBO            PUNCH BLANK CARD                   DSEQ1350
                                196         WAIT  CARDCCBO            WAIT FOR I/O                       DSEQ1360
                                202         EOJ                       END OF JOB                         DSEQ1370
```

```
                                206 ****                                                                      DSEQ1390
                                207 * CHANNEL COMMANDS                                                        DSEQ1400
                                208 ****                                                                      DSEQ1410

                                210 CARDCCBI CCB  SYSIPT,CARDCCWI                                             DSEQ1430
000182 000000000000            221 CARDCCWI CCW  X'02',CARDINIO,X'00',80                                     DSEQ1440
00018B 0200021000000050        222 CARDCCBO CCB  SYSPCH,CARDCCWO                                             DSEQ1450
                                233 CARDCCWO CCW  X'81',CARDOUT,X'00',80                                     DSEQ1460
0001D0 8100026000000050        234 PRTCCB   CCB  SYSLST,SKIPCCW                                              DSEQ1470
0001E8 8B0001E840000001        245 SKIPCCW  CCW  X'8B',*,X'40',1                                             DSEQ1480
0001F0 090002B000000050        246 PRTCCW   CCW  X'09',PRTIO,X'00',80                                        DSEQ1490
                                247 CONCCB   CCB  SYSLOG,CONCCW                                              DSEQ1500
000208 0900031200000022        258 CONCCW   CCW  X'09',CONMSG,X'00',L'CONMSG                                DSEQ1510
```

LOC	OBJECT CODE	ADDR1	ADDR2	STMT	SOURCE STATEMENT		DOS CL3-5 08/26/70
				260	****		DSEQ1530
				261	*I/O AREAS, CONSTANTS, ETC.		DSEQ1540
				262	****		DSEQ1550
000210				264	CARDINIO DS	OCL80	DSEQ1570
000210				265	NAMEI DS	CL8	DSEQ1580
000218				266	DS	CL1	DSEQ1590
000219				267	NUMBERI DS	CL6	DSEQ1600
00021F				268	DS	CL4	DSEQ1610
000223				269	IDI DS	CL8	DSEQ1620
00022B				270	DS	CL2	DSEQ1630
00022D				271	INCRI DS	CL2	DSEQ1640
000210				272	ORG	CARDINIO	DSEQ1650
000210				273	CBLCD DS	OCL80	DSEQ1660
000210				274	PGLN DS	CL6	DSEQ1670
000216				275	DS	CL66	DSEQ1680
000258				276	COBID DS	CL8	DSEQ1690
000210				277	ORG	CARDINIO	DSEQ1700
000210				278	ASSEMLD DS	OCL80	DSEQ1710
000210				279	DS	CL72	DSEQ1720
000258				280	ASSEMID DS	CL8	DSEQ1730
000260				282	CARDOUT DS	CL80	DSEQ1750
000280				284	PRTIO DS	CL80	DSEQ1770
000300				286	NUMBPACK DS	CL4	DSEQ1790
000304				287	INCRPACK DS	CL2	DSEQ1800
000306				288	HOLDID DS	CL8	DSEQ1810
00030E				289	HOLDNUMB DS	CL2	DSEQ1820
000310	000C			290	LNCOUNT DC	PL2'0'	DSEQ1830
000312	C9D5E5C1D3C9C440			291	CONMSG DC	C'INVALID CONTROL CARD-JOB CANCELLED'	DSEQ1840
				292	END		DSEQ1850
000338	C1E2E2C5D4C2D3E8			293		=C'ASSEMBLY'	
000340	000001A2			294		=A(CARDCCBI)	
000344	000001F8			295		=A(CONCCB)	
000348	000001C0			296		=A(CARDCCBO)	
00034C	000001D8			297		=A(PRTCCB)	
000350	250C			298		=P'250'	
000352	615C			299		=C'/*'	
000354	055C			300		=P'55'	
000356	C3D6C2D6D3			301		=C'COBOL'	
00035B	01000C			302		=P'1000'	
00035E	1C			303		=P'1'	

PROGRAMMING ASSIGNMENT

INSTRUCTIONS

Using physical IOCS, write a program to reproduce the test data used in the programming assignment in Chapter 3.

APPENDICES

A. HEXADECIMAL TO DECIMAL CONVERSION

B. DECIMAL TO HEXADECIMAL CONVERSION

C. MACRO – I/O MODULE NAMES

D. CHANNEL COMMAND OPERATION CODES

E. SYSTEM/360 CHARACTER SET

F. SYSTEM/360 INSTRUCTION SET

G. CONDITION CODES

H. JOB CONTROL AND SORT CONTROL

I. CATALOGUING PROGRAMS IN CORE IMAGE LIBRARY

J. TEST DATA FOR PROGRAMMING ASSIGNMENTS

APPENDIX A

HEXADECIMAL TO DECIMAL CONVERSION

Whenever binary values are used on the System/360, they will be displayed as hexadecimal in a core dump or file listing. Therefore, the hexadecimal number must be converted to decimal in order to find the value of a number.

The conversion from hexadecimal to decimal is based upon the place value in a hexadecimal number.

	1	1	0	
4096	256	16	1	Place Value
16^3	16^2	16^1	16^0	Base

In the illustration above, the hexadecimal number 110 is represented. Note that the decimal place values are under the number. Thus, to convert the hexadecimal value 110 to decimal the following steps would be done.

1. Multiply each of the hexadecimal digits by its place value.

$$
\begin{aligned}
1 \times 256 &= 256 \\
1 \times 16 &= 16 \\
0 \times 1 &= 0
\end{aligned}
$$

2. Add the results.

$$
\begin{aligned}
  256 \\
+ \ \ 16 \\
+ \ \ \ \ 0 \\
\hline
  272
\end{aligned}
$$

Thus, the decimal equivalent of the hexadecimal value 110 is 272.

To convert the hexadecimal value 2FC to decimal, the following steps would be taken.

1. Multiply the decimal equivalent of each of the hexadecimal digits by its place value.

$$
\begin{array}{rcrcr}
2 & \times & 256 & = & 512 \\
15 & \times & 16 & = & 240 \\
12 & \times & 1 & = & 12
\end{array}
$$

2. Add the results.

$$
\begin{array}{r}
512 \\
+\ 240 \\
+\ \underline{12} \\
762
\end{array}
$$

Thus, the decimal equivalent of the hexadecimal value 2FC is 762.

The following table is helpful in converting hexadecimal numbers to decimal.

BYTE				BYTE				BYTE			
0123		4567		0123		4567		0123		4567	
HEX	DEC	HEX	DEC	HEX	DEC	HEX	DEC	HEX	DEC	HEX	DEC
0	0	0	0	0	0	0	0	0	0	0	0
1	1,048,576	1	65,536	1	4,096	1	256	1	16	1	1
2	2,097,152	2	131,072	2	8,192	2	512	2	32	2	2
3	3,145,728	3	196,608	3	12,288	3	768	3	48	3	3
4	4,194,304	4	262,144	4	16,384	4	1,024	4	64	4	4
5	5,242,880	5	327,680	5	20,480	5	1,280	5	80	5	5
6	6,291,456	6	393,216	6	24,576	6	1,536	6	96	6	6
7	7,340,032	7	458,752	7	28,672	7	1,792	7	112	7	7
8	8,388,608	8	524,288	8	32,768	8	2,048	8	128	8	8
9	9,437,184	9	589,824	9	36,864	9	2,304	9	144	9	9
A	10,485,760	A	655,360	A	40,960	A	2,560	A	160	A	10
B	11,534,336	B	720,896	B	45,056	B	2,816	B	176	B	11
C	12,582,912	C	786,432	C	49,152	C	3,072	C	192	C	12
D	13,631,488	D	851,968	D	53,248	D	3,328	D	208	D	13
E	14,680,064	E	917,504	E	57,344	E	3,584	E	224	E	14
F	15,728,640	F	983,040	F	61,440	F	3,840	F	240	F	15
6		5		4		3		2		1	

Note in the table that both the hexadecimal and decimal values are given for each hexadecimal place position. Thus, it can be seen that x'10' = 16, x'100' = 256, x'1000' = 4096 and x'10000' = 65536. In order to convert the hexadecimal number 5C9A, using the table, the following steps would be taken.

1. From the fourth column from the right, which is equivalent to the position held by the number 5 in 5C9A, extract the corresponding decimal number.

$$X'5xxx' = 20480$$

2. From the third column from the right, which is equivalent to the position held by the number C, extract the corresponding decimal number.

$$X'xCxx' = 3072$$

3. From the second column from the right, which is equivalent to the position held by the number 9, extract the corresponding number.

$$X'xx9x' = 144$$

4. From the first column on the right, which is equivalent to the position held by the number A, extract the corresponding decimal number.

$$X'xxxA' = 10$$

5. Add the decimal values.

$$
\begin{array}{r}
20480 \\
3072 \\
144 \\
\underline{10} \\
23706
\end{array}
$$

Thus, the number 5C9A in the hexadecimal number system is the same as the decimal number 23706.

DECIMAL TO HEXADECIMAL CONVERSION

There are certain applications in which it is desirable to know the hexadecimal equivalents of decimal numbers. The following examples illustrate a method to use for the conversion.

EXAMPLE 1: Convert the decimal number 15 to hexadecimal.

Step 1: Divide the decimal number by 16.

$$16 \overline{\smash{\big)}\, \begin{array}{r} 0 \\ 15 \\ \underline{0} \\ 15 \end{array}}$$

The answer is 0 with a remainder of 15.

Step 2: Convert the remainder to hexadecimal.

Dec 15 = Hex F

Therefore, the hexadecimal equivalent of decimal 15 is F.

EXAMPLE 2: Convert the decimal number 30 to hexadecimal.

Step 1: Divide the decimal number by 16.

$$16 \overline{)\begin{array}{c} 1 \\ 30 \\ 16 \\ \hline 14 \end{array}}$$

Step 2: Convert the remainder to hexadecimal.

Dec 14 = Hex E

The first remainder is the low - order hexadecimal digit.

Step 3: Divide the quotient by 16.

$$16 \overline{)\begin{array}{c} 0 \\ 1 \\ 0 \\ \hline 1 \end{array}}$$

Step 4: Convert the remainder to hexadecimal.

Dec 1 = Hex 1

The remainder from the second division becomes the second digit in the hexa-decimal number, numbering from right to left.

Step 5: Since the quotient is = 0, no more division can take place. Therefore, the hexadecimal number 1E is equivalent to the decimal number 30.

EXAMPLE 3: Convert the decimal number 322 to hexadecimal.

Step 1: Divide the decimal number by 16.

```
          20
   16  ⌐322
          32
           2
           0
           2
```

Step 2: Convert the remainder to hexadecimal.

Dec 2 = Hex 2

Step 3: Divide the quotient by 16.

```
           1
    16  ⌐20
          16
           4
```

Step 4: Convert the remainder to hexadecimal.

Dec 4 = Hex 4

Step 5: Divide the quotient by 16.

```
           0
    16  ⌐1
          0
          1
```

Step 6: Convert the remainder to hexadecimal.

Dec 1 = Hex 1

Step 7: Since the quotient is = 0, no more division can take place. Therefore, the hexadecimal number 142 is equivalent to the decimal number 322.

The following table can be useful in converting decimal numbers to hexadecimal numbers.

BYTE		BYTE		BYTE	
0123	4567	0123	4567	0123	4567
HEX DEC	HEX DEC	HEX DEC	HEX DEC	HEX DEC	HEX DEC
0 0	0 0	0 0	0 0	0 0	0 0
1 1,048,576	1 65,536	1 4,096	1 256	1 16	1 1
2 2,097,152	2 131,072	2 8,192	2 512	2 32	2 2
3 3,145,728	3 196,608	3 12,288	3 768	3 48	3 3
4 4,194,304	4 262,144	4 16,384	4 1,024	4 64	4 4
5 5,242,880	5 327,680	5 20,480	5 1,280	5 80	5 5
6 6,291,456	6 393,216	6 24,576	6 1,536	6 96	6 6
7 7,340,032	7 458,752	7 28,672	7 1,792	7 112	7 7
8 8,388,608	8 524,288	8 32,768	8 2,048	8 128	8 8
9 9,437,184	9 589,824	9 36,864	9 2,304	9 144	9 9
A 10,485,760	A 655,360	A 40,960	A 2,560	A 160	A 10
B 11,534,336	B 720,896	B 45,056	B 2,816	B 176	B 11
C 12,582,912	C 786,432	C 49,152	C 3,072	C 192	C 12
D 13,631,488	D 851,968	D 53,248	D 3,328	D 208	D 13
E 14,680,064	E 917,504	E 57,344	E 3,584	E 224	E 14
F 15,728,640	F 983,040	F 61,440	F 3,840	F 240	F 15
6	5	4	3	2	1

To convert the decimal number 573 to hexadecimal, using the table, the following steps would be taken.

Step 1: Find the number 573 or the next value lower than 573 in the decimal side of the table.

Step 2: The hexadecimal digit equivalent to 512 (the decimal number found in the table) becomes the high-order digit in the hexadecimal value. Thus, 2 is the high-order digit.

Step 3: Subtract the number found from 573.

$$
\begin{array}{r}
573 \\
- 512 \\
\hline
61
\end{array}
$$

Step 4: Find the number 61 (the result of the subtraction in Step 3) or the next value lower than 61 in the decimal side of the table.

Step 5: The hexadecimal digit equivalent to 48 (the decimal number found in the table) becomes the next high-order digit in the hexadecimal value. Thus, 3 is the next high-order digit.

Step 6: Subtract the number found from 61.

$$
\begin{array}{r}
61 \\
- \ 48 \\
\hline
13
\end{array}
$$

Step 7: Find the number 13 (the result of the subtraction in Step 6) or the next value lower than 13 in the decimal side of the table.

Step 8: The hexadecimal equivalent of 13 (the decimal number found) becomes the low-order digit because the value found was in the right-most column of the table. Thus, D is the low-order digit.

Step 9: Thus, the hexadecimal equivalent of the decimal value 573 is 23D.

APPENDIX C

MACROS — I/O MODULE NAMES

The following macros are used in the sample programs presented in this text and must be on the source statement library in order for the sample programs to be assembled.

MACROS:			
GET	DTFCD	WAITF	LOAD
PUT	DTFMT	SETFL	WAIT
OPEN	DTFSD	ENDFL	DUMP
OPENR	DTFIS	SETL	CANCEL
CLOSE	COMRG	ESETL	
CLOSER	EOJ	CCB	
CNTRL	READ	EXCP	
PRTOV	WRITE	DTFPR	

For any additional information about these macros, refer to IBM System Reference Library Manual C24-5037, Supervisor and Input/Output Macros.

I/O MODULES

I/O modules are IBM written routines which provide input and output processing in conjunction with the file defined by the user in DTFs. Although a module may be given any name desired by the user, it is suggested that the standard IBM names be used.

Five I/O modules are used in this text: the printer module, the card module, the tape module, the sequential disk module and the indexed sequential module. The derivation of the module names is defined below.

PRMOD – PRINTER I/O MODULE

The printer module is used for printer output functions.

Every printer module begins with the prefix IJD followed by five options to be entered in the name depending upon the features desired by the programmer.

PRMOD = IJDabcde

a = F if the RECFORM =FIXUNB (fixed unblocked)
a = V if the RECFORM = VARUNB (variable length, unblocked).
a = U if the RECFORM = UNDEF (record form is undefined)

b = A if CTLCHR = ASA is specified (use of the ASA control character)
b = Y if CTLCHR = YES is specified (use of 360 control character)
b = C if CONTROL = YES is specified (use of the CNTRL macro is desired)
b = S if STLIST is specified (use of the selective tape listing feature)
b = Z if none of the above entries for b are specified

c = P if PRINTOV = YES is specified (use of the PRTOV macro)
c = Z if PRINTOV = YES is NOT specific

d = I if IOAREA2 = YES is specified (use of two I/O areas)
d = Z if IOAREA2 = YES is not specified

e = W if WORKA = YES is specified (use of a work area)
e = Z if WORKA = YES is not specified

CDMOD – CARD I/O MODULE

The CDMOD is used for card input and output operations.

Every card is module name begins with the prefix IJC followed by five options depending upon the users needs.

CDMOD Name = IJCabcde

a = F if RECFORM = FIXUNB (record form is fixed unblocked)
a = V if RECFORM = VARUNB (record form is variable unblocked)
a = U if RECFORM = UNDEF (record form   undefined)

b = A if CTLCHR = ASA (use of ASA control chatacter)
b = Y if CTLCHR = YES (use of 360 control characters)
b = C if CONTROL = YES (use of CNTRL macro)
b = Z if none of the other entries for B are specified

c = I if TYPEFLE = Input (An input file, read cards)
c = O if TYPFLE = OUTPUT (An output file – punch cards)
c = C if TYPEFLE = CMBND (punch & read cards)

d = Z if neither WORKA nor IOAREA2 are specified
d = W if WORKA = YES is specified (a work area will be used with one I/O area)
d = I if IOAREA2 = YES (two I/O areas and no work area)
d = B if both IOAREA2 = YES and WORKA =YES

e = 0 if DEVICE = 2540
e = 1 if DEVICE = 1442
e = 2 if DEVICE = 2520
e = 3 if DEVICE = 2501
e = 4 if DEVICE = 2540 & CRDERR is specified (repunch card errors)
e = 5 if device = 2520 and CRDERR is specified

MTMOD — TAPE I/O MODULE

The MTMOD macro is used for tape input and output operations. Every tape module begins with the prefix IJF followed by five options depending upon the user's needs.

MTMOD Name = IJFabcde

a = F if RECFORM = FIXUNB or FIXBLK
a = V if RECFORM = VARUNB or VARBLK
a = U if RECFORM = UNDEF
a = S if RECFORM = SPNUNB or SPNBLK
b = B if READ = BACK
b = Z if READ = FORWARD or if READ is not specified

c = C if CKPTREC = YES
c = Z if CKPTREC = YES is not specified

d = W if WORKA = YES
d = Z if WORKA = YES is not specified

e = M if ERREXT = YES and RDONLY = YES
e = N if ERREXT = YES
e = Y if RDONLY = YES
e = Z if ERREXT and RDONLY not specified

SDMODxx — SEQUENTIAL DISK I/O MODULE

The SDMODxx macro is used for sequential disk input and output operations. The sequential disk macro used to generate the I/O module differs from all other I/O module macros because the file characteristics are separated into ten categories and a separate macro is used for each. The macros are shown below.

Macro	Module Generated
SDMODFI	Sequential direct-access device, fixed-length records, input file.
SDMODFO	Sequential direct-access device, fixed-length records, output file.
SDMODFU	Sequential direct-access device, fixed-length records, update file.
SDMODVI	Sequential direct-access device, variable-length records, input file.
SDMODVO	Sequential direct-access device, variable-length records, output file.
SDMODVU	Sequential direct-access device, variable-length records, update file.
SDMODUI	Sequential direct-access device, undefined records, input file.
SDMODUO	Sequential direct-access device, undefined records, output file.
SDMODUU	Sequential direct-access device, undefined records, update file.
SDMODW	Sequential direct-access device, work file.

Every sequential direct-access module name begins with the prefix IJG followed by five options depending upon the user's needs.

SDMODxx Name = IJGabcde

a = C if SDMODFx specifies HOLD = YES
a = F if SDMODFx does not specify HOLD = YES
a = R if SDMODUx specifies HOLD = YES
a = U if SDMODUx does not specify HOLD = YES
a = P if SDMODVx specifies HOLD = YES (spanned records)
a = Q if SDMODVx does not specify HOLD = YES (spanned records)
a = S if SDMODVx specifies HOLD = YES

b = U if SDMODxU
b = I if SDMODxI
b = O if SDMODxO

c = C if ERROPT = YES and ERREXT = YES
c = E if ERROPT = YES
c = Z if neither is specified

d = M if TRUNCS = YES and FEOVD = YES
d = T if TRUNCS = YES
d = W if FEOVD = YES
d = Z if neither is specified

e = B if CONTROL = YES and RDONLY = YES
e = C if CONTROL = YES
e = Y if RDONLY = YES
e = Z if neither is specified

ISMOD – INDEXED SEQUENTIAL I/O MODULE

The ISMOD macro is used to generate an I/O module for indexed sequential input and output operations.

Every indexed sequential module begins with the prefix IJH followed by five options.

ISMOD Name = IJHabcde

a = A if RECFORM = BOTH and IOROUT = ADD or ADDRTR
a = B if RECFORM = FIXBLK and IOROUT = ADD or ADDRTR
a = U if RECFORM = FIXUNB and IOROUT = ADD or ADDRTR
a = Z if RECFORM is not specified (that is, IOROUT = LOAD or RETRVE)

b = A if IOROUT = ADDRTR
b = I if IOROUT = ADD
b = L if IOROUT = LOAD
b = R if IOROUT = RETRVE

c = B if TYPEFLE = RANSEQ
c = G if IOAREA2 = YES and TYPEFLE = SEQNTL or IOROUT = LOAD
c = R if TYPEFLE = RANDOM
c = S if TYPEFLE = SEQNTL
c = Z if neither is specified (that is, IOROUT = LOAD or ADD)

d = C if CORINDX = YES
d = Z if CORINDX = YES is not specified

e = F if CORDATA = YES and ERREXT = YES and RDONLY = YES
e = G if CORDATA = YES and ERREXT = YES
e = O if CORDATA = YES and RDONLY = YES
e = P if CORDATA = YES
e = S if ERREXT = YES and RDONLY = YES
e = T if ERREXT = YES
e = Y if RDONLY = YES
e = Z if none of the above are specified

APPENDIX D

CHANNEL COMMAND OPERATION CODES

The following table contains all of the commands which are available for the peripheral devices on the System/360. For a detailed explanation of each operation code, consult the IBM hardware manual for the particular device.

CHANNEL COMMAND CODES

Device	Command for CCW		0	1	2	3	4	5	6	7	Hex	Dec
1052	Read Inquiry BCD		0	0	0	0	1	0	1	0	0A	10
	Read Reader 2 BCD		0	0	0	0	0	0	1	0	02	02
	Write BDC, Auto Carriage Return		0	0	0	0	1	0	0	1	09	09
	Write BDC, No Auto Carriage Return		0	0	0	0	0	0	0	1	01	01
	No Op		0	0	0	0	0	0	1	1	03	03
	Sense		0	0	0	0	0	1	0	0	04	04
	Alarm		0	0	0	0	1	0	1	1	0B	11
2540	Read, Feed, Select Stacker SS	Type AA	S	S	D	0	0	0	1	0		
	Read	Type AB	1	1	D	0	0	0	1	0		
	Read, Feed (1400 compatability mode only)		1	1	D	1	0	0	1	0		
	Feed, Select Stacker SS	Type BA	S	S	1	0	0	0	1	1		
	PFR Punch, Feed, Select Stacker SS	Type BA	S	S	D	0	1	0	0	1		
	Punch, Feed, Select Stacker SS	Type BB	S	S	D	0	0	0	0	1		

SS	Stacker		D	Data Mode
00	R1		0	EBCDIC
01	R2		1	Column Binary
10	RP3			

1442 N1

Command	M	M	M	M	Description
Read	0	0	X		Eject and SS1
Read	1	0	X		Eject and SS1
Read	0	1	X		Eject and SS2
Read	1	1	X		Eject and SS2
Write	0	0	X		SS1
Write	1	0	X		Eject and SS1
Write	0	1	X		SS2
Write	1	1	X		Eject and SS2
Control	1	0			Eject and SS1
Control	0	1			SS2
Control	1	1			Eject and SS2
Sense			1	1	Punch diagnostic
Sense			0	1	Read diagnostic

	0	1	2	3	4	5	6	7
Read	M	M	M	0	0	0	1	0
Write	M	M	M	0	0	0	0	1
Control	M	M	0	0	0	0	1	1
No Op	0	0	0	0	0	0	1	1
Sense	0	0	M	M	0	1	0	0

X = 0 means EBCDIC mode
X = 1 means Column Binary Mode

Device	Command for CCW	0	1	2	3	4	5	6	7	Hex	Dec
1403 or 1443	Write, No Space	0	0	0	0	0	0	0	1	01	01
	Write, Space 1 After Print	0	0	0	0	1	0	0	1	09	09
	Write, Space 2 After Print	0	0	0	1	0	0	0	1	11	17
	Write, Space 3 After Print	0	0	0	1	1	0	0	1	19	25
	Write, Skip To Channel N After Print	1	C	H	A	N	0	0	1		
	Diagnostic Read (1403)	0	0	0	0	0	0	1	0	02	02
	Diagnostic Read (1443)	0	0	0	0	0	1	1	0	06	06
	Sense	0	0	0	0	0	1	0	0	04	04
Carriage Control	Space 1 Line Immediately	0	0	0	0	1	0	1	1	0B	11
	Space 2 Line Immediately	0	0	0	1	0	0	1	1	13	19
	Space 3 Line Immediately	0	0	0	1	1	0	1	1	1B	27
	Skip To Channel N Immediately	1	C	H	A	N	0	1	1		
	No Op	0	0	0	0	0	0	1	1	03	03

C	H	A	N	Channel	C	H	A	N	Channel
0	0	0	1	1	0	1	1	1	7
0	0	1	0	2	1	0	0	0	8
0	0	1	1	3	1	0	0	1	9
0	1	0	0	4	1	0	1	0	10
0	1	0	1	5	1	0	1	1	11
0	1	1	0	6	1	1	0	0	12

Device	Command for CCW	0	1	2	3	4	5	6	7	Hex	Dec
UCS	Allow buffer loading	1	1	1	0	1	0	1	1	EB	235
	Load buffer (no folding)	1	1	1	1	1	0	1	1	FB	251
	Load buffer (folding)	1	1	1	1	0	0	1	1	F3	243
	Block data check latch	0	1	1	1	0	0	1	1	73	121
	Reset block data check latch	0	1	1	1	1	0	1	1	7B	129

2400 Tape*															Hex	Dec
	Read Backward (Overrides Data Converter On)					0	0	0	0	1	1	0	0		0C	12
Sense		N	N	N		0	0	0	0	0	1	0	0		04	04
Write	0	0	0	1600 bpi P.E. **		0	0	0	0	0	0	0	1		01	01
Read	0	0	1	800 bpi NRZ1		0	0	0	0	0	0	1	0		02	02
Control						0	0	C	C	C	1	1	1			
						D	D	M	M	M	0	1	1			
						1	1	N	N	N	0	1	1			

C	C	C	Control Codes	Hex	Dec
0	0	0	REW	7	7
0	0	1	RUN	0F	15
0	1	0	ERG	17	23
0	1	1	WTM	1F	31
1	0	0	BSR	27	39
1	0	1	BSF	2F	47
1	1	0	FSR	37	55
1	1	1	FSF	3F	63

D	D	7 Track Density	
0	0	200	
0	1	556	7 Track
1	0	800**	
1	1	***	

M	M	M	(Mode Modifiers)	Set Density	Set Odd Parity	Set Even Parity	Data Converter On	Data Converter Off	Translator On	Translator Off	Request TIE (Track in Error)
0	0	0	No Op								
0	0	1	Not Used								
0	1	0	Reset Condition	X	X		X			X	
0	1	1	Nine-track only								X
1	0	0		X			X		X		
1	0	1		X		X	X	X			
1	1	0	Reset Condition	X	X		X			X	
1	1	1		X	X		X	X			

*9 track op. forces 800 BPI and odd parity; also, it overrides 7 track but does not reset 7 track. Load/Sys Reset forces 7 track to 800 BPI, odd parity, data converter on, translator off.

** Reset condition

*** Set 9 Track mode, Models 4-6

DASD CHANNEL COMMAND CODES (see A26-5988 and A26-3599)

Command for CCW		Count	(M-T)Off Hex Dec		(M-T)On Hex Dec	
Control	No Op	(not zero)	03	03		
	Seek	6	07	07		
	Seek Cylinder	6	0B	11		
	Seek Head	6	1B	27		
	Set File Mask	1	1F	31		
	Space Count	(not zero)	0F	15		
	Transfer in Channel	X	X8			
	Recalibrate (Note 1)	(not zero)	13	19		
	Restore (2321 only)	X	17	23		
Sense Switching	Sense I/O	6	04	04		
	Release Device } (Note 2)	(not zero)	94	148		
	Reserve Device	(not zero)	B4	180		
Search†	Home Address EQ	4 (usually)	39	57	B9	185
	Identifier EQ	5 (usually)	31	49	B1	177
	Identifier HI	5 (usually)	51	81	D1	209
	Identifier EQ or HI	5 (usually)	71	131	F1	241
	Key EQ	1 to 255	29	41	A9	169
	Key HI	1 to 255	49	73	C9	201
	Key EQ or HI	1 to 255	69	105	E9	233
	Key & Data EQ		2D	45	AD	173
	Key & Data HI		4D	77	CD	205
Continue Scan	Key & Data EQ or HI		6D	109	ED	237
	Search EQ	(Note 3)	25	37	A5	165
	Search HI		45	69	C5	197
	Search HI or EQ		65	101	E5	229
	Set Status Modifier*		35	53	B5	181
	Set Status Modifier*		75	117	F5	245
Read†	No Status Modifier		55	85	D5	213
	Home Address	5	1A	26	9A	154
	Count	8	12	18	92	146
	Record R0		16	22	96	150
	Data	Number of bytes transferred	06	06	86	134
	Key & Data		0E	14	8E	142
	Count, Key & Data		1E	30	9E	158
	IPL		02	02		
Write	Home Address	5 (usually)	19	25		
	Record R0	8+KL+DL of R0	15	21		
	Count, Key & Data	8+KL+DL	1D	29		
	Special Count, Key & Data	8+KL+DL	01	01		
	Data	DL	05	05		
	Key & Data	KL+DL	0D	13		

*Sense byte determines which command is used.   X=not significant
† M-T On = M-T Off except during Search and Read, bit 0=1 in M-T On.
Note 1. For 2311 or 2314 only.   Note 2. Two channel switch required except for a 2314/2844 combination. , Note 3. Include mask bytes in search argument; these commands are a special feature on 2841.

SYSTEM/360 CHARACTER SET

The following table contains the complete System/360 character set.

RR FORMAT INSTRUCTIONS

Decimal	Hexadecimal	Mnemonic	Graphic & Control Symbols BCDIC	EBCDIC	(2) 7-Track Tape BCDIC	Punched Card Code	System/360 8-Bit Code
0	00			NUL		12-0-1-8-9	0000 0000
1	01			SOH		12-1-9	0000 0001
2	02			STX		12-2-9	0000 0010
3	03			ETX		12-3-9	0000 0011
4	04	SPM		PF		12-4-9	0000 0100
5	05	BALR		HT		12-5-9	0000 0101
6	06	BCTR		LC		12-6-9	0000 0110
7	07	BCR		DEL		12-7-9	0000 0111
8	08	SSK				12-8-9	0000 1000
9	09	ISK				12-1-8-9	0000 1001
10	0A	SVC		SMM		12-2-8-9	0000 1010
11	0B			VT		12-3-8-9	0000 1011
12	0C	(EBCDIC +)		FF		12-4-8-9	0000 1100
13	0D	(EBCDIC −)		CR.		12-5-8-9	0000 1101
14	0E			SO		12-6-8-9	0000 1110
15	0F			SI		12-7-8-9	0000 1111
16	10	LPR		DLE		12-11-1-8-9	0001 0000
17	11	LNR		DC1		11-1-9	0001 0001
18	12	LTR		DC2		11-2-9	0001 0010
19	13	LCR		TM		11-3-9	0001 0011
20	14	NR		RES		11-4-9	0001 0100
21	15	CLR		NL		11-5-9	0001 0101
22	16	OR		BS		11-6-9	0001 0110
23	17	XR		IL		11-7-9	0001 0111
24	18	LR		CAN		11-8-9	0001 1000
25	19	CR		EM		11-1-8-9	0001 1001
26	1A	AR		CC		11-2-8-9	0001 1010
27	1B	SR		CU1		11-3-8-9	0001 1011
28	1C	MR		IFS		11-4-8-9	0001 1100
29	1D	DR		IGS		11-5-8-9	0001 1101
30	1E	ALR		IRS		11-6-8-9	0001 1110
31	1F	SLR		IUS		11-7-8-9	0001 1111
32	20	LPDR		DS		11-0-1-8-9	0010 0000
33	21	LNDR		SOS		0-1-9	0010 0001
34	22	LTDR		FS		0-2-9	0010 0010
35	23	LCDR				0-3-9	0010 0011
36	24	HDR		BYP		0-4-9	0010 0100
37	25	LRDR		LF		0-5-9	0010 0101
38	26	MXR		ETB		0-6-9	0010 0110
39	27	MXDR		ESC		0-7-9	0010 0111
40	28	LDR				0-8-9	0010 1000
41	29	CDR				0-1-8-9	0010 1001
42	2A	ADR		SM		0-2-8-9	0010 1010
43	2B	SDR		CU2		0-3-8-9	0010 1011
44	2C	MDR				0-4-8-9	0010 1100
45	2D	DDR		ENQ		0-5-8-9	0010 1101
46	2E	AWR		ACK		0-6-8-9	0010 1110
47	2F	SWR		BEL		0-7-8-9	0010 1111
48	30	LPER				12-11-0-1-8-9	0011 0000
49	31	LNER				1-9	0011 0001
50	32	LTER		SYN		2-9	0011 0010
51	33	LCER				3-9	0011 0011
52	34	HER		PN		4-9	0011 0100
53	35	LRER		RS		5-9	0011 0101
54	36	AXR		UC		6-9	0011 0110
55	37	SXR		EOT		7-9	0011 0111
56	38	LER				8-9	0011 1000
57	39	CER				1-8-9	0011 1001
58	3A	AER				2-8-9	0011 1010
59	3B	SER		CU3		3-8-9	0011 1011
60	3C	MER		DC4		4-8-9	0011 1100
61	3D	DER		NAK		5-8-9	0011 1101
62	3E	AUR				6-8-9	0011 1110
63	3F	SUR		SUB		7-8-9	0011 1111

Decimal	Hexadecimal	Mnemonic	Graphic & Control Symbols BCDIC	EBCDIC	(2) 7-Track Tape BCDIC	Punched Card Code	System/360 8-Bit Code	(4)
64	40	STH		SP	(2)	no punches	0100 0000	
65	41	LA				12-0-1-9	0100 0001	
66	42	STC				12-0-2-9	0100 0010	
67	43	IC				12-0-3-9	0100 0011	
68	44	EX				12-0-4-9	0100 0100	
69	45	BAL				12-0-5-9	0100 0101	
70	46	BCT				12-0-6-9	0100 0110	
71	47	BC				12-0-7-9	0100 0111	
72	48	LH				12-0-8-9	0100 1000	
73	49	CH				12-1-8	0100 1001	
74	4A	AH	•	¢		12-2-8	0100 1010	
75	4B	SH	•	•	B A 8 2 1	12-3-8	0100 1011	
76	4C	MH	¤)	<	B A 8 4	12-4-8	0100 1100	
77	4D			(	B A 8 4 1	12-5-8	0100 1101	(
78	4E	CVD	<	+	B A 8 4 2	12-6-8	0100 1110	+
79	4F	CVB	‡			B A 8 4 2 1	12-7-8	0100 1111	
80	50	ST	& +	&	B A	12	0101 0000	
81	51					12-11-1-9	0101 0001	
82	52					12-11-2-9	0101 0010	
83	53					12-11-3-9	0101 0011	
84	54	N				12-11-4-9	0101 0100	
85	55	CL				12-11-5-9	0101 0101	
86	56	O				12-11-6-9	0101 0110	
87	57	X				12-11-7-9	0101 0111	
88	58	L				12-11-8-9	0101 1000	
89	59	C				11-1-8	0101 1001	
90	5A	A		!		11-2-8	0101 1010	
91	5B	S	$	$	B 8 2 1	11-3-8	0101 1011	
92	5C	M	•	•	B 8 4	11-4-8	0101 1100	
93	5D	D	]	)	B 8 4 1	11-5-8	0101 1101	)
94	5E	AL	;	;	B 8 4 2	11-6-8	0101 1110	
95	5F	SL	Δ	¬	B 8 4 2 1	11-7-8	0101 1111	
96	60	STD		−	B	11	0110 0000	
97	61		/	/	A 1	0-1	0110 0001	
98	62					11-0-2-9	0110 0010	
99	63					11-0-3-9	0110 0011	
100	64					11-0-4-9	0110 0100	
101	65					11-0-5-9	0110 0101	
102	66					11-0-6-9	0110 0110	
103	67	MXD				11-0-7-9	0110 0111	
104	68	LD				11-0-8-9	0110 1000	
105	69	CD				0-1-8	0110 1001	
106	6A	AD				12-11	0110 1010	
107	6B	SD	,	,	A 8 2 1	0-3-8	0110 1011	
108	6C	MD	%(	%	A 8 4	0-4-8	0110 1100	
109	6D	DD	Y	_	A 8 4 1	0-5-8	0110 1101	
110	6E	AW	\	>	A 8 4 2	0-6-8	0110 1110	
111	6F	SW	⧻	?	A 8 4 2 1	0-7-8	0110 1111	
112	70	STE				12-11-0	0111 0000	
113	71					12-11-0-1-9	0111 0001	
114	72					12-11-0-2-9	0111 0010	
115	73					12-11-0-3-9	0111 0011	
116	74					12-11-0-4-9	0111 0100	
117	75					12-11-0-5-9	0111 0101	
118	76					12-11-0-6-9	0111 0110	
119	77					12-11-0-7-9	0111 0111	
120	78	LE				12-11-0-8-9	0111 1000	
121	79	CE				1-8	0111 1001	
122	7A	AE	ƀ	:	A	2-8	0111 1010	
123	7B	SE	# =	#	8 2 1	3-8	0111 1011	
124	7C	ME	@	@	8 4	4-8	0111 1100	
125	7D	DE	:	'	8 4 1	5-8	0111 1101	'
126	7E	AU	>	=	8 4 2	6-8	0111 1110	=
127	7F	SU	√	"	8 4 2 1	7-8	0111 1111	

Decimal	Hexa-decimal	Mnemonic	Graphic & Control Symbols BCDIC	EBCDIC	(2) 7-Track Tape BCDIC	Punched Card Code	System/360 8-Bit Code
128	80	SSM				12-0-1-8	1000 0000
129	81			a		12-0-1	1000 0001
130	82	LPSW		b		12-0-2	1000 0010
131	83	(Diagnose)		c		12-0-3	1000 0011
132	84	WRD		d		12-0-4	1000 0100
133	85	RDD		e		12-0-5	1000 0101
134	86	BXH		f		12-0-6	1000 0110
135	87	BXLE		g		12-0-7	1000 0111
136	88	SRL		h		12-0-8	1000 1000
137	89	SLL		i		12-0-9	1000 1001
138	8A	SRA				12-0-2-8	1000 1010
139	8B	SLA				12-0-3-8	1000 1011
140	8C	SRDL				12-0-4-8	1000 1100
141	8D	SLDL				12-0-5-8	1000 1101
142	8E	SRDA				12-0-6-8	1000 1110
143	8F	SLDA				12-0-7-8	1000 1111
144	90	STM				12-11-1-8	1001 0000
145	91	TM		j		12-11-1	1001 0001
146	92	MVI		k		12-11-2	1001 0010
147	93	TS		l		12-11-3	1001 0011
148	94	NI		m		12-11-4	1001 0100
149	95	CLI		n		12-11-5	1001 0101
150	96	OI		o		12-11-6	1001 0110
151	97	XI		p		12-11-7	1001 0111
152	98	LM		q		12-11-8	1001 1000
153	99			r		12-11-9	1001 1001
154	9A					12-11-2-8	1001 1010
155	9B					12-11-3-8	1001 1011
156	9C	SIO				12-11-4-8	1001 1100
157	9D	TIO				12-11-5-8	1001 1101
158	9E	HIO				12-11-6-8	1001 1110
159	9F	TCH				12-11-7-8	1001 1111
160	A0					11-0-1-8	1010 0000
161	A1					11-0-1	1010 0001
162	A2			s		11-0-2	1010 0010
163	A3			t		11-0-3	1010 0011
164	A4			u		11-0-4	1010 0100
165	A5			v		11-0-5	1010 0101
166	A6			w		11-0-6	1010 0110
167	A7			x		11-0-7	1010 0111
168	A8			y		11-0-8	1010 1000
169	A9			z		11-0-9	1010 1001
170	AA					11-0-2-8	1010 1010
171	AB					11-0-3-8	1010 1011
172	AC					11-0-4-8	1010 1100
173	AD					11-0-5-8	1010 1101
174	AE					11-0-6-8	1010 1110
175	AF					11-0-7-8	1010 1111
176	B0					12-11-0-1-8	1011 0000
177	B1					12-11-0-1	1011 0001
178	B2					12-11-0-2	1011 0010
179	B3					12-11-0-3	1011 0011
180	B4					12-11-0-4	1011 0100
181	B5					12-11-0-5	1011 0101
182	B6					12-11-0-6	1011 0110
183	B7					12-11-0-7	1011 0111
184	B8					12-11-0-8	1011 1000
185	B9					12-11-0-9	1011 1001
186	BA					12-11-0-2-8	1011 1010
187	BB					12-11-0-3-8	1011 1011
188	BC					12-11-0-4-8	1011 1100
189	BD					12-11-0-5-8	1011 1101
190	BE					12-11-0-6-8	1011 1110
191	BF					12-11-0-7-8	1011 1111

Decimal	Hexa-decimal	Mnemonic	Graphic & Control Symbols BCDIC	EBCDIC	(2) 7-Track Tape BCDIC	Punched Card Code	System/360 8-Bit Code
192	C0		?		B A 8 2	12-0	1100 0000
193	C1		A	A	B A 1	12-1	1100 0001
194	C2		B	B	B A 2	12-2	1100 0010
195	C3		C	C	B A 2 1	12-3	1100 0011
196	C4		D	D	B A 4	12-4	1100 0100
197	C5		E	E	B A 4 1	12-5	1100 0101
198	C6		F	F	B A 4 2	12-6	1100 0110
199	C7		G	G	B A 4 2 1	12-7	1100 0111
200	C8		H	H	B A 8	12-8	1100 1000
201	C9		I	I	B A 8 1	12-9	1100 1001
202	CA					12-0-2-8-9	1100 1010
203	CB					12-0-3-8-9	1100 1011
204	CC					12-0-4-8-9	1100 1100
205	CD					12-0-5-8-9	1100 1101
206	CE					12-0-6-8-9	1100 1110
207	CF					12-0-7-8-9	1100 1111
208	D0		!		B 8 2	11-0	1101 0000
209	D1	MVN	J	J	B 1	11-1	1101 0001
210	D2	MVC	K	K	B 2	11-2	1101 0010
211	D3	MVZ	L	L	B 2 1	11-3	1101 0011
212	D4	NC	M	M	B 4	11-4	1101 0100
213	D5	CLC	N	N	B 4 1	11-5	1101 0101
214	D6	OC	O	O	B 4 2	11-6	1101 0110
215	D7	XC	P	P	B 4 2 1	11-7	1101 0111
216	D8		Q	Q	B 8	11-8	1101 1000
217	D9		R	R	B 8 1	11-9	1101 1001
218	DA					12-11-2-8-9	1101 1010
219	DB					12-11-3-8-9	1101 1011
220	DC	TR				12-11-4-8-9	1101 1100
221	DD	TRT				12-11-5-8-9	1101 1101
222	DE	ED (3)				12-11-6-8-9	1101 1110
223	DF	EDMK (3)				12-11-7-8-9	1101 1111
224	E0		‡		A 8 2	0-2-8	1110 0000
225	E1					11-0-1-9	1110 0001
226	E2		S	S	A 2	0-2	1110 0010
227	E3		T	T	A 2 1	0-3	1110 0011
228	E4		U	U	A 4	0-4	1110 0100
229	E5		V	V	A 4 1	0-5	1110 0101
230	E6		W	W	A 4 2	0-6	1110 0110
231	E7		X	X	A 4 2 1	0-7	1110 0111
232	E8		Y	Y	A 8	0-8	1110 1000
233	E9		Z	Z	A 8 1	0-9	1110 1001
234	EA					11-0-2-8-9	1110 1010
235	EB					11-0-3-8-9	1110 1011
236	EC					11-0-4-8-9	1110 1100
237	ED					11-0-5-8-9	1110 1101
238	EE					11-0-6-8-9	1110 1110
239	EF					11-0-7-8-9	1110 1111
240	F0		0	0	8 2	0	1111 0000
241	F1	MVO	1	1	1	1	1111 0001
242	F2	PACK	2	2	2	2	1111 0010
243	F3	UNPK	3	3	2 1	3	1111 0011
244	F4		4	4	4	4	1111 0100
245	F5		5	5	4 1	5	1111 0101
246	F6		6	6	4 2	6	1111 0110
247	F7		7	7	4 2 1	7	1111 0111
248	F8	ZAP (3)	8	8	8	8	1111 1000
249	F9	CP (3)	9	9	8 1	9	1111 1001
250	FA	AP (3)				12-11-0-2-8-9	1111 1010
251	FB	SP (3)				12-11-0-3-8-9	1111 1011
252	FC	MP (3)				12-11-0-4-8-9	1111 1100
253	FD	DP (3)				12-11-0-5-8-9	1111 1101
254	FE					12-11-0-6-8-9	1111 1110
255	FF					12-11-0-7-8-9	1111 1111

APPENDIX F

SYSTEM/360 INSTRUCTION SET

The following table contains the standard instruction set and the decimal feature instruction set.

STANDARD INSTRUCTION SET

NAME	MNEMONIC	TYPE	CODE	OPERAND
Add	AR	RR	1A	R1, R2
Add	A	RX	5A	R1, D2 (X2, B2)
Add Halfword	AH	RX	4A	R1, D2 (X2, B2)
Add Logical	ALR	RR	1E	R1, R2
Add Logical	AL	RX	5E	R1, D2 (X2, B2)
AND	NR	RR	14	R1, R2
AND	N	RX	54	R1, D2 (X2, B2)
AND	NI	SI	94	D1 (B1), I2
AND	NC	SS	D4	D1 (L, B1), D2 (B2)
Branch and Link	BALR	RR	05	R1, R2
Branch and Link	BAL	RX	45	R1, D2 (X2, B2)
Branch on Condition	BCR	RR	07	M1, R2
Branch on Condition	BC	RX	47	M1, D2 (X2, B2)
Branch on Count	BCTR	RR	06	R1, R2
Branch on Count	BCT	RX	46	R1, D2 (X2, B2)
Branch on Index High	BXH	RS	86	R1, R3, D2 (B2)
Branch on Index Low or Equal	BXLE	RS	87	R1, R3, D2 (B2)
Compare	CR	RR	19	R1, R2
Compare	C	RX	59	R1, D2 (X2, B2)
Compare Halfword	CH	RX	49	R1, D2 (X2, B2)
Compare Logical	CLR	RR	15	R1, R2
Compare Logical	CL	RX	55	R1, D2 (X2, B2)
Compare Logical	CLC	SS	D5	D1 (L, B1), D2 (B2)
Compare Logical	CLI	SI	95	D1 (B1), I2
Convert to Binary	CVB	RX	4F	R1, D2 (X2, B2)
Convert to Decimal	CVD	RX	4E	R1, D2 (X2, B2)
Diagnose		SI	83	
Divide	DR	RR	1D	R1, R2
Divide	D	RX	5D	R1, D2 (X2, B2)
Exclusive OR	XR	RR	17	R1, R2
Exclusive OR	X	RX	57	F1, D2 (X2, B2)
Exclusive OR	XI	SI	97	D1 (B1), I2
Exclusive OR	XC	SS	D7	D1 (L, B1), D2 (B2)
Execute	EX	RX	44	R1, D2 (X2, B2)
Halt I/O	HIO	SI	9E	D1 (B1)
Insert Character	IC	RX	43	R1, D2 (X2, B2)
Load	LR	RR	18	R1, R2
Load	L	RX	58	R1, D2 (X2, B2)
Load Address	LA	RX	41	R1, D2 (X2, B2)
Load and Test	LTR	RR	12	R1, R2
Load Complement	LCR	RR	13	R1, R2
Load Halfword	LH	RX	48	R1, D2 (X2, B2)
Load Multiple	LM	RS	98	R1, R3, D2 (B2)
Load Negative	LNR	RR	11	R1, R2
Load Positive	LPR	RR	10	R1, R2
Load PSW	LPSW	SI	82	D1 (B1)
Move	MVI	SI	92	D1 (B1), I2
Move	MVC	SS	D2	D1 (L, B1), D2 (B2)
Move Numerics	MVN	SS	D1	D1 (L, B1), D2 (B2)
Move with Offset	MVO	SS	F1	D1 (L1, B1), D2 (L2, B2)
Move Zones	MVZ	SS	D3	D1 (L, B1), D2 (B2)
Multiply	MR	RR	1C	R1, R2
Multiply	M	RX	5C	R1, D2 (X2, B2)
Multiply Halfword	MH	RX	4C	R1, D2 (X2, B2)

OR	OR	RR	16	R1, R2
OR	O	RX	56	R1, D2 (X2, B2)
OR	OI	SI	96	D1 (B1), I2
OR	OC	SS	D6	D1 (L, B1), D2 (B2)
Pack	PACK	SS	F2	D1 (L1, B1), D2 (L2, B2)
Set Program Mask	SPM	RR	04	R1
Set System Mask	SSM	SI	80	D1 (B1)
Shift Left Double	SLDA	RS	8F	R1, D2 (B2)
Shift Left Single	SLA	RS	8B	R1, D2 (B2)
Shift Left Double Logical	SLDL	RS	8D	R1, D2 (B2)
Shift Left Single Logical	SLL	RS	89	R1, D2 (B2)
Shift Right Double	SRDA	RS	8E	R1, D2 (B2)
Shift Right Single	SRA	RS	8A	R1, D2 (B2)
Shift Right Double Logical	SRDL	RS	8C	R1, D2 (B2)
Shift Right Single Logical	SRL	RS	88	R1, D2 (B2)
Start I/O	SIO	SI	9C	D1 (B1)
Store	ST	RX	50	R1, D2 (X2, B2)
Store Character	STC	RX	42	R1, D2 (X2, B2)
Store Halfword	STH	RX	40	R1, D2 (X2, B2)
Store Multiple	STM	RS	90	R1, R3, D2 (B2)
Subtract	SR	RR	1B	R1, R2
Subtract	S	RX	5B	R1, D2 (X2, B2)
Subtract Halfword	SH	RX	4B	R1, D2 (X2, B2)
Subtract Logical	SLR	RR	1F	R1, R2
Subtract Logical	SL	RX	5F	R1, D2 (X2, B2)
Supervisor Call	SVC	RR	0A	I
Test and Set	TS	SI	93	D1 (B1)
Test Channel	TCH	SI	9F	D1 (B1)
Test I/O	TIO	SI	9D	D1 (B1)
Test Under Mask	TM	SI	91	D1 (B1), I2
Translate	TR	SS	DC	D1 (L, B1), D2 (B2)
Translate and Test	TRT	SS	DD	D1 (L, B1), D2 (B2)
Unpack	UNPK	SS	F3	D1 (L1, B1), D2 (L2, B2)

DECIMAL FEATURE INSTRUCTIONS

Add Decimal	AP	SS	FA	D1 (L1, B1), D2 (L2, B2)
Compare Decimal	CP	SS	F9	D1 (L1, B1), D2 (L2, B2)
Divide Decimal	DP	SS	FD	D1 (L1, B1), D2 (L2, B2)
Edit	ED	SS	DE	D1 (L, B1), D2 (B2)
Edit and Mark	EDMK	SS	DF	D1 (L, B1), D2 (B2)
Multiply Decimal	MP	SS	FC	D1 (L1, B1), D2 (L2, B2)
Subtract Decimal	SP	SS	FB	D1 (L1, B1), D2 (L2, B2)
Zero and Add	ZAP	SS	F8	D1 (L1, B1), D2 (L2, B2)

CONDITION CODES

The following table gives the condition code settings and masks to test after arithmetic instructions and logical operations.

CONDITION CODES

	0	1	2	3
Condition Code Setting	0	1	2	3
Mask Bit Position	8	4	2	1

FLOATING-POINT ARITHMETIC

Add Normalized S/L	zero	<zero	>zero	– –
Add Unnormalized S/L	zero	<zero	>zero	– –
Compare S/L (A:B)	equal	A low	A high	– –
Load and Test S/L	zero	<zero	>zero	– –
Load Complement S/L	zero	<zero	>zero	– –
Load Negative S/L	zero	<zero	– –	– –
Load Positive S/L	zero	– –	>zero	– –
Subtract Normalized S/L	zero	<zero	>zero	– –
Subtract Unnormalized S/L	zero	<zero	>zero	– –

FIXED-POINT ARITHMETIC

Add H/F	zero	<zero	>zero	overflow
Add Logical	zero, no carry	not zero, no carry	zero, carry	not zero, carry
Compare H/F (A:B)	equal	A low	A high	– –
Load and Test	zero	<zero	>zero	– –
Load Complement	zero	<zero	>zero	overflow
Load Negative	zero	<zero	– –	– –
Load Positive	zero	– –	>zero	overflow
Shift Left Double	zero	<zero	>zero	overflow
Shift Left Single	zero	<zero	>zero	overflow
Shift Right Double	zero	<zero	>zero	– –
Shift Right Single	zero	<zero	>zero	– –
Subtract H/F	zero	<zero	>zero	overflow
Subtract Logical	– –	not zero, no carry	zero, carry	not zero, carry

DECIMAL ARITHMETIC

Add Decimal	zero	<zero	>zero	overflow
Compare Decimal (A:B)	equal	A low	A high	– –
Subtract Decimal	zero	<zero	>zero	overflow
Zero and Add	zero	<zero	>zero	overflow

LOGICAL OPERATIONS

AND	zero	not zero	– –	– –
Compare Logical (A:B)	equal	A low	A high	– –
Edit	zero	<zero	>zero	– –
Edit and Mark	zero	<zero	>zero	– –
Exclusive OR	zero	not zero	– –	– –
OR	zero	not zero	– –	– –
Test Under Mask	zero	mixed	– –	one
Translate and Test	zero	incomplete	complete	– –

The table below illustrates the extended mnemonic instruction codes which can be used after compare instructions, arithmetic instructions and the test under mask instruction.

EXTENDED MNEMONIC INSTRUCTION CODES

GENERAL

Extended Code	Machine Instruction	Meaning
B D2(X2,B2)	BC 15, D2(X2,B2)	Branch Unconditionally
BR R2	BCR 15, R2	Branch Unconditionally
NOP D2(X2,B2)	BC 0, D2(X2,B2)	No Operation
NOPR R2	BCR 0, R2	No Operation (RR)

AFTER COMPARE INSTRUCTIONS (A:B)

BH D2(X2,B2)	BC 2, D2(X2,B2)	Branch on A High
BL D2(X2,B2)	BC 4, D2(X2,B2)	Branch on A Low
BE D2(X2,B2)	BC 8, D2(X2,B2)	Branch on A Equal B
BNH D2(X2,B2)	BC 13, D2(X2,B2)	Branch on A Not High
BNL D2(X2,B2)	BC 11, D2(X2,B2)	Branch on A Not Low
BNE D2(X2,B2)	BC 7, D2(X2,B2)	Branch on A Not Equal B

AFTER ARITHMETIC INSTRUCTIONS

BO D2(X2,B2)	BC 1, D2(X2,B2)	Branch on Overflow
BP D2(X2,B2)	BC 2, D2(X2,B2)	Branch on Plus
BM D2(X2,B2)	BC 4, D2(X2,B2)	Branch on Minus
BZ D2(X2,B2)	BC 8, D2(X2,B2)	Branch on Zero
BNP D2(X2,B2)	BC 13, D2(X2,B2)	Branch on Not Plus
BNM D2(X2,B2)	BC 11, D2(X2,B2)	Branch on Not Minus
BNZ D2(X2,B2)	BC 7, D2(X2,B2)	Branch on Not Zero

AFTER TEST UNDER MASK INSTRUCTIONS

BO D2(X2,B2)	BC 1, D2(X2,B2)	Branch if Ones
BM D2(X2,B2)	BC 4, D2(X2,B2)	Branch if Mixed
BZ D2(X2,B2)	BC 8, D2(X2,B2)	Branch if Zeros
BNO D2(X2,B2)	BC 14, D2(X2,B2)	Branch if Not Ones

APPENDIX H

JOB CONTROL AND SORT CONTROL

The following listings contain the job control and sort control cards which were used to execute the sample programs presented in the text.

```
// JOB SALESUPD
// OPTION LINK,DUMP                          CHAPTER 2
   INCLUDE
      ___
      ___

   OBJECT DECK — CHAPTER 2
      ___
      ___
/*
// LBLTYP TAPE
// EXEC LNKEDT
// ASSGN SYS010,X'180'
// ASSGN SYS011,X'181'
// UPSI 10000000 — USED IF "FIRST-TIME"
// TLBL MSTRIN,'SALES MASTER'
// TLBL MSTROUT,'SALES MASTER'
// EXEC
      ___
      ___

   SORTED INPUT DATA
      ___
      ___
/*
/&
```

```
      // JOB TESTINV                                          CHAPTER 3
      // ASSGN SYS004,X'091'
      // ASSGN SYS005,X'091'
      // ASSGN SYS006,X'091'
      // OPTION LINK,DUMP
       ACTION MAP
       INCLUDE
          ---
          ---
       OBJECT DECK - CHAPTER 3
          ---
          ---


      /*
      // EXEC LNKEDT
      // DLBL SEQDISK,'CARD OUTPUT',69/001,SD
      // EXTENT SYS004,111111,1,0,1600,3
      // EXEC
          ---
          ---
       TEST DATA TO LOAD MASTER FILE
          ---
          ---

      /*
      // DLBL FILEA,'CARD OUTPUT',69/001,SD       CHAPTER 4
      // EXTENT SYS004,111111,1,0,1600,3
      // DLBL FILEO,'SORT OUTPUT',69/001,SD
      // EXTENT SYS005,111111,1,0,1603,3
      // DLBL FILEW,'SORT WORK',69/001,DA
      // EXTENT SYS006,111111,1,0,1606,6
      // EXEC DSORT
       SORT FIELDS=(1,7,A),FORMAT=BI,SIZE=25
       INPFIL INPUT=D,BLKSIZE=(3600,X),VOLUME=1
       RECORD TYPE=F,LENGTH=(80,,90)
       OUTFIL OUTPUT=D,BLKSIZE=3600
       OPTION PRINT,VERIFY
       END
      /*
      // OPTION LINK
       ACTION MAP
       INCLUDE
          ---
          ---
       OBJECT DECK - CHAPTER 4
          ---
          ---

      /*
      // LBLTYP NSD(04)
      // EXEC LNKEDT
      // DLBL DISKIN,'SORT OUTPUT',69/001,SD
      // EXTENT SYS006,111111,1,0,1603,3
      // DLBL INVMSTR,'INVENTORY MASTER',69/001,ISC
      // EXTENT SYS005,111111,4,0,1630,1
      // EXTENT SYS005,111111,4,1,1631,5
      // EXTENT SYS005,111111,1,2,1640,30
      // EXTENT SYS005,111111,2,3,1670,10
      // EXEC
      /*
```

```
// OPTION LINK                                              CHAPTER 5
  ACTION MAP
  INCLUDE
     __
     __

  OBJECT DECK — CHAPTER 5
     __
     __
/*
// LBLTYP NSD(04)
// EXEC LNKEDT
// DLBL MSTRIN,'INVENTORY MASTER',69/001,ISE
// EXTENT SYS005,111111,4,0,1630,1
// EXTENT SYS005,111111,4,1,1631,5
// EXTENT SYS005,111111,1,2,1640,30
// EXTENT SYS005,111111,2,3,1670,10
// EXEC
// OPTION LINK
  ACTION MAP
  INCLUDE                                                   CHAPTER 6
     __
     __

  OBJECT DECK — CHAPTER 3
     __
     __
/*
// EXEC LNKEDT
// DLBL SEQDISK,'CARD OUTPUT',69/001,SD
// EXTENT SYS004,111111,1,0,1600,3
// EXEC
     __
     __

  TEST DATA TO UPDATE MASTER FILE
     __
     __

/*
// DLBL FILEA,'CARD OUTPUT',69/001,SD
// EXTENT SYS004,111111,1,0,1600,3
// DLBL FILEO,'SORT OUTPUT',69/001,SD
// EXTENT SYS005,111111,1,0,1603,3
// DLBL FILEW,'SORT WORK',69/001,DA
// EXTENT SYS006,111111,1,0,1606,6
// EXEC DSORT
 SORT FIELDS=(1,7,A),FORMAT=BI,SIZE=25
 INPFIL INPUT=D,BLKSIZE=(3600,X),VOLUME=1
 RECORD TYPE=F,LENGTH=(80,,80)
 OUTFIL OUTPUT=D,BLKSIZE=3600
 OPTION PRINT,VERIFY
 END
/*
```

```
// OPTION LINK
 ACTION MAP
 INCLUDE
   ──
   ──
 OBJECT DECK – CHAPTER 6
   ──
   ──

/*
// LBLTYP NSD(04)
// EXEC LNKEDT
// DLBL DISKIN,'SORT OUTPUT',69/001,SD
// EXTENT SYS006,111111,1,0,1603,3
// DLBL INVMSTR,'INVENTORY MASTER',69/001,ISE
// EXTENT SYS005,111111,4,0,1630,1
// EXTENT SYS005,111111,4,1,1631,5
// EXTENT SYS005,111111,1,2,1640,30
// EXTENT SYS005,111111,2,3,1670,10
// EXEC                                                    CHAPTER 7
/*
// DLBL DISKFLE,'INVENTORY MASTER',69/001,ISE
// EXTENT SYS005,111111,4,0,1630,1
// EXTENT SYS005,111111,4,1,1631,5
// EXTENT SYS005,111111,1,2,1640,30
// EXTENT SYS005,111111,2,3,1670,10
// LBLTYP NSD(03)
// EXEC MSTRLSTR
/&                                                         CHAPTER 8
// JOB PRINT
// OPTION DUMP
// ASSGN SYS004,X'091'
// ASSGN SYS005,X'091'
// ASSGN SYS006,X'091'
// DLBL DISKFLE,'INVENTORY MASTER',69/001,ISE
// EXTENT SYS005,111111,4,0,1630,1
// EXTENT SYS005,111111,4,1,1631,5
// EXTENT SYS005,111111,1,2,1640,30
// EXTENT SYS005,111111,2,3,1670,10
// TLBL TAPEFLE,'TAPE OUTPUT'
// LBLTYP NSD(04)
// EXEC MSTRUTIL
     PRINT,MASTER
/*
/&
```

For a detailed description of the job control cards, see IBM SRL C24-5036, SYSTEM
CONTROL AND SYSTEM SERVICE PROGRAMS. The sort cards are described in detail
in IBM SRL C24-3444, DOS DISK SORT.

APPENDIX I

CATALOGUING PROGRAMS IN CORE IMAGE LIBRARY

The following listing illustrates the job control cards used to catalog the sample program in Chapter 7. In addition, the link-edit map is illustrated.

```
// JOB ASSEM
// OPTION CATAL,XREF
 ACTION MAP
 PHASE MSTRLSTR,+0
// EXEC ASSEMBLY
    ══════

 SOURCE DECK

    ══════

/*



 INCLUDE DISK1
 INCLUDE PRINT1
// EXEC LNKEDT



 JOB   ASSEM     08/24/70   DISK LINKAGE EDITOR DIAGNOSTIC OF INPUT

 ACTION TAKEN    MAP
 LIST     PHASE MSTRLSTR,+0
 LIST     INCLUDE DISK1
 LIST     INCLUDE PRINT1
 LIST     AUTOLINK   IJDFAZZZ
 LIST     AUTOLINK   IJHZRSZZ
 LIST     ENTRY
```

08/24/70	PHASE	XFR-AD	LOCORE	HICORE	DSK-AD	ESD TYPE	LABEL	LOADED	REL-FR
	MSTRLSTR	000000	000000	001B55	4A 08 2	CSECT	PRTMASTR	000000	000000
						CSECT	DISK1	000548	000548
						ENTRY	DISKFLE	000548	
					* ENTRY	DISKKEY	000670	
					* ENTRY	DISKIO1	000677	
					* ENTRY	DISKIOW	00146E	
						CSECT	IJHZRSZZ	001628	001628
						CSECT	PRINT1	0014A8	0014A8
						ENTRY	PRTIO1	0014D8	
						ENTRY	PRTDTF	0014A8	
						CSECT	IJDFAZZZ	001560	001560

For additional information on cataloguing programs, see IBM SRL C24-5036, SYSTEM CONTROL AND SYSTEM SERVICE PROGRAMS.

TEST DATA FOR PROGRAMMING ASSIGNMENTS

This appendix contains suggested test data to be used in the programming assignments presented in Chapters 2, 3, 6, and 9. The input to the programs in the other chapters are disk files created from this input. In addition, the printed results of each program are presented provided that this test data is used in the program.

CHAPTER 2 — Sequential Update

For this assignment, two sets of data are used. The first set is to load the sequential master file and the second set is to update the master file. In addition to valid data for the program, invalid data is provided. It is suggested that the program first be tested using the valid data to ensure that all major functions of the program are being performed. The data with errors can then be included to check out the error routines.

Data To Create The Master File

Valid Data:

	1-10	11-20	21-30	31-40	41-50	51-60	61-70	71-80
1	6Ø1ØØBATES, TONY F.		Ø819Ø66	Ø4	4			
2	6Ø179DAMSON, ERIC C.		Ø3525Ø2	Ø2	4			
3	6Ø292EVERLEY, DONNA M.		Ø332ØØØ	Ø2	4			
4	6Ø4Ø9ICK, MICK W.		Ø41Ø122	Ø2	4			
5	6Ø6Ø7ODELLE, NICHOLAS P		Ø5825Ø7	Ø3	4			
6	6Ø825TILLMAN, DON M.		123Ø444	Ø5	4			
7	7Ø214EDMONSON, RICK T.		ØØ79Ø67	Ø3	4			
8	7Ø31ØGORMALLY, MARIE N.		Ø389ØØ2	Ø6	4			
9	7Ø332HELD, ANNA J.		Ø244ØØØ	Ø9	4			
10	7Ø689OWNEY, REED M.		Ø437788	Ø9	4			
11	7Ø8Ø2SHEA, MICHAEL H.		Ø642Ø33	Ø8	4			
12	8Ø1Ø2BELLSLEY, ARTHUR A.		Ø883ØØØ	Ø9	4			
13	8Ø282ESTABAN, JUAN L.		1984Ø55	1Ø	4			
14	8Ø322HARLETON, JEAN H.		Ø78Ø899	Ø6	4			
15	8Ø5Ø5LAMBERT, JERRY O.		Ø154ØØ1	Ø4	4			
16	8Ø921ULL, GEORGE A.		18Ø2ØØØ	Ø9	4			
17	9Ø1Ø5BOYLE, RALPH P.		Ø878Ø44	Ø6	4			
18	9Ø215EDSON, WILBUR S.		Ø6Ø7Ø5Ø	Ø7	4			
19	9Ø315HALE, ALAN A.		1274ØØØ	Ø8	4			
20	9Ø574MELTZ, FRANK K.		Ø754366	1Ø	4			

Invalid Data:

NOTES:

FIELD IDENTIFICATION								
1-10	11-20	21-30	31-40	41-50	51-60	61-70	71-80	
1234567890	1234567890	1234567890	1234567890	1234567890	1234567890	1234567890	1234567890	

1 7φ21AEDMONSON, RICK T.   φφ79φ67   φ3   4   - INVALID S.M. NUMBER -

2 7φ31φGORMALLY, MARIE N.   7φ35   φ8   4   - INVALID SALES AMOUNT -

3 9φ315HALE, ALAN A.   φ973642   φ3   2   - INVALID TYPE CODE

4

5

Data To Update The Master File

Valid Data:

NOTES:

FIELD IDENTIFICATION								
1-10	11-20	21-30	31-40	41-50	51-60	61-70	71-80	
1234567890	1234567890	1234567890	1234567890	1234567890	1234567890	1234567890	1234567890	

1 6φ179   φφφ4φ67   3

2 6φ4φ9   φφ27643   3

3 6φ6φ7   2

4 6φ825   φφφφ1φφ   3

5 6φ927HILLARY, JAMES H.   φφ2φ1φ5   φ1   1

6 8φ5φ5   φφ36742   3

7 9φ215   2

8 9φ574   φφφ7243   3

9

10

11

Invalid Data:

NOTES:

FIELD IDENTIFICATION								
1-10	11-20	21-30	31-40	41-50	51-60	61-70	71-80	
1234567890	1234567890	1234567890	1234567890	1234567890	1234567890	1234567890	1234567890	

1 6φ1φφ   φ74   3   - INVALID SALES AMOUNT -

2 7φ214EDMONSON, RICK T.   φφ27385   φ6   1   - DUPLICATE MASTER RECORD -

3 7φ31A   2   - INVALID S.M. NUMBER -

4 8φ914   2   - NO MASTER RECORD -

5 85213   φφφ2167   3   - NO MASTER RECORD -

6

7

CHAPTER 3 — Card to Disk

The program written for the programming assignment in Chapter 3 is used for two purposes: To build the sequential disk file which will be input to load the Sales Master file (Chapter 4) and to build a sequential disk file which will contain transactions to update the master file (Chapter 6). Thus, one set of data is presented for loading the master file and one set of data for updating the master. As in Chapter 2, both valid and invalid data is included.

Data To Load The Master File

Valid Data

NOTES:

	1-10	11-20	21-30	31-40	41-50	51-60	61-70	71-80
1	10004ACHER, WILLIAM C.			00675241ø	000001			
2	10185DONNEMAN, THOMAS M.			0090019 1ø	0010201			
3	10300FELDMAN, MIKE R.			003000010	000001			
4	10325HATFIELD, MARK I.			0020539 1ø	0002201			
5	10730REEDE, OWEN W.			010514410	0023101			
6	10960WINGLAND, KEITH E.			003500010	000001			
7	20111CARTOLER, VIOLET B.			00750612	0011401			
8	20304FROMM, STEVE V.			01200012	0018231			
9	2059ØNEIL, CLARENCE N.			00950312	0023241			
10	20801SCHEIBER, HARRY T.			003250812	000520 1			
11	20956WANGLEY, THEO. A.			001500012	0002751			
12	30030ALLOREN, RUTH W.			00000015	000001			
13	30181DELBERT, EDWARD D.			013055415	000001			
14	30318HANEY, CAROL S.			014500015	0060191			
15	30487KING, MILDRED J.			01804 29 15	0053221			
16	30834TRAWLEY, HARRIS T.			00550015	0013291			
17	40027ALHOUER, ELAINE E.			00220612	000401			
18	40171COSTA, NAN S.			00560212	009031			
19	40317HANBEE, ALETA O.			00395012	0011801			
20	40721RASSMUSEN, JOHN J.			010000 12	0023461			

Invalid Data

FIELD IDENTIFICATION

	1-10	11-20	21-30	31-40	41-50	51-60	61-70	71-80
1	1004BSHEA, MICHAEL H.			008200910		0046801	— INVALID S.M. NO. —	
2	10050GROLER, GRACE B.			020542015		0483696	— INVALID TYPE CODE —	
3	7A214EDMONSON, RICK T.			003305710		0000001	— INVALID DEPT NO —	
4	60179DAMSON, ERIC C.			0180888 2C		0002231	— INVALID CURRENT SALES —	
5	90574MELTZ, FRANK K.			005903012		000000A	— INVALID TYPE CODE —	
6	40721RASSMUSEN, JOHN J.			010000012		0023461	— DUPLICATE LOAD REC. —	
7								
8								

Data To Update The Master File

Valid Data

FIELD IDENTIFICATION

	1-10	11-20	21-30	31-40	41-50	51-60	61-70	71-80
1	10004ACHER, WILLIAM J.					2		
2	10004			0006467		3		
3	10004					0005005		
4	10730		12			4		
5	20111			0005000		3		
6	20304			0065000		3		
7	20590		15			4		
8	20590			0072024		3		
9	20590					0006005		
10	20673TELLER, STEPHEN U.			017700912		0322226		
11	20956					7		
12	30030					7		
13	30318HANEY, MARIE S.					2		
14	30487		10			4		
15	40171COSTA, NANCY S.					2		
16	40317			0001700		3		
17	40317					0034005		
18	50734OWNEY, REED M.			005306610		0011326		

Invalid Data

FIELD IDENTIFICATION

1–10	11–20	21–30	31–40	41–50	51–60	61–70	71–80
1234567890	1234567890	1234567890	1234567890	1234567890	1234567890	1234567890	1234567890

```
1  1Ø185DONNEMAN, THOMAS M.        ØØ9ØØ19 1Ø      ØØ1Ø2Ø6    - DUPLICATE ADDITION REC.-
2  1Ø3Ø4                                                 7    - RECORD NOT ON FILE -
3  2Ø3ØØ                           ØØØ6437              3    - RECORD NOT ON FILE -
4  4Ø171 COSTA, NAN S.             ØØ56ØØ212       ØØØ9Ø36    - DUPLICATE ADDITION REC-
5  4Ø721                               15              1    - INVALID TYPE CODE -
6
7
8
```

It should be noted that the invalid test data used as input for the program is necessary only to test the error routines in the program and need not be corrected or used in subsequent programs.

Since the program is run for two purposes, two exception reports will be created. The exception reports should contain the following information when all of the test data is used.

CHAPTER 3 – EXCEPTION REPORT

(LOAD FUNCTION)

DEPT. NO.	S.M. NO.	ERROR
10	04B	INVALID SALESMAN NO.
7A	214	INVALID DEPARTMENT NO.
60	179	INVALID CURRENT SALES
90	574	INVALID TYPE CODE

CHAPTER 3 — EXCEPTION REPORT

(UPDATE FUNCTION)

NO ERRORS

CHAPTER 4 — Loading The Indexed Sequential File

The input to the program assignment presented in Chapter 4 is the disk file created in the Chapter 3 programming assignment. The output, in addition to the indexed sequential master file, is an exception report. If all the data was used in Chapter 3, the exception report should contain the following errors.

CHAPTER 4 — EXCEPTION REPORT

DEPT. NO.	S.M. NO.	ERROR
10	050	INVALID TYPE CODE
40	721	DUPLICATE LOAD RECORD

CHAPTER 5 — Sequential Retrieval of Indexed Sequential File

The input to the program in the assignment in this chapter is the indexed sequential Sales Master file. The output is a listing of the master. If all the test data was used to create the master file, the report should contain the following information.

CHAPTER 5 — MASTER LIST

(BEFORE UPDATE)

DEPT. NO.	S.M. NO.	S.M. NAME	COMM. RATE
10	004	ACHER, WILLIAM C.	10%
10	185	DONNEMAN, THOMAS M.	10%
10	300	FELDMAN, MIKE R.	10%
10	325	HATFIELD, MARK I.	10%
10	730	REEDE, OWEN W.	10%
10	960	WINGLAND, KEITH E.	10%
20	111	CARTOLER, VIOLET B.	12%
20	304	FROMM, STEVE V.	12%
20	590	NEIL, CLARENCE N.	12%
20	801	SCHEIBER, HARRY T.	12%
20	956	WANGLEY, THEO A.	12%
30	030	ALLOREN, RUTH W.	15%
30	181	DELBERT, EDWARD D.	15%
30	318	HANEY, CAROL S.	15%
30	487	KING, MILDRED J.	15%
30	834	TRAWLEY, HARRIS T.	15%
40	027	ALHOUER, ELAINE E.	12%
40	171	COSTA, NAN S.	12%
40	317	HANBEE, ALETA O.	12%
40	721	RASSMUSEN, JOHN J.	12%

CHAPTER 6 — Random Update

The input to the program in the assignment is the Sales Master file and the sequential disk file created from the program in Chapter 3. If all the test data is used, the exception report from this program should contain the following errors.

CHAPTER 6 — EXCEPTION REPORT

DEPT. NO.	S.M. NO.	ERROR
10	185	DUPLICATE ADDITION RECORD
10	304	RECORD NOT ON FILE
20	300	RECORD NOT ON FILE
40	171	DUPLICATE ADDITION RECORD
40	721	INVALID TYPE CODE

CHAPTER 7 — Self-Relocating Programs

The input to this program is the Sales Master file. The output is a listing of the master file. If all the test data is used, the following is the information which should be contained on the report after the master file has been updated by the program in Chapter 6.

CHAPTER 7 — REPORT

(AFTER UPDATE)

DEPT. NO.	S.M. NO.	S.M. NAME	COMM. RATE
10	004	ACHER, WILLIAM J.	10%
10	185	DONNEMAN, THOMAS M.	10%
10	300	FELDMAN, MIKE R.	10%
10	325	HATFIELD, MARK I.	10%
10	730	REEDE, OWEN W.	12%
10	960	WINGLAND, KEITH E.	10%
20	111	CARTOLER, VIOLET B.	12%
20	304	FROMM, STEVE V.	12%
20	590	NEIL, CLARENCE N.	15%
20	673	TELLER, STEPHEN U.	12%
20	801	SCHEIBER, HARRY T.	12%
30	181	DELBERT, EDWARD D.	15%
30	318	HANEY, MARIE S.	15%
30	487	KING, MILDRED J.	10%
30	834	TRAWLEY, HARRIS T.	15%
40	171	COSTA, NANCY S.	12%
40	317	HANBEE, ALETA O.	12%
40	721	RASSMUSEN, JOHN J.	12%
50	734	OWNEY, REED M.	10%

The input to this program is the Sales Master file. The output of the program is a tape containing the master file and two reports — the Net Sales report and the Commission report. The two reports should contain the following information after the master file has been updated by the program in Chapter 6.

CHAPTER 8 — NET SALES REPORT

(AFTER UPDATE)

DEPT. NO.	S.M. NO.	S.M. NAME	Y-T-D SALES	Y-T-D RETURNS	Y-T-D NET
10	Q04	ACHER, WILLIAM J.	739.91	5.00	734.91
10	185	DONNEMAN, THOMAS M.	900.19	10.20	889.99
10	300	FELDMAN, MIKE R.	300.00	.00	300.00
10	325	HATFIELD, MARK I.	205.39	2.20	203.19
10	730	REEDE, OWEN W.	1051.44	23.10	1028.34
10	960	WINGLAND, KEITH E.	350.00	.00	350.00
20	111	CARTOLER, VIOLET B.	800.06	11.40	788.66
20	304	FROMM, STEVE V.	1850.0^	18.23	1831.77
20	590	NEIL, CLARENCE N.	1670.47	29.24	1641.23
20	673	TELLER, STEPHEN U.	1770.09	322.22	1447.87
20	801	SCHEIBER, HARRY T.	325.08	5.20	319.88
30	181	DELBERT, EDWARD D.	1305.54	.00	1305.54
30	318	HANEY, MARIE S.	1450.00	60.19	1389.81
30	487	KING, MILDRED J.	1804.29	53.22	1751.07
30	834	TRAWLEY, HARRIS T.	550.00	13.29	536.71
40	171	COSTA, NANCY S.	560.02	9.03	550.99
40	317	HANBEE, ALETA O.	412.00	45.80	366.20
40	721	RASSMUSEN, JOHN J.	1000.00	23.46	976.54
50	734	OWNEY, REED M.	530.66	11.32	519.34

CHAPTER 8 — COMMISSION REPORT

(AFTER UPDATE)

DEPT. NO.	S.M. NO.	S.M. NAME	Y-T-D NET	COMM. RATE	COMMISSION
10	004	ACHER, WILLIAM J.	734.91	10%	73.49
10	185	DONNEMAN, THOMAS M.	889.99	10%	89.00
10	300	FELDMAN, MIKE R.	300.00	10%	30.00
10	325	HATFIELD, MARK I.	203.19	10%	20.32
10	730	REEDE, OWEN W.	1028.34	12%	123.40
10	960	WINGLAND, KEITH E.	350.00	10%	35.00
20	111	CARTOLER, VIOLET B.	788.66	12%	94.64
20	304	FROMM, STEVE V.	1831.77	12%	219.81
20	590	NEIL, CLARENCE N.	1641.23	15%	246.18
20	673	TELLER, STEPHEN U.	1447.87	12%	173.74
20	801	SCHEIBER, HARRY T.	319.88	12%	38.39
30	181	DELBERT, EDWARD D.	1305.54	15%	195.83
30	318	HANEY, MARIE S.	1389.81	15%	208.47
30	487	KING, MILDRED J.	1751.07	10%	175.11
30	834	TRAWLEY, HARRIS T.	536.71	15%	80.51
40	171	COSTA, NANCY S.	550.99	12%	66.12
40	317	HANBEE, ALETA O.	366.20	12%	43.94
40	721	RASSMUSEN, JOHN J.	976.54	12%	117.72
50	734	OWNEY, REED M.	519.34	10%	51.93

CHAPTER 9 — Physical IOCS

The input to the program is the data used for Chapter 3 and the output is an 80-80 listing of the cards and a punched deck.

PROGRAM SEQUENCE

The following job control cards are samples of cards which could be used to execute the programming assignments. Changes may be necessary to device addresses, volume serial numbers, and extents used but the general sequence can be followed.

1. Chapter 2   Sequential Update

```
// JOB   SALESUPD
// OPTION LINK,DUMP
// EXEC  ASSEMBLY
     ——
     ——
   SOURCE DECK — CH 2
     ——
     ——
/*
// LBLTYP   TAPE
// EXEC   LNKEDT
// ASSGN  SYS010,X'180'
// ASSGN  SYS011,X'181'
// TLBL   MSTRIN,'SALES MASTER'
// TLBL   MSTROUT,'SALES MASTER'
// EXEC
     ——
     ——
   TEST DATA
/*
/&
```

2. Chapter 3   Card to Disk

It is suggested that an object deck be produced when the program is debugged. This object deck can then be used in the programming assignments in subsequent chapters.

```
// JOB   CDTODISK
// OPTION  LINK,DUMP,DECK
// EXEC   ASSEMBLY
    ——
    ——
    SOURCE  DECK — CH 3
    ——
    ——
/*
// EXEC  LNKEDT
// ASSGN  SYS004,X'091'
// DLBL   SEQDISK,'CARD OUTPUT',69/001,SD
// EXTENT  SYS004,111111,1,0,1600,3
// EXEC
    ——
    ——
    TEST DATA FOR LOAD
    ——
    ——
/*
/&
```

It should be noted that the assumption is made that the student will not be able to retain his disk files on a disk pack for future reference. Therefore, the Job Control shown for each chapter will contain all the necessary cards to build the files each time.

3. Chapter 4   Loading The Indexed Sequential File

The card data can be arranged in an ascending order, thus eliminating the need of the DOS SORT.

```
// JOB  LOADMSTR
// OPTION  LINK,DUMP,DECK
   INCLUDE
      ___

      ___
   OBJECT DECK — CH 3
      ___

      ___
/*
// EXEC  LNKEDT
// ASSGN  SYS004,X'091'
// DLBL  SEQDISK,'CARD OUTPUT',69/001,SD
// EXTENT  SYS004,111111,1,0,1600,3
// EXEC
      ___

      ___
   TEST DATA FOR LOAD
      ___

      ___
 /*
// OPTION  LINK
// EXEC  ASSEMBLY
      ___

      ___
   SOURCE DECK — CH 4
      ___

      ___
 /*
// LBLTYP  NSD(03)
// EXEC LNKEDT
// ASSGN SYS005,X'091'
// ASSGN SYS006,X'091'
// DLBL  DISKIN,'CARD OUTPUT',,SD
// EXTENT  SYS006,111111,1,0,1600,3
// DLBL  SALMSTR,'SALES MASTER',69/001,ISC
// EXTENT  SYS005,111111,4,1,1630,1
// EXTENT  SYS005,111111,1,2,1640,10
// EXTENT  SYS005,111111,2,3,1650,5
// EXEC
/*
/&
```

```
// JOB   PRTMASTR
// OPTION  LINK,DUMP,DECK
  INCLUDE
     ---
     ---
  OBJECT DECK – CH 3
     ---
     ---
/*
// EXEC  LNKEDT
// ASSGN  SYS004,X'091'
// DLBL  SEQDISK,'CARD OUTPUT',69/001,SD
// EXTENT  SYS004,111111,1,0,1600,3
// EXEC
     ---
     ---
  TEST DATA FOR LOAD
     ---
     ---
/*
// OPTION  LINK
  INCLUDE
     ---
     ---
  OBJECT DECK – CH 4
     ---
     ---
/*
// LBLTYP  NSD(03)
// EXEC  LNKEDT
// ASSGN  SYS005,X'091'
// ASSGN  SYS006,X'091'
// DLBL  DISKIN,'CARD OUTPUT',,SD
// EXTENT  SYS006,111111,1,0,1600,3
// DLBL  SALMSTR,'SALES MASTER',69/001,ISC
// EXTENT  SYS005,111111,4,1,1630,1
// EXTENT  SYS005,111111,1,2,1640,10
// EXTENT  SYS005,111111,2,3,1650,5
// EXEC
/*
// OPTION  LINK
// EXEC  ASSEMBLY
     ---
     ---
     ---
  SOURCE DECK – CH 5
     ---
     ---
/*
// LBLTYP  NSD(03)
// EXEC  LNKEDT
// DLBL  MSTRIN,'SALES MASTER',69/001,ISE
```

```
// EXTENT   SYS005,111111,4,1,1630,1
// EXTENT   SYS005,111111,1,2,1640,10
// EXTENT   SYS005,111111,2,3,1650,5
// EXEC
/*
/&
```

5. Chapter 6   **Random Update**

```
// JOB  UPDATMST
// OPTION  LINK,DUMP,DECK
   INCLUDE
   ___
   ___
   OBJECT DECK — CH 3
   ___
   ___
/*
// EXEC  LNKEDT
// ASSGN  SYS004,X'091'
// DLBL  SEQDISK,'CARD OUTPUT',69/001,SD
// EXTENT  SYS004,111111,1,0,1600,3
// EXEC
   ___
   TEST DATA FOR LOAD
   ___
   ___
/*
// OPTION  LINK
   INCLUDE
   ___
   ___
   OBJECT DECK — CH 4
   ___
   ___
/*
// LBLTYP  NSD(03)
// EXEC  LNKEDT
// ASSGN  SYS005,X'091'
// ASSGN  SYS006,X'091'
// DLBL  DISKIN,'CARD OUTPUT',,SD
// EXTENT  SYS006,111111,1,0,1600,3
// DLBL  SALMSTR,'SALES MASTER',69/001,ISC
// EXTENT  SYS005,111111,4,1,1630,1
// EXTENT  SYS005,111111,1,2,1640,10
// EXTENT  SYS005,111111,2,3,1650,5
// EXEC
/*
// OPTION  LINK
```

```
    INCLUDE
    ──
    ──
    OBJECT DECK — CH 3
    ──
    ──
/*
// EXEC  LNKEDT
// DLBL  SEQDISK,'UPDATE OUTPUT',69/001,SD
// EXTENT  SYS004,111111,1,0,1660,3
// EXEC
    ──
    ──
    TEST DATA FOR UPDATE
    ──
    ──
/*
// OPTION  LINK
// EXEC  ASSEMBLY
    ──
    ──
    SOURCE DECK — CH 6
    ──
    ──
/*
// LBLTYP  NSD(03)
// EXEC  LNKEDT
// DLBL  DISKIN,'UPDATE OUTPUT',,SD
// EXTENT  SYS004,111111,1,0,1660,3
// DLBL  MSTRIN,'SALES MASTER',69/001,ISE
// EXTENT  SYS005,111111,4,1,1630,1
// EXTENT  SYS005,111111,1,2,1640,10
// EXTENT  SYS005,111111,2,3,1650,5
// EXEC
/*
/&
```

6. Chapter 7   Self-Relocating Programs

The job control cards shown for this chapter and for Chapter 8 will assume that
the master has been created and updated as shown in step 5. The only change which
should be made to that job stream is to insert the object deck for Chapter 6 in place
of the source deck, as was done for the other programs.

```
// JOB   PRTMST
// ASSGN  SYS004,X'091'
// DLBL  MSTRIN,'SALES MASTER',69/001,ISE
// EXTENT  SYS004,111111,4,1,1630,1
// EXTENT  SYS004,111111,1,2,1640,10
// EXTENT  SYS004,111111,2,3,1650,5
// LBLTYP  NSD(03)
// EXEC   PRTMAST
/&
```

It should be noted that the program was catalogued on the core image library with
the phase name PRTMAST.

7. Chapter 8   Overlays

```
// JOB   MSTRUTIL
// ASSGN  SYS004,X'180'
// ASSGN  SYS005,X'091'
// TLBL   BACKUP,'MASTER BACKUP'
// DLBL  MSTRIN,'SALES MASTER',69/001,ISE
// EXTENT  SYS005,111111,4,1,1630,1
// EXTENT  SYS005,111111,1,2,1640,10
// EXTENT  SYS005,111111,2,3,1650,5
// LBLTYP  NSD(03)
// EXEC   MSTRUTIL
    -- CONTROL CARD --
/*
/&
```

It should be noted that the three phases comprising the program in Chapter 8 have
been catalogued on the Core Image Library. When a program is catalogued on the
core image library, any program already on the library with the same name is no longer
available. Therefore, when students are cataloguing programs, care must be taken to
ensure that all phase names are unique.

INDEX